Environmental Law in Transformation

Moritz Reese · Till Markus · Romina Schaller
Editors

Environmental Law in Transformation

Springer

Editors
Moritz Reese
Department of Environmental and Planning Law
Helmholtz Centre for Environmental Research
GmbH - UFZ
Leipzig, Germany

Till Markus
Department of Environmental and Planning Law
Helmholtz Centre for Environmental Research
GmbH - UFZ
Leipzig, Germany

Romina Schaller
Department of Environmental and Planning Law
Helmholtz Centre for Environmental Research
GmbH - UFZ
Leipzig, Germany

ISBN 978-3-032-31566-3 ISBN 978-3-032-31567-0 (eBook)
https://doi.org/10.1007/978-3-032-31567-0

This work was supported by Bundesministerium für Forschung, Technologie und Raumfahrt.

This Springer imprint is published by the registered company Springer Nature Switzerland AG
The registered company address is: Gewerbestrasse 11, 6330 Cham, Switzerland

Preface

Exponential growth in population and resource consumption has led humanity into an existential environmental crisis. Anthropogenic global warming, rapid biodiversity loss, and increasing environmental pollution with persistent pollutants have long exceeded planetary and local boundaries and threaten the livelihoods of humans and nature. The causes of this triple ecological crisis are rooted in the prevailing economic, energy, and land use systems. It is clear that a profound transformation of these systems is needed to make them ecologically sustainable, a transformation to renewable energies and climate neutrality, to extensive agriculture and ecological nutrition, to complete, low-pollutant material cycles, and to adequate materials management.

The need for ecological transformation has long been obvious and has also been recognized by European policymakers in particular. In 2019, the EU Commission initiated a comprehensive program of "deeply transformative policies" with its European Green Deal and, in the following years, took a variety of regulatory measures to curb unsustainable economic practices and promote innovative, sustainable approaches. The EU Climate Law, the Nature Restoration Law, and the new Ecodesign Regulation are central pillars of this transformative environmental legislation, which is primarily aimed at establishing a comprehensive, long-term framework for ecological transformation. Numerous more specific regulations have also been enacted to promote transformation in the energy, industry, food, transport, raw materials, and finance sectors. In the spirit of ecological transformation, environmental law is also undergoing a fundamental transformation. It is increasingly changing from a law that sets peripheral frameworks to a transformative law that is much more focused than before on ensuring and steering profound and long-term change processes.

The aim of this book is to take a closer look at this shift in environmental law towards a law of ecological transformation and to identify the key challenges, strategies, and approaches of transformative legal governance. To this end, the book focuses on three main areas. The first section begins by exploring the fundamental normative, strategic and constitutional challenges that must be overcome when developing transformative environmental law. These include long-termism, uncertainty, complexity and adaptability problems in transformative governance, as well as fundamental questions about the legal demands required for sustainable, transformative change with regard to fundamental rights and the precautionary principle. The second section then focuses more specifically on the governance of (sustainable) innovation and on the question how innovations can be promoted and regulated in light of the precautionary principle. Finally, the third part deals with various aspects of a formative development associated with the transformative shaping of environmental law, namely an increasingly long-term, planning-oriented approach that aims to commit not only the executive and private actors, but also the legislature to long-term transformation goals and paths. The regulations on EU climate governance and the EU Nature Restoration Law are only the most prominent examples of this planning approach which is also spreading beyond this area and raising numerous questions, particularly regarding the limits of predictability and the binding nature of legislation. Challenges of multifunctional land use and regarding for the knowledge base of planning are also discussed as important aspects of transformative planning law.

The book and the contributions are the results of the joint project "Competence Network Challenges of Environmental Law" (KomUR—https://www.ufz.de/komur/), which was funded by the German Federal Ministry of Education and Research from 2020 to 2026 to analyze the future challenges of environmental law through a series of doctoral theses, conferences, and workshops. The editors would like to express their sincere thanks to the authors for their contributions and for their patient cooperation in the production of this volume.

Leipzig, Germany
December 2025

Moritz Reese
Till Markus
Romina Schaller

Contents

Editors and Contributors

About the Editors

Moritz Reese is Head of the Department of Environmental and Planning Law at the UFZ in Leipzig. He is also professor for European environmental law at the Faculty of Law of Leipzig University. His research focuses on European and national environmental law, particularly in the areas of water law, circular economy law, climate adaptation law, nature conservation law, immission control law, and urban and infrastructure planning law. In addition, his work addresses the theoretical foundations of environmental law and the overarching legal dimensions of the sustainability transformation. He is also Chair of the European Environmental Law Form (EELF), co-editor of the *Zeitschrift für Umweltrecht* (Journal of Environmental Law) and co-editor of the Journal for European Environmental & Planning Law (JEEPL).

Till Markus has served as Deputy Head of the Department of Environmental and Planning Law at the Helmholtz Centre for Environmental Research (UFZ) in Leipzig since April 2024. Since February 2020, he has been a Privatdozent at the Faculty of Law at the University of Bremen. He is Co-Chief Editor of the *Zeitschrift für Umweltrecht* (Journal of Environmental Law, ZUR) and Editor of the book series *Climate Change Law and Governance* (Nomos). His research and teaching focus on international, European, and comparative law, with a particular emphasis on environmental law, the law of the sea, and legal theory.

Romina Schaller is a Postdoctoral Researcher in the Department of Environmental and Planning Law at the Helmholtz Centre for Environmental Research-UFZ (Germany). She also coordinates the "Competence Network Challenges of Environmental Law" (KomUR). Her work focuses on international and European environmental law, particularly in climate change mitigation (nature conservation, forest and soil law) as well as on ecosystem services and sustainable development. Her current research explores the legal aspects for the regulation of carbon dioxide removal technologies (CDR) and the emerging challenges linked to their governance.

Contributors

Ivo Appel Chair of Public Law, Environmental Law and Philosophy of Law, University of Hamburg, Hamburg, Germany

Christian Calliess Chair of Public Law, Environmental and European Law, Free University of Berlin, Berlin, Germany

Pascale Cancik Faculty of Law, University of Osnabrück, Osnabrück, Germany

Wolfgang Durner Chair of Public Law, Rheinische Friedrich-Wilhelms-Universität Bonn, Bonn, Germany

Kurt Faßbender Institute for Environmental and Planning Law, Leipzig University, Leipzig, Germany

Claudio Franzius Chair of Public Law, Administrative Law and Environmental Law, University of Bremen, Bremen, Germany

Matti Gurreck Law School, Faculty of Social Sciences and Business Studies, University of Eastern Finland, Joensuu, Kuopio, Finland

Till Markus Department of Environmental and Planning Law, Helmholtz Centre for Environmental Research-UFZ, Leipzig, Germany

Moritz Reese Department of Environmental and Planning Law, Helmholtz Centre for Environmental Research-UFZ, Leipzig, Germany

Sabine Schlacke Chair of Public Law, in Particular Administrative and Environmental Law, University of Greifswald, Greifswald, Germany

Michael von Landenberg-Roberg Privatdozent at Faculty of Law, Humboldt–Universität zu Berlin, Berlin, Germany

Environmental Law and Precaution in the Anthropocene

Fundamental Legal Issues in the Anthropocene

Till Markus

Abstract This chapter examines how legal scholarship has employed the Anthropocene concept to diagnose structural weaknesses in existing legal systems and to outline potential pathways for reform. It first considers law's historical role in enabling the economic growth and resource use that have contributed to humanity's entry into the Anthropocene. It then surveys emerging scholarly debates and reform proposals in environmental and natural-resource law. These include revising foundational legal doctrines, reinterpreting or introducing new guiding principles, reforming constitutions, and strengthening polycentric regulatory approaches. The article also identifies five overarching challenges for law in the Anthropocene: a growing loss of orientation and increasing doubts about the prevailing anthropocentric paradigm; the need to curb resource overuse; shrinking civil liberties; fragmented regulatory authority; and the difficulty of adapting legal frameworks to an increasingly dynamic Earth system. It concludes that environmental law must move beyond merely mitigating harm and instead begin to support the societal transformation required to ensure long-term Earth-system stability.

1 Introduction

Environmental policy and law face major challenges now and in the future. Global population growth, ever-increasing resource consumption, changing consumer behaviour around the world, unsustainable technologies and the slowing but continuing globalisation of trade are all increasing pressure on the environment. While

The author thanks Prof. Dr. Wolfgang Köck (UFZ), Prof. Dr. Moritz Reese (UFZ) and Dr. Nadja Salzborn (Federal Environment Agency) for many valuable comments. All remaining errors are solely his.

T. Markus (✉)
Department of Environmental and Planning Law, Helmholtz Centre for Environmental Research-UFZ, Leipzig, Germany
e-mail: till.markus@ufz.de

M. Reese et al. (eds.), *Environmental Law in Transformation*,
https://doi.org/10.1007/978-3-032-31567-0_1

just over half a century ago scientists were pointing to "limits to growth",[1] today they are urgently warning against exceeding "planetary boundaries", using geological terminology to characterise human impact on the environment to the point of epochal change.[2] At the same time, environmentally harmful activities often have transboundary or even global impacts and require effective transnational governance. In addition, the globalisation of most social activities is changing both societies and their cultural practices, as well as their respective public and private institutions. Against this background, ensuring relatively stable environmental conditions and adapting to unavoidable environmental changes will require a fundamental, structural change in the way we live, particularly in our economic activities. These challenges have implications for law: Environmental law is being transformed, and it must itself enable and promote far-reaching transformations.

The current multi- and interdisciplinary debate on the Anthropocene significantly enriches both the analysis of current problems and challenges and the search for appropriate political and legal responses. The range of topics covered is very broad; creating an almost unmanageable plethora of interpretations and ideas which are subsumed and discussed under the concept of the Anthropocene. Much of the analysis remains vague, however, and it is precisely this lack of clarity that provides an opportunity to take stock and integrate previously unconnected problems, discourses and theories. The concept's fundamental argument about the relationship between humans and nature enables it to function as a comprehensive analytical framework for a wide range of related and often interdependent questions. This also applies to current and future fundamental issues and challenges in environmental law.

The conceptual overview of ideas, arguments and conclusions on the Anthropocene presented here in the form of a review article is intended to highlight their analytical added value for environmental law. Of course, some of the ideas developed in the Anthropocene debate are not entirely new. Various works on the Anthropocene draw on, develop and reinterpret previously existing concepts. Thus, guiding principles of environmental policy and law remain relevant, such as the "Great Transformation", the "transnationalisation of environmental law", "ecological liberalism", "environmental constitutionalism", "sustainable development" and "precaution", etc.[3] They too have their place in the Anthropocene discourse.

The following article will therefore begin by looking at the origin, content and scientific reception of the Anthropocene concept (2). The second step is to trace the causes and effects of humanity's entry into the Anthropocene epoch (3). In particular, this will entail an analysis of the contribution of law to its emergence. Clarifying this contribution is fundamental to understanding the role of law in the Anthropocene. The majority of the article focuses on the current debate concerning the possible

---

[1] See Meadows et al. (1972).

[2] Rockström et al. (2009a); Steffen et al. (2015b).

[3] For "strict", "strong" or "ambitious" sustainability, see Köck (2007), p. 419; Winter (2003). For transformation, see in particular WBGU (2011) (english version available). For *environmental constitutionalism,* see Kotzé (2016); Winter (2013). For ecological liberalism, see e.g., Kersten (2016). For sustainable environmentally sound development, see SRU (1997).

developments, challenges and strategies of law in the Anthropocene (4). This is followed by a critical discussion of the ideas presented (5). The conclusions present a schematic overview of the principal environmental policy and legal challenges associated with the Anthropocene. This enables the identification of their position within broader trajectories and discursive contexts, as well as the initial formulation of conclusions regarding their significance for environmental law in the Anthropocene (6).

2 The Anthropocene: Concept, Findings, Reception

The concept of the Anthropocene started to receive attention from the scientific community when a Nobel Prize winner for chemistry, Paul Crutzen, used it prominently at a conference on Earth system science in 2000, and later defined it in several publications.[4] The word Anthropocene is made up of the ancient Greek terms *anthropos* (human) and *kainos* (new). It integrates insights from Earth system science with stratigraphic questions and suggests that the influence of humans on the biological, chemical and physical processes of the Earth system can now be traced in the Earth's sediments. According to Crutzen, the geosignatures of the Anthropocene differ significantly from those of the preceding Holocene.[5]

In response, extensive scientific debates emerged around the concept of the Anthropocene, first in the natural sciences and later in the social sciences and humanities, including law. The debate also led to the creation of a number of new scientific journals: *Anthropocene*, *The Anthropocene Review*, *Elementa: Science of the Anthropocene*, and *Anthropocene Coasts*. The term has also been—and still is—widely recognised and discussed among the general population.[6] Its meaning, its normative content and the precise beginning of the new epoch have been the subject of controversial debate.[7] More than a decade after the term was introduced, Crutzen himself, together with other scientists, attempted to clarify its meaning and function:

> The concept of the Anthropocene, proposed by one of us a decade ago, was introduced to capture this quantitative shift in the relationship between humans and the global environment. The Anthropocene suggests: (i) that the Earth is now moving out of its current geological epoch, called the Holocene and (ii) the human activity is largely responsible for this exit from the Holocene, that is, that humankind has become a global geological force in its own right.[8]

---

[4] See his obituary, The Economist (2021). Crutzen explained his use of the term shortly afterwards in two scientific articles, see Crutzen and Stoermer (2000), p. 17; Crutzen (2002).

[5] See also Waters et al. (2016).

[6] See, e.g., Stegemann (2021), p. 241 et seq.; Jardine in Neue Züricher Zeitung (2019); Kenigsberg (2019); Schrader in Süddeutsche Zeitung (2015). For planetary boundaries, see in particular Calliess in Frankfurter Allgemeine Zeitung (2019). See earlier, The Economist (2011).

[7] See the literature cited in the subsequent text.

[8] Steffen et al. (2011); see also Steffen et al. (2007).

The qualification of humans as a "global geological force" responsible for the end of the Holocene ("moving out of"/ "exit from the Holocene") is based on the finding that humans fundamentally changed the environmental conditions of the Holocene through a variety of activities—including the exploitation of material and energy resources.[9] There is some debate as to the exact date of the beginning of these activities. Alternatively, the start of European colonisation, the beginning of industrialisation, or the end of World War II have been suggested.[10] What is indisputable, however, is that the processes underlying these changes have accelerated dramatically, particularly since the end of World War II. This dynamic is also referred to as the "Great Acceleration".[11]

While the Holocene provided comparatively stable environmental conditions in which humanity could thrive, the Anthropocene is characterised by a significantly higher degree of instability, unpredictability and risk.[12] Although humanity has the power to shape the world, it has only a limited ability to predict and control the dynamics it has set in motion. It is essentially instability, unpredictability and risk that motivate the question of how people should act in the face of such threatening prospects.[13] For most authors from the social sciences, humanities and law, this is probably the starting point when considering the Anthropocene.[14]

Different disciplines read and interpret the Anthropocene differently.[15] Thinking of humanity as a geological force which is putting its own future at risk has led to:

- a fundamental rethinking of the relationship between human beings, their cultures and their relationship with nature(s)[16];
- discussing the self-understanding and the future tasks of the sciences[17];

---

[9] The discussion about the beginning of the Anthropocene is illustrative in this respect, see, e.g., Zalasiewicz et al. (2015); Davies (2016).

[10] Zalasiewicz (2015).

[11] Steffen et al. (2015a); see also Jouffray et al. (2020).

[12] Keys et al. (2019).

[13] Epistemologically, a precise distinction may be made between the descriptive-analytical findings on the one hand and the normative-consequential aspects of the Anthropocene on the other ("no ought follows from is"). From the outset, however, the term has been characterised by an evaluative character and political-normative imprint (not least by *Crutzen* himself). The term may therefore be understood as an analytical-normative hybrid. On the normativity of the term, see Leinfelder (2017); Dalby (2015).

[14] See e.g., Lorimer (2017); Hoffman and Jennings (2018), p. 5; Biermann et al. (2016); Clark (2015); Chakrabarty (2009).

[15] A typology is offered, for example, by Bonneuil (2015).

[16] See, e.g., Thomas et al (2020), p. 112 et seq.; Hamilton (2017), p. 36 et seq.; Ellis, Anthropocene, 2018, p. 75 et seq.; Latour (2017), p. 64 et seq.; Latour (2015), p. 193 et seq.

[17] See generally Renn (2020); Brondizio et al. (2016). With regard to legal studies, see, e.g., Stephens (2018); Lövbrand et al. (2015).

- identifying visions of the future, actions and thresholds, especially those in which the Anthropocene could possibly remain *Holocene-like* (in particular how humankind can stay within the so-called planetary boundaries)[18];
- fundamentally questioning existing economic ideas, consumer habits and the associated consumption of resources (especially the growth paradigm)[19];
- designing strategies for taking actions and specific measures[20];
- contemplating geopolitical and security issues[21];
- developing political and legal concepts for describing as well as constructing normative strategies for coping with the Anthropocene (models, principles, regulatory approaches)[22];
- identifying and conceptualising actors and institutions that can govern effectively under the conditions of the Anthropocene.[23]

Not all of these ideas are new.[24] In most cases, existing ideas have been developed, reinterpreted and adapted, sometimes radically.

Nevertheless, the idea of the Anthropocene has been referred to as a "paradigm shift" and compared to the "Copernican revolution".[25] According to this way of thinking, the Anthropocene offers a new description and interpretation of reality, a new worldview or meta-narrative, especially with regard to the interplay between humanity, culture and nature.[26] Seen in this light, humankind is no longer only an important and powerful component of a largely stable environment, but has become a force that dominates the entire, rapidly changing Earth system.[27] In terms of environmental protection, human actions are no longer understood as small or large

[18] Rockström et al (2009a); Steffen et al (2015b). *Gerten* and *Schellnhuber* talk of a "biophysical orientation framework", Gerten and Schellnhuber (2016), p. 17. See also WBGU (2011), p. 34.

[19] See in particular Angus (2016); von Weizsäcker and Weijkman (2018); Kelly (2019), p. 43 et seq.; see contributions in Brown and Timmermann (2015); see also Winter (2017).

[20] WBGU (2011); see also Schneidewind (2019).

[21] Dalby (2020). The security policy aspect is also emphasised by the German Advisory Council on the Environment (SRU), see SRU (2019).

[22] E.g., Biber (2017); Franzius (2019); Robinson (2014); Kotzé (2016); Kotzé (2019b); Hoffmann (2019); Burdon (2020b); Vidas et al. (2015); Winter (2017); Kersten (2014a, b), p. 378; SRU (2019); SRU (2016); Viñuales (2018); Berros (2019); Steffen and Smith (2013). See also WBGU (2011).

[23] The following contributions are exemplary in this respect, Dryzek (2019); Biermann (2014); Franzius (2019); Winter (2017); WBGU (2011).

[24] Conceptually, many of the ideas developed in the context of the Anthropocene debate are closely related to the concept of "strong" or "strict sustainability". See Köck (2007); Winter (2003); SRU (1997).

[25] Hamilton (2017), p. 13; Angus (2016), p. 27. With further references from the German literature, see Leinfelder (2017), p. 260.

[26] *Claudio Franzius* puts it succinctly: "One can put it in a nutshell and describe the Anthropocene as a new climax to the old question of the relationship between nature and culture." See Franzius (2019), p. 498.

[27] *Hamilton* speaks of humans as a "world-making creature" and of a "new anthropocentrism", see Hamilton (2017), p. 36 et seq., p. 58 et seq.

interventions in specific media or ecosystems that must be merely limited, prohibited or reversed if they have negative consequences for humans. In the Anthropocene, humans need to control their earth-altering powers, which could potentially destroy the entire biosphere, i.e. their very basis of existence.[28] In this new Anthropocene world, it is these epochal forces with which humanity must plan and manage its future. Bruno Latour puts it aptly:

> (...) The term Anthropocene sums up (...) that the earth system reacts henceforth to your action in such a way that you no longer have a stable indifferent framework in which you lodge your desires for modernisation.[29]

The responses and interpretations of the social sciences and humanities presented here illustrate the intellectual, discursive and normative power of a term that succinctly sums up the increasingly clear findings of the natural sciences as well as contemporary evaluations and socio-political reactions.[30] Against this background, it does not matter whether or not the International Commission on Stratigraphy (ICS) of the International Union of Geological Sciences formally defines the Anthropocene as a new geological epoch, the Anthropocene has already made its impact.[31]

3 Law's Contributions to the Emergence of the Anthropocene

As noted above, the processes driving the transition to the Anthropocene have accelerated rapidly since the end of World War II. Important factors include a growing world population, technological progress, increasing urbanisation, global growth in land use, trade, industry and transport, rising global economic output, and the increasing mobility and informational connectedness of people. The effects of these developments are clearly visible in the Earth's biogeochemical cycles (e.g. for carbon, nitrogen and phosphorus), in the increasing atmospheric concentration of greenhouse gases, in the acidification of the oceans, in the decline of biodiversity, and so on.[32] There is no fundamental trend reversal in any of these indicators today.[33] The multiple impacts of all these developments on the various components of the natural world are legion and are regularly documented in the reports of international, intergovernmental and national commissions, agencies and organisations.[34]

---

[28] Hamilton and Grinevald (2015).

[29] Latour (2017), p. 84.

[30] For more information, see Baskin (2015).

[31] See Zalasiewicz et al. (2017); *Angus* aptly formulates: "The Anthropocene already has a robust geological basis, is in widespread use, and indeed is becoming a central, integrating concept in the consideration of global change", see Angus (2016), p. 58.

[32] Rockström et al. (2009a, b), Art. 32.

[33] Steffen et al. (2015b). See also Steffen et al. (2018).

[34] Instead of a plethora of reports, see most recently UNEP (2019).

The social causes of the processes triggering the Anthropocene are the subject of research in various disciplines. Economics in particular is concerned with the conditions and drivers of economic growth and the associated increase in interventions in nature. Traditionally, there has been disagreement about the relative importance of individual framework conditions and factors, and whether or to what extent they should be relevant to economic policy (e.g. property, competition, etc.).[35] However, there is widespread agreement on basic causal relationships.[36] Although the "IPAT-equation" is very simple and was developed back in the 1970s, it accurately identifies three central drivers of environmental change, which are also featured in the analysis of the Great Acceleration:

$$I = P \times A \times T$$

Human impact on the environment and natural resources (I) is defined here as the product of population (P), affluence (A) and technology (T).[37] All three factors have increased significantly in recent centuries, leading to a significant increase in both resource use and the intensity of interventions in nature.

In addition to these three factors, many other conditions are also considered to contribute to growth,[38] such as free trade, a high degree of competition, and national economic policies (e.g. the financing of research, social benefits, public services, or the permanent subsidisation of entire sectors of the economy).[39]

Four historical conditions have been identified as central to the onset of the Great Acceleration in the mid-twentieth century (Their broadly simultaneous emergence shows that they were catalytically reinforcing in their growth-enhancing effects.)[40]:

- the availability of cheap energy in the form of fossil fuels
- a wave of mechanisation triggered by the Second World War
- the liberalisation of world markets
- the increasing physical and informational interconnectedness of the world's population

Discussion of the Anthropocene thus far, however, has only sporadically and haphazardly touched on how law has contributed to its emergence.[41] This relative lack of interest is surprising for a number of reasons: First, it is becoming increasingly clear that more than half a century of increasingly systematic and ambitious national

---

[35] See most recently Jäger and Springer (2012); Cohen (2015).

[36] The model was developed in the 1970s in a trialogue between *Barry Commoner, Paul Ehrlich* and *John Holdren*. See Chertow (2000); Goudie (2013), p. 20 et seq.

[37] Population (P), Affluence (A), Technology (T).

[38] The various conditions are also the subject of the studies that have significantly shaped today's discussion about the "Great Acceleration" and the "Great Transformation". See in particular Polanyi (1973).

[39] See a more recent overview, e.g., in Aghion and Howitt (2009), p. 19 et seq.; Mills (2002). See also Boianovsky and Hoover (2014).

[40] See, with further references, e.g., WBGU (2011), p. 89 et seq.; see also SRU (2019), p. 35.

[41] See further below in this section.

and international legal efforts to protect the environment have failed to reverse the environmental trends outlined above.[42] Second, clarifying its impact is fundamental to understanding its own role in the Anthropocene: If law is to help govern the Anthropocene, it is necessary to clarify how it has helped to create it.

Trying to understand the contribution of law to the emergence of the Anthropocene requires a more general consideration of its function as a driver of social change. In this respect, it is important to remember that law is only one social driver among many (something lawyers sometimes tend to forget). From a sociological point of view, its main function is to pacify conflicts and to stabilise social expectations with regard to individual or collective behaviour.[43] Law is omnipresent in society and influences it in many different ways. It is both a reflex and an impulse, it limits and enables, it defines and structures social relations. With regard to the onset of the Anthropocene, it is important to understand that the increasingly complex, technologized and resource-intensive social processes of modernity leading up to the Anthropocene took place within the framework of relatively stable, increasingly formalised and state-supported legal systems.[44]

Law has authorised, promoted and secured the rapid growth of economic activity, for example, by providing systematically regulated and institutionalised use and property rights[45] (including intellectual property rights[46]), contract law, commercial and company law (e.g. by introducing limited liability[47]), bankruptcy law,[48] labour law and competition law.[49]

Jorge Viñuales illustrates this point by recalling that James Watt not only invented a new version of the steam engine that was so important for industrialisation, but also had it patented under English law.[50] The questions posed above should therefore be formulated more precisely: What social developments have led to the Anthropocene, and to what extent have they been enabled or constrained by law? With regard to the significance of environmental law, it is particularly important to ask whether it has up to this point taken sufficient account of the social and technical processes that are partly responsible for the challenges of the Anthropocene.

---

[42] Many environmental law scholars are now asking themselves this question, see, e.g., Köck and Markus (2018); Kotzé (2018), pp. 140-144. See also WBGU (2011), pp. 33–34. Of course, this fundamental question is not entirely new either. See Doran et al. (1974) and Köck (2009).

[43] Luhmann (1971), p. 27 et seq.

[44] See, e.g., Weber (1921/1972), p. 503 et seq.; see Williamson (1990). The relative importance of the emergence of the modern state for the development of law is traditionally assessed differently in the sociology of law.

[45] See most recently Pistor (2021).

[46] On the history and significance of copyright in this context, see Rehbinder and Peukert (2018), p. 1 et seq.

[47] See, e.g., Ireland (2010); see also Hansmann et al. (2006).

[48] Informative Skeel (2001).

[49] For ideas regarding the effects of competition and rivalry in economic processes, see with further references the overview in Markus (2015).

[50] See Viñuales (2016), p. 7.

So far, very few authors have offered concrete assessments of the contribution of law in general and environmental law in particular to the emergence of the Anthropocene. In this respect, some contributions by legal scholars have taken the form of (hypo-)theses. The central arguments of three such attempts are presented here by way of example:

Jorge Viñuales puts forward two main theses. First, he argues that the contribution of law to the emergence of the Anthropocene has so far been neglected by scholars. In particular, he outlines the enabling role of corporate, labour and commercial law in the industrialisation of England and the USA. Second, environmental law has not prevented the onset of the Anthropocene. Its main function has been to limit the negative external effects of social (especially economic) activities on uninvolved third parties or the environment. In most cases, environmental law does not fundamentally limit economic activities, especially not their expansion, but merely addresses the negative impacts they generate.[51] In Viñuales's words, it is as follows:

> Whether it is through personal-injury based techniques (e.g., through tort law doctrine of nuisance or civil law doctrine of *abus de droit*, and more recently environmental liability and human rights litigation) or through impact limitation techniques (environmental impact assessments, environmental permitting, zoning and protection of designated areas, pollution limitation standards, taxation, or market mechanisms), the assumption is that the legal system first organises social processes, such as defining subjects, rights, duties, devolution of powers, general taxations, corporate structures, economic freedoms, labour relations, (…), etc., and only then it adds a layer of regulation aimed at protecting the environment. It sets bounds to (it 'regulates') the effects of a pre-established system.[52]

Gerd Winter points out that environmental law traditionally and primarily aims to make infrastructure, production processes and products environmentally friendly. It limits the impact of social and economic freedoms on natural resources. However, the problem of quantitative growth has been neglected. As a result, qualitative improvements have often been offset by quantitative growth, which has been—to this day—the core element of economic growth. Economic growth not only undermines the regulatory system through resistance to new regulation, but also asserts itself within the system. This is done, among other things, by exploiting the scope for discretion and consideration, by accepting rather than punishing legal violations and by shifting problems from one environmental medium to another and from one region of the world to another.[53]

Louis J. Kotzè, Louise Du Toit and Duncan French argue that not only has international environmental law not been effective in preventing climate change, it may even have accelerated climate change and the injustices associated with it.[54] They accuse it of "complicity". According to these authors, the "ethically deficient anthropocentrism" underlying large parts of international environmental law is one of the

---

[51] See Viñuales (2016), p. 19.

[52] Viñuales (2016), p. 21.

[53] Winter (2017), p. 268.

[54] Kotzé et al. (2020); somewhat more generally, see Kotzé (2018). With a similar argumentative thrust Grear (2015).

root causes of the socio-ecological crisis and the injustices of the Anthropocene. Moreover, international environmental law is imbued with (post-)colonial power structures, which means, among other things, that it does not adequately regulate the exploitation of natural resources by powerful actors, to the detriment of weak states and people. They argue that the principle of state sovereignty, on which international environmental law is based, ultimately promotes the exploitation of nature.

The theses presented here illustrate three elementary facets of the law's role in the emergence of the Anthropocene in general and environmental law in particular. First of all, law is both the result of social developments and a factor in shaping them. It makes possible and promotes many of the social activities and processes that are partly responsible for the Anthropocene. In this respect, law in general, and environmental law in particular, is never the sole cause, but always a contributing cause—not the central problem, but an important part of a complex situation. Ultimately, however, this also means that it can contribute to solving the challenges of the Anthropocene.[55] Second, Viñuales and Winter both point to the totality of social activities that have led to the onset of the Anthropocene, including the legal issues that affect them. In doing so, they broaden the scholarly perspective beyond environmental law. Third, all three contributions explicitly point to the limited power of environmental law to bring about or redirect social change and its structural deficits (its regulatory successes remain undisputed). The first two contributors in particular emphasise that much of the law has been and continues to be designed to facilitate economic growth. Although environmental law restricts these activities, it does not fundamentally address its enabling and facilitating effects.

4 The Transformation of Environmental Law in the Anthropocene

Legal science is also increasingly concerned with the implications of the Anthropocene. Interest in this area has grown noticeably over the last five years.[56] As in the social sciences, analyses and assessments of the legal significance of the Anthropocene vary (both in terms of the scientific evidence, the concept and the term itself). The debate is broadly organised and presented here according to the following epistemological and research interests. (Other organising principles are, of course, conceivable.)

The various contributions will, *inter alia*,

- examine the general and specific implications of the onset of the Anthropocene for law;

---

[55] Worth reading in this respect Ebbeson (2010).

[56] Compared to the social sciences, the discussion in the legal sciences therefore began comparatively late. The earliest contributions in Germany - as far as is evident - come from the WBGU and *Jens Kersten*, see WBGU (2011); Kersten (2014b).

- reflect on the theoretical foundations of law and consider new paradigms, goals and principles;
- seek to advance existing legal frameworks and institutions conceptually;
- discuss possible contributions of law to the management of growth processes;
- search for appropriate actors and constellations of actors to meet emerging governance demands;
- attempt to determine the basic role and function of law, and to
- identify ideas and options for the reorientation of the law.

In the following subsections, key arguments in the debate will be presented in line with these research interests. At best, this will provide an initial map of the relevant problems, issues and tasks of law in the Anthropocene, as well as their interrelationships. In some cases, specific individual contributions to the debate will be brought up as they relate to the ideas, arguments and theses being presented. These specific contributions are examples of certain categories of ideas, arguments or propositions and it is not always possible to follow the outlined categories in a direct linear fashion, especially as many authors pursue several research interests.

4.1 Effects of the Anthropocene on the Law

Various legal articles on the Anthropocene consider the potential legal implications of Anthropocene-related environmental conditions.[57]

For example, Davor Vidas et al. argue that increasingly unstable, unpredictable and risky environmental conditions will affect law at two fundamental levels. First, law aims to stabilise social orders, and second, central areas of law have developed within the stable environmental conditions of the Holocene. The authors illustrate their thesis with the example of rising sea levels.[58] Rising sea levels could challenge the entire maritime zone regime that has been negotiated over centuries. The zone regime is based on the assumption that coastal states have largely stable land masses from which their powers over the seas extend. If, as a result of sea-level rise, land masses were to change significantly or even disappear altogether, it would have to be determined whether the maritime boundaries of the states concerned would also change and to what extent, and whether states would continue to be entitled to the maritime areas previously allocated to them under international law.[59] The possible speed of change could destabilise existing orders and become a source of conflict. The possibility of abrupt or catastrophic events also poses particular challenges for the development of the law and the conduct of international relations.

With regard to the potential impact of the Anthropocene on existing law, legal scholars also discuss genuinely new regulatory needs that are likely to arise. The need

[57] See, for example, the contribution by *Eric Biber,* who examines the various effects of the Anthropocene on different institutions in US law, Biber (2017).

[58] Vidas et al. (2015); see also Vidas (2011).

[59] Vidas et al. (2015).

for regulatory action is seen as particularly likely in order to control the development and use of new technologies (e.g., in the field of geoengineering,[60] or designing genetic resources[61]), as well as disaster prevention and management.[62]

4.2 *Questioning Theoretical Foundations*

As outlined above in Sect. 2, the diagnosis of an Anthropocene triggers considerable pressure to act. For many authors, the prospect of a comparatively crisis-ridden future provides a strong incentive to look for possible ways for law to the creation of a more stable future.[63] In some cases, this search triggers basic theoretical and ethical considerations. Established assumptions about the law are questioned and new analytical and normative foundations are developed.[64] In particular, some authors ask whether and to what extent existing concepts are still suitable for guiding environmental policy and law.[65] At this point, the various contributions on the theoretical foundations of law can be divided into two categories. A first group of authors argues on a basic epistemological and ethical level. Part of this group calls for nature to be endowed with its own rights. The other part calls for a reconsideration of the meaning of the normative concepts of 'obligation' and 'responsibility' and is rather sceptical about the development of inherent rights for nature. In the second category, authors respond to the diagnosis of the Anthropocene by reinterpreting or further developing familiar legal models and principles.

4.2.1 Inherent Rights of Nature

The debate on nature's rights dates back to the 1970s.[66] Not least against the backdrop of worsening environmental problems, the topic has also received more attention in recent years.[67] Due to the ever-expanding scope of the debate, it is not possible to summarise it comprehensively here,[68] but it is crucial to note two things at this

[60] Scott (2013).

[61] Vidas et al. (2015).

[62] See, for example, Stephens (2016), p. 153.

[63] It is quite rightly pointed out in the literature that inequalities will also exist in the Anthropocene. Not all actors are therefore likely to be equally addressed and motivated by the concept of the Anthropocene, as (a) people will be affected to varying degrees by the challenges of the Anthropocene, and (b) not everyone will benefit equally from tackling the problems of the Anthropocene. See in particular Grear (2015).

[64] See, e.g., Philippopulos-Mihalopoulos (2017); Vermeylen (2017).

[65] See for example Bridgewater et al. (2015). See also Bosselmann (2014).

[66] Stone (1972). See also the 2010 reissue of the author's book of the same name, Stone (2010).

[67] Most recently Wolf (2022); Mührel (2022); Gutmann (2021); Köck and Markus (2018).

[68] For an overview, see most recently Boyd (2017); Krämer (2020); Ramsauer (2019); Gutmann (2019); Schröter and Bosselmann (2018); Fischer-Lescano (2018), p. 205.

point. First, various legislators and courts around the world are already using the legal concept of nature's rights. For example, the constitutions of Ecuador and Bolivia grant nature its own rights, and courts in Colombia, India, Bangladesh and New Zealand recognise the rights of rivers, forests, or mountains.[69] Second, the discussion about inherent rights is also taken up in the debate of the Anthropocene.[70]

One may argue that both discourses—Anthropocene and nature's rights—are based on a holistic understanding of nature; one is rooted in the scientific world view of Earth system sciences (Anthropocene), while the other is based on cosmological or animistic ideas (nature's rights). The foundations of the Anthropocene concept arguably underpin the notion of inherent rights. Linking the two concepts could, in turn, illuminate the normative implications of the concept of the Anthropocene and thereby stimulate the development of new normative and political ideas and policies capable of advancing sustainability. As the strongest normative institution or image of modernity, the attribution of subjective rights to nature could restructure political communication and potentially contribute to the creation of safe normative spaces for the preservation of the environment.[71]

4.3 The Principle of Responsibility (Hans Jonas Revisited)

Some authors question the positive value of rights for nature as law's normative foundation in the Anthropocene and instead postulate a revitalisation of "obligations" and "responsibilities" in the law.[72] Proponents of this view generally rely on two principle arguments. First, the diagnosis of an incipient Anthropocene changes the basic assumptions of various modern and critical strands of environmental law (ecological law, earth law, wilderness law), which are mostly rooted in ecology.[73] Although humans are obviously part of nature (which is in line with earlier ideas), they now ultimately occupy a unique position within nature, particularly in relation to its development in the Anthropocene.[74] The concept of the Anthropocene thus represents post-ecological thinking. Although humans are not a priori more valuable than other elements of nature, the sheer scale of their impact requires that they be placed at the centre of environmental policy and legal thinking. This is the only way to develop a realistic assessment of our responsibility towards nature ("descriptive anthropocentrism").[75] Second, by virtue of their specific position, human beings have a unique ethical obligation or responsibility to ensure the well-being of their

---

[69] See, e.g., Gutmann (2019); Wolf (2022), p. 451 et seq.

[70] See, e.g., Berros (2019); Chapron et al. (2019); Knauß (2018).

[71] See Knauß (2018).

[72] See in particular Burdon (2020b); Matthews (2019).

[73] Burdon (2020b); Matthews (2019).

[74] Burdon (2020a).

[75] Burdon (2020a), p. 37 et seq. See also Hamilton (2017), p. 36 et seq., p. 58 et seq.

fellow human beings and to protect the natural foundations of life.[76] In terms of the development of law, it is important to operationalise this responsibility. Conceptually a legal obligation or responsibility is better suited to this task than rights (especially nature's rights).[77] According to this view, rights have always been subordinated to duties throughout the history of law and have so far proved ineffective in protecting the environment (despite their increasing prevalence).[78]

4.4 *The Quest for New Guiding Principles*

In addition to these more philosophical considerations, the diagnosis of an incipient Anthropocene has also triggered a discussion about the sources of legal legitimacy, as well as legal paradigms, principles and imperatives. The basic assumption is as follows: The political and legal processes and measures needed to cope with the conditions of the Anthropocene in the future will require normative underpinnings and frameworks. New approaches and principles are needed to better understand these processes and to legitimise and guide action. In this respect, they can have significant governance implications.

This subsection presents three approaches that are argumentative variations on this basic assumption. The first approach is strongly influenced by scientific evidence on the limited carrying capacity of the environment. The second approach develops existing principles of environmental law, and the third seeks to identify a core set of universal norms that can guide the way in which the challenges of the Anthropocene can be addressed. The practical significance of such considerations manifests itself, e.g., in the efforts of the "*club des jurists*", a number of well-known environmental lawyers, who try to find recognition of central principles of environmental law by means of an internationally binding treaty.[79]

4.4.1 Using Planetary Boundaries as a Normative Foundation

First, both the German Advisory Council on Global Change (WBGU) and the German Advisory Council on the Environment (SRU) take the concept of "planetary boundaries" as a starting point for their quest to establish a normative foundation for law in the Anthropocene,[80] i.e. they are oriented towards "qualitatively definable thresholds of damage, the exceeding of which would have intolerable consequences now

[76] In this respect, the authors refer to Jonas (1979).

[77] Burdon (2020b); Matthews (2019).

[78] In this respect, the studies refer above all to the work of Weil (1984/2005), p. 221.

[79] https://globalpactenvironment.org/en/the-pact/.

[80] Similarly, see Chapron et al. (2017).

or in the future (…)".[81] However, planetary boundaries themselves do not yet constitute a normative concept, principle or imperative; rather, they serve as science-based reference points for a framework of action deemed necessary to avert an undesirable future.[82]

WBGU develops the idea of a global social contract as a normative foundation for the Anthropocene. The contract functions as an imagined framework for the measures required to stay within the 'planetary boundaries' and to move towards a sustainable global economic order ('Great Transformation').[83] This global social contract is based on the idea that individuals and groups (including businesses and science) as well as states and groups of states have a responsibility to avert existential threats to humanity. The central actor in the implementation of this imaginary contract is the 'active' or 'creative' state, which leads the transformation through a wide range of nationally and internationally coordinated measures, setting priorities and at the same time involving and motivating its citizens.[84]

The SRU also takes the Planetary Boundaries as a starting point for its legal considerations, but takes a narrower view by focusing on the German constitution as the normative framework that requires the German state to contribute to governing in the Anthropocene. In this context, the SRU strongly reminds us of two central constitutional functions of the state: the protection of individual liberties and the maintenance of security. With the possibility of overshooting planetary boundaries and the prospect of a potentially devastating Anthropocene, environmental law must no longer be seen as a restriction on individual freedom, but as a prerequisite for ensuring freedom and security. Constitutional objectives such as the maintenance of security, the protection of the "natural foundations of life" and the obligation to protect fundamental rights provide a strong source of legitimacy for government action to protect the environment. In particular, the goal of protecting the "natural foundations of life" (Article 20a of the Basic Law), in combination with the precautionary principle, includes an obligation to take action to stay away from the planetary boundaries.[85] This requirement is not a priori exempt from having to balance against other legally protected rights. However, the more serious the consequences of exceeding the limits, the greater the need for action to keep away from these limits.

[81] See definition of planetary boundaries, WBGU (2011), p. 34.

[82] The WBGU formulates as follows: "The central requirements facing this comprehensive transformation arise from the limits of the Earth system, which force a restructuring of national economies and the global economy within these limits in order to avoid irreversible damage to the world's ecosystems and their impact on humanity." See WBGU (2011), p. 87. The SRU formulates as follows: The findings of the Earth system sciences should be the basis of a "legitimising self-assurance about the ethical and legal framework for action", see SRU (2019), p. 15.

[83] WBGU (2011), p. 87 et seq., 282, 293 et seq.

[84] WBGU (2011), p. 7 et seq., 215 et seq., 295 et seq.

[85] See Faßbender, in this volume, subsection 3.1.6. See also Calliess, in this volume, section 1.

4.4.2 Developing the Principles of Precaution and Sustainability

Jens Kersten takes a different approach.[86] He is particularly interested in the conflict dimensions of the Anthropocene and seeks legal perspectives and concepts within or with which individual freedoms can be safeguarded in the face of Anthropocene conditions. Kersten particularly addresses and develops the principles of precaution and sustainability.[87]

Kersten conceives of the Anthropocene as an "age of local, regional and global conflicts".[88] According to him, the advent of the Anthropocene fundamentally affects our understanding of freedom, both in terms of time and space. The Anthropocene expands our time horizon by highlighting the importance of our actions for the future, but it also creates considerable pressure to act in the present. The later we respond to Anthropocene pressures, the more severe the restrictions on individual and collective freedoms will be.[89] In terms of the spatial dimension, Kersten sees the concept of planetary boundaries as risky. Such a "claustrophobic framework" could block innovative and imaginative thinking and discourage social, economic and environmental innovation.[90] Against this background, he turns to the principles of precaution and sustainability. With regard to precaution, he argues that the transition to the Anthropocene should be used as an opportunity to rethink the different thresholds of risk, danger and threat. In his view, they should and must be redefined when discussing the precautionary principle in the Anthropocene: "Climate change, species extinction and nuclear catastrophes are not 'just' risks, they are already dangerous".[91] The concept of risk needs to be reconceptualised in a way that does not restrict any exercise of freedom. With regard to the principle of sustainability, Kersten notes that it will fail to guide protection in cases where an appropriate balance between different interests is no longer possible. "What does sustainable development mean in the face of the global collapse of biodiversity?" According to Kersten, many developments and processes have entered a "post-sustainable" phase. Here humanity faces a clear danger and must act accordingly.

Kersten's work also considers how sustainability might be conceptualised in the Anthropocene and suggests ways to adapt it. According to him, sustainability will be about ensuring "resistance", "resilience" and "persistence". These are three "types of conflict" that need to be further defined and contoured in order to adequately govern and manage the Anthropocene. *Resistance* must be ensured when there is a risk of an ecosystem "ceasing to function completely". In this case, a balance must be struck "which may lead to a ban on intervention if the ecosystem's resistance cannot be guaranteed by technical intervention". Resilience must be ensured where "adaptation of culture and nature is likely". The potential for resilience depends on

[86] Kersten (2014a); Kersten (2014b); Kersten (2016).

[87] See also Verschuuren (2017); Gonzalez (2017).

[88] Kersten (2014a), p. 73.

[89] Kersten (2016), p. 314.

[90] Kersten (2016), p. 315 et seq.

[91] Kersten (2016), p. 317.

the vulnerability of the ecosystem, the level of stress, and its sensitivity and potential for adaptation. Persistence must be pursued where an ecosystem is to be maintained in the long term. Cultural or technical intervention may be required to maintain the system.

4.4.3 Establishing Universal Norms as a Foundation

A third approach was developed by Nicholas A. Robinson.[92] Robinson begins by pointing out that the Anthropocene will pose major challenges for humanity.[93] These challenges will bring about changes that create a considerable need for orientation, both at an individual and collective level.

Law can contribute to orientation above all if it is based on universal values and norms, reinforces them and also adapts them to the conditions of the Anthropocene. Robinson identifies such values and norms, and justifies their universality on the basis of evolutionary biology. His argument goes something like this: Humans have evolved as social beings in nature, and in the process have developed certain universal traits and abilities. These characteristics and abilities essentially determine their physical, biological and psychological existence. According to Robinson, certain patterns of behaviour and expectations can be derived from these traits and abilities, which can be found ubiquitously as fundamental norms in world religions, philosophies, politics and law. Such principles therefore already exist, but in view of the Anthropocene they need to be remembered, critically reflected upon and contextually concretised.

According to Robinson, for example, humans as social beings are dependent on and capable of cooperation. Accordingly, humans have established the principle of cooperation as a fundamental norm in many societies and most normative systems (Robinson lists many examples from different legal systems). Other human qualities and capacities that manifest themselves as somewhat universal norms in different systems include the love of nature (biophilia), the capacity to be resilient, and the ability to plan ahead and act with moderation (where necessary). It is also important to note that people's well-being is strongly dependent on their perception of being treated fairly in the distribution and allocation of material and non-material resources. According to Robinson, nature is increasingly being included in global thinking about justice. These developments need to be strengthened.

---

[92] Robinson (2014).

[93] He is particularly concerned about the remaining radioactivity in the earth's crust, the amount of greenhouse gases in the atmosphere, the melting of ice masses, changing coastal land masses, the rapid change in ecosystems (in particular the loss of biodiversity), the large quantities of anthropogenic waste and global population growth and its consequences.

4.4.4 Highlights of the New Principles

Certain aspects of these different approaches should certainly be critically reflected upon and discussed in greater depth than is possible here.[94] At this point, however, it is worth highlighting the constructive elements that the authors bring to the discussion on the requirements of law in the Anthropocene.

First, the WBGU and SRU's focus on planetary boundaries addresses the physical, chemical and biological framework conditions of humanity. As it gradually gets hotter and windier, as species disappear and water levels rise, such changes lead to conditions in which peaceful coexistence becomes increasingly difficult or even impossible. The law must deal with these thresholds, limits and possible tipping points in the Earth system—some of which are difficult to identify and measure—and with the technical and social factors that can enable humanity to remain within these limits.

Second, in the face of the Anthropocene, the liberty- and security-preserving function of environmental law restrictions becomes increasingly evident. At the same time, concerns about drastic restrictions on civil liberties and their potential effects on creativity and innovation need to be taken into account.[95]

Ultimately, Robinson's contribution underlines the value of an ongoing, systematic and global discussion of shared values and norms for the Anthropocene. Although evolution appears to be an inappropriate and undesirable biologistic-normative framework for identifying values and legal principles, the principles Robinson identifies are indeed important elements and reference points for guiding political and legal processes and legitimising action.

4.5 *The Advancement of the Existing Legal Framework and Existing Institutions*

Much of the legal literature on the Anthropocene is concerned with the adaptation and development of existing legal and institutional structures in order to respond to Anthropocene challenges. Such considerations can be found in almost all publications in the field. Two lines of argument stand out. The first argues in favour of strengthening existing instruments that are seen as beneficial to environmental protection, and conversely, removing instruments that are detrimental to the environment. The second line of argument is in favour of promoting environmental protection through the development and application of high(er) ranking law.

---

[94] See, for example, the critical discussions in *Jens Kersten* and *Claudio Franzius* regarding the WBGU approach and the ideas of the WBGU and *Jens Kersten*. See Kersten (2016); Franzius (2019).

[95] This was also the case for the Federal Constitutional Court with its considerations on the intertemporal protection of liberty in its so-called "climate decision". See BVerfG, Beschluss vom 24. März 2021 (1 BvR 2656/18, 1 BvR 96/20, 1 BvR 78/20, 1 BvR 288/20, 1 BvR 96/20, 1 BvR 78/20).

Many arguments are based on the assumption that certain legal instruments and institutions have either strengthened or weakened environmental protection in recent decades. The strengthening instruments and institutions should now be consolidated as far as possible and, where necessary, further developed. Innovative or underdeveloped approaches are also considered.[96] For example, there are calls for improved information, participation and legal protection, more international coordination and cooperation, ongoing adaptation of laws and greater effectiveness of the existing mix of instruments.[97] In developing international institutions, it is increasingly important to take account of the complexity of the Earth system[98] and to establish effective disaster management systems.[99] Suggested concepts and tools considered worthy of development include the requirement to assess and consider alternatives in project development ("alternative assessments"), the concept of "nature's trusts",[100] "ecological proportionality"[101] and comprehensive "future impact assessments".[102] At the same time, structures and legal measures that weaken environmental protection should be phased out (e.g. the reduction of environmentally harmful subsidies).[103]

It is also argued that the protection of the environment should increasingly be safeguarded by a higher law ("constitutionalisation of environmental law").[104] The central idea is that nation states will commit themselves—both individually and collectively—more strongly by developing environmental constitutional law and thus strengthen the protection of nature in legislative and administrative practice.[105] The constitutional principles and rights originally developed in the national context should also become increasingly applicable and effective at the international level, thus promoting the protection of the environment, e.g., through an *"environmental rule of law"*, a *"global environmental judiciary"*, a *"global environmental democracy"*, a *"superior basic norm"* or a *"human right to a healthy environment"*.[106]

---

[96] See in particular the contribution by Leinfelder (2017), but see also the contribution by *Gerd Winter*, who argues in favour of the development of the legal concept of "public goods", see Winter (2017), p. 275.

[97] The WBGU (2011), p. 215 et seq. is certainly again exemplary in this respect; see also Baker (2015); Markus (2016).

[98] See in particular Biermann (2014), p. 81 et seq.

[99] Stephens (2016), p. 153.

[100] *Gerd Winter*, who argues in favour of the development of the legal concept of 'alternatives assessment' and 'public goods', see Winter (2017), p. 273 et seq. Fundamental to the development of the legal concept of public goods in law Wood (2014). Fundamental for the assessment of alternatives as an instrument of environmental law Winter (1997).

[101] Winter (2013).

[102] Leinfelder (2017).

[103] Winter (2017), p. 274. On the topic of environmentally harmful subsidies, see also Burger and Brettschneider (2021).

[104] Kotzé (201b), Kotzé (2019a).

[105] See, e.g., Hudson (2015); see the overviews in Boyd (2011); May and Daly (2015).

[106] For details, see Kotzé (2016), p. 201 et seq.; Markus and Silva-Sánchez (2019); Kim and Bosselmann (2013).

The first line of argumentation is part of an extensive series of legal publications aimed at progressively improving the instruments of environmental law. It takes into account the particular challenges of the Anthropocene. In this respect, the analyses and proposals are more comprehensive than previous publications on individual issues of environmental law. The second line of thought is closely related to the first. Well-known principles of constitutional law should be increasingly applied to environmental problems. Their special status and legal weight should contribute to solving the particular challenges of the Anthropocene.[107] The desire to support environmental protection through constitutional law also reflects a scepticism towards parliamentary legislation and the instruments of lower-ranking environmental law.

4.6 Possible Contributions of Law to the Management of Growth Processes

The Anthropocene thesis has inspired many non-lawyers to examine the problems of growth and resource depletion.[108] In the emerging legal debate on the Anthropocene, this issue has so far been discussed only rarely and hardly in a systematic way. Most of the individual contributions on the Anthropocene make only passing reference to the need for a legal approach to these issues.[109] Systematic considerations can be found, however, in the contributions of the WBGU and Gerd Winter.[110]

In a number of fundamental contributions on the "Great Transformation", the WBGU has put forward a wide range of proposals for dealing with the resource problem and the necessary legal adjustments. In developing its proposals, the Council tends to proceed in two steps: First, it analyses the problem and seeks solutions, for example with regard to the transformation of individual sectors (e.g. energy, digitalisation, etc.) or entire problem areas (e.g. oceans, cities, climate, etc.).[111] In a second step, the Council develops and designs transformative measures to implement the solutions. Specifically, it makes proposals for the further development of existing or new legal instruments—at national, European and international levels.

This is precisely where Gerd Winter's argument begins, asking what might need to be added to the WBGU's analysis and proposals. His starting point is the above-mentioned observation that the instruments of environmental law have so far been unable to change or halt the negative global environmental trends. Achievements

[107] Kotzé's book, Global Environmental Constitutionalism in the Anthropocene, 2016, is certainly exemplary for this argument.

[108] Outside of the Anthropocene debate, there are of course studies on the relationship between law and resources, see in particular Faßbender, in this volume, Section 5; Roßnagel and Hentschel (2017).

[109] See, e.g., Kersten (2016), p. 313; Franzius (2019), p. 503. See also the contribution by *Reinhold Leinfelder* (a geologist) on environmental law, Leinfelder (2017), p. 263 et seq.

[110] See also recently the contributions in Reese et al. (2023). See also SRU (2024).

[111] WBGU (2020); WBGU (2016); WBGU (2014); WBGU (2013). For further reports, see https://www.wbgu.de/de/publikationen/alle-publikationen.

have been offset by economic growth and the associated quantitative increase in resource use. Neglecting this is a problem both for environmental protection and for the necessary "Great Transformation". According to him, we need a "transformation before the transformation"[112]; That is to say, legal environmental protection in the Anthropocene must address growth itself., and for this a revision of growth policy is needed.[113] Such a process of change could be supported, among other things, by a change in ethical and anthropological guiding principles, as well as by reforms of regular legislation, constitutions and transnational governance formations.[114] For example, in terms of regular legislation, the waste law should be developed into an ambitious circular economy law,[115] the resource management law should be further developed, and the requirements regarding an "overall economic needs assessment" and the instrument of "alternative assessments" should be strengthened.[116] Economic legislation that promotes growth also needs to be revised (e.g. subsidy legislation, tax and social security legislation). At the constitutional level, for example, economic objectives such as the achievement of macroeconomic equilibrium could be redefined, a fundamental obligation to protect resources could be developed (in addition to existing fundamental rights), and a legal concept of public trust could be strengthened.[117]

The many ideas by the WBGU, as well as the article by Gerd Winter, highlight the role of law in addressing the problems of growth and resource overexploitation. They make it clear that economic and quantitative growth requires legal regulation. Moreover, the transformation of specific policies also requires legal support. In order to achieve this objective, it is necessary to develop and implement a wide range of legal measures. In certain instances, this will entail a radical alteration of existing legislation. The range of legal approaches and measures is diverse and, in some cases fundamentally interferes with existing legal concepts and guiding principles.

4.7 Governance of the Transformation(s) in the Anthropocene

Some legal and political science contributions to the Anthropocene debate consider the social actors that should provide the necessary governance in an Anthropocene future. Many publications focus primarily on the sovereign, territorially delimited

[112] Winter (2017), p. 268.

[113] Winter (2017), p. 269.

[114] Winter (2017), p. 273 et seq.

[115] See Faßbender, in this volume, subsection 5.1.

[116] When managing resources, it is particularly important to avoid the over-flexibilisation of flexible instruments. A reform must emphasise the regulatory elements more strongly. See Winter (2017), p. 273 et seq. For the instrument of demand planning, see also Köck et al. (2017).

[117] For example, Germany is required within the framework Article 109(2) of the German Constitution to aim for economic equilibrium.

nation-state bound by international law.[118] Given the global dimension of the Anthropocene, international organisations are given particular importance. Most publications assume that the national and international system will have to evolve in the face of the Anthropocene, but also that its basic structures will have to remain intact. For example, the creation of new or the adaptation of existing treaty regimes is proposed,[119] and new international organisations or other "global political bodies" are imagined (e.g., a "*Global Environmental Assessment Commission*", "*World Environment Organisation*",[120] "*World Ocean Organisation*",[121] a "*global subject*"[122]). Their roles and responsibilities are essentially defined by familiar or slightly modified legal forms.

Some authors also point to the increasing importance of transnational rule-making and rule-implementation. Alongside the state, such formations provide a wide range of regulatory and governance services that need to be activated and utilised.[123] Such formations consist, for example, of private and public actors that interact across borders.[124] This proposal is based on the observation of the growing regulatory power of such actors and actor constellations. These lower-level actors are becoming more important in the face of growing divisions in the international community and the limited effectiveness of existing international treaties.[125]

4.8 Rethinking Legal Scholarship in the Anthropocene

A number of legal publications address the perspectives, methods and objectives of law in the Anthropocene. The debate on the Anthropocene thus seems to be fuelling an already incipient development in the discussion of methods.[126] The following paragraphs outline four contributions that explore ways of describing and understanding the Anthropocene from a legal perspective, and derive some conclusions in terms of goals and methods from such a perspective.

Tim Stephens, for example, argues that the emerging Anthropocene requires a reorientation of the academic debate on international environmental law. The main task of legal scholarship must be to identify the elements of a just and effective international environmental law. Stephens outlines four features of a preliminary research

---

118 Vidas et al. (2015). See also WBGU (2011), p. 7 et seq., p. 215 et seq., p. 295 et seq.

119 See, for example, the efforts to consolidate international law as part of a *Global Pact for the Environment*. For the current status, see: https://globalpactenvironment.org/en/the-pact/.

120 Biermann (2014), pp. 72-79.

121 WBGU (2013), p. 269 et seq.

122 Schellnhuber (1999).

123 See, e.g., Winter (2017), p. 275 et seq.; Franzius (2019).

124 Overview most recently in Markus and Dilling (2020); and Hayvaert (2018).

125 Franzius (2019), p. 501, 503, 505 et seq.

126 See, e.g., Fisher et al. (2009). See also contributions in Pedersen (2018); Fisher (2016); Philippopoulos-Mihalopoulos and Brooks (2017).

programme: First, existing principles of international environmental law should be developed to protect or, where necessary, restore the life-supporting functions of the earth. Second, international regimes should be developed so that their objectives take into account the findings of Earth system science—in particular the findings on planetary boundaries. Third, the actions needed to stay within planetary boundaries will generate benefits and costs, and these would need to be distributed fairly. Fourth, the process by which global targets are set and national commitments are assigned must also be fair.[127]

Claudio Franzius searches for a fundamental legal concept that can describe the complexities and challenges of the Anthropocene. He finds it in the "transnationalisation of existing legal systems".[128] Its starting point is that the challenges of the Anthropocene cannot be met by national or international law alone.[129] It is therefore necessary for lawyers to broaden their perspective and move away from their traditional state-centred approach.[130] Only such a broadening of perspectives opens the way to a broader understanding of the law's capacity to solve problems.[131] He sees the "transnationalisation of law" as the appropriate perspective or method for such an endeavour, which makes it possible to better understand and clarify the "interplay of different orders, actors and controls"[132] and to observe the "change of national and international law in its transnational problem-solving capacity".[133] From this perspective, there is no need to hope for and conceptualise a "global actor". Rather, from the perspective of the transnationalisation of law, the world appears as a "composite of different strands", characterised by transnational paths and linkages. Power is distributed widely around the globe.[134]

Louis Kotzé argues that the Anthropocene forces the legal sciences to address the limitations and deficits of environmental law. Such an examination could, among other things, lead to a second generation of environmental law (a "*lex anthropocena*" or an "*earth system law*"). Furthermore, environmental law would have to take into account all nine planetary boundaries and the complexity of the Earth system as a whole. Single issues such as climate change cannot be addressed in isolation. Moreover, existing inequalities, injustices and hierarchies must be taken into account in relation to the causes and consequences of the Anthropocene. These, however, are currently manifested, stabilised and reinforced in and by existing environmental law.

---

127 Stephens (2018).

128 With regard to the state of the international discussion on transnational law in the Anthropocene, which has yet to take shape, reference should be made in particular to the editorial by *Emily Webster* and *Laura Mia* in the special issue of the journal Transnational Legal Theory. See Webster and Mai (2020).

129 Franzius (2019), p. 505.

130 Franzius (2019), p. 506.

131 Franzius (2019), p. 506.

132 Franzius (2019), p. 506.

133 Franzius (2019), p. 506.

134 Franzius (2019), p. 504.

In this respect, Kotzé stresses the urgent need for a committed and critical environmental law scholarship that speaks out against "neoliberal anthropocentrism" and for more justice among humans and towards other species. In this respect, environmental law must also become more critically reflective and sensitive to the interests of marginalised groups. Kotzé also calls for more transdisciplinarity and a strengthening of a transnational perspective.

In view of the Anthropocene, there is a growing interest in the methods and findings of comparative legal studies.[135] The basic argument goes something like this: The increasing urgency of many environmental problems in the Anthropocene demands that the global reservoir of legal ideas, experiences and solutions be fully exploited. Because of its knowledge and methods, comparative law is well-suited to inform and shape this process. The various contributions examine the significance of comparative law for the development of national and international environmental law, and seek methods for researching and transferring appropriate legal solutions to problems.

5 Criticism and Discussion

The following section aims to summarise and critically discuss the main findings of the discourse presented. Particular attention will be paid to their (added) scientific or epistemic value of the Anthropocene concept for legal scholarship.

The concept of the Anthropocene is based in particular on the analyses of Earth system science. These analyses describe the whole Earth as a system and humans within it as a powerful factor of global change. Accordingly, Earth system science provides a more complex analysis than the individual scientific disciplines that preceded it. The development of such a complex perspective has only been possible since the 1980s, especially due to the use of satellites and increasingly powerful computers.[136] The Earth system perspective opens up a view of the entirety of the complex interrelationships in the Earth system. In this narrative, humans and nature are part of a dynamic system whose development is largely determined by humans.[137] In this respect, the boundary between humans and nature has become blurry, as has the boundary between specific anthropogenic impacts such as land use, climate change, biodiversity loss, and ocean acidification, among others. While in the past these phenomena may have been treated separately from each other, at a fundamental epistemological level, none of these things can be considered anymore to exist independently of the others. While climate change has often been described as 'humanity's greatest challenge' because of its potential consequences, scale and complexity, "Earth system stability" is humanity's real challenge in the Anthropocene. Merely shifting problems within this one system (or putting them off to a

[135] See most recently Markus (2020); Viñuales (2019); and Morgera (2015); Mehling (2015).

[136] Angus (2016), pp. 29-38.

[137] Steffen et al. (2004); Schellnhuber (1999).

future time) will simply not be possible anymore. At the same time, it must be emphasised that looking at the interdependencies and relationships in the Earth System must not lead to overlooking important local environmental protection and resource issues.

Crutzen's description of the Anthropocene over 20 years ago succinctly summarised the state of scientific knowledge at the time and thus stimulated a public and interdisciplinary scientific debate. The concept of the Anthropocene has proved to be open to interpretation, leading to very different analyses and conclusions. In this respect, it is important to stress that Crutzen's choice of term was also a normative one from the outset. It may not be possible to derive an 'ought' from an 'is', but Crutzen's pinpointing of scientific evidence has already generated a wide range of concerns about the future, as well as considerable political pressure for action, and will certainly continue to do so for years to come.

In the debate on the Anthropocene, it is particularly interesting for environmental law to consider the contributions of law to its emergence. Significantly, law has enabled and supported many of the social processes that have contributed to it. The contributions by Viñuales and Winter, in particular, suggest that environmental law has so far taken insufficient account of these processes and, in particular, has neglected quantitative growth. Two additional ideas should be added to these certainly correct observations. First, the discussion of the contribution of law to the emergence of the Anthropocene makes clear that environmental protection in general is critical in free societies. Under normal circumstances, the social benefits of innovations are initially assumed. As a result, the development and introduction of new technologies, products and applications does not require the prior approval of the democratic legislator,[138] rather, governments need justifiable reasons to restrict the marketing of new products and technological applications. Traditionally, justifiable reasons for restricting activities have come mainly from knowledge of risks, but in many cases, these are not fully known until long after new products and technologies have been introduced. Second, it can be added that since the 1990s environmental law has included elements that at least indirectly address the quantitative problem. The setting of targets for air quality, the (conservation) status of water bodies, habitats and species, and not least the international 2 °C objective in the climate regime, certainly take the quantitative problem into account. However, there is a significant lack of effective enforcement mechanisms in these areas.[139] In the future, it will be increasingly important to control quantitative growth in a more systematic and effective way, both politically and legally, in the light of planetary boundaries. At some point, permissible levels of many activities and uses will have to be established and allocated in accordance with global environmental targets; sufficiency and substitution requirements will receive greater attention. In this respect, the concept of a CO_2 budget has an exemplary function.

Several contributions rightly point out how changing environmental conditions in the emerging Anthropocene will affect existing law and create a need for regulation. What becomes particularly clear in this discussion is that the pace of change

138 Köck (2005), p. 86.

139 Reese (2021); see also Köck and Dilling (2018).

in the Anthropocene will likely increase significantly and may also be characterised by unpredictable, abrupt and potentially catastrophic events. Many authors stress the need for a change in the theoretical and normative foundations of law. This is understandable, given the global environmental trends and the growing unease in the scientific community and the general public about prevailing ideas about the relationship between humans and nature. These debates about the theoretical foundations of law in the Anthropocene should not be dismissed as a self-referential academic exercise, but rather appreciated for what they are: a practical source of guidance which helps us to reflect on the terms and concepts that shape our preconceptions and presuppositions, which in turn influence how we perceive, interpret and normatively evaluate the external world. They thus enable and structure scientific, political and legal debates. Accordingly, both the call for the recognition of the rights of nature and the demand for the strengthening of a fundamental sense of responsibility are essentially motivated by ethical and aesthetic-phenomenological considerations. Nothing is to be said here about the potential value of these claims. What is important here is that their inclusion in the Anthropocene debate points to a perceived need for a reorientation of the ethical foundations of law. It appears that many deem the current foundations to be inadequate to guide the law in managing the relationship between humanity and nature. Such concerns should be taken seriously for many reasons, not least because the effectiveness and legitimacy of the law depend to a large extent on it aligning with prevailing social conceptions of justice in the long term.

In addition to these fundamental considerations, the search for appropriate specific points of reference and guiding principles of law in the Anthropocene is also a key issue. This paper presents three approaches as illustrative examples: While the WBGU and SRU reports focus on the natural foundations of life and emphasise the freedom- and security-preserving function of environmental law, Kersten develops existing principles of environmental law with a view to safeguarding degrees of freedom in the Anthropocene, and Robinson's paper highlights the value of a systematic and global discussion of shared values and norms for the Anthropocene. What can be learnt from the above considerations? On the one hand, aligning legal objectives with planetary boundaries appears prima facie rational; Using the analytical methods available to them, experts identify boundaries or limits in which humanity can survive and where potential existential threats are relatively low. Keeping humanity within these limits becomes an important function of law. However, such an approach faces challenges. Scientific findings may be correct, but the distribution of responsibilities, benefits and burdens takes place within extremely complex social negotiations and existing interest and power structures. Climate change law is an example of this. Agreeing on global emission reduction targets, pledging national contributions, allocating the burdens of reduction between generations, and assigning liability for the emission contributions of individual actors in "climate lawsuits" are extremely complicated, both politically and legally.[140] Moreover, fundamental aspects of the

[140] Kloepfer and Neugärtner (2021), p. 31. See in particular the decision of the BVerfG of 24 March 2021 (1 BvR 2656/18, 1 BvR 96/20, 1 BvR 78/20, 1 BvR 288/20, 1 BvR 96/20, 1 BvR 78/20).

order established by territorial nation-states will be severely challenged in the Anthropocene. Linear implementation and enforcement of rationally justified policies may become even more difficult in the future than it is now. Last but not least, this model could also run into legitimacy problems. The orientation towards planetary boundaries has an expertocratic character. Clear-cut boundaries leave little room for political negotiations and participatory processes, both necessary sources of legitimacy for legal action.[141] In view of politically divided or overburdened (sub)societies in the Earth system, it is questionable how much persuasive power a global threshold that is difficult to precisely determine and scale can develop in the long term. The legitimising power of a somewhat *distant* and abstract boundary as well as an imagined global social contract could quickly be exhausted. National constitutions and laws may have a stronger influence in this respect, but here too exists the practical question of how far individual citizens' loyalty to the constitution will extend under the conditions of the Anthropocene. It will also be important to develop innovative mechanisms and possibly new institutions to strengthen the political legitimacy of Earth system function-oriented scientific expertise. The IPCC and IPBES can provide initial guidance in this regard. Both institutions have global environmental developments as their object of observation and enjoy a high scientific reputation worldwide, and both voices carry considerable weight in public, scientific, political and legal contexts. The creation of a new institution focusing on Earth system functions and stability is conceivable. This could possibly be enriched with participatory and bottom-up elements and, if necessary, convene international conferences ("Earth Summits").

Kersten's and Robinson's approaches, as well as the Global Pact initiative, focus on developing principles and assessing their sources of legitimacy. In the face of the Anthropocene, there is little to argue against the development or improvement of basic principles, and no argument at all against adapting them to make them fit for purpose. At this point, however, it remains questionable whether and to what extent the proposed revisions can actually help to overcome the emerging and worsening problems. Kersten's reinterpretation of precaution and sustainability through a redifferentiation of hazard and risk, and through securing resistance, resilience and persistence, may contain valuable suggestions for a legal approach appropriate to the looming conflict situations of the Anthropocene, but it does not address the underlying problems. Robinson's attempt to root the validity of certain principles in human evolution seems to stem from a desire to emphasise the unity of people and societies in the Earth system. The principles mentioned indeed seem conducive to peace and the preservation of nature. For example, there is nothing to be said against strengthening precaution[142] and cooperation. However, the evolutionary aspect of the argument bears the hallmarks of natural law thinking and pre-positivism, which can have difficult ethical consequences. Quite apart from the fact that the theory of evolution is not universally accepted—as surprising as this may seem to scientists—one

[141] See also Franzius (2019), p. 501; Kersten (2016), p. 315 et seq.

[142] See Faßbender, in this volume, subsection 5.1.2 and section 6.

could draw completely contradictory conclusions from it. It would be more appropriate to justify the principles outlined on the basis of their ubiquitous presence in many positive legal systems (i.e. systems which resonate with the idea of democracy), which could be detected and proven in particular by means of comparative law.[143]

In practice, the most important part of the legal contribution to the Great Transformation will undoubtedly be the development of both new and existing regulatory systems. This will be accompanied by the dismantling of environmentally damaging legal structures. It is crucial that the law will also take into account the fundamental "transformation before transformation" mentioned above. This will include a realistic assessment of the contribution of law in general, and environmental law in particular, to the sustainable use of resources. As a result, fundamental questions of growth objectives and distributive justice are increasingly coming to the fore in environmental law.

In the literature, the role of legal science is also seen in a variety of ways. For example, it is deemed necessary to protect the life-supporting functions of the Earth, to take into account the comprehensive Earth system perspective (in particular the planetary boundaries), to promote global justice (in particular the interests of disadvantaged groups and many animal species), to strengthen the transnational perspective, and to work increasingly in an inter- and transdisciplinary and comparative legal approach. The unifying element of these demands is probably above all the desire for a reorientation and a broadening of perspectives. For example, one goal is to contribute to the adaptation of existing law to better address the problems of the Anthropocene. In particular, fundamental structural deficits will need to be analysed. More to the point, legal scholarship in the Anthropocene will be progressively forced to look beyond its own disciplinary boundaries, to analyse the transformation of statehood and of national as well as international law, to grasp regulatory formations beyond state-imposed orders, and to explore the interdependence of individual problems and their legal management with other problem constellations from an Earth system perspective. Such demands are not fundamentally new, however, many of the arguments put forward in the course of the debates on the Anthropocene have rightly gained new support. Against this background, a debate on the objectives and methods of environmental law appears essential.

Finally, the contributions by Kersten and the SRU in particular draw attention to the increasingly apparent tension between environmental problems and civil liberties. On the one hand, the SRU points out that legally mediated interventions in individual freedoms to protect the environment increasingly serve to preserve those very freedoms, as well as individual and collective security. On the other hand, Kersten's contributions illustrate the conflict between a traditional ordoliberal understanding of freedom and the ecological limits to the exercise of freedom that have now been reached in many cases. In this respect, the preservation of freedoms in the face of

[143] For the methodological issues of deriving general principles from different normative orders, see Markus (2021), p. 85 et seq.

the challenges of the Anthropocene is possibly one of the most important tasks of societies committed to democracy and the rule of law.

In fact, such societies do not appear to be a priori superior to the dictatorships of this world when it comes to overcoming environmental challenges, but they are definitely preferable in terms of enabling the enjoyment of fundamental and human rights. The development of a global-ecological concept of freedom—one which is also against the polemical position of "eco-dictatorship"—is a pertinent ethical-legal objective of transformation.

6 Conclusion: Fundamental Problems and Challenges for Law in the Anthropocene

The diagnosis of an emerging Anthropocene in the Earth system sciences challenges the very foundations of law. In particular, it offers a new account of the relationship between humans and nature, and thus unpacks new problematic dimensions that need to be addressed both politically and legally. Humanity is responsible for the end of the Holocene—it has pierced planetary boundaries with its resource consumption and created an environment that is increasingly unpredictable, unstable and risky. In the future, it will be necessary to regulate humanity's Earth-altering forces. The Anthropocenic diagnosis thus broadens the view of environmental policy and environmental law and alarms both to the interdependence of specific global problems such as climate change and biodiversity loss. Preserving the stability of the Earth system becomes humanity's main task in the Anthropocene. It has become clear that problems cannot be shifted within this singular system anymore, neither spatially nor temporally.

Against this background, the debate on the Anthropocene also opens up new perspectives for law, and especially environmental law. Fundamental structural problems become much clearer, which in turn provides orientation for assessing and dealing with specific challenges, e.g. with regard to the importance of sufficiency, precaution, and more systematic planning of resource demand, or with regard to the role of states as important shaping actors in the Anthropocene.

The first fundamental challenge for environmental law in the Anthropocene may be the growing doubts over current assumptions, ideas, and narratives about the relationship between humans and nature. At worst, these doubts lead to a loss of confidence in the law's guiding principles, objectives and regulatory approaches. The anthropocentric nature of law in general—and environmental law in particular—is increasingly being questioned and criticised. Discussions in this context cover a range of issues: the value of assuming a fundamental human responsibility for the environment that derives from our powerful position in nature; the strengthening of the rights of nature itself (including animal rights); the constitutional protection of environmental protection (including a human right to a healthy environment); or a clear commitment to "strong sustainability", to name just a few. This search may reflect the changing perception of many that traditional values and guiding principles have led to the onset of the Anthropocene, i.e. an environment that is increasingly hostile to (human) life. The discourse on law in the Anthropocene can facilitate orientation in such matters.

The second fundamental problem that emerges from the debate on law in the Anthropocene is that law itself is partly responsible for the onset of the Anthropocene, especially in regard to the continuous increase in resource consumption (quantitative growth). The analysis shows that in free societies, environmental protection is subject to persistent structural pressure. Innovative products, applications and technologies are generally considered desirable and do not require prior approval by governments. As a result, many key laws and legal institutions have enabled and promoted growth over long periods of time by incentivising economic activity and competition, and reducing business risk. Environmental law has not yet been able to effectively mitigate this quantitative growth. However, with limited resources and planetary boundaries on the one hand, and ever-increasing demand for resources on the other, mitigation will have to be achieved in the near future.[144] The law will have to operationalise environmental limits to growth through quantitative and qualitative targets and reconcile these with the continued consumption of resources.[145] This requires, among other things, the generation of legal knowledge, the determination of thresholds, the organisation of demand planning, the fair distribution of increasingly scarce resources, and the move towards an effective circular economy and sufficiency (i.e. the absolute reduction of resource consumption).[146]

The third fundamental challenge for the law in the Anthropocene arises from the paradox that preserving civil liberties will require restricting them. It is increasingly evident that direct interventions into individual freedoms to protect nature also serve to secure freedoms in the long term. The preservation of freedoms in this tense situation, especially the freedoms of future generations, appears to be one of the most important challenges for democratic and constitutional states.

The fourth fundamental legal issue in the Anthropocene is the search for appropriate regulatory actors and governance units capable of transforming the law and using it effectively. The state clearly remains important in its local, national, supranational and international domains. At the same time, it operates in a world of transnational social, economic, political and legal processes. In this situation, it must be able to adapt to shifts in power and new power constellations. If it is to achieve its environmental policy and legal objectives, it must identify the most effective governance actors and mechanisms and use them systematically and strategically (in the sense of polycentric governance).

For example, in times of weak multilateralism, states or other actors may rely more extensively on unilateral measures with extraterritorial effects (e.g. supply chain law, carbon border tax, etc.). While states have a fundamental and human rights obligation to take such measures to protect global environmental goods beyond

[144] See in particular OECD (2019).

[145] See, e.g., Reese (2020), p. 641 et seq.

[146] Most recently Ekhardt (2021); Faßbender, in this volume, subsections 3.1.5, 5.1.2 and section 6.

their own borders,[147] they also have a self-interest in creating an advantage for their own actors in global competition. The practical challenge of generating political legitimacy for ambitious environmental policy goals in relation to globally shared resources is significant, especially in the face of sometimes rather abstract goods or concepts, such as the 2 °C target, staying within planetary boundaries, or aiming for Earth system stability.[148]

A fifth and final fundamental problem is the implementation of existing environmental policy and environmental law principles. The precautionary principle is probably one of the most pertinent examples of this.[149] With several planetary boundaries being breached, it appears that the precautionary principle in its traditional dogmatic form does not provide sufficient answers to the environmental problems of the Anthropocene and therefore needs to be adapted. The perspective of Earth system science shifts the spatial, temporal and qualitative reference points of precaution. Precautionary preparedness and adaptation to impending planetary environmental hazards becomes increasingly important. In such a context, issues of knowledge arise, which are inter alia epistemic and institutional. It is absolutely essential that the conservation or safeguarding of special natural resources for future generations is successful, and the best way to ensure success is for precautionary measures to be taken today.[150] A peculiar qualitative challenge is posed by the tension between precautionary environmental protection on the one hand, and precautionary problem-prevention and adaptation on the other. It will be important to make a clear analytical, political and legal distinction between the different measures: Precautionary measures to prevent the emergence of environmental hazards have a different objective than precautionary measures that aim to prevent the negative effects that follow from these hazards. One group of measures is aimed at "keeping a distance" from danger (e.g. reducing greenhouse gas emissions), the other at proactively preparing for problems resulting from these emissions (e.g. employing negative emission technologies, or growing genetically modified drought-resistant plants) or adapting to permanently changed environmental conditions (e.g. dike construction).[151] The precautionary approach is and will remain applicable to these actions, although it will be more of a risk balancing exercise than an actual precautionary action to prevent harm. The principle must not be abandoned, even when boundaries have already been crossed.

[147] See BVerfG vom 24. März 2021 (1 BvR 2656/18, 1 BvR 96/20, 1 BvR 78/20, 1 BvR 288/20, 1 BvR 96/20, 1 BvR 78/20); Markus and Silva-Sánchez (2019).

[148] See Markus (2023).

[149] For further aspects, see Faßbender, in this volume, subsection 3.1.5.

[150] See also Calliess (2019a, b); Calliess (2021).

[151] See, for the example of negative emission technologies, Markus et al. (2021a, b).

References

Aghion P, Howitt P (2009) The economics of growth. MIT Press, Cambridge
Angus I (2016) Facing the Anthropocene: Fossil capitalism and the crisis of the earth system. Monthly Review Press, New York
Baker SH (2015) Adaptive law in the Anthropocene. Chic-Kent L Rev 90(2):563–584
Baskin J (2015) Paradigm dressed as epoch: the ideology of the Anthropocene. Environ Values 24(1):9–29
Berros MV (2019) Rights of nature in the Anthropocene: Towards the democratization of environmental law. In: Lim M (ed) Chartering environmental law futures in the Anthropocene. Springer, Singapore, pp 21–31
Biber E (2017) Law in the Anthropocene Epoch. Georgetown L Rev 106(1):1–68
Biermann F (2014) Earth system governance—world politics in the Anthropocene. MIT Press, Cambridge
Biermann F, Bai X, Bondre N et al (2016) Down to earth: contextualizing the Anthropocene. Glob Environ Chang 39:341–351
Boer B (1984) Social ecology and environmental law. Environ Plan Law 1(3):233–257
Boianovsky M, Hoover KD (2014) In the Kingdom of Solovia: The rise of growth economics at MIT, 1965–1970. Hist Polit Econ 46:198–228
Bonneuil C (2015) The geological turn: narratives of the Anthropocene. In: Hamilton C, Bonneuil C, Gemenne F (eds) The Anthropocene and the global environmental crisis. Routledge, London, pp 17–31
Bosselmann K (1999) When two worlds collide: society and ecology. RSVP Publishing, Auckland
Bosselmann K (2014) The rule of law grounded in the earth: Ecological integrity as a grundnorm. In: Westra L, Vilela M (eds) The earth charter, ecological integrity and social movements. Routledge, London, pp 3–12
Boyd DR (2017) The rights of nature: A legal revolution that could save the world. Ingram Publisher Services, LaVergne
Boyd DR (2011) The environmental rights revolution: a global study of constitutions, human rights, and the environment. University of British Columbia Press, Vancouver
Bridgewater P, Kim RE, Bosselmann K (2015) Ecological integrity: a relevant concept for international environmental law in the Anthropocene? Yearbook Int Environ Law 25(1):61–78
Brondizio ES, O'Brien K, Bai X et al (2016) Re-conceptualizing the Anthropocene: a call for collaboration. Glob Environ Chang 39:318–327
Brown PG, Timmermann P (2015) Ecological economics for the Anthropocene. Columbia University Press, New York
Burdon PD (2014) Earth jurisprudence: private property and the environment. Routledge, London
Burdon PD (2020a) Ecological law in the Anthropocene. Transnational Legal Theory 11(1–2):33–46
Burdon PD (2020b) Obligations in the Anthropocene. Law Critique 31:309–328
Burger A, Brettschneider W (2021) Umweltschädigende Subventionen in Deutschland. UBA Texte:43
Calliess C (2019a) Abstand halten! Frankfurter Allgemeine Zeitung Vom 11(09):2019
Calliess C (2019b) Abstand halten: Rechtspflichten der Klimaschutzpolitik aus planetaren Grenzen. ZUR 20(7–8):385–386
Calliess C (2021) Klimapolitik und Grundrechtsschutz—Brauchen wir ein Grundrecht auf Umweltschutz? Zeitschrift Für Umweltrecht (ZUR) 32(6):323–332
Chapron G, Epstein Y, Trouwborst A, López-Bao JV (2017) Bolster legal boundaries to stay within planetary boundaries. Nat Ecol Evol 1:1–5
Chapron G, Epstein Y, López-Bao JV (2019) A rights revolution for nature. Science 363(6434):1392–1395
Chertow MR (2000) The IPAT equation and its variants. J Ind Ecol 4(4):13–29
Chakrabarty D (2009) The climate of history: Four theses. Crit Inq 35(2):197–222

Clark T (2015) Ecocriticism on the edge: the Anthropocene as a threshold concept. Bloomsbury Academic, London
Cohen SM (2015) Reintroducing macroeconomics—a critical approach. Routledge, London
Crutzen PJ, Stoermer EF (2000) The “Anthropocene”. IGBP Global Change Newsletter
Crutzen PJ (2002) The geology of mankind. Nature 415:23
Dalby S (2015) Framing the Anthropocene: the good, the bad, and the ugly. Anthropocene Rev 3(1):33–51
Dalby S (2020) Anthropocene geopolitics: globalization, security, and sustainability. University of Ottawa Press, Ottawa
Davies J (2016) The birth of the Anthropocene. University of California Press, Berkeley
Doran CF, Hinz MO, Mayer-Tasch PC (1974) Umweltschutz—Politik des peripheren Eingriffs. Luchterhand, Darmstadt
Dryzek JS (2019) The politics of the Anthropocene. Oxford University Press, Oxford
Ebbeson J (2010) The rule of law in governance of complex socio-ecological changes. Glob Environ Chang 20(3):414–422
Ekhardt F (2021) Suffizienz als Governance und Rechtsproblem—Unter besonderer Berücksichtigung der nachhaltigen Digitalisierung. ZUR 32(9):472–480
Ellis EC (2018) Anthropocene. Oxford University Press, Oxford
Fischer-Lescano A (2018) Natur als Rechtsperson—Konstellationen der Stellvertretung. ZUR 29(4):205–216
Fisher D (2016) Research handbook of fundamental concepts of environmental law. Edward Elgar Publishing, Cheltenham
Fisher E, Lange B, Scotford E, Carlarne C (2009) Maturity and methodology: starting a debate about environmental law scholarship. J Environ Law 21(2):213–250
Franzius C (2019) Klimaschutz Im Anthropozän. EurUP 17(4):498–508
Gerten D, Schellnhuber HJ (2016) Planetare Grenzen, globale Entwicklung. In: Leitschuh H, Michelsen G, Simonis UE et al (eds) Jahrbuch Ökologie. S. Hirzel, Stuttgart, pp 11–19
Gonzalez CG (2017) Global justice in the Anthropocene. In: Kotzé L (ed) Environmental law and governance for the Anthropocene. Hart Publishing, Oxford, pp 219–240
Goudie AS (2013) The human impact on the natural environment: past, present, and future, 7th edn. Wiley-Blackwell, Hoboken
Grear A (2015) Deconstructing the Anthropos: a critical legal reflection on “Anthropocentric” law and Anthropocene “humanity.” Law Critique 26:225–249
Gutmann A (2021) Hybride Rechtssubjektivität. Die Rechte der „Natur oder Pacha Mama“ in der ecuadorianischen Verfassung von 2008. Nomos, Baden-Baden
Gutmann A (2019) Pachamama als Rechtssubjekt? ZUR 30(11):611–617
Hamilton C (2017) Defiant earth: the fate of humans in the Anthropocene. Polity, Cambridge
Hamilton C, Grinevald J (2015) Was the Anthropocene anticipated? Anthropocene Rev 2(1):1–14
Hansmann H, Kraakman R, Squire R (2006) Law and the rise of the firm. Harv Law Rev 119:1333–1403
Hartzell-Nichols L (2017) A climate of risks: precautionary principles catastrophes, and climate change. Routledge, New York
Hayvaert V (2018) Transnational environmental regulation and governance. Cambridge University Press, Cambridge
Hoffmann J (2019) Anthropozän und Recht—Reaktionsmuster am Beispiel des Umweltrechts. Umwelt- und Planungsrecht 39(2):52–59
Hoffman AJ, Jennings PD (2018) Re-engaging with sustainability in the Anthropocene. Cambridge University Press, Cambridge
Hudson B (2015) Structural Environmental Constitutionalism. Wide L Rev 21:201–216
Ireland P (2010) Limited liability, shareholder rights, and corporate irresponsibility. Camb J Econ 34(5):837–856
Jäger J, Springer E (2012) Ökonomie der Internationalen Entwicklung—Eine kritische Einführung in die Volkswirtschaftslehre. Mandelbaum, Wien

Jardine A (2019) Wir haben den Planeten mit seinem stabilen, milden Klima in ein neues Erdzeitalter geführt: das Anthropozän. Neue Zürcher Zeitung Vom 27(09):2019
Jonas H (1979) Das Prinzip Verantwortung: Versuch einer Ethik für die technologische Zivilisation. Suhrkamp, Frankfurt am Main
Jouffray JB, Blasiak R, Norström AV, Österblom H, Nyström M (2020) The blue acceleration: the trajectory of human expansion into the ocean. One Earth 2(1):43–54
Kelly D (2019) Politics of the Anthropocene. Polity, Cambridge
Kenigsberg B (2019) Anthropocene: the human epoch. New York Times Vom
Kersten J (2014a) Das Anthropozän-Konzept. Nomos, Baden-Baden
Kersten J (2014b) Das Anthropozän-Konzept. Rechtswissenschaft 5(3):378–416
Kersten J (2016) Ökologischer Liberalismus—Der anthropozäne Wandel der Welt. Zeitschrift Für Europäisches Umwelt- und Planungsrecht (EurUP) 14(4):312–323
Keys PW, Galaz V, Dyer M et al (2019) Anthropocene risk. Nat Sustain 2:667–673
Kim RE, Bosselmann K (2013) International environmental law in the Anthropocene: towards a purposive system of multilateral environmental agreements. Transnat Environ Law 2(2):285–309
Kloepfer M, Neugärtner RD (2021) Liability for climate damages, sustainability and environmental justice. In: Kahl W, Weller, MP (eds) Climate change litigation, pp 21–44
Knauß S (2018) Conceptualizing human stewardship in the Anthropocene: the rights of nature in Ecuador, New Zealand and India. J Agric Environ Ethics 31(6):703–722
Köck W (2005) Die Entwicklung des Vorsorgeprinzips im Recht—ein Hemmnis für Innovationen zum nachhaltigen Wirtschaften? In: Hansjürgens B, Nordbeck R (eds) Chemikalienregulierung und Innovationen zum nachhaltigen Wirtschaften, pp 85–120
Köck W (2007) Nachhaltigkeit Im Verwaltungsrecht. Die Verwaltung 40:419–439
Köck W (2009) Zukunftsfähigkeit des Umweltrechts—eine Artikelserie anlässlich des 20-jährigen Bestehens der Zeitschrift für Umweltrecht. ZUR 20(9):401–402
Köck W, Bovet J, Fischer H et al (2017) Das Instrument der Bedarfsplanung—Rechtliche Möglichkeiten für und verfahrensrechtliche Anforderungen an ein Instrument für mehr Umweltschutz. UBA-Texte:55
Köck W, Dilling O (2018) Was bleibt? Deutsches Umweltrecht in vergleichender Perspektive. Die Öffentliche Verwaltung (DöV) 15:594–605
Köck W, Markus T (2018) 30 Jahre „Robbenklage": Zur Aktualität der Eigenrechte der Natur. ZUR 29(4):193–194
Kotzé LC (2015) The Anthropocene's global environmental constitutional moment. Yearbook Int Environ Law 25(1):24–60
Kotzé LC (2016) Global environmental constitutionalism in the Anthropocene. Hart Publishing, Oxford
Kotzé LC (2018) Reflections on the future of environmental law scholarship and methodology in the Anthropocene. In: Pedersen OW (ed) Perspectives on environmental law scholarship. Cambridge University Press, Cambridge, pp 140–161
Kotzé LC (2019a) A global environmental constitution for the Anthropocene? Transnat Environ Law 11–33
Kotzé LC (2019b) Earth system law for the Anthropocene. Sustainability 11(23):6796
Kotzé LC (2020) Earth system law for the Anthropocene: rethinking environmental law alongside the earth system metaphor. Transnational Legal Theory 11(1–2):75–104
Kotzé LC, Du Toit L, Louise FD (2020) Friend or Foe? International environmental law and its structural complicity in the Anthropocene's climate injustices. Oñati Socio-Legal Series 11(1):180–206
Krämer L (2020) Rights of nature and their implementation. J Eur Environ Plan Law 17(1):47–75
Latour B (2015) Kampf um Gaia. Suhrkamp, Berlin
Latour B (2017) Down to earth: Politics in the new climate regime. Polity, Cambridge
Leinfelder R (2017) Das Zeitalter des Anthropozäns und die Notwendigkeit der großen Transformation—welche Rollen spielen Umweltpolitik und Umweltrecht? ZUR 28(5):259–266

Lorimer J (2017) The Anthropo-scene: a guide for the perplexed. Soc Stud Sci 47(1):117–142
Lövbrand E, Beck S, Chilvers J et al (2015) Who speaks for the future of earth? How critical social sciences can extend the conversation on the Anthropocene. Glob Environ Chang 32:211–218
Luhmann N (1971) Rechtssoziologie. Springer VS, Wiesbaden
Markus T (2015) Die Wirtschafts- und Wettbewerbsordnung der Europäischen Union. In: Liebert U, Wolff J (eds) Interdisziplinäre Europastudien. Springer VS, Wiesbaden, pp 209–231
Markus T (2016) Die Problemwirksamkeit des internationalen Klimaschutzrechts—Ein Beitrag zur Diskussion um die Effektuierung völkerrechtlicher Verträge. Zeitschrift Für Ausländisches Öffentliches Recht und Völkerrecht (ZaöRV) 76:715–752
Markus T (2020) Zur Rechtsvergleichung im nationalen und internationalen Umweltrecht. ZaöRV 649–707
Markus T (2021) Rechtsvergleichung im Völkerrecht. Mohr Siebeck, Tübingen
Markus T (2023) Unilaterales Umweltrecht als Baustein einer globalen Umweltgovernance—Strukturen, Wirkungen, Grenzen, Legitimation. In: Markus T, Reese M, Köck W (eds) Zukunfsfähigkes Umweltrecht III: Unilaterale Beiträge zur globalen Nachhaltigkeitsordnung. Nomos, Baden-Baden
Markus T, Dilling O (2020) Interglobalsuprasubandtransialidocious‘: disentangling and mapping transnational environmental governance. In: Heyvaert V, Duvic-Paoli A (eds) Research handbook on transnational environmental law. Edward Elgar Publishing, Cheltenham, pp 67–87
Markus T, Silva-Sánchez PP (2019) Der Schutz der Umwelt durch die Amerikanische Menschenrechtskonvention: Das Gutachten des IAGMR OC-23/2017. ZUR 30(3):150–156
Markus T, Schaller R, Gawel E, Korte K (2021a) Negativemissionstechnologien als neues Instrument der Klimapolitik: Charakteristiken und klimapolitische Hintergründe. Natur und Recht (NuR) 43(2):90–99
Markus T, Schaller R, Gawel E, Korte K (2021b) Negativemissionstechnologien und ihre Verortung im Regelsystem internationaler Klimapolitik. NuR 43(3):153–158
Matthews D (2019) Law and aesthetics in the Anthropocene: from the rights of nature to the aesthesis of obligations. Law Cult Human 19(2):1–21
May JR, Daly E (2015) Global environmental constitutionalism. Cambridge University Press, Cambridge
Meadows DH, Randers J, Meadows DL (1972) The limits to growth. Yale University Press, New Haven
Mehling M (2015) The comparative law of climate change: a research agenda. Rev Eur Commun Int Environ Law 24(3):341–352
Morgera E (2015) Global environmental law and comparative legal methods. RECIEL 24(3):254–263
Mills J (2002) A critical history of economics. Palgrave Macmillan, London
Mührel J (2022) Welche Natur? Zur Spezifizierung des Trägers der Rechte der Natur im Globalen Norden. ZUR 33(9):464–471
OECD (2019) Global material resources outlook to 2060—economic drivers and environmental consequences. OECD Publishing, Paris
Pedersen OW (2018) Perspectives on environmental law scholarship. Cambridge University Press, Cambridge
Philippopulos-Mihalopoulos A (2017) Critical environmental law in the Anthropocene. In: Kotzé L (ed) Environmental law and governance for the Anthropocene. Hart Publishing, Oxford, pp 131–155
Philippopoulos-Mihalopoulos A, Brooks V (2017) Research methods in environmental law—a handbook. Edward Elgar Publishing, Cheltenham
Pistor K (2021) Der Code des Kapitals—Wie das Recht Reichtum und Ungleichheit schafft. Suhrkamp, Berlin
Polanyi K (1973) The great transformation—political and economic origins of societies and economic systems

Ramsauer U (2019) Vom Umweltrecht zu Eigenrechten der Natur? In: Schlacke S, Beaucamp G, Schubert M (eds) Infrastruktur-Recht. Festschrift für Wilfried Erbguth zum 70. Geburtstag. Duncker & Humblot, Berlin, pp 465–477

Reese M (2020) Das EU-Klimagesetz—Nachhaltigkeit durch Umweltpolitikplanungsrecht. ZUR 31(12):641

Reese M (2021) Offenbarungseid Zur Wasserrahmenrichtlinie. ZUR 32(6):321

Reese M, Köck W, Markus T (2023) Zukunftsfähiges Umweltrecht II: Suffizienz im Recht. Nomos, Baden-Baden

Rehbinder M, Peukert A (2018) Urheberrecht, 18th edn. C.H. Beck, München

Renn J (2020) The evolution of knowledge—rethinking science for the Anthropocene. Princeton University Press, Princeton

Robinson NA (2014) Fundamental principle of law for the Anthropocene? Environ Policy Law 44(1–2):13–27

Rockström J, Steffen W, Noone K et al (2009a) A safe operating space for humanity. Nature 461:472–474

Rockström J, Steffen W, Noone K et al (2009b) Planetary boundaries: exploring the safe operating space for humanity. Ecol Soc 14(2):32

Roßnagel A, Hentschel A (2017) Rechtliche Instrumente des allgemeinen Ressourcenschutzes. UBA-Texte:23

Sachverständigenrat für Umweltfragen (SRU) (1997) Zur Umsetzung einer dauerhaft-umweltgerechten Entwicklung

SRU (2016) Impulse für eine integrative Umweltpolitik, Berlin

SRU (2019) Demokratisch regieren in ökologischen Grenzen—Zur Legitimation von Umwelt-politik, Berlin

SRU (2024) Sufficiency as a "strategy of the enough": a necessary debate, Berlin

Schellnhuber HJ (1999) 'Earth system' analysis and the second Copernican revolution. Nature 402:19–23

Schneidewind U (2019) Die Große Transformation—Eine Einführung in die Kunst gesellschaftlichen Wandels. S. Fischer, Frankfurt am Main

Schrader C (2015) Am Limit. Süddeutsche Zeitung Vom 16(01):2015

Schröter MW, Bosselmann K (2018) Die Robbenklage im Lichte der Nachhaltigkeit. ZUR 29(4):195–205

Scott KN (2013) International law in the Anthropocene: responding to the geoengineering challenge. Mich J Int Law 34(2):309–358

Skeel DA (2001) Debt's dominion: a history of bankruptcy law in America. Princeton University Press, Princeton

Steffen W, Smith SM (2013) Planetary boundaries, equity and global sustainability: why wealthy countries could benefit from more equity. Curr Opin Environ Sustain 5(3–4):403–408

Steffen W, Sanderson RA, Tyson PD et al (2004) Global change and the earth system: a planet under pressure. Springer, Berlin, Heidelberg

Steffen W, Crutzen PJ, McNeill JR (2007) The Anthropocene: are humans now overwhelming the great force of nature? Ambio 36(8):614–621

Steffen W, Grinevald J, Crutzen PJ, McNeill J (2011) The Anthropocene: conceptual and historical perspectives. Philos Trans R Soc 369(1938):842–867

Steffen W, Broadgate W, Deutsch L et al (2015a) The trajectory of the Anthropocene: the great acceleration. Anthropocene Rev 2(1):81–89

Steffen W, Richardson K, Rockström J et al (2015b) Planetary boundaries: guiding human development on a changing planet. Science 347(6223):1259855

Steffen W, Rockström J, Richardson K (2018) Trajectories of the earth system in the Anthropocene. Proc Nat Acad USA 115(33):8252–8259

Stegemann B (2021) Die Öffentlichkeit und ihre Feinde. Klett-Cotta, Stuttgart

Steel D (2015) Philosophy and the precautionary principle—science, evidence, and environmental policy. Cambridge University Press, Cambridge

Stephens T (2016) Disasters, international law and the Anthropocene. In: Breau SC, Samuel KLH (eds) Research handbook on disasters and international law. Edward Elgar Publishing, Cheltenham, pp 153–176

Stephens T (2018) What's the point of international environmental law scholarship in the Anthropocene? In: Pedersen OW (ed) Perspectives on environmental law scholarship. Cambridge University Press, Cambridge, pp 121–139

Stone C (1972) Should trees have standing? towards legal rights for natural objects. South Calif Law Rev 45(2):450–501

Stone C (2010) Should trees have standing? Law, morality and the environment, 3rd edn. Oxford University Press, Oxford

The Economist from 26.05.2011, Welcome to the Anthropocene

The Economist from 13.02.2021, Seer of the Anthropocene

Thomas JA, Williams M, Zalasiewicz J (2020) The Anthropocene: a multidisciplinary approach. Polity, Cambridge

United Nations Environment Programme (UNEP) (2019) Global environmental outlook 6. Cambridge University Press, Cambridge

Vermeylen S (2017) Materiality and the ontological turn in the Anthropocene: establishing a dialogue between law, anthropology and eco-philosophy. In: Kotzé L (ed) Environmental law and governance for the Anthropocene. Hart Publishing, Oxford, pp 137–162

Verschuuren J (2017) The role of sustainable development and the associated principles of environmental law, and governance in the Anthropocene. In: Kotzé L (ed) Environmental law and governance for the Anthropocene. Hart Publishing, Oxford, pp 3–30

Vidas D (2011) The anthropocene and the international law of the sea. Phil Trans R Soc A 369(1938):909–929

Vidas D, Fauchald OD, Jensen O et al (2015) International law for the Anthropocene? shifting perspectives in regulation of the ocean, environment and genetic resources. Anthropocene 9:1–13

Viñuales JE (2016) Law and the Anthropocene. C-EENRG Working Paper

Viñuales JE (2018) The organisation of the Anthropocene: in Our hands? Brill, Leiden

Viñuales JE (2019) Comparative environmental law: structuring a field. In: Lees E, Viñuales JE (eds) Oxford handbook of comparative environmental law. Oxford University Press, Oxford, pp 3–34

Von Weizsäcker EU, Weijkman A (2018) Come on! capitalism, short–termism, population and the destruction of the planet—a report to the club of Rome. Springer, New York

Waters C, Zalasiewicz J, Summerhayes CP et al (2016) The anthropocene is functionally and stratigraphically different from the holocene. Science 351(6269):6269

Weber M (1921/1972) Wirtschaft und Gesellschaft. Mohr Siebeck, Tübingen

Webster E, Mai L (2020) Transnational law in the Anthropocene. Transnat Legal Theory 11(1–2):1–15

Weil S (1984/2005) An anthology. Penguin Books, London

Wiener JB (2018) Precautionary principle. In: Krämer L, Orlando E (eds) Principles of environmental law—elgar encyclopedia of environmental law—volume VI. Edward Elgar Publishing, Cheltenham, pp 174–185

Williamson OE (1990) Die ökonomischen Institutionen des Kapitalismus. Mohr Siebeck, Tübingen

Winter G (1997) Alternativenprüfung in der administrativen Entscheidungsfindung—Zugleich ein Beitrag zu einer Grundpflicht ökologischer Verhältnismäßigkeit. Werner, Düsseldorf

Winter G (2003) Umweltrechtliche Prinzipien des Gemeinschaftsrechts. ZUR Sonderheft:137–145

Winter G (2013) Ökologische Verhältnismäßigkeit. ZUR 24(7–8):387–395

Winter G (2017) Rechtsprobleme im Anthropozän: Vom Umweltschutz zur Selbstbegrenzung. ZUR 28(5):267–276

Wissenschaftlicher Beirat der Bundesregierung Globale Umweltveränderungen (WBGU) (2011) Welt im Wandel—Gesellschaftsvertrag für eine Große Transformation, Berlin

WBGU (2011) World in transition—a social contract for sustainability. Berlin

WBGU (2013) Welt im Wandel—Menschheitserbe Meer. Berlin

WBGU (2014) Klimaschutz als Weltbürgerbewegung. Berlin
WBGU (2016) Der Umzug der Menschheit: Die transformative Kraft der Städte. Berlin
WBGU (2020) Landwende im Anthropozän: Von der Konkurrenz zur Integration. Berlin
Wolf R (2022) Eigenrechte der Natur oder Rechtsschutz für intertemporalen Freiheitsschutz? ZUR 33(9):451–463
Wood MC (2014) Nature's trust—environmental law for a new ecological age. Cambridge University Press, Cambridge
Zalasiewicz J (2015) Disputed start dates for the Anthropocene. Nature 520:436
Zalasiewicz J, Waters CN, Summerhayes CP et al (2017) The working group on the Anthropocene: summary of evidence and interim recommendations. Anthropocene 19:55–60

Till Markus is Professor of Public Law specialising in environmental and climate law at the Faculty of Law, University of Bremen, and Deputy Head of the Department of Environmental and Planning Law at the Helmholtz Centre for Environmental Research (UFZ) in Leipzig. He is Co-Chief Editor of the Zeitschrift für Umweltrecht (Journal of Environmental Law, ZUR) and Editor of the book series Climate Change Law and Governance (Nomos). His research and teaching lie international, European, and comparative law, with a particular focus on environmental law, climate law, the law of the sea, and legal theory.

Planetary Boundaries and Constitutional Law: Towards Environmental Sustainability by Enforcing the Precautionary Principle

Christian Calliess

Abstract This chapter explores the relationship between the scientific concept of planetary boundaries and German constitutional law. Building on Article 20a of the Basic Law (environmental protection as a state objective), the author argues that the so called "safe operating space" inherent in the concept corresponds to the precautionary principle embedded in the constitution. The article develops a legal framework that regarding ways to handle the challenge of uncertainty moves beyond classical hazard prevention towards risk precaution, with particular focus on avoiding ecological tipping points by a shift of the burden of proof. Drawing on the Federal Constitutional Court's landmark climate decision of 2021, the author demonstrates how this approach can be made judicially enforceable in the framework of climate litigation. The article concludes by outlining both substantive and procedural requirements, including risk identification, risk assessment, shift of the burden of proof and proportionate protective measures, as a legal framework for sustainable environmental governance.

1 Planetary Boundaries, Science and Law

With Article 20a of the Basic Law, the protection of the environment was anchored in constitutional law as a binding state objective.[1] In this respect, the concept of planetary boundaries as defined by planetary system science, underlines that this state task is of existential importance for the continued existence of our planet and humanity.[2] This is because planetary boundaries formulate a science-based concept that describes the limits of ecological systems (absorption capacity), particularly for climate protection, but also for biodiversity, nitrogen and phosphorus input into the

[1] On this, Calliess (2001a), p. 74 et seq.

[2] In this regard, SRU (2019), para. 9 et seq.

C. Calliess (✉)
Chair of Public Law, Environmental and European Law, Free University of Berlin, Berlin, Germany
e-mail: europarecht@fu-berlin.de

M. Reese et al. (eds.), *Environmental Law in Transformation*,
https://doi.org/10.1007/978-3-032-31567-0_2

environment, land use change, freshwater use, ozone loss of the stratosphere and ocean acidification and its interactions.[3]

The core concern of the concept of planetary boundaries is to identify a "safe operating space" for humanity in which it can most likely live under stable Earth system conditions. It is true that ecosystems can compensate for impairments to a certain extent. However, once a certain level of stress is exceeded, disturbances and eventually irreversible damage occur.[4]

The starting point for determining planetary stress limits are scientific findings. In this respect, science has sophisticated methods to determine Earth system interactions, possible dysfunctions, thresholds and probabilities of occurrence. Nevertheless, despite all expertise, scientific uncertainties and prognostic ranges remain. The reasons for this include discontinuous processes that can occur, for example, when Earth system functions change in a non-linear or even abrupt manner when certain thresholds are reached—the exact location of which cannot be determined with certainty. In this respect, Earth system sciences speak of tipping points. The previously mentioned nine dimensions of planetary stress limits also interact with each other, which complicates the already complex prediction of possible damage processes and consequences.[5] If these tipping points are exceeded, irreversible environmental damage looms, which can result in a kind of "devastation scenario" and thus endanger the survival of humans and the environment.[6] Considering this, as well as the remaining scientific uncertainties outlined above, the concept of planetary boundaries draws on a science-based safety margin in determining the "safe operating space", specifically in the context of quantifying critical thresholds, which must be further concretized by political decision-makers.

Particularly in climate protection, the international climate protection goals laid out in the Paris Agreement, which call for limiting man-made global warming to well below 2 °C compared to pre-industrial levels, but preferably to 1.5 °C,[7] define a science-based global ecological limit.[8] The German Constitutional Court's climate decision of March 2021 also attaches a standard-setting significance to the agreement for defining the state goal of environmental protection in climate policy. In this respect, the BVerfG looks to the findings of climate science. With reference to the work of the Intergovernmental Panel on Climate Change (IPCC) as well as two expert reports of the interdisciplinary and advisory German Advisory Council on

[3] Thus in 2009, Rockström et al. (2009), p. 472 et seq.; followed in 2015 by an update: Steffen et al. (2015).

[4] On this, SRU (2019), para. 85 et seq.

[5] SRU (2019), para. 57 et seq.

[6] SRU (2019), para. 13 et seq.

[7] Art. 2 para. 1 (a) of the Paris Agreement (adopted 12 December 2015, entered into force 4 November 2016) 5156 UNTS 79.

[8] Intergovernmental Panel on Climate Change (IPCC) (2018), p. 11 et seq. and 17 et seq.; on development, Schlacke (2014), p. 93 et seq.

the Environment (SRU),[9] the court convincingly links[10] to the findings of the Earth system sciences on planetary boundaries and the budget approach broken down by the SRU[11] to the European Union (EU) and Germany.[12] Even if the latter does not constitute a statement on climate-related planetary boundaries in the narrow sense of the term, but is rather to be classified as a normative statement on budget distributions between the global North and South, it has the function to apply an identified planetary boundary unilaterally to the jurisdiction of a nation state. In view of the actual complexity of the issue, this method seems appropriate and legitimate.[13]

Since the results of Earth system research show that in light of planetary boundaries, measures are necessary, but cannot be established concretely for the community of states or individual states, the science must be assessed normatively and politically in order to derive concrete conclusions.[14] As will be worked out in the following, there is indeed political discretion and scope for action in this respect. However, it is limited by a legal framework that can be controlled by the courts.

Especially through the safety margin mentioned above, the concept of planetary impact limits—as will be shown in this paper—contains a normative component that corresponds with the state task of environmental protection in Article 20a of the Basic Law and the preventative principle immanent in this norm: For both risk prevention and resource precaution seek to avoid,[15] as is the thesis here, critical thresholds or tipping points, which, if reached, threaten serious and irreparable damage to the environment.[16]

---

[9] On this advisory body, established as early as 1971, and its work, the contributions in Merkel (1997).

[10] However, the author, who was a legal member of the SRU from 2008–2020 and contributed to the reports in this capacity, may be biased.

[11] SRU (2020), p. 37 et seq.; on the global approach already Wissenschaftlicher Beirat der Bundesregierung Globale Umweltveränderungen (WBGU) (2009), p. 9 et seq.

[12] BVerfGE 157, 30, para. 16-21 as well as para. 33 ff. in connection with para. 122 and 216 et seq.

[13] On this, Köck (2017), p. 257 et seq.; in general, see the contributions in Dreier and Willoweit (2010); Wischmeyer (2016), p. 253 et seq.; crit. Vierhaus (1993), p. 36 et seq.; Voland (2019), pp. 114, 119; against Buser (2020), p. 1394 et seq.; Kahl (2021), p. 124.

[14] Köck (2017), p. 257 et seq.; Schlacke (2014), pp. 93, 96 et seq.

[15] See here only Appel (2005), p. 299 et seq.; Calliess (2001a, b), p. 176 et seq.

[16] Calliess (2019), p. 385; similarly on the determination of planetary boundaries or ecological impact boundaries as a mix of knowledge-based and precautionary principle already Köck (2017), p. 257 et seq.; agreeing on the relevance of tipping points Meyer (2020), p. 897 et seq. as well as Buser (2020), p. 1392.

2 Concretisation of the Precautionary Principle in Law

2.1 Starting Point

Above all, in the form of the aforementioned safety margin, the concept of planetary boundaries contains a normative component that corresponds with the state objective of environmental protection in Article 20a of the Basic Law and the precautionary principle[17] immanent to this norm.

In its sustainability strategy, the German government correctly describes the planetary boundaries as "absolute guard rails" for political decisions.[18] Nevertheless, there is a gap between scientific findings and the political promise to commit to the planetary boundaries as guard rails for sustainable action on the one hand, and the level of ambition of the adopted government strategies and programs, including the necessary concrete measures to be taken, on the other. This gap widens as soon as it comes to their binding implementation in law and their enforcement in everyday life. With regard to the German Climate Protection Act, the Federal Constitutional Court has addressed this gap with the construct of "intertemporal safeguarding of freedom" and formulated requirements for the political actors.

A significant reason for this gap in political action is that even the concept of planetary boundaries, given the complexity of Earth system science, cannot provide exact "scientific evidence" of when exactly a threshold and tipping point is crossed. At this point, the findings of earth system science must be assessed normatively and politically. In doing so, the political level must operate with the concepts of scientific uncertainty and insecurity typical of a risk society.[19] In this framework, the safety margin formulated by the earth system sciences—according to my core thesis—represents the decisive connecting factor for the political coupling with the precautionary principle under environmental law.

2.2 Legal Basis

The word "protects" in connection with the formulation "also in responsibility for future generations" in Article 20a GG includes contents of the precautionary principle as well as the principle of sustainable development.[20] This is underlined in a historical and systematic interpretation by the Unification Treaty. Article 34 of the Unification Treaty makes it the task of the legislature "to protect the natural foundations of

[17] Calliess (2001a), p. 114 et seq. and p. 181 et seq.

[18] Bundesregierung (2016), p. 12.

[19] See Markus, in this volume, section 2 and subsection 4.1.

[20] This is also the prevailing opinion in the literature: Bernsdorff (1997), pp. 328, 332; Steiger (1997), paras. 87 et seq.; Murswiek (2021) Art. 20a, paras. 32 et seq.; Kloepfer (1996), p. 78; Waechter (1996), p. 326; Di Fabio (1997), pp. 807, 812, 814.

human life, taking into account the preventive, polluter and cooperation principles, and to promote the balance of ecological living conditions at a high level, or at least at the level achieved in the Federal Republic of Germany". According to its Article 45 (2), the Unification Treaty continues to apply as federal law even after the execution of accession. Although it does not have the rank of constitutional law, it has a "special dignity" as former treaty law, on the basis of which it continues to have a higher-ranking binding effect that must be observed.[21] Within the framework of the state's fundamental rights obligations to protect the individual, not only the prevention of danger but also risk prevention is recognised.[22] The precautionary principle is explicitly standardised in European environmental law in Article 191 (2) sentence 2 TFEU.[23] The Commission and the ECJ even regard it as a general legal principle of all Union law beyond European environmental law.[24] In addition, the democratic legislator has anchored and concretised the precautionary principle in many German and European laws. The leading laws in this respect are immission control law, nuclear law, genetic engineering law and chemicals law.[25]

2.3 From Hazard Prevention to Risk Prevention

In view of the consequences (including the unintended side-effects) of industrialisation, scientific progress and the resulting new technologies, the entire legal system—this is currently only most evident in environmental and climate protection law—is constantly confronted with new challenges. The law is thus faced with the task of ensuring rational, risk-adequate and efficient control of this scientific and technological development, corresponding to the state's task of security. The crisis of the governance by law in the risk society[26] illustrates that the tried and tested legal system must in part tread new paths: While security was essentially defined as the absence of dangers—brought about by the state instrument of hazard prevention—until around the mid-1970s,[27] since then the question has been raised whether and, if so, to what extent security also encompasses the absence of risks or the mitigation of risks – brought about by state risk prevention.[28]

---

21 Thus, Klein (1991), p. 732; Kloepfer (1991), p. 34 et seq.

22 On all this Calliess (2001a), p. 179 et seq.

23 Faßbender, in this volume, subsection 4.2.

24 European Commission (2000), p. 12; on this Appel (2001), p. 395 et seq.; in detail Arndt (2009), p. 80 et seq.; Calliess (2022b), paras. 28 et seq.

25 On this, Calliess (2001a), pp. 182 et seq.; overview of the specialised case law in Köck (2005), p. 96 et seq.

26 Concept in Beck (1986), pp 35 et seq. and p. 300 et seq., from a legal perspective, Köck (1996), p. 1 et seq.; Wolf (1991), p. 378, as well as in detail Calliess (2001a), p. 2 et seq. and p. 158 et seq. with further references.

27 Cf. only Isensee (1983), p. 26; Di Fabio (1994), p. 30 et seq.; Köck (1999), p. 144 et seq.

28 Ipsen (1990), pp. 177, 186 et seq.; Murswiek (1990), p. 208 et seq.; Preuß (1994), p. 523 et seq.; Scherzberg (1993), p. 484 et seq.; Schmidt (1994), p. 749 et seq.; Köck (1996), p. 1 et seq.; Grimm

Generally, environmental legislation, parallel to the history of the development of environmental law,[29] is modelled after the traditional basic structures of administrative police law and its forms in commercial law. Accordingly, the polluter-pays principle in environmental law also adopts the attribution triad of danger, causal connection and liable disturber, inherent to police law.[30] The existence of a danger is determined by the knowledge of facts from which, by way of rule of experience and subsequent prognosis, damage to a protected legal asset can be predicted.[31] The "knowledge" of a potential damaging event, based on general rules of experience, is therefore at the centre of effective safety assurance.[32] The greater and more serious the latter is, the lower the probability requirements demanded for the danger judgement; the mere possibility of a damage occurrence, however, is never sufficient for the assumption of a danger.[33] The classical hazard prevention outlined in this way as "damage prevention" thus initially became the cornerstone of environmental law.[34]

However, where there are no experiments confirming the causality of damage and no scientific evidence, a probability sufficient under police law can no longer be established for lack of the necessary certainty of assessment. However, if certain indications point to an abstract possibility of damage, the transition between danger on the one hand and risk on the other is reached.[35]

In certain cases, in view of this lack of knowledge, it will also be possible in the future to proceed according to the law of hazard prevention according to the *trial-and-error method*. However, this method is only appropriate for potential damage that is reversible. If, on the other hand, certain projects, techniques and interventions in the environment can be reasonably expected to have irreversible effects from the outset, the *trial-and-error method* also faces the aforementioned constitutional limits arising from the state's duty to protect. In addition to the task of averting hazards, which could be carried out on the basis of proximity calculations and short, linear causal processes, the complex task of risk prevention—mediated by the precautionary principle—has subsequently emerged.[36]

(1991), p. 197 et seq.; Wahl and Appel (1995), p. 13 et seq.; Wolf (1991), p. 382 et seq.; Köck (1999), p. 147 et seq.

[29] Kloepfer (1994), p. 30 et seq.

[30] Di Fabio (1994), p. 30 et seq.

[31] See only BVerwGE 45, 51 (57); Kingreen and Poscher (2020), para. 8 marginal no. 1 et seq.

[32] Pitschas (1989), p. 785 et seq.; Preuß (1994), p. 527; in detail, Ladeur (1995), p. 9 et seq., p. 69 et seq.

[33] See only Kingreen and Poscher (2020), para. 8 marginal no. 6 et seq.; critical of the prevailing approaches to the definition of probability, Darnstädt (1983), p. 35 et seq.

[34] Wolf (1991), p. 382 et seq.; Di Fabio (1996), p. 568.

[35] Di Fabio (1996), p. 568; Wahl and Appel (1995), p. 86.

[36] For a detailed discussion of all this, see Calliess (2001a), p. 153 et seq.

2.4 Content and Requirements of the Precautionary Principle

In the literal sense, prevention primarily means the creation of a stock for the future by doing without in the present: Natural resources, which are becoming increasingly scarce, must be used sparingly in the present in order to preserve them as a stock for future generations in the interest of their viability. At the same time, this resource precaution serves the purpose of conserving environmental resources in the interest of their future use by not exhausting the ecological limits. In this way, "free spaces" are to be preserved in the form of "future habitats" for humans and nature, as well as in the form of reserves for pollution and ecological resilience.[37]

However, precaution is also designed to cope with risk situations defined by uncertainty and insecurity (risk prevention). In expansion of the concept of danger oriented on the concept of probability, risk can be defined as a situation in which, in the case of an unhindered course of events, a condition or behaviour possibly leads to an impairment of legal assets. The decisive factor is therefore the replacement of the concrete, sufficient probability by the mere possibility, the abstract concern, of the occurrence of damage.[38] In this way, the object of risk prevention becomes danger instead of damage, with the aim of avoiding the misjudgement of a danger.[39] The decisive consequence of the extension of the classic danger prevention model by the precautionary model is shifting the permissible time of intervention for state measures to a prior point.[40]

If damage is either completely uncertain or its realisation can be practically ruled out with certainty, then—as the BVerfG has also ruled—the democratically elected legislature can decide that this so-called residual risk is acceptable.[41] This political decision only becomes legally relevant insofar as there is an obligation that the residual risk is always kept as low as possible according to the latest state of science and technology.[42]

2.5 Material and Procedural Requirements of the Precautionary Principle

The scope of the precautionary principle cannot be unlimited in a free constitutional state. In this respect, it is first necessary to concretise the precautionary principle in a way that conforms to the rule of law. The aim must therefore first be to prevent

---

[37] Lübbe-Wolff (1997), p. 55 et seq. and p. 68 et seq. with further references.

[38] Murswiek (1985), pp. 81, 86; Ipsen (1990), p. 186 et seq.; Wahl and Appel (1995), p. 88; also Darnstädt (1983), p. 36 et seq.

[39] Cf. Hansen-Dix (1982), p. 21; Scherzberg (1993), p. 497 et seq.; Wahl and Appel (1995), p. 76; Köck (1996), p. 1, 19.

[40] For more details, see Calliess (2001a), p. 154 et seq.

[41] BVerfGE 53, 30 (59); BVerfGE 49, 89 (137 et seq.).

[42] In-depth, Calliess (2001a), p. 167 et seq.

precaution from becoming a "shot in the dark".[43] Against this backdrop, an objective, exhaustive determination of all information relevant to the precautionary measure is required in the context of risk assessment.[44] For precaution, an abstract potential for concern is sufficient, i.e. a theoretical—in contrast to pure speculation, however, based on scientific plausibility reasons—initial suspicion which, however, must not yet be empirically solidified or even scientifically proven in the sense of a majority opinion.

2.5.1 Risk Identification with the Aid of Science and Technology

In a first step, therefore, it must be scientifically determined and continuously researched what the respective risk potential consists of and how extensive it is (preliminary scientific risk determination). Based on relief and concern criteria—with scientific help—formulas can be developed that serve to determine this initial suspicion. Based on such formulas, concrete rules for a precautionary approach to uncertainty can be formulated.[45]

2.5.2 Risk Assessment

This risk identification must be separated from the risk assessment, i.e. the evaluative consideration of the cause of precaution characterised by the abstract concern potential.[46] Within this framework, it must be decided whether the respective risk potential is tolerable or not and with which measures it should be countered according to the sliding scale of safety dogmatics (hazard-risk-residual risk) (preliminary political risk assessment). This assessment is first and foremost the responsibility of the legislator, who, within the framework of the aforementioned constitutional requirements, has a scope for assessment, evaluation and prognosis.

2.5.3 Precautionary Measure

Concept of Protection

With regard to the precautionary measure to be taken, it is then possible—taking into account the principle of proportionality—to identify different levels of interference

[43] Ossenbühl (1986), p. 166.

[44] Calliess (2001a), p. 207 et seq.

[45] Cf. the proposals of the German Advisory Council on the Environment: SRU (2011), paras. 430 et seq.

[46] Cf. on the whole Murswiek (1990), p. 217 et seq.; Wahl and Appel (1995), p. 109; Calliess (2001a), p. 214 et seq.; similarly, Scherzberg (1993), p. 499 et seq.; European Commission (2000), p. 14 et seq

with the economic freedom guaranteed by fundamental rights. In this respect, it is not a matter of preventive bans with licensing requirements from the outset, but often of generating information accompanying the preliminary risk assessment, which is suitable for clarifying the existing uncertainty. Following from this, it is a matter of creating transparency and enabling traceability in the event that a substance in a product that was initially considered harmless turns out to be dangerous due to new findings.[47]

Moreover, the precautionary principle requires state authorities to act in a forward-looking manner, which includes special consideration of risks and their short- and long-term effects.[48] Furthermore, according to the precautionary principle, state authorities are constitutionally obliged to preserve economic space for newcomers (i.e., those companies that start their activities and thus burden the environment for the first time) as well as future generations.[49] This requirement corresponds with the approach of "intertemporal safeguarding of freedom" in the BVerfG's climate decision. Finally, in the case of complete or partial irreversibility of environmental pollution, the precautionary principle requires decision-makers to act with foresight, which includes special consideration of long-term risks.[50] Accordingly, the legal assessment of environmental harm by pollutants must not only focus on the current effects, but also take into account their summation over years.[51]

Measured against these normative requirements, Article 20a of the Basic Law (together with the fundamental rights to life and health, Art. 2 (2) Basic Law) in conjunction with the precautionary principle results in a judicially controllable mandate to act, in the course of which the German state authorities (analogously, this applies to those of the EU via Article 191 TFEU) must visibly steer away from the planetary boundaries and avert a (further) overstepping of the ecological stress limits by means of a suitable, effective as well as long-term, coherent and legally binding protection concept.[52]

Proportionality in Consideration of Conflicting Interests ("Opportunities and Risks")

It is precisely the dynamic, precautionary character of the environmental state,[53] which is expressed not least in the understanding of its constitutional basis in Article

---

[47] Calliess and Stockhaus (2011), p. 924 et seq.; in detail on the example of nanomaterials, SRU (2011), paras. 438 et seq

[48] Murswiek (1996), p. 225; Kloepfer (1996), p. 77 et seq.; Steiger (1997), para. 103.

[49] Waechter (1996), p. 326; Calliess (2001a), p. 182 et seq.

[50] Murswiek (1996), p. 225; Kloepfer (1996), p. 77 et seq.; Steiger (1997), para. 103.

[51] Reiter (1998), p. 48 et seq. and 133 et seq.; also Feldhaus (1987), p. 5 Wahl and Appel (1995), p. 133 et seq.

[52] For a detailed discussion, see Calliess (2001a), p. 125 et seq. and p. 235 et seq.

[53] On the emergence of the term, Calliess (2001a), p. 30 et seq.

20a of the Basic Law as well as the precautionary principle concretising and optimising it, that it almost inevitably comes up against the rights, legal goods and legal principles united under the principle of the rule of law designed to ensure permanence and legal certainty. In this respect, the Federal Constitutional Court states:

> The requirement of the rule of law, when viewed in conjunction with the general presumption of liberty in Article 2 (1) of the Basic Law in favour of the citizen, requires that the individual be protected from unnecessary interference by public authority. If a legislative intervention is indispensable, the means must be suitable for achieving the legislative objective and must not impose an excessive burden on the individual.[54]

From this follows that under the rule of law (also) every state precautionary measure must be proportionate. It is therefore no coincidence that the principle of proportionality is unanimously described in practice and literature as the limit of the precautionary principle.[55] However, if done in an abstract and undifferentiated manner, this insight is of little help. This is especially true because the starting point of the proportionality test under the rule of law remains unclear.[56]

Against this background, it is above all the positioning of the proportionality test to fundamental rights that is important, which thus marks the actual constitutional limit of the precautionary principle. Accordingly, it follows from the modern understanding of fundamental rights that every law legitimising interference is in turn examined for its suitability, necessity and appropriateness, in order to carry out the encroachment on fundamental rights as sparingly as possible.[57] Accordingly, part of the literature correctly points out that the principle of proportionality can only develop its control effect where individual legal positions are affected, especially when state precautionary measures interfere with fundamental rights.[58] The attempt to further substantiate the principle of proportionality in general terms with regard to precautionary measures under uncertainty does not lead anywhere.[59] However, these authors leave it at this correct statement. In particular, they overlook the necessity of anchoring the proportionality test for precautionary measures in the fundamental rights test. If one wants to determine the limits of the precautionary principle and thus the constitutional limits of the environmental state at a relatively higher level of abstraction, fundamental rights and the proportionality test based on them provide

---

[54] BVerfGE 55, p. 159 (165); E 17, p. 306 (313 et seq.).

[55] BVerwGE 69, p. 37 (44); European Commission (2000), p. 20 et seq.; Sendler (1983), p. 256 et seq.; Ossenbühl (1986), p. 167 et seq.; Rengeling (1989), p. 37 et seq.; Trute (1998), p. 72 et seq; Di Fabio (1997), p. 828 et seq.; Lübbe-Wolff (1997), p. 63 et seq.

[56] Instructive on this, Köck (2005), p. 103 et seq.

[57] BVerfGE 55, p. 159 (165); E 17, p. 306 (313 et seq.); Wendt (1979), p. 414 et seq.; Di Fabio (1997), p. 829.

[58] Trute (1998), p. 56 et seq.; Di Fabio (1997), pp. 807, 833. It is nevertheless surprising that the above-mentioned authors nevertheless discuss the principle of proportionality in abstract terms in advance. In general, on the concretised fundamental rights connecting factor of the principle of proportionality Wendt (1979), p. 461 et seq.; Schnapp (1989), p. 854 et seq.

[59] Ossenbühl (1986), p. 167; Lübbe-Wolff (1997), p. 64 et seq.

a sufficiently concrete framework for examination. From this follows which legislative and subsequently administrative limits the rule of law sets for the environmental state.

In a concrete case, the balancing has to take place within the framework of a multipolar proportionality test, which can admittedly only be outlined here.[60] The prohibition of excess of defensive rights on the one hand and the prohibition of inadequate protection of the state obligation to protect on the other hand form a kind of corridor,[61] within which the legislature has the leeway required by the separation of powers to weigh and balance the conflicting interests. This results in the following structure for judicial review of the legislative distribution of freedom: Its starting point lays at the respective legal positions of the multipolar constitutional law system. For each of them, the first and second step of the proportionality test must be carried out individually. Thus, for environmental polluters, the first and second step of the prohibition of excess under their defensive rights must be examined. In the case of the party affected by pollution, the first and second steps of the prohibition of insufficient protection under protective laws must be examined.

Correspondingly, the same must be done for the public interest concerns affected (embodied in Article 20a of the Basic Law in the case of environmental protection relevant here). At the third stage of the multipolar proportionality test, all three test strands converge. Figuratively speaking, this means that the walls of the corridor on the third level are no longer considered independently of each other—one-dimensionally, as it were—but that the corridor now only arises in a multidimensional manner in the first place. This is done through the instrument of a multipolar interest balancing, in the framework of which the interrelationships between the legal positions of the multipolar constitutional law relations are taken into account and brought into balance.[62]

Based on these specifications, the significance of the various interests to be weighed in the legislative distribution of freedoms can be defined. It is recognised that parallel interests shift the weighting within the balancing process. Accordingly, the interests of the duty to protect fundamental rights (e.g. Article 2 (2) of the Basic Law) and the common good (e.g. Article 20a of the Basic Law) can be added up, provided they are identical in content, and thus strengthen a specific objective pursued with the state measure (e.g. air pollution control) as well as the interests it protects. The balancing determined in this way is a framework-like specification for the legislative development of a concrete protection concept, or—if a protection concept already exists—a yardstick for its judicial review and (possibly) further development or redesign.[63]

---

[60] In depth, Calliess (2001a), p. 577 et seq.

[61] The views of Canaris (1989), p. 163 et seq.; Jarass (1985), p. 382 et seq.; Scherzberg (1989), p. 221 et seq.; Isensee (2011), para. 191 marginal nos. 303 et seq. such a model; Hoffmann-Riem (1994), p. 1384 et seq. explicitly speaks of such a corridor; likewise, Cremer (2003), p. 310 et seq.; Brönneke (1999), p. 274 et seq. constructs—under the same premises—a star-shaped model.

[62] In this regard, Cremer (2004), p. 314 et seq. critically.

[63] Calliess (2001a), p. 580 et seq.

As a concretising component of the multipolar proportionality test, an alternative test must be carried out[64]—viewing all legal positions involved: It opens up not only the state's scope for action, but also that of individual freedom. Thus, a variant can be compatible with the requirements of the prohibition of excess as well as with those of the prohibition of inadequacy. The alternatives assessment thus aims precisely at the described corridor between both prohibitions. It becomes an instrument of the overall balancing within the framework of the multipolar proportionality test, which serves to establish practical concordance between the individual legal positions of the multipolar constitutional law system. For by bringing about flexibility, the alternatives test helps to find the "right balance" between favouring and burdening and thus to establish the balance of the distribution of freedom in the multipolar constitutional rights system.[65] In this context, for example, the authorisation of pilot projects as an alternative to bans can be expedient.[66]

3 Towards Environmental Sustainability

3.1 Environmental Sustainability and Precaution Through Integration

The so-called *"integration principle"* or *"cross-cutting clause"* of the EU enshrined in Article 11 TFEU offers a good example for legal pathways to achieve the goal of environmental sustainability. It reads as follows: *"Environmental protection requirements must be integrated into the definition and implementation of the Union's policies and activities, in particular with a view to promoting sustainable development."* According to the conception and intention of Article 11 TFEU, the integration clause is a significant instrument for implementing the principle of sustainable development in EU Law.[67] In conjunction with the Preamble and Article 3(3) sentence 2 TEU, it implies even a general principle of sustainability for the EU.

Article 11 TFEU can be understood as a primary law requirement for conducting a strategic environmental impact assessment, which applies not only to individual measures, but also to policies, programs, plans and laws.[68] However, within the framework of Article 11 TFEU, the requirements of environmental protection must be balanced against conflicting interests (such as economic freedom and the principle of the welfare state).

---

64 In general, Winter (1997).

65 Calliess (2001a), p. 592 et seq.; with concrete examples, see Calliess (2009), p. 221 seq.

66 SRU (2009).

67 Calliess (1998), p. 559 et seq. and SRU (2019), paras. 270 et seq. and paras. 309 et seq.; in this sense as well European Commission, see document SEC (93) 785.

68 Appel (2018), para. 2 marginal no. 44.

In this regard, politics, and in particular the legislator, have a political margin of discretion in implementing the provision. Nevertheless, when balancing environmental protection against conflicting economic and social interests, two specific aspects must be taken into account. Article 11's demands have to be implemented in conjunction with the goals of Article 191(1) and the precautionary principle in Article 191(2) TFEU.[69] In addition, fundamental rights obligations that guarantee an *"ecological minimum subsistence level"* by respecting a *"safe operating space"* have to be taken into account. In the balancing process, this is further supplemented by a prohibition of insufficient means or actions (*"Untermaßverbot"*) on the part of the legislature.

Secondly, the concept of integration implies that environmental considerations cannot simply be disregarded.[70] Instead, they must be an integral part and visibly shape the content of the individual EU measure.[71]

Apart from these substantive requirements, the integration clause also has a procedural dimension, that demands effective monitoring of the fulfilment of the substantive side in European decision making and the Member States' implementation process[72] by institutionally established scrutiny mechanisms or *"watch dogs"*. Article 11 TFEU has gained significance as environmental burdens have increased and the recognition has grown that environmental assets such as ecosystems, environmental media, and the climate are often closely interconnected, giving rise to strong interdependencies between various environmental sectors and issues.[73] The legislative scope of discretion in this respect is exceeded when a measure is visibly designed to the detriment of environmental protection. Such a measure, which is very likely to result in significant damage to the environment may not be adopted under Article 11 TFEU. A policy that crossed this boundary would be unlawful, as it would be in breach of Article 11 TFEU.[74]

This leads to the assumption that Article 11 TFEU has great potential for realising the ecological transformation of both of its addressees, the Union and its Member States. Nevertheless, it can be said that the *explicit* inclusion of an ecological clause in highly complex areas, such as economic policy, could be beneficial, in particular, considering the difficulty regarding the implementation and legal enforcement of Article 11 TFEU.[75] The implementation of goals is the responsibility of the Member States and too often lost in the complexity of the political process. Therefore, it is

---

[69] Calliess (2022a), para. 14.

[70] See Calliess (1998), p. 565 et seq. as well as Calliess and Dross (2020), p. 461.

[71] Hailbronner (1992), p. 20 et seq.; Durán and Morgera (2020), ch. 1 section 4.2.1; Epiney (2013), p. 162; Appel (2018), para. 2 marginal no. 4 et seq.; Scheuing (1989), p. 176 et seq.; Kahl (2018); contra Nettesheim (2023), para. 22, who also refers in para. 23 et seq. to European jurisdiction.

[72] On this already Calliess (1998), p. 566 et seq.

[73] Calliess and Dross (2020), p. 461.

[74] In contrast, AG Geelhoed argues that Article 6 EC [now Article 11 TFEU] can only serve as a criterion for the legality of Community acts if environmental concerns have obviously not been taken into account or completely disregarded, Opinion in Case C-161/04, ECR 2006, I-7183, para. 59 (no decision in this case due to withdrawal).

[75] Equally Kahl (2018), para. 50 et seq.; Calliess and Dross (2020), p. 461.

very welcome that as part of the European Green Deal, the European Commission has announced that it will work to strengthen efforts to ensure that existing legislation and measures relevant to the European Green Deal are enforced and effectively implemented.[76] If the proclaimed strategy of the European Green Deal is not to be lost in everyday politics, Article 11 TFEU must fulfil its potential for realising the transformation towards an ecological legal system. The provision points the way to an ecologically sustainable and thus future-oriented economic policy that makes environmental policy one of its integral parts and is aligned with the sustainability and viability of ecological systems. Ultimately, the contribution of Article 11 TFEU to the realisation of an *"ecological European Union"* depends on how it is handled in practice.

3.2 Environmental Sustainability and Precaution Through Procedure

Even though there is further room for unfolding the potential of Article 11 TFEU, it is evident that there are already instruments and tools, which provide for an operationalisation of environmental principles, such as the reversal of the burden of proof in the context of the precautionary principle.[77] If, however, an appropriate level of protection cannot be derived directly from scientific results in view of continuing uncertainties, there is a growing need to safeguard environmental sustainability by means of suitable procedural rules.

3.2.1 Lowering the Standard of Proof in the Legislative Precautionary Measure

Procedural regulations shall ensure that the scope for assessment and evaluation given in the gauging of scientific data and findings is disclosed. Above all, if the scientific risk assessment does not arrive at unambiguous evaluations, the decision-making procedure fulfils an important compensatory function; it must be *"socially robust"*.[78] This is the only way to ensure social acceptance.[79] The precautionary principle is therefore also interpreted in the literature as a process requirement, in the course of which various procedural requirements are formulated.[80] In this respect, various aspects must be taken into account:

[76] European Commission (2019), p. 4; on proposals for strengthening enforcement of European Environmental Law, see SRU (2020), paras. 753-754.

[77] See on the precautionary principle, Calliess (2022b), paras. 28-37; see in detail, Calliess (2001a), p. 207 et seq.

[78] In depth, Nowotny et al. (2001).

[79] In detail, Grunwald (2005), p. 54 et seq., especially 58 et seq.

[80] Wahl and Appel (1995), p. 1 et seq.

The question will often arise as to what should be done if the existing uncertainty cannot (yet) be determined due to a lack of sufficient research or cannot be resolved with the available means of investigation in view of an existing dispute between experts. If, as in the area of classical hazard prevention, the sufficient probability of the occurrence of damage must be proven, then the burden of proof lies with the potentially affected party of the risk or—corresponding to the state's duties to protect from Article 20a GG and the fundamental rights—with the state.

Outside the legal discussion, for example in philosophy and environmental ethics, a general reversal of the burden of proof ("in dubio contra projectum") has therefore been demanded for certain risks.[81] From this point of view, the precautionary principle implies a reversal of the burden of proof. The problems of a general reversal of the burden of proof under the rule of law, in particular under fundamental rights,[82] cannot be further discussed here.[83]

Against this backdrop, the introduction of a rebuttable presumption of danger could be considered.[84] Within the framework of the abstract potential for concern, or the much-cited situation of non-liquidity, in which the existing uncertainty cannot be clarified with the available means of investigation, the precautionary principle acts according to the legal model of a rebuttable presumption of danger, which—as the Commission rightly states in its statement on the precautionary principle[85]—can lead to a reversal of the burden of proof.[86] Of course, for reasons of the rule of law, the requirements for the burden of proof must not reach the level of positive proof for the possibility or impossibility of harm.[87]

In order to shake this presumption, the entity causing the risk is required to present facts and prove, in the sense of a reasonable probability, that there is no threat of harm from its substance, manufacturing process or product. This puts the onus on the causer, from whose sphere the risk originates, with the consequence that the state institutions—starting with the legislator up to the administration deciding in the individual case (on the basis of the adopted law)—are relieved in this situation of uncertainty. Such a shifting of the burden of proof can be enacted by the legislator as law within the framework of its risk decisions for individual cases. It acts as an incentive for the risk causer to conduct their own impact research parallel to development research in order to rebut the legal presumption of danger in a—where

[81] Jonas (1984), p. 70 et seq.; Böhler (1993), p. 389.

[82] See the in this regard questionable decisions of German administrative courts like VGH Kassel, NJW 1990, p. 336; VG Gelsenkirchen, ZUR 1993, p. 119 et seq.

[83] Calliess (2001a), p. 19 et seq. and p. 431 et seq. with further references.

[84] Calliess (2001b), p. 1725, esp. p. 1732 et seq.

[85] European Commission (2000), p. 24; in this respect, Rengeling (2000), p. 1479 et seq.; in turn, Appel (2001), pp. 396, 398.

[86] In detail, Calliess (2001a), p. 223 et seq.; also, Arndt (2009), p. 290 et seq. and p. 295 et seq., who assumes as a direct consequence of the precautionary principle only a reduction of the standard of proof, but not a reversal of the burden of proof, but sees such a reversal realised within the framework of the authorisation procedures under secondary law.

[87] Rehbinder (1989), p. 9 et seq.; Ritter (1992), p. 648 et seq.; in depth, Calliess (2001a), p. 223 et seq.

necessary, set up specifically for this purpose—procedure in which the concerns of those affected by the risk are also taken into account.[88]

3.2.2 Transparency in the Legislative and Administrative Process

Procedural regulations must ensure that the scope for assessment and evaluation given in the evaluation of scientific data and findings is disclosed. A transparent decision-making process requires that the entire range of scientifically justifiable risk assessments, from optimistic to pessimistic assumptions, be presented and alternative solutions be developed in the process of concretisation. Consideration of the entire spectrum of scientifically justifiable positions also includes minority opinions.[89] Only if precautionary measures are justified in a sufficiently transparent manner in the political process can a loss of credibility be avoided, which can result, for example, from adaptation to new findings. Therefore, in order to improve the political implementation of measures, the lack of scientific knowledge must be addressed. This requires a change in the political risk culture.[90]

3.2.3 Appropriate Participation of Social Groups in the Legislative and Administrative Process

In view of the political character of risk assessment, the decision-making process must not only be transparent, but must also allow for a plural discourse on values and therefore take place with the institutionalised participation of the representatives of social groups involved in public life.[91] It is crucial, however, that the political and the scientific-technical levels are appropriately linked with each other procedurally, so that each side can fulfil the function to which it is entitled. The institutionalised participation of social groups increases the political legitimacy of decisions and should ensure that a broad spectrum of risk assessment criteria is taken into account.[92]

3.2.4 Monitoring the Implementation of the Precautionary Principle in the Legislative and Administrative Process

If the protection of future generations required by Article 20a of the Basic Law is to be given practical significance, then the (constitution-amending) legislature is obliged to

---

[88] For more details on all this, see Calliess (2001a), p. 223 et seq with further references; SRU (2011), paras. 438 et seq.

[89] European Commission (2000).

[90] European Commission (2000). For this purpose, using the example of nanomaterials, SRU (2011), paras. 438 et seq.

[91] Fundamentally, Stern and Fineberg (1996).

[92] Hey (2000), p. 85 et seq.; Calliess (2001a), p. 463 et seq.

institutionalise the state's long-term responsibility flowing from it through regulated procedures and forms of organisation.[93] The obligation of procedural implementation, which is aimed at helping the substantive core of the norm to become effective, is essential, especially in the case of those norms which—like Article 20a of the Basic Law—are only accessible to a limited extent to substantive concretisation.[94] In this sense, the procedure compensates for the indeterminacy of the content of a legal norm. A procedural concretisation of the provisions of Article 20a GG requires above all institutional precautions. A decisive political reason for this is the realisation that sustainability concerns have a comparatively weak standing in the system of electoral periods and party democracy.

In this respect, it is possible to build on existing institutions or establish new ones.[95] For example, one could start with the administrative state and either use existing administrative decision-making structures in the interest of sustainability or entrust newly established administrative institutions with the protection of specific sustainability concerns.[96] Further possibilities open up with monitoring along the legislative process.[97] This monitoring can take place with the institutionalised involvement and participation of scientific policy advice in the political decision-making process.[98] Among others, a permanent committee to be set up by the Bundestag to examine the ecological consequences of laws and to assess the impact of technology,[99] an independent council of experts for future issues as well as similar models of an environmental council,[100] an ecological council,[101] a sustainability council[102] or also a council for intergenerational justice[103] are being discussed, each of which would have to be included in the decision-making processes as representatives of environmental concerns.

[93] Likewise, Kloepfer (1996), p. 78; in detail, Gethmann et al. (1993), p. 35 et seq.

[94] In this sense also Steinberg (1996), pp. 1989, 1991.

[95] Overview in Calliess (2016), p. 277 et seq.

[96] In detail, Ruffert (1998), p. 897 et seq.

[97] Calliess (2016), p. 288 et seq.; in-depth, SRU (2019), paras. 323 et seq.

[98] Gethmann et al. (1993), p. 38 et seq.; cf. also the—tendentially critical—overview of the existing institutionalised expertise by Vierhaus (1993), p. 36 et seq.

[99] Cf. for example Kuratorium für einen demokratisch verfassten Bund deutscher Länder, Verfassungsentwurf, p. 44 et seq., 114, according to which in Art. 45 a technology impact committee is to be appointed by the Bundestag, which is to be granted the rights of a committee of enquiry.

[100] Steinberg (1998), p. 345 et seq.

[101] Cf. Calliess (2001a), p. 515 et seq.

[102] Calliess (2016), p. 277 et seq.

[103] SRU (2019), paras. 340 et seq.

4 Environmental Sustainability and Precautionary Principle in the Context of Planetary Boundaries

4.1 *Concretising Requirements From Article 20a GG in the Light of the BVerfG's Climate Decision*

The legal interface between the precautionary principle and planetary boundaries is first and foremost the state objective of environmental protection in Article 20a of the Basic Law.

Although this legal connection with regard to the precautionary principle is not developed with sufficient clarity by the BVerfG in its climate decision, the building blocks are laid out and can be elaborated as follows: Via the Climate Protection Act, which concretises Article 20a of the Basic Law and in this way acquires quasi-constitutional status,[104] the BVerfG states that the legislature has a duty, flowing from the state objective of Article 20a of the Basic Law, to distribute the "necessary reductions in CO_2 emissions up to climate neutrality over time with foresight and in a manner that protects fundamental rights". In view of this, the current climate protection law must be improved.[105] For if the reaction to climate change is too hesitant until 2030, much stricter measures would have to be taken in the period until 2050, so that comparatively severe restrictions on freedom may occur in the future.[106] The objection that "the global character of climate and global warming precludes a solution to climate change by one state alone" is convincingly answered in the sense of the open constitutional state conceived by the Basic Law, so that Article 20a GG obliges international cooperation, but also—and this is very significant in view of the climate protection goals[107]—in the "mutual trust" of states to "implement agreed solutions". An obligation to dynamise protection is also correctly derived from Article 20a of the Basic Law.[108] Since Article 20a of the Basic Law, with its focus on "future generations", provides the standard of the precautionary principle, the BVerfG could have examined on this basis, both in the context of a procedural review and a substantive review of justifiability,[109] whether the legislature has fulfilled its resulting duties of care.[110]

[104] BVerfGE 157, 30, paras. 19-21, 120 with 158 et seq., 216 et seq.

[105] BVerfGE 157, 30, paras. 256 et seq.

[106] Kment (2020), p. 1540; generally, Calliess (2001a), p. 24 et seq. and p. 344 et seq.

[107] Instructive on this point, Cremer (2019), p. 278 et seq.; Franzius (2017), p. 515 et seq.

[108] BVerfGE 157, 30, paras. 200 et seq.

[109] Cf. after all BVerfGE 157, 30, paras. 139 et seq.

[110] On this Calliess (2001a), p. 181 et seq. with p. 125 et seq.

4.2 *Concretising Requirements from the "Ecological Subsistence Minimum"*

In this context, however, there is another legal aspect that was recognised (albeit too restrictively) by the Federal Constitutional Court in the climate decision,[111] but was not developed further: Via the ecological minimum subsistence level of the individual human being, which is anchored in human dignity, the planetary boundaries with their tipping points also convey an absolute legal limit to every political consideration. This, in conjunction with Article 20a of the Basic Law, is the link between the precautionary principle in climate protection and the intertemporal rights of freedom according to the BVerfG's climate decision.[112]

If, when the tipping points are exceeded, irreversible environmental damage threatens to result in a kind of "devastation scenario", then, from a legal perspective, the constitutional right of every citizen to the ecological minimum subsistence level, which flows from human dignity, the basic right to life and health and the environmental state objective (Article 1 (1) in conjunction with Article 2 (2) of the Basic Law and Article 20a of the Basic Law), is violated.

However, taking into account the orientation of Article 20a of the Basic Law towards future generations and thus the principle of sustainability, including the precautionary principle, the ecological subsistence level is not only affected when these minimum levels are no longer guaranteed but—since irreversible environmental damage is at stake—already when extreme ecological hardship in the form of the aforementioned "devastation scenario" is possible. In this respect, the planetary boundaries, together with their tipping points, i.e., in the field of climate protection the 1.5 to 2-degree target, formulate a rebuttable presumption. Accordingly, the claimants are not obliged to present and prove their case; rather, the opponents of the claim, i.e., the state institutions as addressees by the fundamental rights, must present and prove that with their protection concept, they have taken all necessary measures with regard to effectively steering away ("keeping their distance")[113] from the planetary boundaries and can thus safely guarantee the ecological minimum subsistence level.

Since the results of Earth system research show that measures are necessary in the light of planetary boundaries, but cannot specify them concretely for the community of states or individual states, the scientific state of affairs must be assessed normatively and politically in order to derive concrete conclusions.[114] For this reason alone, it is primarily up to the legislator to draw consequences from scientific findings on

---

[111] Cf. BVerfGE 157, 30, paras. 113 et seq.; critical of its approach, Calliess (2022c), paras. 185 et seq.

[112] For more details, see Calliess (2021), p. 328 et seq.

[113] Thus already, Calliess (2019), p. 385; agreeing on the relevance of tipping points in the area of fundamental rights protection obligations also: Meyer (2020), p. 897 et seq., as well as Buser (2020), p. 1392; similarly on the determination of planetary boundaries or ecological load limits as a mix of knowledge-based and precautionary principle already, Köck (2017), p. 257 et seq.

[114] Köck (2017), p. 257 et seq.; Schlacke (2014), p. 93, 96 et seq.

ecological limits. Since environmental protection aspects have to be weighed against conflicting constitutional concerns (economic freedom, principle of the welfare state), the state institutions, first and foremost the democratic legislature, necessarily have a political scope for shaping and weighing up the implementation of the protection concept.

Beyond the ecological minimum subsistence level defined in this way, the material target core of the state and Union target definition pursuant to Article 20a GG and Article 191, 11 TFEU, as well as the fundamental right to life and health (Article 2 para. 2 GG or Article 3 GrCh of the EU), set a framework for state legislation and the associated distribution of freedom via the aforementioned prohibition of inadequacy.[115] In this respect, the leeway of state institutions in concretising the concept of protection—for example via environmental quality targets[116]—is greater. Regarding this, they "only" have an optimisation mandate that is open to consideration,[117] but the more serious the foreseeable consequences of exceeding the planetary boundaries, the greater the weight to be attached to keeping a distance from the planetary boundaries in the political decision.[118]

All this has consequences for the scope of judicial review. Analogous to the decisions on the social subsistence minimum, in which the BVerfG does not give the legislature any guidelines on the exact amount of the entitlement, the ecological subsistence minimum is also about determining the minimum protection on the basis of the planetary boundaries. Analogous to the social subsistence minimum, the BVerfG can also control the procedure for determining the ecological subsistence minimum.[119] Specifically, the legislature must have sufficiently grasped and circumscribed the goal. Furthermore, it must have chosen a suitable calculation method within the scope of its discretion. At the same time, it must be ensured that the legislature has ascertained all the necessary facts and has kept within the bounds of what is justifiable in all calculation steps, as well as disclosing the methods and calculation steps used for constitutional court review.[120]

Measured against these normative requirements, the fundamental right to an ecological minimum subsistence level in conjunction with Article 20a GG results in a judicially controllable mandate to act. This implies a mandate to act, in the course of which the institutions of Germany and the EU must visibly steer away from the planetary boundaries and avert a (further) overstepping of the ecological limits of the Earth by means of a suitable and effective as well as long-term, coherent and legally binding protection concept. Within this framework, the constitutional and European law requirement to maintain a certain distance acts as a concrete requirement to take action via the prohibition of inadequate measures if an unchanged continuation

[115] In detail, Calliess (2001a), p. 451 et seq. and 563 et seq.; similarly, Brönneke (1999), p. 272 et seq. and p. 471 et seq.; Sommermann (1997), p. 439 et seq.

[116] Reese (2010), p. 345.

[117] Brönneke (1999), p. 269 et seq.; Sommermann (1997), p. 360 et seq.

[118] Calliess (2019), p. 385; approvingly, Meyer (2020), p. 897 et seq.; Buser (2020), p. 1392.

[119] BVerfGE 125, 175, para. 142.

[120] BVerfGE 125, 175, para. 144; in principle, Calliess (2001a), p. 125 et seq.

of environmental use exceeds (or, as in the case of climate protection, has already exceeded) the planetary load limits and thus endangers the stability of the Earth system as well as the ecological foundations of human life with a very high likelihood. As a result, the constitutionally recognised prohibition of under-protection thus requires a safety concept that is enacted by the legislature as an "absolute guard rail" of politics in the form of a binding guiding law—modelled on the benchmarks once suggested by the Federal Constitutional Court for financial constitutional law.[121]

For climate protection in particular, the Paris Climate Agreement and the European 2030 climate protection targets already provide a legal framework to which Germany and the EU are bound and which they must comply with as part of their climate protection policy.[122] In this context, the German Climate Protection Act (KSG)[123] represents a target-oriented approach. However, the law is still too weak, especially with regard to the monitoring of the implementation of the agreed targets,[124] as the independent "Expert Council for Climate Issues" established in §§ 11 and 12 of the KSG performs a mere emergency function, but not a real monitoring function.[125] Within the framework of the implementation of the "European Green Deal" on 29.7.2021, the EU has now also enacted a European climate protection law,[126] which considering its goals—not least in implementation of the requirements of the environmental integration clause of Article 11 TFEU—should lead to an institutional monitoring process beyond the modest approaches.[127]

5 Conclusion

1. In climate protection, but also with regard to other areas of environmental policy such as biodiversity, the concept of planetary boundaries, determined within the framework of Earth system sciences, has been shaping the discussion for several years. The international climate protection goals agreed in the Paris Agreement, which call for limiting man-made global warming to well below 2 °C compared to pre-industrial levels, but preferably to 1.5 °C, represent a concrete planetary boundary.

---

[121] For a detailed discussion, see Calliess (2001a), p. 125 et seq. and p. 235 et seq.

[122] Saurer (2017), p. 1574.

[123] Scharlau et al. (2020), p. 1.

[124] For more details, see the special report of the SRU (2019), pp. 175-185.

[125] Scharlau et al. (2020), p. 4 et seq.

[126] Cf. Regulation (EU) 2021/1119 of the European Parliament and of the Council of 30 June 2021 establishing the framework for achieving climate neutrality and amending Regulations (EC) No 401/2009 and (EU) 2018/1999 ('European Climate Law'), OJ L 243, 9.7.2021; on this, Schlacke (2022), p. 905 et seq.

[127] On the legal necessity, Calliess and Dross (2020), p. 461 et seq.; with regard to the EU's climate governance: Knodt et al. (2021), p. 287 et seq.

2. There is a gap between scientific knowledge and the political commitment to planetary boundaries as “guard rails” for sustainable action on the one hand, and the level of ambition of the state authorities’ strategies and programs adopted in this respect on the other. This gap deepens as soon as it comes to binding implementation in law and their enforcement.
3. A decisive reason for this gap in political action is that the concept of planetary boundaries cannot present any “scientific evidence” with regard to the thresholds and tipping points, but must operate with the concepts of scientific uncertainty and insecurity typical of the risk society. At this point, the situation determined by Earth system science must be normatively and politically evaluated. This is an important starting point for linking the planetary boundaries with the precautionary principle.
4. The legal interface to planetary boundaries is first and foremost the state objective of environmental protection in Article 20a of the Basic Law, including the precautionary principle immanent to this norm. This is because both risk precaution and resource precaution aim to avoid critical burdens and to keep a distance from the tipping points identified by Earth system science, so that serious and irreparable damage to humans and the environment is avoided. With regard to scientific uncertainty and insecurity, the precautionary principle implies a reversal of the burden of proof in the form of a science-based rebuttable presumption of danger.
5. The legal concept of climate protection, which state authorities, according to Article 20a of the Basic Law are supposed to deliver, must be balanced against fundamental rights as well as legal principles united under the umbrella of the rule of law (e.g. legal stability and certainty). It is therefore no coincidence that the principle of proportionality is unanimously described in practice and literature as a limit of the precautionary principle. In the triangle between the environmental state objective of Article 20a of the Basic Law, state authorities’ duties to respect and protect fundamental rights, a multipolar constitutional law relationship arises, in the framework of which a multipolar proportionality test forms the yardstick for the precautionary measure with regard to the protection concept.
6. Through the ecological minimum subsistence level of the individual human being, which is anchored in human dignity, the planetary boundaries with their tipping points also convey an absolute legal limit to political discretion. In conjunction with Article 20a of the Basic Law and the precautionary principle, this formulates a legal triad with the intertemporal preservation of freedom according to the climate decision of the BVerfG. Within this framework, the planetary boundaries together with their tipping points, i.e., in the area of climate protection the 1.5 to 2-degree target, formulate a rebuttable presumption. In the course of this, the claimants are not obliged to present and prove their case, rather, the state institutions as addressees of fundamental rights must present and prove that within their protection concept, they have taken all necessary measures with regard to an effective steering away from planetary boundaries.

References

Appel I (2001) Europas Sorge um die Vorsorge—Zur Mitteilung der Europäischen Kommission über die Anwendbarkeit des Vorsorgeprinzips. NVwZ 20(4):395–398

Appel I (2005) Staatliche Zukunfts- und Entwicklungsvorsorge. Mohr Siebeck, Tübingen

Appel I (2018) Europäisches und nationales Umweltverfassungsrecht. In Koch HJ et al. (eds) Handbuch Umweltrecht, 5th ed. C.H. Beck, München

Arndt B (2009) Das Vorsorgeprinzip im EU-Recht. Mohr Siebeck, Tübingen

Beck U (1986) Risikogesellschaft—Auf dem Weg in eine andere Moderne. Suhrkamp, Berlin

Bernsdorff N (1997) Positivierung des Umweltschutzes im Grundgesetz (Art. 20 a GG). NuR:328-334

Böhler D, Böhler B (1993) Gebt der Zukunft ein Recht! Plädoyer für Technologie- und Zukunftsverantwortung im Sinne des dialogischen Prinzips. ZRP 26(10):389–394

Brönneke T (1999) Umweltverfassungsrecht, 1st ed. Nomos, Baden-Baden

Bundesregierung (2016) German sustainability development strategy—new version 2016. https://www.bundesregierung.de/resource/blob/2196306/188836/3926a67a336e2a6d545beddc67d44c01/2017-06-20-nachhaltigkeit-neuauflage-engl-data.pdf?download=1. Accessed 22 Sep 2025

Buser A (2020) Ein Grundrecht auf Klimaschutz? Möglichkeiten und Grenzen grundrechtlicher Klima-klagen in Deutschland. Dvbl 21:1389–1396

Calliess C (1998) Die neue Querschnittsklausel des Art. 6 ex 3c EGV als Instrument zur Umsetzung des Grundsatzes der nachhaltigen Entwicklung. DVBl:559–568

Calliess C (2001a) Rechtsstaat und Umweltstaat—Zugleich ein Beitrag zur Grundrechtsdogmatik im Rahmen mehrpoliger Verfassungsrechtsverhältnisse. Mohr Siebeck, Tübingen

Calliess C (2001b) Vorsorgeprinzip und Beweislastverteilung Im Verwaltungsrecht. Dvbl 22:1725–1733

Calliess C (2009) Innovationsförderung durch Koppelung von Genehmigung und Alternativenprüfung? In: Eifert M, Hoffmann-Riem W (eds) Innovationsfördernde Regulierung. Duncker & Humblot, Berlin, pp 221–242

Calliess C (2016) Nachhaltigkeitsräte. In: Kahl W (ed) Nachhaltigkeit durch Organisation und Verfahren. Mohr Siebeck, Tübingen, pp 275–295

Calliess C (2019) Abstand halten: Rechtspflichten der Klimaschutzpolitik aus planetaren Grenzen. ZUR 30(7–8):385–386

Calliess C (2021) Klimapolitik und Grundrechtsschutz—Brauchen wir ein Grundrecht auf Umweltschutz? ZUR 32(6):323–332

Calliess C (2022a) Art. 11 TFEU. In: Calliess C, Ruffert M (eds) EUV/AEUV, 6th ed. C.H. Beck, München, pp 533–541

Calliess C (2022b) Art. 191 TFEU. In: Calliess C, Ruffert M (eds) EUV/AEUV, 6th ed. C.H. Beck, München, pp 1854–1876

Calliess C (2022c) Art. 20a GG para. 185–195. In: Dürig G et al. (eds) Grundgesetz-Kommentar, 99th supplement September 2022

Calliess C, Dross M (2020) Umwelt- und Klimaschutz als integraler Bestandteil der Wirtschaftspolitik. ZUR 31(9):456–464

Calliess C, Stockhaus H (2011) Regulierung von Nanomaterialien—reicht REACH? Dvbl 15:921–929

Canaris CW (1989) Grundrechtswirkungen und Verhältnismäßigkeitsprinzip in der richterlichen Anwendung und Fortbildung des Privatrechts. JuS:161–172

Cremer W (2004) Freiheitsgrundrechte. Mohr Siebeck, Tübingen

Cremer W (2019) Verfassungskräftiger Klimaschutz nach Maßgabe völkerrechtlich verbindlicher Verpflichtungen und Ziele. ZUR 30(5):278–283

Darnstädt T (1983) Gefahrenabwehr und Gefahrenvorsorge—eine Untersuchung über Struktur und Bedeutung der Prognose-Tatbestände im Recht der öffentlichen Sicherheit und Ordnung. Metzner, Frankfurt am Main

Di Fabio U (1994) Risikoentscheidungen im Rechtsstaat. Mohr Siebeck, Tübingen
Di Fabio U (1996) Gefahr, Vorsorge, Risiko: Die Gefahrenabwehr unter dem Einfluss des Vorsorgeprinzips. JURA 18(11):566–573
Di Fabio U (1997) Voraussetzungen und Grenzen des umweltrechtlichen Vorsorgeprinzips. In: Kley MD, Ritter W (eds) Festschrift für Wolfgang Ritter. O. Schmidt, Köln, pp 807–838
Dreier H, Willoweit D (eds) (2010) Wissenschaft und Politik, 1st edn. Steiner, Stuttgart
Durán G, Morgera E (2012) Environmental integration in the EU's external relations. Hart Publishing, Oxford and Portland, Oregon
Epiney A (2013) EU Environmental law: sources, instruments and enforcement: reflections on major developments over the last 20 years. Maastricht Journal of European and Comparative Law 20(3):403–422. https://doi.org/10.1177/1023263X1302000305
European Commission (2000) Communication from the commission on the precautionary principle, COM(2000) 1 final, 2.2.2020
European Commission (2019) Communication from the commission—The European Green Deal, COM(2019) 640 final, 11.12.2019
Feldhaus G (1987) Rechtliche Instrumente zur Bekämpfung von Waldschäden. UPR 7:1–11
Franzius C (2017) Das Paris-Abkommen zum Klimaschutz—Auf dem Weg zum transnationalen Klimaschutzrecht? ZUR 28(10):515–525
Gethmann F et al (1993) Langzeitverantwortung im Umweltstaat. Economica Verlag, Bonn
Grimm D (1991) Die Zukunft der Verfassung, 1st edn. Suhrkamp, Berlin
Grunwald A (2005) Zur Rolle von Akzeptanz und Akzeptabilität in der Bewältigung von Technikkonflikten. Technikfolgenabschätzung Theorie und Praxis. TATuP—Zeitschrift für Technikfolgenabschätzung in Theorie Und Praxis 14(3):54–60. https://doi.org/10.14512/tatup.14.3.54
Hailbronner K (1992) Stand und Perspektiven der EG-Umweltgesetzgebung. In: Calliess C, Wegener B (eds) Europäisches Umweltrecht als Chance: die Umweltpolitik der EG und die Einflussmöglichkeiten der Umweltverbände. Blottner, Taunusstein, pp 15–28
Hansen-Dix F (1982) Die Gefahr im Polizeirecht, im Ordnungsrecht und im Technischen Sicherheitsrecht. Heymann, Köln, Berlin, Bonn, München
Hey C (2000) Zukunftsfähigkeit und Komplexität: Institutionelle Innovationen in der EU. In: Prittwitz V (ed) Institutionelle Arrangements in der Umweltpolitik. VS Verlag für Sozialwissenschaften, Wiesbaden, pp 85–100
Hoffmann-Riem W (1994) Reform des Allgemeinen Verwaltungsrechts—Vorüberlegungen. DVBl:1381–1390
Intergovernmental Panel on Climate Change (IPCC) (2018) Global warming of 1.5°C. See summary for policymakers. https://www.ipcc.ch/sr15/chapter/spm/. Accessed 25 Aug 2025
Ipsen J (1990) Die Bewältigung der wissenschaftlichen und technischen Entwicklungen durch das Verwaltungsrecht. In: Veröffentlichungen der Vereinigung der Deutschen Staatsrechtslehrer (VVDStRL), Staatszwecke im Verfassungsstaat nach 40 Jahren Grundgesetz. De Gruyter, pp 177–203. https://doi.org/10.1515/9783110894929
Isensee J (1983) Das Grundrecht auf Sicherheit. De Gruyter, Berlin, New York
Isensee J (2011) Das Grundrecht als Abwehrrecht und als staatliche Schutzpflicht. In: Isensee J, Kirchhof P (eds) Handbuch des Staatsrechts, vol. IX, 3rd ed. C.F. Müller, Heidelberg, München, Landsberg
Jarass H (1985) Grundrechte als Werteentscheidungen bzw. objektivrechtliche Prinzipien in der Rechtsprechung des Bundesverfassungsgerichts. AöR 110(3):363–397
Jonas H (1984) Das Prinzip Verantwortung, 1st ed. Suhrkamp, Frankfurt
Kahl W (2018) Art. 11 TFEU. In: Streinz R (ed) EUV/AEUV, 3rd ed. C.H. Beck, München
Kahl W (2021) Klimaschutz und Grundrechte. Juristische Ausbildung 43(2):117–129
Kingreen T, Poscher R (2020) Polizei- und Ordnungsrecht, 11th edn. C.H.Beck, München
Klein HH (1991) Staatsziele im Verfassungsgesetz—Empfiehlt es sich, ein Staatsziel Umweltschutz in das Grundgesetz aufzunehmen? DVBl:729–739

Kloepfer M (1991) Das Umweltrecht in der deutschen Einigung: zum Umweltrecht im Einigungsvertrag und zum Umweltrahmengesetz, Schriften zum Umweltrecht 22. Duncker und Humblot, Berlin

Kloepfer M (1994) Zur Geschichte des deutschen Umweltrechts, Schriften zum Umweltrecht 50. Duncker und Humblot, Berlin

Kloepfer M (1996) Umweltschutz als Verfassungsrecht: Zum neuen Art. 20a GG. DVBl:73–80

Martin K (2020) Klimaschutzziele und Jahresemissionsmengen—Kernelemente des neuen Bundes-Klimaschutzgesetzes. NVwZ 39(21):1537–1544

Knodt M et al (2021) (Un)fit for 55! Ohne eine verschärfte Governance-Verordnung sind die Klimaziele 2030 nicht zu erreichen. Integration 44(4):287–300. https://doi.org/10.5771/0720-5120-2021-4-287

Köck W (1996) Risikovorsorge Als Staatsaufgabe. Aör 121(1):1–23

Köck W (1999) Grundzüge des Risikomanagements im Umweltrecht. In: Bora A (ed) Rechtliches Risikomanagement. Duncker & Humblot, Berlin, pp 129–192

Köck W (2005) Die Entwicklung des Vorsorgeprinzips im Recht—ein Hemmnis für Innovationen zum nachhaltigen Wirtschaften? In: Hansjürgens B, Nordbeck R (eds) Chemikalienregulierung und Innovationen zum nachhaltigen Wirtschaften. Physica-Verlag, Heidelberg, pp 85–120

Köck W (2017) Editorial: Erfordernisse des Umweltrechts im Anthropozän—Rechtskonzepte für eine „Große Transformation". ZUR 28(5):257–259

Ladeur KH (1995) Das Umweltrecht der Wissensgesellschaft: Von der Gefahrenabwehr zum Risikomanagement. Schriften zur Rechtstheorie 167. Duncker & Humblot, Berlin

Lübbe-Wolff G (1997) Präventiver Umweltschutz - Auftrag und Grenzen des Vorsorgeprinzips im deutschen und europäischen Recht. In: Bizer J, Koch H-J (eds) Sicherheit, Vielfalt, Solidarität: Ein neues Paradigma des Verfassungsrechts? Nomos, Baden-Baden, pp 47–74

Merkel A (ed) (1997) Wissenschaftliche Politikberatung für die Umwelt. Analytica, Berlin

Meyer S (2020) Grundrechtsschutz in Sachen Klimawandel? NJW 73(21):894–902

Murswiek D (1985) Die Staatliche Verantwortung für die Risiken der Technik. Duncker & Humblot, Berlin

Murswiek D (1990) Die Bewältigung der wissenschaftlichen und technischen Entwicklungen durch das Verwaltungsrecht. In: Veröffentlichungen der Vereinigung der Deutschen Staatsrechtslehrer (VVDStRL), Staatszwecke im Verfassungsstaat nach 40 Jahren Grundgesetz. De Gruyter, pp 207–234. https://doi.org/10.1515/9783110894929

Murswiek D (1996) Staatsziel Umweltschutz (Art. 20a GG)—Bedeutung für Rechtsetzung und Rechtsanwendung. NVwZ 15(3):222–230

Murswiek D (2021) Art. 20a. In: Sachs M (ed) GG, 9th ed. C.H. Beck, München

Nettesheim M (2023) Art. 11 TFEU. In: Grabitz E et al (eds) Das Recht der Europäischen Union, 78th supple-ment January 2023

Nowotny H et al (2001). Re-Thinking Science: Knowledge and the Public in an Age of Uncertainty. https://doi.org/10.2307/3089636

Ossenbühl F (1986) Vorsorge als Rechtsprinzip im Gesundheits-Arbeits- und Umweltschutz. NVwZ 5(3):161–171

Pitschas R (1989) Die Bewältigung der wissenschaftlichen und technischen Entwicklungen durch das Verwaltungsrecht. DÖV 42(18):785–800

Preuß U (1994) Risikovorsorge als Staatsaufgabe. In Grimm D (ed) Staatsaufgaben, 1st ed. Nomos, Baden-Baden, pp 523–551

Reese M (2010) Leitbilder des Umweltrechts. ZUR 21(7–8):339–346

Rehbinder E (1989) Grenzen und Chancen einer ökologischen Umorientierung des Rechts. IKO-Verlag, Frankfurt

Reiter B (1998) Entschädigungslösungen für durch Luftverunreinigungen verursachte Distanz- und Summationsschäden. Erich Schmidt Verlag, Berlin

Rengeling HW (1989) Umweltvorsorge und ihre Grenzen im EWG-Recht. Carl Heymanns Verlag, Köln, Berlin, Bonn, München

Rengeling HW (2000) Bedeutung und Anwendbarkeit des Vorsorgeprinzips im europäischen Umweltrecht. Dvbl 20:1473–1483
Ritter EH (1992) Von den Schwierigkeiten des Rechts mit der Ökologie. DÖV 45(15):641–649
Rockström J et al (2009) A safe operating space for humanity. Nature 461:472–475. https://doi.org/10.1038/461472a
Ruffert M (1998) Interessensausgleich im Verwaltungsorganisationsrecht. DÖV: 897–907
Saurer J (2017) Klimaschutz global, europäisch, national—Was ist rechtlich verbindlich? NVwZ 36(21):1574–1579
Scharlau J et al (2020) Das Bundes-Klimaschutzgesetz. NVwZ 39(1–2):1–8
Scherzberg A (1989) Grundrechtsschutz und "Eingriffsintensität", Schriften zum öffentlichen Recht 573. Duncker & Humblot, Berlin
Scherzberg A (1993) Risiko als Rechtsproblem - Ein neues Paradigma für das technische Sicherheitsrecht. VerwArch 84:484–513
Scheuing D (1989) Umweltschutz auf der Grundlage der Einheitlichen Europäischen Akte. EuR 34(3):152–192
Schlacke S (2014) Grenzwert oder Politikziel? Dogmatik und Legitimität der 2 Celsius-Leitplanke. In: Dilling O, Markus T (eds) Ex Rerum Natura Ius?—Sachzwang und Problemwahrnehmung im Umweltrecht. Nomos, Baden-Baden, pp 93–104
Schlacke S (2022) Klimaschutzrecht Im Mehrebenensystem. NVwZ 41(13):905–912
Schmidt R (1994) Der Staat Als Umweltvorsorge. DÖV 18:749–756
Schnapp F (1989) Die Grundrechtsbindung der Staatsgewalt. JuS:1ff
Sendler H (1983) Grundprobleme des Umweltrechts. JuS 23:255–260
Sommermann KP (1997) Staatsziele und Staatszielbestimmungen, 1st ed. Mohr Siebeck, Tübingen
SRU (2009) Capture, transport and storage of carbon dioxide—the federal government bill in the context of the energy debate. https://www.umweltrat.de/SharedDocs/Pressemitteilungen/EN/2009/2009_01_PressRelease.html. Accessed 22 Sep 2025
SRU (2011) Vorsorgestrategien für Nanomaterialien. Sondergutachten. https://t1p.de/aj4zc. Accessed 22 Sep 2025
SRU (2019) Demokratisch regieren in ökologischen Grenzen—Zur Legitimation von Umweltpolitik, https://t1p.de/iq7k2. Accessed 22 Sep 2025
SRU (2020) Umweltgutachten 2020: Für eine entschlossene Umweltpolitik in Deutschland und Europa. https://t1p.de/a0zl. Accessed 22 Sep 2025
Steffen W et al. (2015) Planetary boundaries: guiding human development on a changing planet. Science 347(6223). https://doi.org/10.1126/science.1259855
Steiger H (1997) Verfassungsrechtliche Grundlagen. In: Arbeitskreis für Umweltrecht (ed) Grundzüge des Umweltrechts, 2nd ed. Erich Schmidt, Berlin
Steinberg R (1996) Verfassungsrechtlicher Umweltschutz durch Grundrechte und Staatszielbestimmung. NJW 49(31):1985–1994
Steinberg R (1998) Der ökologische Verfassungsstaat. Suhrkamp, Frankfurt
Stern P, Fineberg H (1996) Understanding risk: informing decisions in a democratic society. National Academy Press, Washington DC
Trute HH (1998) Vorsorgestrukturen und Luftreinhalteplanung im Bundesimmissionsschutzgesetz. V. Decker, Heidelberg
Vierhaus HP (1993) Sachverstand als Vierte Gewalt? NVwZ 12(1):36–41
Voland T (2019) Zur Reichweite von Menschenrechten im Klimaschutz—Wäre die „Urgenda-Entscheidung" auch im deutschen Recht zu erwarten? NVwZ 38(3):114–120
Waechter K (1996) Umweltschutz als Staatsziel. NuR:321–327
Wahl R, Appel I (1995) Prävention und Vorsorge: Von der Staatsaufgabe zur rechtlichen Ausgestaltung. In: Wahl R (ed) Prävention und Vorsorge: von der Staatsaufgabe zu den verwaltungsrechtlichen Instrumenten. Economica-Verlag, Bonn, pp 1–216
Wendt R (1979) Der Garantiegehalt der Grundrechte und das Übermaßverbot. Zur maßstabsetzenden Kraft der Grundrechte in der Übermaßprüfung. Aör 104:414–474

Winter G (1997) Alternativen in der administrativen Entscheidungsbildung: zugleich ein Beitrag zu einer Grundpflicht ökologischer Verhältnismäßigkeit. Umweltrechtliche Studien vol. 23, 1st ed. Werner, Düsseldorf

Wischmeyer T (2016) Nachhaltige Gesetzgebung und Sachverständigenberatung. In: Kahl W (ed) Nachhaltigkeit durch Organisation und Verfahren. Mohr Siebeck, Tübingen, pp 253–274

Wissenschaftlicher Beirat der Bundesregierung Globale Umweltveränderungen (WBGU) (2009) Kassensturz für den Weltklimavertrag—Der Budgetansatz, Sondergutachten. https://www.wbgu.de/en/publications/publication/kassensturz-fuer-den-weltklimavertrag-der-budgetansatz#section-downloads. Accessed 22 Sep 2025

Wolf R (1991) Zur Antiquiertheit des Rechts in der Risikogesellschaft. In: Beck U (ed) Politik in der Risikogesellschaft, 1st edn. Suhrkamp, Frankfurt am Main, pp 357–377

Christian Calliess is Professor for Public, Environmental and European Law at Freie Universität Berlin, Germany. In 2000 he finished his habilitation with a book on the rule of law, environmental law, the precautionary principle and fundamental rights ("Rechtsstaat und Umweltstaat"), which was awarded the prize of the German Gesellschaft für Umweltrecht (GfU). From 2008 till 2020 Christian Calliess served as a member of the Advisory Council on the Environment of the Federal Government of Germany (SRU). In 2013 he became a member of the Club of Rome, German branch. From 2015 till 2019 he was on leave from academia in order to work as Legal Adviser to the European Political Strategy Center (EPSC), the In-House-Think-Tank of the President of the European Commission.

The Precautionary Principle in Selected Areas: Status and Development Prospects for Resource Precaution

Kurt Faßbender

Abstract The following contribution analyses the role that the precautionary principle under environmental law could and should play in overcoming the challenges caused by the overuse of natural resources, particularly of the three environmental media of air, water and soil. The main focus here will be on resource precaution as the most widely recognised form of the precautionary principle in German environmental law. However, this raises the fundamental question of whether and to what extent such an interpretation is compatible with European Union and international law, since the precautionary principle is widely interpreted as being reduced to its risk dimension. Therefore, some argue in favour of locating the essential elements of resource precaution rather in the sustainability principle. This article argues against such a view and puts forward the hypothesis that it makes perfect sense and is compatible at both EU and international level to (continue to) develop the concept of resource precaution as an independent element of the precautionary principle. This argument will be substantiated and illustrated in abstract terms and then by using examples from the circular economy, land use and water resource management.

The article was commissioned by the Federal Environment Agency as part of the project "Challenges for a sustainable environmental law". Essential parts of the article were previously presented at a workshop. The author would like to thank the participants of this workshop, especially Moritz Reese, for their insightful contributions to the discussion. Finally, the author would like to thank his research assistant Carolin Heinzel for her valuable support in the preparation of this paper. All citations of German literature and court decisions were translated by the author.

K. Faßbender (✉)
Institute for Environmental and Planning Law, Leipzig University, Leipzig, Germany
e-mail: fassbender@uni-leipzig.de

M. Reese et al. (eds.), *Environmental Law in Transformation*,
https://doi.org/10.1007/978-3-032-31567-0_3

1 Introduction

Today's environmental law faces enormous challenges. Humanity increasingly reaches ecological boundaries both regional and global with its economic and other activities.[1] Anthropogenic climate change is a paradigmatic example of the argument that we have entered the new geological era of the Anthropocene since the end of the Second World War at the latest. Mankind has itself become a formative geological force, not only through its CO_2 emissions but also, for example, through the modification of biochemical and water cycles and the irreversible destruction of biodiversity.[2] The main cause of the ensuing global environmental crisis is the overuse of natural resources, particularly of the three environmental media of air, water and soil.

Against this backdrop, the following section will first analyse the role that the precautionary principle under environmental law could and should play in overcoming the challenges outlined above. The main focus here will be on resource precaution as the most widely recognised form of the precautionary principle in German environmental law. However, this raises the fundamental question of whether and to what extent such an interpretation is compatible with European Union and international law. Afterall, the precautionary principle is widely interpreted as being reduced to its risk dimension.[3] Therefore, at the workshop of the research project in the context of which this article was written, some argued in favour of locating the essential elements of resource precaution rather in the sustainability principle.

This article argues against such a view and puts forward the hypothesis that it makes perfect sense and is compatible at both EU and international level to (continue to) develop the concept of resource precaution as an independent element of the precautionary principle. This argument will first be substantiated and illustrated in abstract terms and then by using examples from the circular economy, land use and water resource management.

2 Notes on the Genesis of the Precautionary Principle Under Environmental Law

With regard to the question about the compatibility of the German understanding of the precautionary principle, it should be recalled at the outset that, according to the prevailing opinion, the precautionary principle in environmental law is an 'invention' of German environmental policy. Form here, it has it found its way into the international and European environmental legal order and into the environmental

[1] For more details, see SRU (2019); also Calliess (2019).

[2] Cf. for more details Kersten (2014), summarised in Kersten (2016); see also Franzius (2019); Markus, in this volume, Sect. 2.

[3] See in more detail below under Sect. 4.

law of many other nation states.[4] This historical background indicates that German environmental policy and German environmental law can certainly have a formative effect on other legal systems.

For this reason alone, it would seem questionable, especially in the case of the precautionary principle, to prematurely abandon one's own conception due to some—actual or supposed—developments at the international and supranational level, instead of introducing it confidently into the debate. This is all the more true as the discussions on the exact content of the precautionary principle at supra- and international level are not even close to being settled.[5] Finally, it should not be ignored that the dual understanding of the precautionary principle, which is widely acknowledged in Germany, can be evidenced at least in substance in some other national legal systems of the European Union, such as Austria,[6] Sweden,[7] Spain[8] and Greece.[9]

3 Risk and Resource Precaution in German Environmental Law

At the same time, the historical background suggests that the precautionary principle should not only be understood as risk precaution but also as resource precaution. This is because in German environmental law literature,[10] the precautionary principle is primarily traced back to the Federal Government's 1971 environmental programme[11] and the Federal Government's 1976 environmental report, in which, under the heading "precautionary principle", it is stated:

> "Environmental policy is not limited to the defence against imminent dangers and the elimination of damage that has already occurred. Precautionary environmental policy also requires that natural resources are protected and utilised with care. The implementation of the precautionary principle is a prerequisite for ensuring that
>
> - the health and well-being of people is ensured,
> - the efficiency of the ecosystem is maintained,

[4] As summarised by Köck (2005), pp. 88–89. Similarly European Environmental Agency (EEA), Late Lessons from Early Warnings: The Precautionary Principle 1896–2000, 2001, p. 13. From an international perspective, see, for example, Cameron and Abouchar (1996), pp. 29–31; Freestone and Hey (1996), pp. 3–4; Proelß (2022), 3rd section para. 27; Sands and Peel (2018), pp. 229–230.

[5] Cf., for example, Böckenförde (2003), p. 314: "there is still considerable controversy over how to articulate or define a precautionary principle of law".

[6] Cf., for example, Arndt (2009), pp. 67–68; Germann (1993), pp. 5 et seq., 142 et seq and above all pp. 249 et seq, where a "duty to optimise the distribution of emissions" is derived from the precautionary principle.

[7] For more details, see Rehbinder (1991), p. 183 et seq.

[8] For more details, see the references in Sánchez Barroso (2021), p. 118 et seq and passim.

[9] For more details, see Charitopoulos (2009), p. 309 et seq.

[10] See, for example, Köck (2005), p. 89.

[11] This environmental programme can be found in Bundestag-Drucksache VI/2710, where the term "precaution" appears but not the precautionary principle.

- civilisational progress and economic productivity is safeguarded in the long term,
- damage to cultural and economic assets is avoided,
- the diversity of landscape, flora and fauna are preserved.

In order to fulfil these predominantly cross-sectional tasks, ever-increasing demands are being placed on the administrative and planning aspects of environmental policy. In addition, forward-looking and formative planning measures must ensure that all social and governmental forces act in an environmentally friendly manner and take possible environmental impacts into account in their decisions."[12]

In doing so, the Federal Government explicitly assumed that the precautionary principle exceeds the concept of risk precaution and also includes the principle of resource precaution. Nowadays, this framing corresponds to the almost unanimous view in the German environmental law literature.[13] In the following, these two characteristics will first be outlined and situated normatively (Sect. 3.1). Furthermore, the relationship between risk precaution and resource precaution will be clarified in a first approach (Sect. 3.2).

3.1 Essential Contents and Normative Localisation

Before the precautionary principle and its two forms are outlined in terms of content and located normatively, it seems apposite to first unpack the general legal categorisation of principles (Sect. 3.1.1). The development of the precautionary principle in immission control law is then outlined (Sect. 3.1.2), from which in turn core elements of the principle of resource precaution (Sect. 3.1.3) and—after a reference to its judicial recognition (Sect. 3.1.4)—the distance requirement is derived as a concrete manifestation of this principle (Sect. 3.1.5). Finally, the question is briefly discussed of whether the principle of resource precaution must necessarily be underpinned by concretising objectives in order to make it manageable (Sect. 3.1.6).

[12] The environmental report is printed in Bundestag-Drucksache 7/5684, p. 7.

[13] See, for example, Appel (2005), p. 185 et seq.; Calliess (2021), p. 176 et seq.; Fischer (2013), p. 138 et seq.; Kahl/Gärditz (2023), § 4 para. 22–23; Kloepfer, Umweltrecht, 4th ed. 2016, § 4 para. 22 et seq. and p. 54 et seq.; Köck (2005), p. 88; Krüper (2009), p. 69 et seq.; Lübbe-Wolff (1998), p. 53 et seq.; Murswiek (2004), p. 426 et seq.; Rehbinder (2018), ch. 3 para. 19 et seq. and 39 et seq.; Söhnlein (1999), p. 130 et seq.; Wahl and Appel (1995), p. 74 et seq. Similarly Arndt (2009), pp. 26 et seq. and Monien (2014), p. 309 et seq, who speaks of a "resource-economical" variant o form of the precautionary principle in German environmental law.

3.1.1 Notes on the Legal Categorisation of Principles and Policies

The following discussion of the precautionary principle and the principle of resource precaution[14] in German environmental law raises the question of what legal consequences they have. This is because the legal quality of principles can vary considerably.[15] First of all, it is fundamental to distinguish between merely political maxims for action, which are not legally binding, and 'genuine' legal principles, which in turn can be divided into two groups according to their binding nature. On the one hand, there are principles in the form of legal principles that are condensed into a directly applicable standard. This is readily apparent when statutory principles have the function of a norm that legitimises state intervention, such as Section 5(1)(no. 2) of the German Federal Immission Control Act (Bundes-Immissionsschutzgesetz—BImSchG), which will be discussed in more detail below. However, statutory principles also include legalised mandates for the respective legislator, such as the provisions in Art. 20a Basic Law and Art. 191(2) TFEU, since they provide a directly applicable standard in this respect. This already indicates the distinction between the justification and mandate dimension of the precautionary principle, which is correctly emphasised in the literature[16] and will also be discussed in more detail below. Secondly, legal principles include so-called structural or guiding principles that underlie certain regulations and legitimise them but which are not directly applicable.

It follows that the concrete understanding of the precautionary principle can certainly differ in the various sub-areas of environmental and planning law.[17] Therefore, the first step is always to clarify how the respective legislator frames the precautionary principle. Admittedly, there are certain similarities when looking at individual legal norms as a whole, which justify speaking of the precautionary principle as having content that transcends legal norms.[18] This also legitimises its designation as a 'principle' of environmental law.

3.1.2 The Development of the Precautionary Principle in Immission Control Law

The precautionary principle found its first concrete legal manifestation in the Federal Immission Control Act of 1974. According to Section 1 of this Act, one of its purposes is to "prevent the occurrence of harmful environmental impacts" (also

[14] The terms 'guiding principle' ('Grundsatz') and 'principle' ('Prinzip') are used synonymously in this respect.

[15] Cf. on this and the following Rehbinder (2018), ch. 3 para. 17. Similar, but also partly deviating distinctions can be found, for example, in Köck (2005), p. 90 et seq.

[16] See Lübbe-Wolff (1998), p. 62 et seq.

[17] This is emphasised, for example, by Proelß (2022), 3rd section para. 30; Viertel (1995), p. 72.

[18] Krüper (2009), p. 48, even describes it as a "peculiarity" of the precautionary principle that it is derived from a large number of applicable rules and knowledge gained from experience.

today's Section 1(1) BImSchG). Following on from this, Section 5(2) BImSchG of 1974 stipulated that installations requiring authorisation must be constructed and operated in such a way that "precautions are taken against harmful effects on the environment, in particular through measures as are appropriate according to the best available techniques". Today's Section 5(1)(2) BImSchG formulates it in the same way, only requiring additional precautions against "other hazards, significant disadvantages and significant nuisances".

In the case of this precautionary principle, which is turned into a norm in the form of a legal statute, its form as risk or hazard precaution is now essentially undisputed and—at least in principle—clearly defined. According to this principle, risk precaution aims to ensure that measures are taken in advance of danger defence, in particular by means of measures as are appropriate according to the best available techniques, so that environmental hazards or even environmental damage do not occur in the first place.[19] Characterising element here is a cognitive deficit. There is a lack of sufficient knowledge as to whether there is already a danger in the regulatory sense that justifies or even requires state intervention. In this precarious situation, the precautionary principle in its form of risk precaution aims to justify state measures despite remaining uncertainty. This is done in particular in the case of the protection of environmental media by avoiding emissions by using the best available techniques, which must be carried out regardless of specific risks. This is expressed in an almost model way in Section (1)(no. 2) BImSchG, where it is stipulated that precautions against harmful environmental effects and other hazards, significant disadvantages and significant nuisances are to be taken "in particular by means of measures as are appropriate according to the best available techniques".

However, the precautionary principle standardised in Section 5(1)(no. 2) BImSchG also offers the reference point for the first normative form of resource precaution: the so-called open space hypothesis developed in literature at the beginning of the 1980s.[20] In view of Germany's dense population and high degree of industrialisation, it assumes for precautionary reasons that it is necessary to preserve open spaces even in areas that are not yet environmentally endangered. The precautionary principle understood in such a way is not aimed at risk precaution but at "environmental planning in hazard-free areas".[21]

In addition to the areas discussed in more detail below under V., such open space protection is also turned into norms, for example, in the regulation on open space protection and development in Section 1(6) of the German Federal Nature Conservation Act (Bundes-Naturschutzgesetz—BNatSchG).[22] This objective just like the other objectives of nature conservation and landscape management stipulated in

---

[19] On this and the following, see the contributions mentioned above in footnote 13.

[20] Cf. for example Appel (2005), pp. 188-189; Kahl and Gärditz (2023), § 4 para. 23; Kloepfer (2016), § 4 para. 54 et seq; Köck (2005), p. 88; Murswiek (2004), pp. 426–427; Wahl and Appel (1995), p. 78 et seq.

[21] See Petersen (1993), p. 206 et seq.

[22] On the precautionary approaches in Art. 1(1) BNatSchG, see Viertel (1995), pp. 67–68. See also Rehbinder (2018), ch. 3 para. 52: "Nature conservation law is based on the idea of resource conservation".

Section 1 BNatSchG is to be concretised "as a basis for precautionary action" within the framework of landscape planning at a supra-local and local level in accordance with Section 8 BNatSchG. Furthermore, the requirements and measures for the realisation of these objectives within the framework of landscape planning should be presented and justified. This explicit reference to the precautionary principle in Section 8 BNatSchG generally emphasises that landscape planning "represents the central precautionary planning element of nature conservation and landscape management".[23] This also applies specifically to the open space protection required in Section 1(6) BNatSchG.

3.1.3 The First Core Elements and Conceptual Variations of the Principle of Resource Precaution

The 'open space'-hypothesis as well as Sections 1 and 8 BNatschG already reveal three initial core elements that characterise the principle of resource precaution in general and also beyond immission control law—and in contrast to risk or hazard prevention. These core elements are also emphasised as such in different variations in the literature.[24] Firstly, the principle of resource precaution is fundamentally valid *irrespective of any specific threat to an environmental resource*. Secondly, this relates to the basic concern for conserving environmental media and resources in the interest of future uses and needs. In this respect, resource precaution is generally about "future precaution" or "posterity precaution",[25] which in turn is a central form of safeguarding freedom in times of global environmental crisis.[26] In view of this, the principle of resource precaution is widely and rightly used to call for the careful use of available resources.[27] This is then also the reference point for the third characteristic element of the principle of resource precaution; it is conceptually based on *a management law and often planning approach.*

Given all of this, it should be noted from a *terminological point of view* that resource precaution is often semantically detached from the concept of precaution, without this resulting in a significant difference in meaning. Examples include the terms "resource protection" and "resource conservation", which are used synonymously especially but not only in the context of the circular economy.[28] These terms can and should therefore be understood as emanations of resource precaution.

---

[23] See in more detail on "Landscape planning as an instrument of a precautionary environmental policy" Charitopoulos (2009), p. 79 et seq.

[24] Cf. for example Appel (2005), pp. 188-189; Arndt (2009), pp. 37–38; Calliess (2021), pp. 176-177; Söhnlein (1999), p. 130 et seq.

[25] For example, Kloepfer (2016), § 4 para. 22–23.

[26] For more on this context, see Krüper (2009), pp. 59–60.

[27] See, for example, Kahl and Gärditz (2023), § 4 para. 22; Rehbinder (2018), ch. 3 para. 37; Söhnlein (1999), p. 131; Wahl and Appel (1995), p. 74.

[28] See, for example, Murswiek (2021), Art. 20a para. 37–38.

3.1.4 The Judicial Recognition of the Principle of Resource Precaution

Important for the classification as a legal principle is the fact that the concretisation of the precautionary principle has been acknowledged in court rulings. For example, in its Decision of 18 September 1987 on a permit under water law for the extraction and subsequent discharge of cooling and process water of a nuclear power plant, the German Federal Administrative Court (Bundesverwaltungsgericht—BVerwG) stated that the provision of Section 1a(1) of the German Federal Water Act (Wasserhaushaltsgesetz—WHG) in force at the time authorised the water authorities to promote the public interests relevant to water management, to protect them from impairment and to create a fair distribution system with regard to the water available. This also includes "planning provision for future utilisation interests as well as forward-looking conservation of a drinking water reservoir beyond current requirements".[29]

Furthermore, in 1995, the Federal Administrative Court pointed out in a ruling on a subsequent immission control order that the precautionary measures required under Section 5(1)(no. 2) BImSchG also include measures that are intended to counteract a suspected hazard—for example in the sense of as yet unknown cause-effect relationships; however, this by no means exhausts the scope of what precautionary measures cover. The Court then goes on to say: "Precautionary measures in the sense of preventive environmental protection are also aimed at the area beyond specific harmful thresholds and therefore justify avoidance efforts with regard to environmentally harmful air pollutants that are taken with the aim of bringing about or ensuring long-term standards of air quality; they are sufficiently distinct from conditions that specifically suggest or give rise to fears of harmful environmental effects. Precaution is thus not only orientated towards potential effects in the sense of still incomplete knowledge about the harmfulness of certain immissions; it is also linked to a currently given potential effect of substances, against which an appropriate distance should be maintained".[30] The Federal Administrative Court thus also explicitly moves away from mere risk precaution and emphasises—apparently in the interest of future uses—the permissibility of a management law approach.[31]

3.1.5 The Distance Requirement as a Central Aspect of the Principle of Resource Precaution

At the same time, the Federal Administrative Court thus formulates a distance requirement, which as a central concretisation of the principle of resource precaution can be generalised. The backdrop of this argument is the demand, which has been derived

[29] See Bundesverwaltungsgericht, in: Neue Zeitschrift für Verwaltungsrecht 1988, pp. 535–536 and in more detail below under Sect. 5.3.

[30] See Bundesverwaltungsgericht, in: Neue Zeitschrift für Verwaltungsrecht 1995, pp. 994–995.

[31] Cf. Franzius, in this volume, Sect. 2 with footnote 9.

from the precautionary principle in the literature for over 20 years, that the ecological thresholds should not be exhausted.[32] This means nothing other than to maintain a sufficient distance from ecological boundaries.[33] Such action seems objectively necessary because environmental problems, apart from the exceptional case of noise, are, in the words of *Gertrude Lübbe-Wolff*, "typically characterised by a tendency to accumulate". The latter stems from the fact that technical and natural purification processes for emissions caused directly or indirectly by humans do not lead to the pollutants emitted being eliminated; rather, a large proportion is "merely transported zo other places—into the soil, river sediments, the sea—and accumulates there". Therefore, the "ecological carrying capacity" at the end "marks the threshold from which a precautionary *distance* must be kept, if no exceedances are to occur over time".[34]

In its 2019 special report on "Democratic governance within ecological limits", the German Advisory Council on the Environment (*Sachverständigenrat für Umweltfragen*—SRU) also assumed that the precautionary principle could be used as the basis for a distancing requirement, which is justified by the biophysical limitations of the Earth given the availability of natural resources and the absorption capacity of sinks.[35]

3.1.6 The Constitutional Foundation of Resource Precaution

The Sachverständigenrat für Umweltfragen derived the latter requirement for the level of national environmental law from the environmental state objective in Art. 20a of the Basic Law (Grundgesetz—GG).[36] This is to be agreed with. For there are good reasons why the prevailing opinion in the literature has long been that Art. 20a of the Basic Law not only includes the environmental precautionary principle as such but also calls for the precautionary use of resources.[37] This is supported above all by the obligation mentioned in the article's wording to protect the natural foundations of life "also in responsibility towards future generations". From here follows a material obligation to take into account the ecological consequences of today's actions, even far into the future, and not to deprive future generations of the natural foundations of life through overuse.

In its historic climate Decision of 24 March 2021, the German Federal Constitutional Court (Bundesverfassungsgericht—BVerfG) also affirmed the necessity of resource precaution and compliance with a distance requirement understood in this

[32] Cf., for example, Appel (2005), p. 189; Arndt (2009), p. 29; Calliess (2021), pp. 176–177; Lübbe-Wolff (1998), p. 55 et seq.

[33] Cf. also Markus, in this volume, Sect. 5.1.1 at footnote 86.

[34] See Lübbe-Wolff (1998), pp. 57–59 (emphasis in original).

[35] Cf. SRU (2019), p. 15 and p. 72 et seq.; also summarising Calliess (2019), pp. 385–386.

[36] Cf. SRU (2019), p. 15 and p. 72 et seq.

[37] Cf. for example Calliess (2021), pp. 177 and 181; Kahl and Gärditz (2023), § 4 para. 22; Lübbe-Wolff (1998), p. 53 et seq.; Söhnlein (1999), p. 130 et seq.

way. Still, the Decision—regrettably—does not explicitly mention these terms or the precautionary principle in the reasons for the Decision. In this Decision, the Constitutional Court focused primarily on external factors, when reviewing the Federal Climate Protection Act against the standard of fundamental rights and—mediated by them—against the standard of Art. 20a of the Basic Law. In the absence of a clear burden-sharing agreement under international law, it derived a specific CO_2 budget for Germany from expert studies; a budget which must be adhered to, if the constitutionally relevant goal of limiting the increase in the global average temperature to well below 2 °C and, if possible, to 1.5 °C compared to pre-industrial levels—as stipulated by the Paris Agreement—is to be met. These factual considerations in turn form the basis for the First Senate's central legal assumption that, under such conditions, the Basic Law obliges the German state to safeguard freedom protected by fundamental rights over time and to distribute opportunities for freedom proportionately across generations. This is not only objectively required by Article 20a of the Basic Law. Rather, the fundamental rights protect the complainants under subjective law as an "intertemporal safeguarding of freedom" against a one-sided shift into the future of the greenhouse gas reduction burden imposed by Article 20a of the Basic Law.[38]

This focus on a "distributable" amount of freedom, which "according to the current state of ecological knowledge is de facto limited, will be limited or can or should be normatively limited", has rightly been described in the literature as "a mix of the precautionary principle, risk and resource precaution".[39] In view of this argument, the principle of resource precaution and the principle of distancing, which prohibits the exhaustion of ecological limits, are given constitutional status by Article 20a of the Basic Law.

In this respect, it should be noted that, according to Article 20a of the Basic Law, it is initially the responsibility of the legislator to define the principle of distancing in more detail. On the one hand, the principle of resource precaution and the distance requirement serve as justification for restrictions on fundamental rights, in particular those of economic actors. On the other hand, Article 20a of the Basic Law provides a mandate for action, which the Federal Constitutional Court concretised considerably with regard to climate protection. Of great importance here is the Court's finding that the relative weight of the climate protection requirement continues to increase in the weighing of interests as climate change progresses.[40] In this respect, the principle of resource precaution and the resulting requirement to maintain a safe distance must also be taken into account when interpreting existing regulations.

---

[38] See BVerfG, Decision of 24 March 2021, 1 BvR 2656/18 et al, in: Neue Juristische Wochenschrift 2021, p. 1723, headnote 4 and para. 118 et seq., 166 et seq., 183 et seq., 208 et seq., 215 et seq. and 233 as well as Faßbender (2021a), p. 2086 et seq.

[39] See Berkemann (2021), p. 712.

[40] Cf. BVerfG, Decision of 24 March 2021, 1 BvR 2656/18 et al, in: Neue Juristische Wochenschrift 2021, 1723, headnote 2 a and paras. 120, 185 and 198.

3.1.7 The Need for a Target-Based Concretisation of Resource Precaution

The question of whether and to what extent the principle of resource precaution must be underpinned by concrete objectives in order to make it manageable is assessed differently. In this regard, *Ivo Appel* and *Rainer Wahl* argue in relation to immission control law that if environmental protection is (also) to be thought of in terms of the environmental medium or resource, then an idea of the 'state' or 'existence' of this medium is also required. Therefore, the attempt at long-term, spatial and resource-related precautionary measures 'always' requires concretising environmental quality objectives that also take into account the resilience of an environmental medium.[41]

In contrast, *Gertrude Lübbe-Wolff* assumes with regard to the distance requirement that neither the ecological boundary is clearly positioned nor the distance to be maintained is defined in detail. Such a measure "cannot even be specified, because the fundamental priority function of the precautionary principle is not to place a somewhat thinner second wall in front of the wall against which one should not drive, so that it already crashes a little at this wall, but to designate the necessary space for flexible redirection towards sustainability. In *this* sense [...] the precautionary principle has the function of securing free space".[42]

This seems convincing with regard to the distance to be maintained, while the ecological boundary—as the example of climate protection discussed in the previous section shows—can certainly be defined more precisely in certain cases. Furthermore, resource precaution is not always about ecological limits. Rather, resource precaution can also be pursued by the legislator—as in the area of water resource management—in prescribing a good quality of the medium, which must be maintained or strived for in the interests of future utilisation of the water resource.[43] When and to the extent that it is therefore possible to set verifiable targets on a valid professional basis, this noticeably promotes effective resource precaution. Afterall, such targets often bring about two major changes: firstly, the allocation of financial and human resources to achieve the targets and, secondly, the establishment of the necessary administrative structures to manage the respective planning tasks.[44] In this respect, targets that concretise resource precaution are undoubtedly desirable, particularly in the case of media-based environmental protection, yet they are not mandatory in every case. One example where targets are rightly considered as mandatory is climate change law because without climate targets, implemented measures would lack indeed enough ambition and the necessary "planning horizon to promote development" that the Federal Constitutional Court has demanded in the above-mentioned decision for the goal of climate neutrality.

---

[41] See Wahl and Appel (1995), p. 192. Similarly, Appel (2005), p. 185 et seq.; Calliess (2021), p. 316 et seq. Cf. also Krüper (2009), p. 70: "However, state environmental precautionary planning can only provide effective impetus where it pursues sector-specific, concrete projects."

[42] See Lübbe-Wolff (1998), p. 60 (emphasis in original).

[43] See in more detail below under Sect. 5.3.

[44] See Ginzky et al. (2021), p. 450.

3.2 *The Relationship Between Risk Precaution and Resource Precaution: Similarities and Differences*

Even at the national level, the question arises as to how the principle of resource precaution relates to risk precaution. In the past, in immission control law, the idea of risk precaution below a hazard threshold and resource precaution in the sense of preserving open spaces outlined above were sometimes seen as contradicting each other.[45] However, today the view is predominantly held that the precautionary principle should rather be understood as a "multifunctional imperative" that encompasses both aspects.[46]

This is agreed to the extent that there are indeed certain similarities that can be outlined as "elements of a general environmental precautionary principle".[47] However, if this were to remain the case, one could justifiably ask why the two forms should be distinguished at all. The relevant similarities and differences will therefore be summarised in the following.

There are similarities above all in the objectives of the general precautionary principle under environmental law. This is because the precautionary principle pursues two elementary objectives in all areas of environmental law.[48] On the one hand, it involves a more or less pronounced forward shift in the state's approach to action. Secondly, all precautionary regulations in environmental law aim to preserve the natural foundations of human life through cautious and economical utilisation. This is the common core of the general precautionary principle of environmental law.[49]

However, there are also differences, some of which have already been mentioned.[50] Firstly, the principle of resource precaution goes beyond risk precaution in that it applies irrespective of any specific threat to an environmental resource.[51] This is particularly evident in nature conservation law, which is only briefly mentioned here,[52] and in water protection law, which is discussed in more detail below.[53] Next, the question of sufficient risk precaution is typically examined in the assessment and, above all, state authorisation of specific environmentally relevant measures, whereas the principle of resource precaution is regularly based on

---

[45] See the apt summary by Rehbinder (2018), ch. 3 para. 39 with references from the older literature.

[46] Cf. for example Bundesverwaltungsgericht, in: Neue Zeitschrift für Verwaltungsrecht 1995, pp. 994–995; Appel (2005), p. 185 et seq.; Arndt (2009), p. 29 et seq.; Calliess (2021), p. 178; Kahl and Gärditz (2023), § 4 para. 22; Rehbinder (2018), ch. 3 para. 39.

[47] For example, Viertel (1995), p. 73 et seq.

[48] In this respect, I follow the main ideas of Viertel (1995), pp. 73–74. On the other hand, Viertel himself implicitly admits on p. 75 that the "inclusion of expert assessments with regard to risks and avoidance possibilities", which he mentions as a third element, is only provided for in immission control, nuclear and chemicals law.

[49] See also the general paraphrases in Appel (2005), p. 185; Kloepfer (2016), § 4 para. 22.

[50] See above under Sect. 3.1.3.

[51] See also Bundesverwaltungsgericht, in: Neue Zeitschrift für Verwaltungsrecht 1995, pp. 994–995.

[52] See above under Sect. 3.1.2 at the end.

[53] See below under Sect. 5.3.

a management law and often planning approach that goes beyond individual environmentally relevant measures and typically also includes proactive action. Nevertheless, it may also be necessary to observe the principle of resource precaution in specific authorisation procedures. Finally, it should be noted that, as will be shown below, the differences mentioned do not exclude the possibility that the principles of risk precaution and resource precaution can also reinforce each other.

4 The Supra- and International Compatibility of the German Concept

As mentioned in the introduction, however, the question arises as to whether and to what extent this interpretation is compatible with EU and international law, because there the precautionary principle is widely reduced to its risk dimension.[54] Some argue that this is already apparent from the English term "precautionary principle".[55] However, this point is not convincing, because one could just as easily take the view that the English "precautionary principle", like the French "précaution", is generally about foresighted care, which in turn implies a conceptual openness to the idea of resource precaution.

4.1 The Level of International Law

At the level of international law, it is true that the precautionary principle only appears as risk precaution in a number of agreements and also in Principle 15 of the 1992 Rio Declaration on Environment and Development.[56] Nevertheless, the historical background outlined above speaks against such a narrowing of the precautionary principle that claims to apply to international environmental law as a whole. For example, an anthology on "The Precautionary Principle and International Law" states: "the precautionary principle found its way into international law and policy as a result of German proposals made to the International North Sea Ministerial Conferences. These proposals were based on the *precautionary principle* of German Law".[57] In German environmental law, however, it was and is widely recognised that the precautionary principle encompasses not only risk precaution but also resource precaution.

[54] Cf. for example Köck (2005), p. 88; Murswiek (2004), p. 425. Appel (2005), p. 229 and Lübbe-Wolff (1998), p. 55 only speak of a corresponding "tendency" at the international level.

[55] For example, Murswiek (2004), p. 425.

[56] Cf. with further references Freestone and Hey (1996), pp. 3–4; Lübbe-Wolff (1998), pp. 54–55; Monien (2014), p. 255 et seq.

[57] Thus, Freestone and Hey (1996), pp. 3–4.

In addition, the specific environmental law context expressed in this quote also favours a broad understanding of the precautionary principle, as the protection of international waters is naturally not only about risk prevention but also about resource conservation. This is also clearly expressed in a number of documents from the 1990s on the protection of the oceans from pollution.[58] Furthermore, the idea, which also forms the basis of the distance requirement discussed above under Sect. 3.1.5, that consideration must be given to the absorption capacities of an environmental medium, has already found its way into the preamble of the Convention on the Prevention of Marine Pollution by Dumping of Wastes and Other Matter of 1972 (the so-called London Convention).[59]

A particularly revealing example of a broad understanding of the precautionary principle is provided by the Multilateral Agreement of 4 December 1995 for the Implementation of the Provisions of the Convention on the Law of the Sea relating to the Conservation and Management of Straddling Fish Stocks and Highly Migratory Fish Stocks. The Agreement deals in detail with the "application of the precautionary principle" in its Article 6.[60] This is because, as the title suggests, the application of the precautionary principle is ultimately intended to achieve the conservation of fish stocks through appropriate "management" that does not consider human-induced risks and even extends to cases where a "natural phenomenon" has a significant adverse effect on the status of straddling or highly migratory fish stocks. The application of the precautionary principle under the Convention is thus aimed at resource precaution, which contains all the reference points previously identified under Sect. 3.1.3 as core elements of resource precaution.

Such a broad understanding of the precautionary principle can be found not only in international water law, but also, albeit rather sporadically, in other areas of international environmental law, such as air pollution control law. For example, the 1985 Vienna Convention for the Protection of the Ozone Layer explicitly refers to the precautionary principle in its preamble.[61] However, concrete measures to protect the ozone layer are only found in the Montreal Protocol on Substances that Deplete the Ozone Layer, which was adopted in 1987 as part of the Vienna Convention and subsequently updated.[62] In this Protocol, the parties declare their determination "to protect the ozone layer by taking precautionary measures to control equitably total global emissions of substances that deplete it, with the ultimate objective of their elimination on the basis of developments in scientific knowledge". Conceptually,

---

[58] Cf. the references in Freestone and Hey (1996), p. 6 et seq.

[59] See also Monien (2014), p. 251.

[60] This is the official title of Art. 6 of the Convention, which can be found in Bundesgesetzblatt III No. 21 of 18 February 2005, p. 1 et seq.

[61] On the significance of the agreement for international environmental law, see also Sands and Peel (2018), p. 231.

[62] A German translation is printed in Bundesgesetzblatt II No. 39 of 15 November 1988, p. 1014 et seq. For an update, see for example the law on the amendment adopted in Beijing on 3 December 1999, which is printed together with the amendments to the Protocol in Bundesgesetzblatt II No. 15 of 29 April 2002, p. 921 et seq.

the Protocol pursues a management law approach that no longer asks about scientific uncertainties, and which incidentally amounts to a distance requirement for the protection of the ozone layer; ultimately then, the Protocol is a matter of resource precaution in the sense outlined above.

In view of all this, those voices in the literature ultimately deserve approval that assume that the precautionary principle under international environmental law *conceptually* encompasses not only risk precaution but also resource precaution.[63]

4.2 The Level of Union Law

It is also controversial whether the German dual understanding of the precautionary principle can be transferred to EU law. This question arises above all at the level of EU constitutional law, because the precautionary principle is expressly elevated to a principle of European environmental policy in Art. 191(2)(2) TFEU alongside the prevention principle, the source principle and the polluter pays principle. There are some analyses to be found in the literature that the precautionary principle standardised in Art. 191(2)(2) TFEU only covers risk precaution but not resource precaution, because otherwise the principle of sustainability referred to in Art. 11 TFEU would be "largely deprived of its legal status (effet utile)".[64]

On closer inspection, this objection is not convincing.[65] For even if one assumes—correctly—that the precautionary principle and the principle of sustainability partially overlap in this case, this would still not call into question the effet utile of Art. 11 TFEU but on the contrary would strengthen it.[66] However, the principle of sustainability must be understood more broadly, because it originates in international environmental law, where it has been given more precise contours, particularly in the Sustainable Development Goals (SDGs) adopted by the UN General Assembly.[67] Accordingly, the principle of sustainability also aims, for example, at combating poverty and hunger, achieving gender equality and promoting peace, justice and strong institutions.[68] This broad understanding is also the basis for the European Union's so-called sustainability strategies.[69] Therefore, there are better

[63] Cf. for example Böckenförde (2003), p. 313 with fn. 1; Lübbe-Wolff (1998), pp 54 et seq.; Wolfrum (1999), p. 207. The same applies to Kloepfer (2016), § 10 para. 80, when he believes that the precautionary principle under international law essentially coincides with the precautionary principle in national environmental law.

[64] See Kahl (2018), Art. 11 TFEU para. 25 et seq. and Art. 191 TFEU para. 83.

[65] Also dissenting Epiney (2019), 5th ch. para. 20.

[66] See also Heselhaus (2023), Art. 191 TFEU para. 67.

[67] See also Calliess (2022), Art. 11 TFEU para. 13.

[68] For more information, see https://www.globalgoals.org/goals.

[69] Cf. in more detail Monien (2014), p. 201 et seq.

reasons for recognising the resource-related variant of the precautionary principle as an independent form or supplement to the principle of sustainability.[70]

Furthermore, a restrictive interpretation of the precautionary principle under EU law cannot be justified by the argument that the EU Commission in its Communication of 2 February 2000 on the applicability of the precautionary principle[71] focused solely on the risk-based version of the precautionary principle.[72] After all, this Communication is not legally binding and the Commission has no authority to interpret primary EU law in a binding manner. Furthermore, problems in health and consumer protection law, such as the BSE crisis in particular, provided the decisive impetus for the Commission's Communication.[73] It was therefore primarily concerned with areas of law in which risk precaution alone is relevant. Moreover, the Commission itself recognises in its Communication that the precautionary principle is not only relevant in cases where risks are to be expected in the short or medium term. It is also relevant when long-term planning is required, and the well-being of future generations is at stake.[74] This can at least be interpreted as an indication that the Commission also recognises the substance of resource precaution.[75]

What is much more important, however, is that the Court of Justice of the European Union, which is called upon to provide the final binding interpretation of EU law in cases of doubt,[76] by no means only refers to the precautionary principle, when there is a lack of sufficiently reliable knowledge in terms of risk precaution described above. Rather, the Court of Justice considers "very different provisions to be manifestations of the precautionary principle or includes the principle in its interpretation, even if their elements do not explicitly refer to potential risks, suspected situations or similar descriptions of insufficiently reliable scientific knowledge."[77] This can be seen not least in circular economy law as one of the areas of environmental law of particular interest here. For when the ECJ explicitly uses the precautionary principle to justify a broad interpretation of the concept of waste under EU law,[78] it is clearly not about a form of scientific uncertainty and thus risk precaution but rather about achieving

[70] Epiney (2019), 5th ch. para. 20; Krüper (2009), p. 92; Lübbe-Wolff (1998), p. 58; Meßerschmidt (2011), § 3 para. 80.

[71] COM 2000 (1) final.

[72] Thus, however, Arndt (2009), pp. 129–130; Kahl (2018), Art. 11 TFEU para. 25–26 and Art. 191 TFEU para. 83.

[73] Cf. in detail on this context Arndt (2009), p. 77 et seq.

[74] See COM (2000) 1, final, p. 9.

[75] This is also recognised by Arndt (2009), pp. 129–130.

[76] This also applies in relation to the Commission, as follows from Art. 17 para. 1 sentence 3 TEU.

[77] Thus, expressis verbis Arndt (2009), p. 173 on the basis of a subsequent differentiated analysis of court rulings.

[78] Cf. for example ECJ, judgement of 15 June 2000, C-418/97 and C-419/97, in: Neue Zeitschrift für Verwaltungsrecht 2000, 1156, para. 39 et seq.; ECJ, judgement of 7 September 2004, Case C-1/03, in: Neue Zeitschrift für Verwaltungsrecht 2004, 1341, para. 42–45.

the broadest possible applicability of European waste management law based on the principle of resource precaution.[79]

Last but not least, on a positive note, several interpretative topoi speak in favour of recognising both dimensions of the precautionary principle at the EU level. Firstly, a historical interpretation of Art. 191(2)(2) TFEU must take into account that the German version of the precautionary principle, which also includes the principle of resource precaution, was also the inspiration here.[80] Secondly, a systematic interpretation of Art. 191(2)(2) TFEU should take account of the fact that Art. 191(1) TFEU specifies a "prudent and rational utilisation of natural resources" as one of the objectives of the Union's environmental policy and thus points to a core element of resource precaution. Thirdly, it would strengthen the effet utile, i.e. the practical effectiveness of the precautionary principle, if its dual nature were recognised. This is all the truer, when we consider, fourthly, that a one-sided normative shift of the concern of resource precaution to the principle of sustainability could lead to a lack of contours and indeterminacy due to its previously described breadth, which covers a wide variety of social factors.[81]

For these reasons and in line with the prevailing opinion in German literature, it can be assumed that the precautionary principle standardised in Art. 191(2)(2) TFEU not only covers risk precaution but also resource precaution in equal terms.[82]

5 The Precautionary Principle in Selected Areas

In the following, it will be shown by way of example that such a broad understanding of the precautionary principle can also be detected in the areas of the circular economy, land use and water resource management. At the same time, it will be shown that this also applies to some regulations of secondary EU environmental law in the areas of the circular economy and water resource management. This in turn further affirms evidence of the broad interpretation of the precautionary principle in EU law which is (also) advocated here.

---

[79] Cf. in more detail on the connection between resource precaution and European waste management law below under Sect. 5.1.

[80] Appel (2001), p. 397 also expressly refers to this fact.

[81] On the problem of the vagueness of the sustainability principle in EU law, see for example Vanhellemont (2021), p. 11 et seq.

[82] See also Appel (2001), p. 397; Calliess (2022), Art. 191 TFEU para. 88 and 94; Epiney (2019), 5th ch. para. 20; Heselhaus (2022), Art. 191 TFEU para. 65; Lübbe-Wolff (1998), p. 53 et seq; Meßerschmidt (2011), § 3 para. 80 and 124–125.

5.1 *The Precautionary Principle in the Circular Economy*

5.1.1 Initial Normative Findings

With regard to the circular economy, it should be noted that the precautionary principle is mentioned at three places in the EU Waste Framework Directive 2008/98/EC.[83] The same applies to the German Circular Economy Act (Kreislaufwirtschaftsgesetz—KrWG).[84] At first glance, risk precaution takes centre stage. However, it is rightly pointed out that the objective of the circular economy formulated in Section 1(1) KrWG, namely to "promote the conservation of natural resources", which can also similarly be found in the Waste Framework Directive,[85] represents a simple legal expression of the principle of resource precaution.[86] This is also supported by the fact that Art. 4(2)(3) of the Waste Framework Directive obliges the Member States to take into account the "general principles of environmental protection" mentioned therein and, in addition to precaution, expressly lists the principle of "the protection of resources", which in turn can be understood as an emanation of resource precaution for the reasons mentioned above under III. 1. c).

In modern recycling management law, the goal of resource precaution is to be achieved first and foremost through the prevention of waste, which 'per se' should be given the highest priority according to the waste hierarchy established in Art. 4(1) of the Waste Framework Directive and Section 6(1) KrWG.[87] This is because the requirement to prevent waste contains the idea of protecting open spaces by safeguarding room for manoeuvre and open spaces developed in the BImSchG.[88] It has been correctly noted that this "unspecific protection of open spaces, which is not oriented towards risk avoidance [...] serves to keep the future open, ultimately also to avoid spatial problems far upstream that may arise in the future and are not attributable to political enforcement problems".[89]

5.1.2 Enforcement Deficits

In practice, however, the sober 2008 statement by the German Advisory Council on the Environment (*Sachverständigenrat für Umweltfragen—SRU*) that "the prioritised

[83] See recital 30, Art. 4(2)(3), Art. 23(1)(lit. c) of Directive 2008/98/EC.

[84] See Section 6(2)(1), Section 36(1)(no. 1)(lit. b); Section 43(2)(1) KrWG; in addition, the precautionary principle is mentioned in Annex 3 to the KrWG.

[85] See in particular the second sentence of recital 6 and Art. 1 of Directive 2008/98/EC.

[86] Kahl and Gärditz (2023), § 4 para. 22. Similarly, Calliess (2021), p. 194, who sees in this legal purpose a "teleological parallelism to the resource-related aspect of the precautionary principle".

[87] For more information on the connection between the waste hierarchy and the principles of precaution and prevention standardised in Art. 191(3) TFEU, see Hahn (2017), p. 39 et seq.

[88] For more details on open space protection, see Sect. 3.1.2 above.

[89] Viertel (1995), p. 63.

prevention of waste is [not] happening" is still valid.[90] This is particularly evident in the case of plastic packaging. In its 2020 environmental report, the SRU pointed out that the amount of plastic packaging produced and disposed of between 1991 and 2017 rose from 20.5 to 38.5 kg per capita per year, of which 12.2 and 25.4 kg respectively were generated by private end consumers.[91] This leads to the conclusion that the concept of product responsibility now standardised in Sections 23 et seq. KrWG has completely failed to achieve its primary goal of preventing waste, at least in the area of packaging. This finding challenges the precautionary principle in both its forms in view of the considerable relevance of the production and disposal of plastics for climate protection, with resource precaution taking centre stage. In its 2020 environmental report, the *SRU* points out that more than 99% of plastics were still produced from petroleum-based primary products in 2017 and that 9 million tonnes of CO_2 are produced annually in Germany when plastics are incinerated.[92]

However, there is also still a lot to be done, when it comes to the utilisation of waste as the second pillar of the circular economy. For example, the SRU's 2020 environmental report states that "raw material consumption" in Germany is still almost twice as high as the global average and that in 2013, raw materials obtained from waste (secondary raw materials) only covered just under 16% of raw material requirements.[93] In its 2020 environmental report, the *SRU* rightly attributes these deficits to three main reasons: firstly, the circular economy is insufficiently integrated into other environmental policies.[94] Secondly, there is a lack of targets for waste prevention and thirdly, recycling is not sufficiently ecologically orientated.[95]

5.1.3 Proposals for Reducing Enforcement Deficits

Against this backdrop, the *SRU* proposes an expansion of the waste hierarchy in its 2020 environmental report. Accordingly, the reduction of material flows and a "circular economy-capable" product design should be at the top of the new waste hierarchy.[96] The next step would be to set binding targets for waste prevention and preparation for reuse, which are currently at the top of the waste hierarchy.[97] Finally, the existing third stage of the waste hierarchy, recycling, is to be both supplemented by the qualification "high quality" and the aspect of removing harmful substances and underpinned by more specific regulations, such as further advanced recycling quotas.[98]

---

[90] SRU (2008), para. 863.

[91] SRU (2020), para. 179.

[92] SRU (2020), para. 177.

[93] SRU (2020), subs. 126.

[94] For more details, see SRU (2020), para. 153 et seq.

[95] For more details, see SRU (2020), para. 160 et seq.

[96] For more details, see SRU (2020), para. 204 et seq.

[97] For more details, see SRU (2020), para. 218–219.

[98] For more details, see SRU (2020), para. 225 et seq.

5.1.4 Evaluation

These proposals deserve strong support for reasons of resource precaution. This applies in particular to the call for waste prevention and preparation for reuse to be underpinned for the first time by binding targets and for recycling quotas to be advanced. After all, as already mentioned, verifiable targets can make effective resource precaution much easier, if they can be defined on a valid professional basis.[99]

5.2 The Precautionary Principle in the Area of Land Use

5.2.1 The Term Land Use and Precautionary Challenges

When considering the validity and significance of the precautionary principle in the area of land use, the first question that arises is what is meant by land use. The narrowest understanding of the term refers only to the use of land-based ecosystems, in particular soil, by agriculture and forestry.[100]

The agriculture referred to here takes up more than half of the land surface in Germany and continues to cause considerable problems, particularly due to the excessive use of fertilisers and pesticides, which are also relevant regarding the precautionary principle.[101]

In a broader sense, the direct use of land both for the private and commercial development of settlements and spatially extensive transport infrastructure are also relevant forms of land use. They are regularly accompanied by corresponding land consumption through soil sealing; the latter of which is already problematic as such from the point of view of resource precaution.[102] In view of the fact that sealing and overbuilding is the most intensive form of land use, the precautionary principle generally requires that the further expansion of settlements and transport areas is limited.[103]

---

[99] See in more detail above under Sect. 3.1.7.

[100] See Söhnlein (1999), p. 195 with further references.

[101] Cf. for example the figures in Kloepfer (2016), § 13 para. 13; also, Möckel (2014), pp. 14–15 with further references, who generally calls for a stronger alignment of agri-environmental law with the precautionary principle. On this and the following, see also SRU (2008), pp. 391–392: "The main soil problems in Germany are soil sealing and the extensive input of pollutants and nutrients from agricultural use."

[102] See here only the figures in Kloepfer (2016), § 13 para. 15.

[103] Thus, convincingly Söhnlein (1999), p. 205 et seq.

5.2.2 Deficits in the Federal Soil Protection Act and the Fertiliser and Plant Protection Act

Accordingly, from the perspective of environmental precaution, land use is first and foremost about protecting the soil, which together with air and water is one of the key environmental media. To protect the soil, the German Federal Soil Protection Act (Bundes-Bodenschutzgesetz—BBodSchG) was (first) enacted in 1998. According to its Section 1(1) BBodSchG, it pursues the purpose of securing or restoring the functions of the soil "sustainably". To this end, according to Section 1(2) BBodSchG, "harmful soil changes must be prevented, the soil and contaminated sites as well as any water pollution caused by them must be remediated and precaution must be taken against detrimental effects on the soil". It can be assumed that the precautionary principle explicitly addressed here also includes the protection of open spaces, which aims to preserve sufficient recreational spaces and areas for development in the interests of future generations. This follows above all from the fact that the BBodSchG has included the utilisation functions of the soil in the protective purpose of the law.[104] Consequently, the precautionary principle on which the BBodSchG is based also contains a resource-related component.

However, the Federal Soil Protection Act does not adequately address this issue.[105] Not only does the Act not contain any instruments to counteract land consumption as one of the central problems of soil protection. On the contrary, the regulations on the scope of application in Section 3(1) BBodSchG stipulate that the Act is only applicable on a subsidiary basis to the sectoral laws listed there.[106] In particular, the reference in Section 3(1)(nos. 8, 9) BBodSchG to the "regulations on the construction, modification, maintenance and operation of transport routes" and to the "regulations of building planning and building regulations law" means that the aforementioned resource-related concerns of the Federal Soil Protection Act, the consistent observance of which would be essential for reducing land consumption, are hardly taken into account in relevant planning and authorisation procedures.[107] Furthermore, the aforementioned provisions mean that the regulation in Section 5 BBodSchG on the unsealing of land that is no longer in permanent use—which is only weakly structured in any case—has no practical significance.[108] In this respect, the precautionary concept of the Federal Soil Protection Act proves to be deficient overall with regard to the pressing problem of land consumption, which was already rightly criticised during the passing of the law.[109]

Section 7(1) BBodSchG then stipulates a precautionary duty that generally obliges property owners, holders of actual power over a property and those who carry out or have carried out activities on a property that may lead to changes in the soil quality to

---

[104] See Charitopoulos (2009), pp. 69–70; Sanden and Schoeneck (1998), § 1 para. 14.

[105] For the following, see also the criticism in Rehbinder (2018), ch. 3 para. 51.

[106] See here only Kahl and Gärditz (2023), § 9 para. 15; Kloepfer (2016), § 13 para. 174.

[107] See also Schink (2018), ch. 6 para. 270.

[108] See Kloepfer (2016), § 13 para. 191 with further references.

[109] See the clear criticism in Peine (1997), pp. 56–59.

take precautions against the occurrence of harmful soil changes caused by their use of the property or within its area of impact. In order to fulfil the precautionary duty, Section 7(3) BBodSchG also stipulates that soil impacts must be avoided or reduced insofar as this is proportionate to the purpose of the use of the property. However, this precautionary duty is relativised to a considerable extent by other provisions of the Federal Soil Protection Act.[110]

The last point also and especially applies to agriculture.[111] Here, the main problems result primarily from the excessive use of fertilisers and pesticides, which also have a negative impact on water management.[112] However, due to the subsidiarity clause in Section 3(1)(no. 4) BBodSchG, the Federal Soil Protection Act leaves this area to the fertiliser and plant protection law,[113] which admittedly also has considerable deficits. To this day, this leads to considerable environmental damage, which not only has a negative impact on soil but also on water bodies and even on the climate.[114] These environmental impairments now also challenge the distancing requirement as a concrete consequence of the principle of resource precaution.[115] This is because the inputs of reactive nitrogen and phosphorus in particular are so high in Germany that they exceed ecosystem boundaries.[116] For precautionary reasons, it is therefore necessary to (further) reform fertiliser and plant protection legislation and supplement it with additional instruments.[117]

Other problems relevant to soil protection legislation result from other agricultural soil management methods, which can lead to excessive soil compaction, erosion, loss of permanent grassland[118] and organic matter.[119] Section 7(5) BBodSchG stipulates that the precautionary requirements for agricultural land use are based on Section 17(1 and 2) BBodSchG. The benchmark for the precautionary obligations is therefore "good professional practice" in accordance with Section 17(1)(1) BBodSchG.

According to Section 17(2)(1) BBodSchG, the principles of good professional practice are "the sustainable safeguarding of soil fertility and soil performance as a natural resource". These principles are unpacked in seven points in Section 17(2)(2) BBodSchG, which address the problems of agricultural land use just mentioned, at least in substance. However, it must be criticised that even the requirements stipulated in Section 17(2)(2) BBodSchG are not specific enough and that further specification

---

[110] In accordance with Section 7(4) BBodSchG, orders to prevent harmful soil changes may only be issued, if requirements are specified in an ordinance in accordance with Section 8(2) BBodSchG.

[111] Cf., for example, the criticism of Ginzky (2010), pp. 1–2.

[112] For the negative effects on the environmental objectives that apply to water bodies, see Köck (2019), p. 69.

[113] See also critically Peine (1997), pp. 56–59.

[114] For more details, see Möckel and Wolf (2020), p. 739 et seq.

[115] See above under Sect. 3.1.5.

[116] See Möckel and Wolf (2020), p. 737 with further references.

[117] See the specific proposals by Möckel and Wolf (2020), p. 742 et seq.

[118] See Möckel (2014), p. 17 et seq. on these problems with reform proposals worth considering—also and especially from a precautionary perspective.

[119] For more details, see SRU (2008), pp. 416–417.

cannot be made by the enforcement authorities due to the lack of a respective basis for authorisation.[120]

In view of this, the precautionary requirements of the German Federal Soil Protection Act are deficient overall, particularly from the point of view of resource precaution, since two essential problems of qualitative and quantitative soil protection are simply ignored. This shortcoming provoked the following harsh but justified criticism in the run-up to the passing of the law: "A law with this limited content does not deserve to be called a soil protection law".[121] It was therefore a sign of hope that the former governing parties at federal level agreed to evaluate the Federal Soil Protection Act in their coalition agreement of December 2021 and adapt it to the challenges of climate protection, climate adaptation and the preservation of biodiversity.[122] Unfortunately, the coalition agreement which was adopted by the newly elected governing parties at federal level in May 2025 did not take up this initiative.[123] Therefore, the conceptual weaknesses of the Federal Soil Protection Act outlined here and elsewhere[124] still needs to be remedied in the future.

5.2.3 Precautionary Deficits in Spatial Planning Law

There is also reason to do so, because the existing requirements for overall spatial planning have also not contributed to permanently limiting soil sealing; still, the prevailing opinion is that quantitative soil protection as a form of resource precaution in the area of settlement and transport area development should be implemented precisely through spatial planning and urban land-use planning.[125] This corresponds not least to the declared intention of the legislator. The legal mandate of spatial planning pursuant to Section 1(1)(2)(no. 2) of the German Spatial Planning Act (Raumordnungsgesetz—ROG) is to generate provisions for individual uses and functions of an area. The guiding principle to fulfil this task is, according to Section 1(2) ROG, "sustainable spatial development that harmonises the social and economic demands on space with its ecological functions and leads to a permanent, large-scale balanced order with equivalent living conditions in the sub-regions." Furthermore, since 2017, Section 2(2)(no. 6)(3) ROG has stipulated the principle that the "first-time use of open spaces for settlement and transport purposes […] must be reduced, in particular through quantified requirements for reducing land use and by giving priority to exploiting the potential for the reuse of land, for redensification and for other measures for the internal development of cities and municipalities and for the development of existing transport areas."

---

[120] Essentially in agreement with Ginzky (2010), p. 2; Ginzky (2019), p. 1; Köck (2019), p. 70.

[121] See Peine (1997), p. 59.

[122] See p. 41 of the coalition agreement, available at https://t1p.de/1stlp. Accessed 22 Sep 2025.

[123] See the coalition agreement, available at https://t1p.de/krb88. Accessed 22 Sep 2025.

[124] See the list of deficits in German soil protection law in SRU (2008), pp. 420–421.

[125] Cf., for example, Appel (2005), p. 189; Kahl and Gärditz (2023), § 4 para. 25; Kloepfer (2016), § 13 para. 234; Rehbinder (2018), ch. 3 para. 53.

And in urban land-use planning, municipalities are obliged under Section 1a(2) of the German Federal Building Code (Baugesetzbuch—BauGB) to use land "sparingly and carefully" and to "limit soil sealing to the extent necessary". However, if we ask how the fundamental problem of excessive land use has a concrete impact on overall spatial planning and construction activity currently, the findings are largely sobering.[126]

On the one hand, this is due to the fact that resource precaution, like climate protection, in concrete planning processes currently has no priority over other relevant concerns.[127] The Decision of the Federal Constitutional Court of 24 March 2021 has not changed this matter, despite the constitutional upgrading of climate protection postulated. However, the Federal Constitutional Court does emphasise that the relative weight of the climate protection requirement in the balancing of interests continues to increase as climate change progresses.[128] In this context, it is also worth to remember the repeated calls to give absolute priority to environmental concerns, at least in cases where there is a threat of serious and long-term destruction of the natural foundations of life.[129] This will have to be taken into account to a greater extent in future spatial planning decisions and reviewed by the courts, not only in overall spatial planning but also in decisions under sectoral planning law, such as those relating to the authorisation of transport infrastructure projects.

Secondly, there is a widespread lack of specific and binding targets in the area of land use.[130] This applies both to soil protection and to the new requirements for land use resulting from climate protection. With regard to the resource function, one should not forget that soil fulfils central natural functions, which are explicitly listed in Section 2(2)(no. 1) BBodSchG for good reason. Accordingly, soil is not only the basis of life and habitat for humans, animals, plants and soil organisms. It is also a component of ecosystems, in particular with its water and nutrient cycles as well as a degradation, equalisation and build-up medium for material impacts due to its filtering, buffering and material conversion properties—in particular for the protection of groundwater. However, these functions are considerably impaired by the ever-increasing use of land.[131]

The matter of limiting the use of new land through binding (federal) legal or spatial planning requirements should therefore be pursued persistently.[132] This also remains

---

[126] See, for example, the analysis and evidence by Schink (2018), ch. 6 para. 278 et seq.; see more recently on the threat to national environmental objectives, including land consumption targets, for example SRU (2019), para. 256 et seq.

[127] Cf. instructive on the problem with regard to the principle of sustainability Appel (2005), p. 422 et seq.

[128] Cf. Bundesverfassungsgericht, Decision of 24 March 2021, 1 BvR 2656/18 et al, in: Neue Juristische Wochenschrift 2021, p. 1723, headnote 2 a and para. 120, 185 and 198.

[129] See Appel (2005), p. 446, with reference to Prof-E about UGB.

[130] See also, with regard to the principle of sustainability, Appel (2005), p. 422 et seq.

[131] See, for example, Bovet (2020), pp. 32–33.

[132] For more details, see Bovet (2020), p. 31 et seq.

a desideratum from the perspective of nature and water law.[133] Not least, the earlier proposal should be considered, namely to stipulate specific targets in soil protection law that are binding for both spatial planning and sectoral planning and cannot be overridden in planning considerations.[134] Contrary to some opinions, such targets may very well be permissible, if they are designed accordingly and, moreover, can be integrated into spatial planning law in a system-compatible manner.[135]

However, it should also be remembered in this context that such spatial planning requirements do not cover an important area of construction activity.[136] After all, local authorities hardly ever draw up development plans that are project independent.[137] The consequence is that most housing development projects are realised in unplanned inner areas in accordance with Section 34 BauGB, where even spatial planning objectives do not play a role in the assessment of permissibility under building planning law according to prevailing opinion.[138] Therefore, clear regulations are needed to ensure that corresponding stipulations must also be observed when making decisions in accordance with Section 34 BauGB.[139] Finally, general consideration should be given to amending Section 34 BauGB in such a way that resource and climate protection and other environmental concerns can and must be given greater consideration when authorising construction projects in unplanned inner areas.[140]

5.2.4 Precautionary Safeguarding of Areas for Wind Energy

With a view to the spatial planning, the *SRU's* demanded in 2021 to designate 2% of the area of the Federal Republic of Germany for the use of onshore wind energy in its latest 'impulse paper' on the expansion of onshore wind energy is indeed justified in view of the precautionary mandate of safeguarding land under spatial planning law.[141] It is to be welcomed as a contribution to risk and resource precaution. The

---

[133] See also the Federal Environment Ministry's National Water Strategy, p. 29 et seq, which is available online; here on p. 33 the "vision" for 2050 is formulated, among other things, that land consumption for settlement and transport has decreased significantly and the transition to a circular economy (net zero land consumption) has been achieved.

[134] This is the proposal of the SRU (2008), pp. 392 and 440, which, however, only mentions specialised planning.

[135] For more details on the whole, see Wagner (2018).

[136] On the parallel problem of spatial planning specifications for flood prevention, see Faßbender (2013), p. 34 et seq. with further references.

[137] Ginzky et al. (2021), p. 450.

[138] Cf. here only Faßbender (2013), p. 34 with further references.

[139] See also Ginzky et al. (2021), p. 450 with regard to the obligation for municipal climate adaptation planning discussed there. However, it should be noted that Section 78 of the German Federal Water Act (WHG) stipulates precautionary requirements for building in floodplains, which must also be observed in unplanned inner areas in accordance with Section 78(4)(1) WHG.

[140] See also Sauthoff (2022), p. 14, who specifically calls for climate protection to be included as a reason for refusal in Art. 34 BauGB.

[141] See SRU (2021), p. 1.

SRU's call to allow wind turbines in the entire outdoor area and not just in areas designated in planning also deserves approval, if the spatial planning authorities do not manage to fulfil the associated state-related quantitative targets within a fixed period.[142] This is because the massive expansion of onshore wind energy is an issue that has also received a significant constitutional boost as a result of the Federal Constitutional Court's climate Decision, if due consideration is given to the actual energy policy situation in Germany.[143]

Given all this, it is to be welcomed that the federal legislator recently passed a law to increase and accelerate the expansion of onshore wind energy installations,[144] which includes a new German Wind Area Requirement Act (Windenergieflächenbedarfsgesetz—WindBG). This sets in advance binding area targets (so-called area contribution values—'Flächenbeitragswerte') for the federal states, which are derived from the expansion targets of the Renewable Energy Sources Act (Section 3(1) in conjunction with Annex 1). Accordingly, a total of 2% of the federal area must be designated for onshore wind energy by the end of 2032, which requires more than doubling the currently designated area (0.8%). The area targets under the Wind Area Requirement Act are incorporated into the Federal Building Code for this purpose. Planning control by designating wind energy areas will only have an exclusionary effect, in case the area targets are met; otherwise, wind turbines are permitted on a privileged basis in the entire planning area (Section 249(2) and (7) BauGB).

5.2.5 Interim Conclusion

The following interim conclusion can therefore be drawn: In the area of land use, the principle of resource precaution fundamentally demands that climate-related concerns and the protection of the soil with its various functions—which justify calling the soil the "foundation of life" in the truest sense of the word[145]—be given much greater consideration in future regulations and decisions relevant to soil protection. Insofar as this involves appropriate legislation, which must also explicitly address agricultural land use and specific construction measures in order to be issue adequate, the focus is first and foremost on the mandate dimension of the precautionary principle; the latter in turn has been significantly upgraded and concretised by the interpretation of Article 20a of the German Basic Law in the Federal Constitutional Court's climate Decision of 24 March 2021.[146] If and to the extent that this legislation is accompanied by restrictions, in particular on the fundamental rights of landowners or the guarantee of municipal self-government, the legislator can also invoke the justification dimension of the precautionary principle. Until then,

[142] SRU (2021), p. 2.

[143] See in more detail Faßbender (2021b), pp. 797–798.

[144] Dated 20 July 2022 (Bundesgesetzblatt I 2022, p. 1353).

[145] Thus Söhnlein (1999), p. 196.

[146] See in more detail above under Sect. 3.1.6.

the courts are also required to take into account the interrelationships described, particularly when reviewing spatial planning decisions.

5.3 The Precautionary Principle in the Area of Water Resource Management

5.3.1 Notes on the Development of the Precautionary Principle in Water Law

When considering the validity and significance of the precautionary principle in the field of water resource management, it should first be noted that for a long time the concept of precaution was neither included in the German Federal Water (Resources Management) Act (Wasserhaushaltsgesetz—WHG) nor the water legislation of the federal states as the relevant legal basis.[147] This changed for the first time with the Act of 27 July 2001 on the Implementation of the EIA Amending Directive, the IPPC Directive and other EC Directives on environmental protection.[148] The Act added a reference to the newly added Annex to the then definition of the state of the art in Section 7a(5) WHG, which in turn had to be observed in accordance with Section 7a(1)(1) WHG when issuing a permit for the discharge of wastewater. In its criteria for determining the state of the art, this new Annex, like Annex IV of the IPPC Directive to be implemented, expressly referred to the precautionary principle.[149]

It is also worth pointing to the Act of 3 May 2005 on the Improvement of Preventive Flood Protection,[150] which explicitly used the term "flood precaution" ('Hochwasser-vorsorge') for the first time concerning the maintenance of floodplains[151] in the regulation and which also significantly strengthened preventive flood protection.

These—rather selective—references to the precautionary principle have essentially not increased to this day. While the Act on the Revision of Water Law of 31 July 2009,[152] which came into force on 1 March 2010, also introduced three regulations that also refer to the precautionary principle; yet, these new regulations served to implement the EU Floods Directive and therefore relate exclusively to flood protection.[153]

Despite the fact that it was not explicitly mentioned for a long time, it has long been recognised that the precautionary principle was and still is the tacit basis for various

[147] This is also the finding of Viertel (1995), p. 86.

[148] Bundesgesetzblatt I No. 40 of 2 August 2001, p. 1950 et seq.

[149] The same applies to today's Annex 1 to Section 3(no. 11) WHG.

[150] Bundesgesetzblatt I No. 40 of 2 August 2001, p. 1950 et seq.

[151] See the former regulation in Section 31b(4)(2)(no. 8) WHG (old version), which can now be found in Section 75(2)(no. 8) WHG.

[152] Bundesgesetzblatt I No. 51 of 6 August 2009, p. 2585 et seq.

[153] See Section 5(2), Section 75(2)(2) and Section 79(2) WHG.

provisions of the Federal Water Act, particularly in its resource-related variant.[154] As early as 1983, *Horst Sendler* stated that with the precautionary principle, the Federal Immission Control Act (BImSchG) had added the additional objective of "doing precisely what has long since been realised in another way in water law by subjecting scarce resources to the discretion of the authorities".[155]

The normative reference point for the assumption that the precautionary principle was already valid in the earlier Federal Water Act was above all Section 1a(1) WHG (old version). In its first version, which dated back to the Fourth Act of 26 April 1976 amending the Federal Water Act,[156] it obliged the water authorities to manage water bodies in such a way that "any avoidable impairment is prevented". This requirement was already interpreted as a manifestation of the precautionary principle.[157] Subsequently, the Fifth Act of 25 July 1986 amending the Federal Water Act[158] added the phrase that water bodies must be managed "as a part of the ecobalance", which further strengthened the idea of resource precaution.[159]

A further point of reference for the application of the precautionary principle in the former Federal Water Act was the fact—not initially explicitly regulated in the law but generally recognised[160]—that the competent authorities have a management discretion even when issuing permits for uses under water law on a case-by-case basis. From this, the conclusion was rightly drawn in the literature that water law is "virtually predestined" for spatial (and thus resource-related) precaution.[161]

Against this background, in its aforementioned[162] Decision of 18 September 1987, the Federal Administrative Court also derived the requirement of "planning precaution" and "forward-looking conservation of the drinking water reservoir beyond current requirements" from both the regulation of Section 1a(1) WHG in force at

[154] See also Krüper (2009), p. 69 et seq. who believes that water law has "always" been a "reference area" for "interpretations of the precautionary principle under management law".

[155] Sendler (1983), p. 38. However, Sendler immediately clarified that, despite this additional objective, the BImSchG had "remained true to its police law origins". Against this background, Sendler posed on p. 40 the question, which is still relevant today, as to whether the BImSchG should not also follow developments that have long since been realised in water law. He provided several reasons for this, which already suggested such a development at a time when climate protection was not yet an issue.

[156] Bundesgesetzblatt I No. 128 of 26 October 1976, p. 3017 et seq.

[157] For more details, see Volkens (1993), p. 25 et seq with further references from the older literature. Cf. from the more recent literature Charitopoulos (2009), p. 52 et seq.

[158] Bundesgesetzblatt I No. 38 of 31 July 1986, p. 1165 et seq.

[159] For more details on the resulting strengthening of the precautionary principle, see Volkens (1993), p. 30 et seq. with references to older literature.

[160] See here only the famous decision of the Federal Constitutional Court (BVerfG) on water law BVerfGE 58, 300, 328–329.

[161] See Viertel (1995), pp. 296ff. Cf. also BVerfGE 58, 300, 347 on the importance of the management discretion for an "orderly control of water utilisation geared towards the future". From this, the BVerfG even draws the conclusion that a preventive authorisation procedure subject to prohibition would not be sufficient to ensure "orderly water management"; a corresponding regulation in water law would therefore be "unjustifiable".

[162] See above under Sect. 3.1.4.

the time and from the management discretion.[163] In this Decision, the three core elements that characterise the principle of resource precaution emerge particularly clearly—also in contrast to risk and hazard precaution.[164]

These considerations in the literature and court rulings continue to apply without restriction even after the new amendment of water law as, on the one hand, the principles of water management stipulated in Section 1a(1) WHG (old version) can be found in Section 6(1) WHG in a partially supplemented form, which is still rightly interpreted as an expression of the precautionary principle.[165] On the other hand, in the course of the revision of water law, the legislator specifically emphasised that the competent authorities have a management discretion even when issuing authorisations for water law uses on a case-by-case basis.[166]

Finally, Section 7a WHG (old version), which in its first version also dated back to the Fourth Act of 26 April 1976 amending the Federal Water Act, served as a normative reference point for the assumption that the precautionary principle also claimed validity in the former Federal Water Act even without an explicit mention. This provision stipulated technology-oriented water body-independent requirements for the discharge of wastewater into water bodies. Since the new regulation of water law, it can now be found in a further advanced form in Section 57 WHG and was interpreted then[167] and now[168] as an expression of the precautionary principle.

Whether the discharge limitations on the basis of Section 7a WHG (old version) have actually been "clearly in the foreground" in the enforcement of water law to date[169] is likely to be questionable in view of the precautionary dimension of Section 1a(1) WHG (old version), which was already widely recognised in the past; ultimately, the effect is likely to depend on the relevant factors. This is due to the management discretion, on the one hand, and the diversity of water law enforcement, on the other hand, which in the past had to deal not only with wastewater discharges but also with other types of water use within the meaning of Section 3 WHG (old version; now Section 9 WHG).

5.3.2 Strengthening Resource Precaution Through the Water Framework Directive

The EU Water Framework Directive (WFD) has without doubt established a further "pillar of precaution" in the area of water resource management "with the concept of

[163] See Bundesverwaltungsgericht, in: Neue Zeitschrift für Verwaltungsrecht 1988, pp. 535–536.

[164] See above under Sect. 3.1.3.

[165] Cf., for example, Czychowski and Reinhardt (2023), § 6 para. 2. More cautious Rehbinder (2018), ch. 3 para. 45.

[166] See Section 12(2) WHG.

[167] See, for example, Charitopoulos (2009), p. 55 et seq.; Viertel (1995), p. 254 et seq.

[168] See, for example, Czychowski and Reinhardt (2023), § 57 para. 5; Rehbinder (2018), ch. 3 para. 44.

[169] Thus Rehbinder (2018), ch. 3 para. 44a.

ambitious quality objectives".[170] This is because the environmental and management objectives (good status or corresponding potential and prohibition of deterioration) stipulated in Art. 4 WFD and the national implementation provisions of Sections. 27–30, 44 and 47 WHG and the other regulations, which—such as Section 34(1) WHG and Section 39(2) WHG—aim at compliance with these objectives, all serve "quality-related precaution, also in the sense of resource precaution".[171]

In this context, the WFD has shaped the principle of resource precaution in an almost exemplary manner,[172] as it firstly contains specific resource-related targets that apply *regardless of any kind of threat* to the environmental resource of water and that, moreover, give measure and direction to resource protection, which facilitates the effectiveness of resource precaution to a considerable extent. Secondly, this is done with the aim of conserving water resources in the interests of *future* uses and needs.[173] Thirdly, the Water Framework Directive not only pursues a *management approach* like the traditional Federal Water (Resources Management) Act. On the contrary, it resolutely calls for a *planning approach*, which was previously pursued only very scantly in Germany,[174] by also specifying in Art. 11 and 13 WFD[175] those planning instruments that must be used by the Member States to implement these objectives. In this respect, the Water Framework Directive functions as a *role model* for resource precaution.

5.3.3 Strengthening Resource Precaution Through a National Water Strategy

The "National Water Strategy", which was adopted by the Federal Government on 15 March 2023, also points out: "Precautionary measures are at the core of this National Water Strategy".[176] In addition, the precautionary principle is explicitly listed as one of the "basic principles of the strategy".[177] Unfortunately, however, the aspect of resource precaution is not mentioned in the text but only in its glossary.[178]

Two environmental policy challenges are rightly emphasised in particular: climate change and the "water pollution caused by nitrogen and phosphorus and various other

---

[170] Rehbinder (2018), ch. 3 para. 44a.

[171] Rehbinder (2018), ch. 3 para. 44a. The precautionary function of environmental and management objectives is also emphasised by Charitopoulos (2009), p. 58 et seq.

[172] See also Appel (2005), p. 455, who believes that the model provided by the WFD is "paradigmatic for other areas of resource protection".

[173] See, for example, Art. 1(1)(lit. b) WFD, according to which the Directive pursues, among other things, the objective of "promoting sustainable water use based on the long-term protection of existing resources".

[174] For more details, see Klingele (2012), p. 85.

[175] The corresponding implementation provisions can be found in Sections 82 and 83 WHG.

[176] Cf. p. 8 of the National Water Strategy which is available in English under https://t1p.de/ym199. Accessed 22 Sept 2025.

[177] Cf. p. 10 of the National Water Strategy.

[178] Cf. p. 108 of the National Water Strategy.

substances (e.g. trace substances) and pollutants (e.g. microplastics)".[179] To tackle these and other challenges, the strategy identifies ten "strategic issues" under the heading "What needs to be done", each of which sets out a vision for the year 2050 and key steps to realise this vision.[180] Finally, an initial "Programme of water measures" sets out specific measures to be taken in stages over the next few years up to 2030.[181]

The "National Water Strategy" contains numerous valuable tips and approaches for advancing risk and resource precaution in the management of water resources. Its conceptual added value lies in the fact that it also makes it clear that key challenges and threats to water resources cannot be tackled by water management and "traditional" water law alone. Instead, cross-sector measures are required.

This applies in particular to the aforementioned pollution of water bodies. To tackle this problem, the "National Water Strategy" proposes concrete measures to mitigate risks caused by pollutants.[182] Inter alia, the zero-pollution action plan at EU level is to be supported and implemented. However, there is hardly any emphasis on short-term restrictions or even bans on chemicals and microplastics, which accumulate in water bodies and are sometimes harmful to health. It would therefore be desirable for reasons of resource precaution and, to some extent, risk precaution,[183] if Germany like other EU Member States were to take prompt regulatory action in this area, if necessary.[184] In this regard, however, it should be remembered that the Water Framework Directive also provides a framework in this respect, for example when it calls for measures and strategies to combat water pollution in surface waters[185] and with regard to groundwater stipulates not only a requirement to reverse any significant and sustained upward trend but also a requirement to progressively reduce pollution of groundwater.[186]

6 Conclusions on the Status and Development Prospects of Resource Precaution

The following can therefore be summarised:

[179] Cf. p. 7 of the National Water Strategy.

[180] Cf. p. 14 et seq. of the National Water Strategy.

[181] Cf. p. 75 et seq. of the National Water Strategy.

[182] Cf. p. 84 et seq. of the National Water Strategy.

[183] On the possibility and necessity of a combination of risk and resource precaution in water law, see the specific example of Lübbe-Wolff (1998), pp. 57–59.

[184] Cf. Stubenrauch and Ekardt (2021), pp. 406–425.

[185] See Art. 4(1)(a)(iv) and Art. 16 WFD.

[186] See Art. 4(1)(b)(i) and (iii) and Art. 17 WFD. Cf. on this and above all on the requirement to minimise pollutants, which has not been sufficiently observed to date, Faßbender (2022), pp. 655–664.

1. The precautionary principle has now found a firm place in current German environmental law not only in the form of risk precaution but also as resource precaution. On the one hand, the principle of resource precaution goes beyond risk precaution in that it applies irrespective of any specific threat to an environmental resource. On the other hand, the question of sufficient risk precaution is typically examined in the assessment and, above all, state authorisation of specific environmentally relevant measures, whereas the principle of resource precaution is regularly based on a management law and often planning approach that goes beyond individual environmentally relevant measures and typically also includes proactive action. Nevertheless, it may also be necessary to observe the principle of resource conservation in specific authorisation procedures. Finally, it should be noted that the aforementioned differences do not rule out the possibility that the principles of risk precaution and resource precaution may reinforce each other.
2. A central concretisation of the principle of resource precaution results from the distance requirement. Behind this is the demand, which has been derived from the precautionary principle in the literature for over 20 years, that ecological boundaries should not be exceeded, and a sufficient distance should be maintained. In its historic climate Decision of 24 March 2021, the Federal Constitutional Court also affirmed the existence of a distance requirement understood in this way, although the Decision regrettably does not explicitly mention this term or the precautionary principle in its reasons.
3. Resource precaution does not necessarily depend on concrete targets that also take into account the resilience of an environmental medium. However, if and insofar as it is possible to set verifiable targets on a valid professional basis, this will noticeably improve effective resource precaution. In this respect, such targets are highly desirable.
4. The dual understanding of the precautionary principle that prevails in Germany is, in its basic features, compatible both with European Union law and international law, despite voices to the contrary. This dual understanding should (continue to) be propagated above all at the EU level, as a one-sided normative shift of the basic concern of resource precaution to the much broader principle of sustainability could lead to a lack of contours and indeterminacy.
5. Both the EU Waste Framework Directive and the German Circular Economy Act aim to minimise the use of resources, primarily through the goal of waste prevention. In practice, however, the sober statement made by the German Advisory Council on the Environment (*Sachverständigenrat für Umweltfragen—SRU*) in 2008 that "the prioritised prevention of waste is [not] happening" is still valid.[187] Therefore, the proposals of the *SRU* in its 2020 Environmental Report deserve emphatic approval, namely to extend the waste hierarchy for reasons of resource precaution. This applies in particular to the suggestion to set binding targets for waste prevention as well as preparation for reuse and to advance

[187] SRU (2008), para. 863.

recycling rates, since, as already mentioned, verifiable targets can make effective resource conservation noticeably easier, if they rest on a valid professional basis.

6. From the perspective of environmental precaution, land use is first and foremost about protecting the soil, which together with air and water amount to the central environmental media. The German Federal Soil Protection Act was (only) enacted in 1998 to protect the soil. It is based on the precautionary principle and contains a resource-related component. However, the law does not adequately implement this concern. Therefore, in the future, the conceptual weaknesses of the Federal Soil Protection Act outlined above under V. 2. b. should be addressed and, ideally, remedied.
7. To date, the guidelines for overall spatial planning have done little to permanently limit soil sealing. On the one hand, this is due to the fact that resource and climate protection are currently not prioritised over other relevant concerns in actual planning processes. Secondly, there is a widespread lack of specific and binding targets in the area of land use. For this reason, the aim of limiting new land use through binding (federal) legal or spatial planning requirements should be persistently pursued, after the federal legislator last expressed in 2017 with the amendment to Section 2(2) (no. 6)(3) ROG that it hopes to see "quantified requirements for reducing land use", particularly in spatial planning.
8. However, it should be noted that spatial planning requirements do not reach an important area of construction activity because most residential development projects are realised in unplanned inner areas in accordance with Section 34 of the German Federal Building Code (Baugesetzbuch—BauGB); here, spatial planning objectives play no role when assessing permissibility under building planning law. Therefore, clear regulations are needed to ensure that corresponding stipulations must also be observed when making decisions under Section 34 BauGB. Finally, general consideration should be given to amending Section 34 BauGB in such a way that resource and climate protection and other environmental concerns can and must be given greater consideration when authorising construction projects in unplanned inner areas.
9. For reasons of risk and resource precaution, it is to be welcomed that the legislator has complied with the latest demands of the *SRU* to designate a general rate of 2% of the area of the Federal Republic of Germany for the use of onshore wind energy. It also permits wind turbines in the entire outdoor area in future and not only in areas designated in planning, when the spatial planning authorities do not succeed in fulfilling the associated state-related quantity targets within a fixed period.
10. In the area of water resource management, it has long been recognised that the precautionary principle—despite not being explicitly mentioned for a long time—was and still is the tacit basis for various provisions of the German Federal Water (Resources Management) Act (Wasserhaushaltsgesetz—WHG), particularly in its resource-related variant. The normative reference point for this assumption was primarily Section 1a(1) WHG (old version) and the fact—initially not expressly regulated in the Act but generally recognised—that the

competent authorities have a management discretion, even when issuing permits for uses under water law on a case-by-case basis. These considerations continue to apply without restriction even after the new regulation of water law.

11. In addition, the EU Water Framework Directive has shaped the principle of resource precaution in an exemplary manner, as it firstly contains specific resource-related targets that apply regardless of any kind of threat to water. This also gives measure and direction to resource precaution, which significantly enhances its effectiveness. Secondly, this is done with the aim of conserving water resources in the interests of future uses and needs. To this end, the Water Framework Directive not merely pursues a management law approach—like the traditional German Water (Resources Management) Act. On the contrary, it also calls for a planning approach that was previously only pursued very scantly in Germany. In this respect, the Water Framework Directive serves as a role model for resource precaution. Fourthly, the ensuing flexibility makes it possible, at least conceptually, to find a solution to the distributive problems triggered by the priority principle in other environmental law, particularly in pollution control law.
12. The "National Water Strategy", which was adopted by the Federal Government on 15 March 2023, contains numerous valuable tips and approaches for advancing risk and resource precaution in the management of water resources. Its conceptual added value lies in the fact that the strategy also makes clear that key challenges and threats to water resources cannot be tackled by water management and "traditional" water law alone. Instead, cross-sector measures are required. In this respect, it should of course be remembered that the Water Framework Directive also provides a framework in this respect, for example, when it calls for measures and strategies to combat water pollution in surface waters and with regard to groundwater stipulates not only a requirement to reverse the trend but also a requirement to minimise pollutants.
13. In contrast, an analysis of the other reference areas reveals that resource precaution in both the circular economy and in the area of land use is still insufficiently underpinned by normative concepts compared to water resource management. If the precautionary principle is indeed to become the "future principle of environmental law par excellence",[188] then the shift from hazard prevention to risk precaution in all three environmental media, including air and soil management, needs to be supplemented by resource precaution worthy of the name.

References

Appel I (2001) Europas Sorge um die Vorsorge – Zur Mitteilung der Europäischen Kommission über die Anwendbarkeit des Vorsorgeprinzips. NVwZ 20(4):395–398

[188] See Franzius (2022), p. 385, who believes that this is already the case, which is certainly the case in view of the above-mentioned change from hazard defense to risk precaution.

Appel I (2005) Staatliche Zukunfts-und Entwicklungsvorsorge, Mohr Siebeck, Tübingen
Arndt B (2009) Das Vorsorgeprinzip im EU-Recht, Mohr Siebeck, Tübingen
Berkemann J (2021) "Freiheitschancen über die Generationen" (Art. 20a GG)—Intertemporaler Klimaschutz im Paradigmenwechsel. DÖV 16:701–713
Böckenförde M (2003) The operationalisation of the precautionary approach in international environmental law treaties—Enhancement or facade ten years after Rio. Zaörv 63:313–331
Bovet J (2020) Kommunaler Ressourcenschutz – Auf der Zielgeraden beim Flächensparen? ZUR 31(1):31–39
Calliess C (2019) Abstand halten—Rechtspflichten der Klimapolitik aus planetaren Grenzen. ZUR 30(7–8):385–386
Calliess C (2021) Rechtsstaat und Umweltstaat. Mohr Siebeck, Tübingen
Calliess C (2022) Commentary on Art. 11 TFEU and on Art. 191 TFEU. In: Calliess C, Ruffert M (eds) EUV/AEUV, 6th ed. C.H. Beck, München
Cameron J, Abouchar J (1996) The status of the precautionary principle in international law. In: Freestone D, Hey E (eds) The precautionary principle and international law. Kluwer Law International, The Hague, London, Boston, pp 29–52
Charitopoulos N (2009) Die Grundprinzipien des deutschen, europäischen und griechischen Umweltrechts. Uni-Verlag, Gießen
Czychowski M, Reinhardt M (2023) Wasserhaushaltsgesetz, 13th edn. C.H. Beck, München
Epiney A (2019) Umweltrecht der Europäischen Union, 4th edn. Nomos, Baden-Baden
Faßbender K (2013) Rechtliche Anforderungen an raumplanerische Festlegungen zur Hochwasservorsorge. Nomos, Baden-Baden
Faßbender K (2021a) Der Klima-Beschluss des BVerfG—Inhalte. Folgen und Offene Fragen. NJW 74(29):2085–2091
Faßbender K (2021b) Die Verfassungsmäßigkeit der sog. 10-H-Regelung in Art. 82 BayBO: Eine Neubewertung nach dem Klima-Beschluss des BVerfG. NuR 43(12):793–803
Faßbender K (2022) PFC im System der Grundwasserbewirtschaftung—Die Gebote der Trendumkehr und der Schadstoffminimierung. ZUR 33(12):655–664
Fischer C (2013) Grundlagen und Grundstrukturen eines Klimawandelanpassungsrechts. Mohr Siebeck, Tübingen
Franzius C (2019) Klimaschutz im Anthropozän. EurUP 17(4):498–508
Franzius C (2022) Prävention durch Verwaltungsrecht: Klimaschutz. Veröffentlichungen der Vereinigung der deutschen Staatsrechtslehrer (VVDStRL) 81:383–436
Freestone D, Hey E (1996) Origins and development of the precautionary principle. In: Freestone D, Hey E(eds) The precautionary principle and international law. Kluwer Law International, The Hague, London, Boston, pp 3–15
Germann M (1993) Das Vorsorgeprinzip als vorverlagerte Gefahrenabwehr. Springer Verlag, Wien, New York
Ginzky H (2010) 10 Jahre Bundes-Bodenschutzgesetz—Nachsorge hui, Vorsorge pfui! ZUR 33(1):1–2
Ginzky H (2019) 20 Jahre Bundes-Bodenschutzgesetz—hinreichend vorsorgend? ZUR 30(1):1–2
Ginzky H, Albrecht J, Pannicke-Prochnow N (2021) Hitze in den Städten—eine Pflicht zur kommunalen Klimaanpassungsplanung tut not! ZUR 32(9):449–450
Hahn T (2017) Die Abfallhierarchie der europäischen Abfallrahmenrichtlinie und ihre Umsetzung im deutschen Kreislaufwirtschaftsgesetz. Carl Heymanns Verlag, Köln
Heselhaus S (2023) Commentary on Art. 191 TFEU. In: Pechstein M, Nowak C, Häde U (eds) Frankfurter Kommentar EUV/GRC/AEUV, 2nd edn. Mohr Siebeck, Tübingen
Kahl W (2018) Commentary on Art. 11 TFEU and Art. 191 TFEU. In: Streinz (ed) EUV/AEUV, 3rd edn. C.H. Beck, München
Kahl W, Gärditz K (2023) Umweltrecht, 13th edn. C.H. Beck, München
Kersten J (2014) Das Anthropozän-Konzept. Nomos, Baden-Baden
Kersten J (2016) Ökologischer Liberalismus—Der anthropozäne Wandel der Welt. EurUP 14(4):312–323

Klingele I (2012) Umweltqualitätsplanung —Zur Integration der gemeinschaftsrechtlichen Luftreinhalte- und Bewirtschaftungsplanung in das nationale Umweltrecht. Verlag Dr. Kovac, Hamburg
Kloepfer M (2016) Umweltrecht, 4th ed. C.H. Beck, München
Köck W (2005) Die Entwicklung des Vorsorgeprinzips im Recht. In: Hansjürgens B, Nordbeck R (eds) Chemikalienregulierung und Innovationen zum nachhaltigen Wirtschaften. Physica-Verlag, Heidelberg, pp 85–120
Köck W (2019) Naturschutz und Landwirtschaft—eine Bilanz aus der Perspektive des Rechts. ZUR 30(2):67–71
Krüper J (2009) Gemeinwohl im Prozess: Elemente eines funktionalen subjektiven Rechts auf Umweltvorsorge. Duncker & Humblot, Berlin
Lübbe-Wolff G (1998) Präventiver Umweltschutz—Auftrag und Grenzen des Vorsorgeprinzips im deutschen und europäischen Recht. In: Bizer J, Koch H-J (eds) Sicherheit, Vielfalt, Solidarität: Ein neues Paradigma des Verfassungsrechts? Nomos, Baden-Baden, pp 47–74
Meßerschmidt K (2011) Europäisches Umweltrecht. C.H. Beck, München
Möckel S (2014) Verbesserte Anforderungen an die gute fachliche Praxis der Landwirtschaft. ZUR 25(1):14–23
Möckel S, Wolf A (2020) Düngung bleibt weiterhin eine ökologische, rechtliche und politische Herausforderung. NuR 42(11):736–746
Monien J (2014) Prinzipien als Wegbereiter eines globalen Umweltrechts? Nomos, Baden-Baden
Murswiek D (2021) Commentary on Art. 20a GG. In: Sachs M (ed) Grundgesetz, 9th edn. C.H. Beck, München
Murswiek D (2004) Schadensvermeidung—Risikobewältigung—Ressourcenbewirtschaftung. In: Osterloh L, Schmidt K, Weber H (eds) Festschrift für Peter Selmer zum 70. Geburtstag. Duncker & Humblot, Berlin, pp 417–442
Peine F-J (1997) Die Bodenschutzkonzeption der Bundesregierung. Umwelt- und Planungsrecht 2:53–39
Petersen F (1993) Schutz und Vorsorge. Duncker & Humblot, Berlin
Proelß A (ed) (2022) Internationales Umweltrecht, 2nd edn. Springer Verlag, Wien-New York
Rehbinder E (1991) Das Vorsorgeprinzip im internationalen Vergleich. Werner-Verlag, Düsseldorf
Rehbinder E (2018) Chapter 3: Ziele, Grundsätze, Strategien und Instrumente. In: Rehbinder E, Schink A (eds) Grundzüge des Umweltrechts, 5th edn. Erich Schmidt Verlag, Berlin
Sachverständigenrat für Umweltfragen (SRU) (2008) Umweltgutachten 2008: Umweltschutz im Zeichen des Klimawandels, Berlin
SRU (2019) Demokratisch regieren in ökologischen Grenzen—Zur Legitimation von Umweltpolitik. Special Report, Berlin
SRU (2020) Umweltgutachten 2020: Für eine entschlossene Umweltpolitik in Deutschland und Europa, Berlin
SRU (2021) Klimaschutz braucht Rückenwind: Für einen konsequenten Ausbau der Windenergie an Land. Impulspapier, Berlin
Sánchez Barroso B (2021) El principio de precaución en España. Congreso de los Diputados, Madrid
Sanden J, Schoeneck S (1998) Bundes-Bodenschutzgesetz: Kurzkommentar. C.F. Müller, Heidelberg
Sands P, Peel J (2018) Principles of international environmental law, 4th edn. Cambridge University Press, Cambridge
Sauthoff M (2022) Durchsetzung des Klimaschutzes im Städtebau—Überlegungen zu Änderungen des Baugesetzbuchs. Klima und Recht 1(1):11–15
Schink A (2018) Chapter 6: Umweltschutz durch Bauplanungsrecht. In: Rehbinder E, Schink A (eds) Grundzüge des Umweltrechts, 5th edn. Erich Schmidt Verlag, Berlin
Sendler H (1983) Wer gefährdet wen: Eigentum und Bestandsschutz den Umweltschutz—oder umgekehrt? Umwelt- und Planungsrecht 2:33–46
Söhnlein B (1999) Landnutzung im Umweltstaat des Grundgesetzes. Boorberg, Stuttgart

Stubenrauch J, Ekardt F (2021) Zur Ausgestaltung eines nationalen Verbots giftiger Chemikalien bei Kunststoffen—Rechtsvergleichende und EU-rechtliche Aspekte. EurUP 19(4):406–425
Vanhellemont A (2021) Towards more sustainable EU environmental law. In: Boeve et al. (eds) Environmental law for transitions to sustainability. Intersentia, pp 11–27
Viertel B (1995) Vorsorge im Abwasserrecht: Zur Funktion der Mindestanforderungen nach § 7a WHG. Erich Schmidt Verlag, Berlin
Volkens B (1993) Vorsorge im Wasserrecht—Der ökologische Schutzzweck des § 1a WHG und seine Verwirklichung im Bereich der Abwassereinleitung, der Abfallablagerung und der Landwirtschaft. Erich Schmidt Verlag, Berlin
Wagner S (2018) Klimaschutz durch Raumordnung. Lexxion, Berlin
Wahl R, Appel I (1995) Prävention und Vorsorge: Von der Staatsaufgabe zur rechtlichen Ausgestaltung. In: Wahl R (ed) Prävention und Vorsorge. Economica-Verlag, Bonn, pp 1–215
Wolfrum R (1999) Precautionary principle. In: Beurier J-P, Kiss A, Mahmoudi S (eds) New technologies and law of the marine environment. Kluwer Law International, The Hague, London, Boston, pp 203–214

A Legal Framework for Sustainable Innovation

The Precautionary Principle and Innovation

Ivo Appel

Abstract The relationship between innovation and precaution is as precarious as it is consequential. It is precarious on the one hand because precaution can prevent unintended consequences of innovations or reduce the associated risks, while too much precaution may also inhibit and limit innovations. On the other hand, innovations, if shaped and used adequately, can also be the basis for appropriate and effective precaution. The relationship is of great consequence in that it helps to determine how open a society is to innovation and development and what risks it is prepared to take or not to take in order to achieve innovations.

1 Rediscovery of Innovation

For some time now, the relationship between precaution and innovation has been back on the agenda. The associated call for greater consideration and protection of innovation in the field of law is nothing new, periodically experiencing a surge in advocacy. In particular, those who consider actors in research and economy to be excessively restricted by legal regulation repeatedly call for greater openness to innovation in the law, demanding that legal regulation should be designed and implemented in a way that does not restrict innovations, but allows for the opportunities they present to be exploited to the greatest extent possible.

The underlying narrative follows a standardised pattern. In connection with allegedly excessive regulatory restrictions in certain scientific und economic areas, such as the new genomic techniques in plants, animals, and micro-organisms, precautionary legal regulation is branded as anti-innovation. At the same time, there are calls for the law to be reformed in a way that does not inhibit innovation but, on the contrary, enables and promotes it. In this context, it is sometimes openly, sometimes covertly insinuated that precautionary legal regulation be anti-innovative, preventing future viability as well as urgently needed successes in science and the economy. In

I. Appel (✉)
Chair of Public Law, Environmental Law and Philosophy of Law, University of Hamburg, Hamburg, Germany
e-mail: ivo.appel@uni-hamburg.de

M. Reese et al. (eds.), *Environmental Law in Transformation*,
https://doi.org/10.1007/978-3-032-31567-0_4

order to ensure the development of new technologies and to promote the economy's potential for innovation, innovations and their relevance should be promoted, also and especially in those areas in which the precautionary principle is applied by law.

1.1 Call for an Innovation Principle

In the course of this renewed debate about the relationship between innovation and precaution, a so-called 'innovation principle' has been advocated for quite some time. The term has been developed and propagated since 2013 by the European Risk Forum (ERF), a think tank with close ties to the chemical, tobacco, and oil industries.[1] Originally understood primarily in economic terms, the idea of an innovation principle, after being brought to the attention of policymakers by corporations and trade associations, has now taken on a life of its own and has found its way into the EU's so-called 'Better Regulation Strategy'.[2] Correspondingly, the term 'innovation principle' has been appearing with increasing frequency in European Commission documents since 2015.[3] According to the European Commission, the innovation principle is an essential part of the EU's approach to better regulation and ensures that any policy or strategy development is fully assessed for its impact on innovation.[4] As a result, a demand emanating from the business community and parts of the scientific community is now reflected in EU-level policy and regulatory strategies.

The intended purpose of an 'innovation principle' in European legislation is obvious. Its goal is to create a framework that is (more) conducive to innovation. Legislation should be designed in such a way that all phases of a potentially innovative technique or product can be fully exploited, all the way from research and development to its commercial use, allowing for the potential economic, social, and/

[1] The European Risk Forum ERF, renamed in 2020 to European Regulation & Innovation Forum ERIF, is according to its self-description 'an independent, not-for-profit think tank in Brussels that aims to promote the adoption by the EU's institutions of world-leading standards of regulatory decision-making, encompassing governance, scientific integrity, and decision-making from inception, through design. legislation, and implementation, to ex post evaluation' (cf. https://www.eriforum.eu/about-us.html. Accessed 22 Sep 2025); the considerations for political and social application were bundled in a short study in 2015: ERF (2015); more on the origins of the 'precautionary principle' concept in: Garnett et al. (2018), p. 1 et seq.; cf. also Federal Ethics Committee on Non-Human Biotechnology (ECNH) (2019), p. 5.

[2] Pelkmans and Renda (2014); European Commission (2017a) Commission Staff Working Document. Better Regulation Guidelines; European Commission (2017b) Better regulation Toolbox; for a summary of the European Commission's REFIT program, see European Commission: REFIT—making EU law simpler, more efficient and future-proof https://ec.europa.eu/info/law/law-making-process/evaluating-and-improving-existing-laws/refit-making-eu-law-simpler-less-costly-and-future-proof_en. Accessed 22 Sept 2025.

[3] European Commission (2016a); European Commission (2017a) Commission Staff Working Document. Better Regulation Guidelines; Renda and Simonelli (2017); for a summary of the developments, see Calliess (2021), p. 125 et seq.

[4] European Commission (2017a) Commission Staff Working Document. Better Regulation Guidelines; Renda and Simonelli (2019).

or environmental benefits associated with an innovative idea to be realised as comprehensively as possible. Even though the principled nature of an innovation principle is only asserted and postulated, while hardly being substantiated to any degree,[5] the political impetus associated with a postulated 'innovation principle' leaves no room for doubt: It is clear that the goal of introducing an 'innovation principle' is to reshape the drafting and application of law in such a way as to promote the development of new technologies, to strengthen the European economy's potential for innovation, and to enable innovation to a greater extent than has been the case to date. This gives rise to the demand that an innovation principle be introduced as comprehensively as possible into European law and the European Treaties.[6]

In contrast, the mere mention of an innovation principle in texts on the EU's 'Horizon Europe' research program has triggered protests from politicians, scientists, associations, and non-governmental organisations. Like some EU member states, they are concerned that the introduction of an innovation principle could compromise the precautionary principle, since it is feared that strengthening the innovation principle would lead to a weakening and partial rollback of precaution and the precautionary principle. In this context, there is every reason to take a closer look at the relationship between innovation and precaution, and in particular, at the relevance and function of a possible 'innovation principle' and its potential implications on the precautionary principle and statutorily regulated precautionary concepts.

1.2 Part of a Longer Tradition

First, however, it is important to recognize that the discussion about the relationship between precaution and innovation is part of a long tradition that is instructive in terms of the comparability of the lines of argument. Similar advances have been made in the past, namely under the labels of 'technology enabling law', 'economization of precaution', 'openness to and responsibility for innovation of the law', as well as in the Anglo-American sphere under the label 'science-based approach'. All of these advances have in common that they aim at limiting the restrictions associated with precautionary regulation for industry, technology, research, and innovation. What is new is that such an advance is being heard in some parts of the political sphere and is being used to influence legislative processes.

[5] Concepts for a justification as a principle can be found in: European Commission (2016b) European Political Strategy Centre. Towards an innovation principle endorsed by better regulation. Issue 14. https://data.europa.eu/doi/10.2872/626511. Accessed 22 Sep 2025.

[6] Cf. BusinessEurope/ERF/ERT (2015); on the question of whether and to what extent an 'innovation principle' is already included in EU law, see Calliess (2021), p. 125 et seq.

1.2.1 Technology-Enabling Law

Preceding the current discussion was the debate about the technology-enabling function of the law.[7] It originated in the observation that the law, especially in the fields of technology and progress-oriented economic activities, has been often perceived as technology prevention law due to the intended preventive avoidance of critical, undesirable consequences.[8] By emphasising the law's potential for enabling advances in technology, on the other hand, the fundamental ambivalence of technology law was and is to be brought to the fore, namely that, in addition to regulating technology in a protective and precautionary manner, it also aims at und effects the enabling of technology, and that without its framework-setting guarantee function, a secure and sustainable development of technology in modern constitutional countries would regularly not be possible at all.

To a certain extent, the debate on the technology-enabling function of the law has identified and highlighted a self-evident fact. After all, the approval procedures for technological and product innovations are routinely designed to identify the underlying conflict between opportunities and risks and to balance the associated multipolar legal positions and underlying interests. In particular, technical safety law for large-scale plants, the approach to the latest information and communication technologies, nuclear and genetic engineering law, environmental impact assessment, and, finally, bio and medical law provide striking examples for legally sophisticated regulatory regimes that are intended to accommodate the awareness for the substantiality of possible effects by anticipating new technological opportunities as well as calculating and combating risks while limiting potential negative repercussions. Since, however, the enabling function is often overlooked and/or taken for granted by developers, operators, and users of technology, whereas the focus is placed on the protective and precautionary restrictive function of regulatory law, an objective in this debate has been to clearly identify both sides, to emphasise the principle openness and fundamental balancing function of the law, and to avert the danger of one-sided perspectives.

Ultimately, it has been a matter of taking into account that environmental and technology law do not only serve a risk management purpose, but are also and especially tasked with enabling and regulating technological innovations in an anticipatory manner. This dual perspective[9] is to be instrumental for the legal oversight of modern technologies such as information and communication technologies, genetic engineering, biotechnology and medical technology, or nanotechnology.

---

[7] Pitschas (2000), p. 73 et seq.; Franzius (2001), p. 507.

[8] Böhret (1989), p. 13 et seq.; Böhret (1991); Bechmann and Jörissen (1992), p. 142 et seq.

[9] For a general overview on. the problem associated with the dual perspective, see von Westphalen and Neubert (1988), p. 257 et seq.

1.2.2 Economization of Precaution

Preceding the debate on the relationship between precaution and innovation were also attempts to subject the precautionary principle and the precautionary requirements derived from it to the proviso of economic efficiency. These tendencies to economize precaution aim at limiting the scope of precautionary regulation in law by subjecting it to the proviso of economic justifiability and a corresponding cost–benefit analysis.[10]

When it comes to precaution, economization tendencies take advantage of the fact that precaution, as a highly indeterminate legal concept in approval law, can generally only be implemented if specifications are made in the law or at the sub-legal level. Accordingly, there are numerous regulations in legal ordinances, administrative provisions, directives, and private standards by means of which the required level of precaution is specified at the national and, as exemplified by the BAT reference documents in the field of industrial emissions plant law,[11] at European level.[12] Increasingly, concerns for economic viability are being incorporated into these stages of specification. As opposed to the traditional German approach, for example, wherein the highest technological level available was to be identified first in order to determine the precautionary measures based on the state of the art, with the proportionality of associated precautionary standards only being determined in a second step, in European Union law, the highest technological level available and the associated state of the art in national law shaped by European law are already subject to the reservation of economic justifiability at the time of their development. This essentially relativises the associated precautionary requirements at the outset.

The goal of applying economization strategies to the precautionary principle and its manifestations is obvious. Precautionary measures are supposed to be implemented, in principle, but only to the extent to which the associated restrictions are economically justifiable. Requirements for the rationale and justification of precautionary measures are increased. The costs and benefits of precautionary regulation are to be weighed and research and economic costs to be kept as low as possible.

1.2.3 Openness to and Responsibility for Innovation of the Law

In its project 'Innovation and Law' conducted between 1996 and 2012, the Centre for Research in Law and Innovation (CERI) at Universität Hamburg focused on the relationship between precaution and innovation.[13] The overall goal of the project was

[10] For a general overview on the economization in environmental law, see Wolff and Gsell (2018); on cost–benefit considerations in administrative law, see Fehling (2004), p. 443 et seq.; for more on the economization of administrative law, see Schneider (2001), p. 317 et seq; Gröpl (2002), p. 459.

[11] For more details, see Appel (2006), p. 67 et seq.; Appel (2008), p. 91 et seq.

[12] Appel (2004), p. 344 et seq.

[13] See Hoffmann-Riem and Schneider (1998); Eifert and Hoffmann-Riem (2002); Eifert and Hoffmann-Riem (2009a, b); consolidating the different threads: Hoffmann-Riem (2016); Cf. previous contributions on the relationship of innovations and administrative law in Hoffmann-Riem and Schmidt-Aßmann (1994).

to conduct a systematic, transdisciplinary and interdisciplinary analysis of existing law with regards to its conducive and inhibiting influences on innovation processes.[14] The project was based on the realisation that significant innovations in technology and society pose challenges to politics, law, and science, and therefore need to be addressed in legal innovation research. This was to gain insights into how the law can influence the development and implementation of social and technological innovations, and how it can guide these processes towards avoiding the risks associated with innovations as much as possible, while at the same time exploiting the associated opportunities.

After identifying the openness to and responsibility for innovation of the law as central points of reference and guidance, the precautionary principle's potentially inhibiting effect on innovations and the underlying relationship between precaution and innovation also played a key role.[15] Accordingly, one outcome of the deliberations was that the focus of the legal review should not be limited to the analysis of the unintended, negative effects of technological developments, but would also have to include the opportunities and potentially positive yields of innovative technologies. This way, the characteristic dual role of innovation and innovation effects was to be brought to the fore—on the one hand, promoting the willingness to innovate and the associated development of new technologies by identifying and assessing the associated opportunities; on the other hand, the comparatively traditional attempt to avoid, or at least mitigate, any negative effects of innovative processes.[16]

1.2.4 Science-Based Approach

Another approach in the long tradition of precaution-related limitation attempts is the 'science-based approach' or 'risk-based approach', which is being pursued primarily in the Anglo-American world, but also to some extent at European Union level.[17] This approach has mainly been focusing on two aspects[18]—on the one hand, avoiding excessive restrictions of application-oriented scientific research due to rigid regulatory requirements, especially if (major) social and/or ecological benefits would be associated with the exploitation of the expected opportunities; on the other hand, ensuring that new, innovative products with (major) economic potential not be subjected to complicated, costly, and potentially restricting regulatory procedures before they can be used and commercialised.

---

[14] For more on this issue related to administrative law as a whole, see Scherzberg and Lepsius (2004).

[15] Cf. Calliess (2009), p. 119 et seq.; Appel (2009), p. 147 et seq.

[16] For more details, see Appel (2009), p. 147 et seq.

[17] For more on that, see Appel and Mielke (2014); Sunstein (2005); Rothstein et al. (2006); Scherzberg (2010); p. 306 et seq.

[18] On the parallel objective of the propagated 'innovation principle', see Garnett et al. (2018); cf. also: Federal Ethics Committee on Non-Human Biotechnology (ECNH) (2019), p. 5.

The main connecting factor has been a precautionary principle that is allegedly too far-reaching and thus too restrictive for research and the economy. Therefore, the extent of the demanded precaution and the precautionary requirements should have been and has to be based on evidence and scientific proof. In contrast to the traditional German and continental European interpretation of the precautionary principle, in which a well-founded suspicion is sufficient,[19] Anglo-American law, which also influences international law significantly, demands sufficient evidence and scientific proof to justify precautionary requirements. While this is a matter of continuous development, it is clearly aimed at restricting the traditional concept of precaution in its approach.

1.3 Comparison with the Distribution Principle of the Rule of Law (Rechtsstaatliches Verteilungsprinzip)

These few examples demonstrate that the discussion about an 'innovation principle' has numerous precursors and has been around for some time. With the postulate of an innovation principle, older concepts are being revived in a slightly different form, but apparently now more successfully at the political level than in previous decades. At the same time, it is remarkable that the desired changes in the relationship between freedom and security associated with balancing precaution and innovation have not yet been addressed at a more fundamental level. After all, these attempts are obviously aimed at reducing the demanded level of security and thus isolating areas of freedom from allegedly excessive restrictions imposed by precaution.

1.3.1 Constitutional Distribution

At first glance, however, the call for the introduction of an innovation principle appears to be a fundamental misjudgement of the distribution principle of the rule of law (*rechtsstaatliches Verteilungsprinzip*) as the constitutional principle for the optimal safeguarding of individual freedoms.[20] According to the distribution principle of the rule of law, public authority is in principle limited, while individual freedom is in principle unlimited. Therefore, it is not the (in principle unlimited) constitutional freedoms that require justification, but the (in principle limited) authority of the state to restrict these freedoms. Consequently, these freedoms can be exercised as long as they are not restricted in a constitutionally justified way when measured against constitutional standards.

This constitutional distribution mechanism also applies to the relationship between freedoms that serve innovations on the one hand and precautionary state

[19] For more on that, see Sect. 2 below.

[20] For more on the distribution principle of the rule of law (rechtsstaatliches Verteilungsprinzip), see Depenheuer (2011), § 194 Recital 57; fundamentally: Schmitt (1928), p. 126.

regulation on the other. If restrictions on fundamental freedoms must in principle remain the exception that can be measured and controlled in terms of its prerequisites and content, any precautionary state regulation that restricts fundamental freedoms requires justification. The precautionary principle serves, among other things, to provide this justification. It provides grounds of justification for restrictions on research and innovation, which are among the fundamentally protected freedoms and therefore do not require justification by default. In contrast to precautionary regulation and precautionary measures, freedoms directed at research and innovation do not require any particular justification or rationale. A general principle of freedom could just as well be postulated, which would be juxtaposed with the state's protection and precaution duties. Since the underlying freedoms are within the constitutional rights and correspond to their basic function, however, a general principle of freedom makes little sense. Applied to these contexts, it is just as redundant as an innovation principle.

1.3.2 The Significance of Approval Law

Above all, it is through approval law that the principle of distribution is given concrete form.[21] Thanks to the more or less open design of the approval requirements, approval law determines the extent to which freedoms are (or may be) restricted for reasons of protection and/or precaution, even if they serve the research, development, or implementation of innovative products or technologies. Especially in the case of new technologies, approval law serves as an indicator for a legal system's and the adopting society's openness to innovation.[22] Therefore, approval law also runs the risk of being in parts characterised as anti-technology and anti-innovation, and of being perceived as an obstacle to and a damper on innovation. Against this background, it is not surprising that the concept of a technology-enabling law[23] and now also the postulate of an innovation principle are primarily oriented towards the state regulation of approval procedures. For approval law is also faced with the challenge of taking appropriate account of the dichotomy of opportunities and risks, especially in the case of new technologies.[24] The goal must be to, with all due precaution, exploit the opportunities new technologies provide and to enable their implementation by creating the necessary legal framework, while simultaneously providing adequate protection and sufficient precaution against the potential risks and dangers that new technologies can pose to humans and the environment.

In the field of new and innovative techniques, materials, and products, the problems of approval law are essentially characterized by the fact that the state of scientific knowledge and, in particular, the assessment of causal relationships and long-term

---

[21] For more on that and the following, see Appel (2022), § 123 Recital 9.

[22] On the underlying relationship of tension, cf. the contributions in Hoffmann-Riem and Eifert (2002, 2009a, b).

[23] Kloepfer (2000b); Kloepfer (2000a), p. 109 et seq.; Franzius (2001), p. 487 et seq.

[24] On genetic engineering law, cf. Appel (2020), § 51.

consequences of the implementation of certain techniques, materials, or products are not always conclusively determined,[25] meaning that actions have to be taken in a state of partial uncertainty. Therefore, it is not surprising that, in these contexts in particular, approval law is subject to the constant pressure to adapt to the influence of dynamically changing factual challenges and must be reviewed in the light of the latest scientific and technological expertise in the ongoing development process[26] in order to be able to justify restrictive requirements for protection and precaution. For this reason, the requirements derived from the precautionary principle are in a constant state of flux and are subject to a dynamic set of requirements designed for constant further development and incorporation of the latest findings.

1.3.3 Innovation Neutrality of the Precautionary Principle

Beyond the mentioned points, these outlined correlations demonstrate that the precautionary principle is neutral towards innovation in its approach. Provided that they are constitutionally justifiable in terms of the rule of law, precautionary measures can restrict a variety of different freedoms while remaining compliant with fundamental rights. It is herein irrelevant whether these freedoms are in any way associated with innovations or not. The determining factor is whether the identified and assessed risks give rise to potential concerns that, according to the legislator, need to be addressed by precautionary measures in order to avoid those risks or reduce them to a level deemed acceptable. The main focus in a precautionary situation by default being on risks and potential harms does not mean that the potential benefits and opportunities inherent in exercising freedom are irrelevant. On the contrary, the benefits and opportunities must always be considered in view of the fundamental freedoms that are restricted and that precautionary measures must be balanced with.[27] For the proportionality and appropriateness of restricting freedoms, considerations of the scope of the loss of freedom and the resulting restriction of potential benefits are also mandatory. Therefore, considerations of the scope and appropriateness of freedom restrictions and their impact on the innovation potential associated with the freedoms are a key component of a precautionary dogma embedded in constitutional law.

The criticism of the precautionary principle being hostile to or inhibiting innovations and that it would have to be supplemented by an innovation principle is not plausible in this context, even at the outset. It is, of course, out of the question that the precautionary principle and the regulations derived from it exist in economic and business contexts and affect the overall fabric of economic, environmental, and

---

[25] On this finding, related to genetic engineering law, see Federal Constitutional Court Germany ('BVerfG') 24 Nov 2010 (1 BvF 2/05) Zur Vereinbarkeit von Vorschriften des Gentechnikgesetzes mit dem Grundgesetz BVerfGE 128, 1–90.

[26] For more details, see Appel (2022), § 123 Recital 9.

[27] Wahl and Appel (1996), p. 135; Hoffmann-Riem (1994), p. 50 et seq.; Petersen (1993), p. 288 et seq.

social concerns. It is also obvious that there is a correlation between innovation, research, and the economy, and that innovations can contribute significantly to the further development of a society, including in terms of sustainable development. However, it is neither constitutionally plausible nor based on ethically sustainable assumptions to conclude from this that precaution and innovation must always be openly weighed against each other.[28] It is equally unjustifiable to invoke an innovation principle to demand a more rapid approval of research, techniques, materials, or products that have been classified as potentially dangerous on the basis of a regulated precautionary approach, even if they may be associated with considerable potential opportunities in terms of social progress or sustainability.[29] If a sufficient level of concern has been identified and assessed and the subsequent precautionary measures are proportionate, the associated restrictions on freedoms can be justified both from an ethical as well as a constitutional perspective.

1.4 Reasons Behind the Call for an Innovation Principle

There must be reasons why the innovation principle and similar concepts are nevertheless propagated and that the debates about them have received a great deal of attention, despite all the comparatively obvious counterarguments. One reason appears to be that the precautionary principle, its specifications, and utilisation in the application of the law have led to shifts in the constitutional structure of distribution that are, at least in part, perceived as problematic and attributed to the precautionary concept.

Here, one of the determining reasons for the perceived shifts is inherent in the concept of precaution itself. Precaution leads to a refusal to accept the risks of certain techniques and/or actions or to the acceptance of these risk only after comparatively extensive measures have been taken to eliminate or reduce them. However, as a way of responding to uncertainty, precaution is designed to be extended indefinitely.[30] It is not conceptually restricted and, therefore, has no immanent limitations. It can be extended indefinitely in objective, spatial, and temporal terms, thus opening up ever more far-reaching obligations in social behaviour. After all, the best precaution seemingly is to allow as little as possible, making it impossible for any risks to materialise or for potential harms to occur.

Corresponding to this is the legitimisation of far-reaching powers of intervention through precaution. For the more comprehensively the protection of certain legal assets by risk-minimising and risk-avoiding precaution is to be strengthened, the more abstract the reasons that can be given to individuals to justify their utilisation will become. Ultimately, this conceptual limitlessness of precaution is the flip side of

---

[28] For more on that in plain clarity, see BVerfG 24 Nov 2010 (1 BvF 2/05) Zur Vereinbarkeit von Vorschriften des Gentechnikgesetzes mit dem Grundgesetz BVerfGE 128, 1–90., p. 6, 13.

[29] Federal Ethics Committee on Non-Human Biotechnology (ECNH) (2019), p. 6, 13.

[30] For more on this and the following, see Appel (2004), p. 334 et seq.

limited knowledge. In contrast to the polluter pays principle, precaution is not based on narrow patterns of allocation, but is largely spatially and temporally neutral.[31]

This structural openness is one of the principal reasons why precaution is, in parts, perceived as problematic and, in some cases, too far-reaching by actors of economy, science, and politics. After all, precaution extends the legal assessment beyond the prevention of harm, which is shaped by the body of experience.[32] Precaution allows the application of the law and the demand for precautionary measures, even when uncertainty prevails and the factual basis for projections is unclear. However, it is often overlooked in this context that the structural openness of the precautionary concept is limited by constitutional and common law. The decisive factor is whether there is sufficient cause for concern, which needs to be specified and substantiated. It is precisely the goal of the precautionary dogma to provide a legal basis for decisions despite of prevailing uncertainties and to restrict associated consequences and costs.[33] Only if this succeeds, precautionary goals and measures can be justified in view of the restrictions of freedoms that they inevitably entail.

What has proven to be a particularly critical point in the precautionary dogma, is the leeway for assessment, evaluation, and judgment on the part of both the regulating legislator and the practitioners of the law. This leeway comes into play dogmatically when sufficient insight to meet the relevant constitutional and/or common law requirements cannot be obtained even with scientific and technological expertise being included, so uncertainties remain, and the essential foundations for legal decisions therefore become fragile. In these cases, leeway for assessment, evaluation, and judgment serves as a dogmatic formula for compromise to justify a less rigid commitment to norms and standards, to legitimise the decision-making powers of the respective decision-makers from the point of view of the separation of powers, and to limit judicial control. As a result, such leeway for assessment within the scope of application of the precautionary principle has the regulating legislator, the sub-legislative standard-setting authority, and/or practitioners of the law deciding, on the basis of less rigid standards and with correspondingly reduced judicial control, whether and to what extent they consider the prerequisites for a precautionary restriction of freedoms to be met or not.[34] Such leeway for assessment, evaluation, and judgment, which has been recognised and dogmatised in other areas of law, is not in and of itself a weak point of the precautionary dogma. It is, however, crucial to clearly define and specify the constitutional limits and legal requirements for its implementation and enforcement, which result in particular from the principle of the separation of powers and the guarantee of legal protection for example in Article 19 (4) of the German Constitution. Only if these limitations are taken into account and observed, precautionary requirements can be regulated and justified by the rule of law.

---

[31] Appel (2004), p. 334 et seq.

[32] Ladeur (1993), p. 209 et seq.; Di Fabio (1994), p. 450 et seq; Di Fabio (1996), p. 147 et seq.

[33] Appel (2011), pp. 468–469; cf. Also, Wahl and Appel (1995), p. 107; Appel (2004), p. 334 et seq.; Karthaus (2001), p. 72 et seq; Scherzberg (2001), p. 134.

[34] For more on that with regards to risk assessments, see Wahl (1991), p. 409 et seq.

2 Challenges of a Legal Limitation of Precaution

At its core, the precautionary principle is based on the premise that potential harm should primarily be addressed by preventive measures and, if possible, by reducing requirements of probability, immanence, and individual accountability to such an extent that adverse effects can be prevented as much as possible rather than having to be counteracted and remedied after the fact.[35] The underlying principle of preventing rather than remedying harm is intended to apply, in particular, in cases where scientific evidence is insufficient, inconclusive, or unclear, but where, on the basis of preliminary and objective scientific risk assessments, there are reasonable grounds for concern that the potentially dangerous consequences for the environment and for the health of humans, animals, and plants may be incompatible with the level of protection sought. This applies not only to suspected hazards or to cases of low probability of harm, but also to hazards or stresses that are more spatially and temporarily remote and are not in themselves problematic, but which, in their aggregate or in interaction with other stresses, may give rise to risks or be harmful.[36] As a result, the precautionary principle reduces the standard of proof and shifts the burden of proof. It does not require conviction that an actual risk exists or that there is no reasonable doubt of it. Rather, plausible or serious indications significantly below the predominant probability are sufficient. If such indicators are present, it is the responsibility of the originator of such a risk to refute the reasonable indications of specific cause-and-effect relationships and to disprove the assumptions underlying the concern.

The challenge for the rule of law lies in the fact that the precautionary principle is, if not further defined and specified in normative terms, comparatively poorly determined in its contentual significance and in need of further specification. It leaves leeway for specification and interpretation, both for the standard-setting authority as well as the practitioner of the law. Nevertheless, the precautionary principle is anything but a non-binding declaration of intent. It has the quality of a legal principle with a directly binding mandate. Despite its need for specification, it is of considerable legal significance, especially with regard to the justification of precautionary regulations and individual measures.[37] It significantly expands the state's scope of action, since, on its basis, restrictions on freedoms can be justified even when there are knowledge deficits and uncertainties. The requirements of the principle of proportionality, which also restricts precautionary measures, are scaled back to the extent

---

[35] For a summary of this and the following, see Appel (2018), § 2 Recital 32 et seq.; on the dogmatics and the legal methods of addressing uncertainty, cf. Jäckel (2010), p. 277 et seq.; Spiecker (2025).

[36] Appel (2018), § 2 Recital 32 et seq.; for a summary of European Law, see Meßerschmidt (2011), § 3 Recital 92 et seq; with further references; on the problem of long latencies between causes and recognizable damages and the immutability of distance and summation damage, see Wahl and Appel (1995), p. 4 et seq.

[37] Cf. BVerfG 23 Oct 2018 (1 BvR 2523/13, 595/14) Rotmilan (2018) BVerfGE 149, 407–421, paras 17 et seq. This corresponds to the assessment that the precautionary principle is comparatively poorly determined in its mandate, but strongly actionable in its justification; cf. Lübbe-Wolff (1997), p. 66 et seq.

that the threshold for proving imminent harm or the suitability of certain means of defence is lowered to a greater or lesser extent. In this way, considerable tension between the precautionary principle and the traditional constitutional requirements can arise.

In order to justify the scaling back of the threshold of intervention associated with the precautionary principle from a constitutional perspective, a number of basic guidelines have emerged in the comparatively comprehensive case law of both national and European courts[38]: Precautionary measures may be taken for the protection of legal assets, even with uncertainties present, without having to prove the existence of risks beyond a reasonable doubt, if there are sufficient grounds for taking precautionary measures. Precautionary (freedom restricting) protective measures can be taken, even in the case of scientific uncertainties, without having to wait for risks and their respective magnitude to be fully proven. However, the cause for precaution must be based on a scientific risk analysis and assessment. If the risk assessment is scientifically controversial, a credible substantial minority among scientists is sufficient to take precautionary measures. Mere hypotheses and inconclusive individual opinions, however, are not sufficient. Even if the precautionary principle entails a shift in the burden of proof, it is not possible to require the originator of such a risk to provide complete proof of harmlessness, which would not be possible in the case of (prevailing) uncertainty. Therefore, the precautionary principle does not require the elimination of all risks. In the presence of a cause for precaution, in addition to sufficient documentation of risks, a risk management appropriate to the identified and assessed risk is required, which may include risk-regulating measures up to and including a total ban.[39]

The correlations outlined above demonstrate that the precautionary principle has a poor mandate, but a strong justificatory quality, which a precautionary state can assert and exploit. According to the continental European concept of precaution, well-founded suspicions may be sufficient to justify, under certain circumstances, far-reaching, freedom-restricting precautionary measures. If the traditional mechanisms of restriction under the rule of law and, in particular, the appropriateness of precautionary measures are difficult to assess in the face of continuing uncertainty, the precautionary dogma works on the assumption that the legislature has more

[38] For a summary, see Appel (2018), § 2 Recital 32 et seq.; for more on the specifications in European case law, see Meßerschmidt (2011), § 3 Recital 91, pp. 108 et seq., 185; from the case law of the German Federal Constitutional Court, cf. BVerfG 24 Nov 2010 (1 BvF 2/05) Zur Vereinbarkeit von Vorschriften des Gentechnikgesetzes mit dem Grundgesetz BVerfGE 128, 1–90; from ECJ case law: ECJ 5 May 1998 (Case C-180/96) United Kingdom of Great Britian and Northern Ireland v Commission of the European Communities (1198) ECR I-2265, para 99; ECJ 5 May 1998 (Case C-157/96) The Queen v Ministry of Agriculture, Fisheries and Food and Commissioners of Customs & Excise, ex parte National Farmers' Union and Others (1998) ECR I-2211, para. 63; ECJ 4 July 2000 (Case C-352/98) Laboratoires pharmaceutiques Bergaderm and Goupil v Commission (2000) ECR I-5291, para. 114 et seq.; ECJ 11 Sept 2002 (Case T-13/99) Pfizer Animal Health v Council (2002) ECR II-3305, para. 114 et seq.; ECJ 11 Sept 2002 (case T-70/99) Alpharma v Council (2002) ECR II-3495, para. 152 et seq.

[39] As already summarised in Appel (2018), § 2 Recital 32et seq., with further references.

or less far-reaching leeway for assessment. It is above all this leeway for assessment that has led to the assumption that precaution is difficult to contain and tends to be boundless. In contrast, it should be noted that legally regulated precaution is not boundless. The leeway for assessment, evaluation, and judgment is just one building block of the precautionary dogma that may come into play at the end of a long cascade of reviews. First and foremost, the decisive factors are the identification and assessment of the potential for concern and the selection of precautionary measures that correspond to the identified and assessed potential for concern. In this context, all available sources of knowledge and the relevant scientific expertise in particular must be used to the greatest extent possible[40] and continuously updated. Also, the regulation based on them has to be promptly improved and adapted if necessary. Any leeway for assessment cannot be assumed as a matter of course, but only if normatively stipulated within the framework of the rule of law and/or if the delegation of authority for evaluation and assessment, including the reduction of judicial control, can also be justified from a constitutional point of view because all available resources of knowledge have been exhausted and uncertainties prevail nonetheless. In such cases, even the legislature can only claim leeway for assessment for itself if all available resources of knowledge have been previously exhausted and knowledge gaps or deficits within the legislative process nevertheless remain and cannot be compensated for over time by knowledge gain and subsequent regulation. In any case, even if leeway for assessment, evaluation, or judgment is assumed, minimum requirements for proper fact-finding, procedure, methodology, and freedom from arbitrariness must be observed and, if necessary, reviewed by the courts.[41] In addition to that, a sub-legal specification of indeterminate precautionary requirements must always be made to the extent possible if the legislature grants leeway for assessment and evaluation. The practitioners of the law must not be left alone with a highly indeterminate concept of precaution and the assumption of far-reaching leeway for assessment, but require the most comprehensive sub-legislative specification possible.

3 Potential Modes of Action of an Innovation Principle

Considering this relationship of precautionary regulation and the precautionary dogma, the question arises as to how and where a postulate of an ‘innovation principle’ affects or would affect the overall system. Even with the call for an innovation principle first and foremost being a political one that seeks to influence legislation, it may, under certain circumstances, have the potential to influence other parameters

[40] For more on that, see Appel (2016), p. 113 et seq.

[41] Cf. BVerfG 17 Apr 1991 (1 BvR 419/81, 1 BvR 213/83) Gerichtliche Prüfungskontrolle BVerfGE 84, 34–58, p. 53–54; BVerfG 23 Oct 2018 (1 BvR 2523/13, 595/14) Rotmilan (2018) BVerfGE 149, 407–421, para 30.

of the precautionary dogma and the application of the law, which may well have far-reaching effects and should therefore be subjected to close scrutiny.

3.1 The Innovation Principle as the Hoped-For Counterpart to Precaution

The hope of the proponents of an innovation principle lies not least in the creation of a political and legal counterpart to the precautionary principle, which they perceive as highly potent and, in their view, difficult to contain. In doing so, this initiative takes advantage of the fact that the concept and the idea of innovation is of high symbolic and legal appeal.[42] In the legislative process, in particular, the precautionary narrative is to be presented with a potent counter-narrative of innovation, which may lead relevant stakeholders to restrict precaution-oriented regulation in actual or supposedly innovative areas at the onset.[43]

3.2 Innovation Principle and Proportionality

Moreover, it is necessary to focus on the legal and legal-dogmatic consequences that may be associated with a strengthening of the innovation concept and the postulate of an innovation principle. In order to understand the functions and potential modes of action of an innovation principle, it is helpful to look at other legal principles. Apart from their theoretical foundations, which for the innovation principle have so far been debatable and not substantiated in detail,[44] the determining legal effects of such principles lie in their guidance role for legislation, their highly potent justificatory quality for a legislator willing to regulate, and their significance for the interpretation and implementation of normative leeway.

In relation to precaution, the impact of a potential innovation principle becomes particularly apparent when assessing the proportionality of precautionary regulation. The principle of proportionality with its four stages of assessment—the constitutionally legitimate pursuit of a particular aim, the suitability, necessity, and appropriateness of means—must also be applied to precautionary regulation and individual precautionary measures. However, it is also important to keep in mind that proportionality in precautionary situations regularly becomes relevant not only in the relationship between an individual citizen and the state, but also in multipolar circumstances, where decisions have to be made with a comparatively broad perspective of the future under conditions of uncertainty. If it is already difficult to assess

[42] For more on that, see 4.1. below.

[43] European Commission (2017b); Renda and Simonelli (2019)

[44] Cf. 1.1. above.

proportionality in multipolar circumstances,[45] performing a future-oriented proportionality assessment, dependent on prognoses and under conditions of uncertainty on the basis of the conventional dogma, will prove challenging. For if one of the basic purposes of the precautionary dogma is to allow for freedom-restricting measures to be taken even with prevailing uncertainties, the proportionality assessment must take this uncertainty into account at every step of the assessment.[46] If uncertainties remain, constitutional case law and the constitutional law dogma grant the legislator more or less far-reaching leeway for assessment, evaluation, and judgment for all aspects of proportionality.[47] In addition to the issue of uncertainty, precaution always raises the question of a spatially and temporally multidimensional proportionality assessment. Since it involves spatial and temporal restrictions of freedoms in different dimensions, proportionality assessments must be conducted in different dimensions and coordinated with each other. However, when proportionality must be maintained in multiple dimensions, the multitude of proportionality assessments becomes a question of distributive justice and burden-sharing justice, as the German Federal Constitutional Court recently stated in its climate decision.[48]

A practicable standard for distributive justice or burden-sharing justice cannot be derived directly from the precautionary principle, just as it could not be derived directly from a potential innovation principle. This is a key reason as to why the German Federal Constitutional Court and the constitutional dogma in this case also operate with leeway for assessment, evaluation, and judgment. In cases where (sufficiently precise) standards are lacking due to remaining uncertainties, they provide the dogmatic hinge to achieve legally justified regulation and to arrive at correspondingly legitimised decisions. At first glance, the implementation of this leeway for assessment, evaluation, and judgment appears to be open decisions, where individual matters and factors could be included in the decision-making process according to their relevance and their relative significance. Postulating an innovation principle appears to aim precisely at countering the precautionary principle with an innovation narrative in the implementation of this leeway in order to influence its implementation and to shift the burden of justification. One possible argument is that the higher the value of an innovation, the greater the effort to justify possible restrictions, and therefore the more obvious would be the conclusion that restrictive precautionary measures should not be taken at all.

However, this argument is already at fault from the outset. After all, by its very nature, the precautionary principle is designed to also influence the implementation

[45] For more on that, see Calliess (2001), p. 566 et seq.

[46] From more recent times, cf. BVerfG 24 Nov 2010 (1 BvF 2/05) Zur Vereinbarkeit von Vorschriften des Gentechnikgesetzes mit dem Grundgesetz BVerfGE 128, 1–90, para. 142, 183.

[47] Cf. BVerfG 24 Nov 2010 (1 BvF 2/05) Zur Vereinbarkeit von Vorschriften des Gentechnikgesetzes mit dem Grundgesetz BVerfGE 128, 1–90, para. 142, 183.

[48] BVerfG 24 Mar 2021 (1 BvR 2656/18) Klimabeschluss (2021) BVerfGE 157, 30–177, para. 193.

of any leeway for assessment, evaluation, and judgment.[49] Precaution applies particularly where uncertainty is high due to possible harm potentials. If, in the assessment of the legislator or other decision-makers, the impending potential for harm is deemed unacceptable in the face of persisting uncertainty, the opportunities or benefits of an innovation are not (or no longer) relevant. In this case, sufficient precautionary regulations and appropriate precautionary measures must be implemented. The exclusive decisive factor is whether the potential for concern the decision to take precautionary measures was based on is sufficiently justified, according to the assessment of the decision-makers implementing the leeway. Thus, precaution and innovation are no commensurable factors.

If, on the other hand, after their assessment, evaluation, and judgment, the legislator or other decision-makers do not believe that there is sufficient potential for concern for implementing the relevant leeway, because the impending consequences are judged to be minor and/or acceptable despite prevailing uncertainties, precautionary regulation and subsequent precautionary measures cannot be justified. This rationale, however, by no means requires recourse to an innovation principle of any kind or even to innovation as a legally relevant concern. These limitations to precautionary regulation, that also apply to the leeway for assessment, evaluation, and judgement, already derive from the fundamental freedoms, which may not be restricted without any constitutional justification. In this context, an innovation principle is just as redundant as it is dispensable.

3.3 Forced Burdens of Analysis and Justification

The debate about the innovation principle can be credited with (once again) drawing attention to and raising awareness of the fact that any recourse to the precautionary principle always requires the precise identification and assessment of the potential for concern, the extensive exploitation of the relevant scientific expertise, and a detailed subsequent justification. Any recourse to the precautionary principle is accompanied by an increased burden of analysis and justification. Risks and potential concerns cannot be assumed and accepted by default but require a detailed and, where necessary, differentiated and graded justification, which in turn must be based on scientific expertise as well as substantiated prognoses and impact assessments. Therefore, legislative, decision-making, environmental, risk, and impact assessments are essential elements, especially in the scope of application of the precautionary principle.

Overall, this results in high demands for the identification, evaluation, and differentiated assessment of precautionary grounds and of associated precautionary measures that restrict freedoms. Fundamentally, this is why the approval of innovative

---

[49] BVerfG 24 Nov 2010 (1 BvF 2/05) Zur Vereinbarkeit von Vorschriften des Gentechnikgesetzes mit dem Grundgesetz BVerfGE 128, 1–90, p. 37; Huber/Voßkuhle/Epiney, GG art. 20a, Recital 71; Steinberg (1998), pp. 101–102; Calliess (2021), p. 121 et seq.

technologies or products is also subject to elaborate legal procedures. Conversely, these procedures are not at issue, even when they prove to be complex and require a considerable amount of time to identify and assess potential causes for concern in a substantiated manner.[50] The fact that this may restrict freedoms, delay innovative developments, or, in extreme cases, lead to their ban, is intrinsic to the overall concept of protection and precaution.

4 The Problematic Openness of the Concept of Innovation and the Limitation of Perspective

The correlations outlined above demonstrate that, from a legal point of view, an 'innovation principle' would not provide any notable added value compared to the already existing constitutional freedoms. Therefore, it should be pointed out only as an additional note that an innovation principle—even if it were to be referred to in legal contexts—would also be virtually impossible to manage in terms of significance, purpose, and scope.

4.1 Prognostic Elements of Innovation

The openness of the concept of innovation, which contains a significant prognostic element, already poses problems for the legal implementation of an innovation principle. Whether or not something can be considered an innovation can regularly only be determined with a certain delay and often in retrospect. The elements 'new' and 'progress', regularly stated as prerequisites for an innovation, require an evaluation for which there is a lack of sufficiently clear standards. This is partially due to the ambiguity of the term 'innovation'. On the one hand, the term 'innovation' refers to something new and of practical use, while, on the other hand, 'innovative' is often associated with going hand in hand with a momentous economic, social, and/or environmental benefit.[51]

When discussing an 'innovation principle', it is the second connotation that is frequently referenced. This has two consequences, which are regularly not substantiated, questioned, and/or justified in detail by those advocating an innovation principle. On the one hand, there is the implicit premise that innovations are fundamentally not only new but also will be, or at least could be, positive and of practical use in the future. It only requires a sideways glance at the example of innovative weapon or espionage technologies to question this issue of an unchallenged positive connotation. On the other hand, the term 'innovation' is in part unintentionally, in

---

[50] Federal Ethics Committee on Non-Human Biotechnology (ECNH) (2019), p. 3.

[51] Federal Ethics Committee on Non-Human Biotechnology (ECNH) (2019), pp. 9, 10; Hoffmann-Riem (2006), pp. 255–256.

part intentionally used to pursue the goal that innovations and new scientific and technological developments 'will be excluded, at least to some degree, from critical discussion',[52] since they are to be assessed as fundamentally positive. While this attempt to single out and isolate innovations from criticism is already problematic in political discourse, it is untenable in legal contexts.

4.2 *Ambiguity of Perspectives*

It is sometimes argued that innovations must be in the service of sustainability, that it would be the best criterion for distinguishing 'good' from 'bad' innovations. This way, innovations could be reconciled with sustainability and, under certain circumstances, with precaution.[53]

Apart from the fact that even limiting the perspective to sustainable innovations would not change the relationship between the precautionary principle and the postulated innovation principle as outlined above,[54] such a limitation of the term 'innovation' to sustainable innovations is neither foreseeable nor feasible. Innovations may be used for precautionary and sustainability purposes, provided there are objectives and standards for such a classification. Innovative activities may also be inspired by precautionary measures and implemented in search of alternative and less risky development paths. However, innovations can also come into considerable conflict with a precautionary and sustainable regulatory strategy. It is not always possible to make clear judgment as to which is the case. This is not surprising, given the inherent openness of innovations and the associated ambiguity of perspectives. Neither do the precautionary principle or the sustainability principle provide clear indications for particularly innovative or environmentally innovative products or services, nor is there an inherent limitation within the term 'innovation' to innovations that are in accord with sustainability and/or precaution. Without further specification, the term 'innovation' is as neutral with regard to sustainability and precaution as the terms 'precaution' and 'sustainability' are with regard to innovation.

Thus, the general question of whether precautionary regulation either restricts freedoms or promotes innovation cannot be fully answered. Both can be the case. Naturally, precautionary regulations and sustainability issues can restrict the freedoms used for innovations. However, provided that the motives for precaution and/or sustainability are clearly and predictably specified in normative terms, they can also provide significant incentives for innovative technologies and promote innovations. Whether one or the other is the case cannot be answered in general terms, and certainly not by narrowing down the definitions of terms.

---

[52] Federal Ethics Committee on Non-Human Biotechnology (ECNH) (2019), p. 5.

[53] For more on the linking of innovation, precaution, and the compatibility with the common good, cf. Calliess (2021), pp. 133, 136 et seq.

[54] For more on independent ethical assessment, see Federal Ethics Committee on Non-Human Biotechnology (ECNH) (2019), p. 6.

4.3 *Comparison with Other Regulatory Restrictions of Freedoms*

Finally, it is important to keep in mind that the focus on innovation-related freedoms often associated with the postulate of an 'innovation principle' obscures the fact that there are a number of other, potentially fundamental freedoms for liberal societies that are also affected by precautionary regulation. The freedoms to develop and use innovations are not the only freedoms that need to be taken into account as constitutional assets. All of these freedoms—regardless of whether they are in any way related to innovations or not—may only ever be restricted by precautionary regulation and individual precautionary measures if they can be constitutionally justified when measured against the requirements of the rule of law. These other freedoms must not be lost sight of by exclusively and one-sidedly focusing on an innovation-oriented perspective, as they run the risk of being overshadowed by the strong innovation narrative.

5 New Genomic Techniques as a Reference Area

The development and use of new genomic techniques (NGT) in plants, animals and micro-organisms, which have been comprehensively placed under the precautionary regime of the genetic engineering legislation by the ECJ[55] and are pending (re)regulation at the European level, provide ample examples for the balancing of precaution and innovation and for the limitations of legal regulation in this context.[56] Issues associated with product approval are particularly evident in the context of new genomic techniques.[57] With the emergence of these techniques, such as the Crispr/CAS9 gene scissors, the question of whether the thereby genetically modified plants should be regulated in the same way as conventional genetically modified organisms, even though most of these techniques do not involve gene transfer, which has characterized the previous regulatory approach of genetic engineering law so far, has become a pressing one. The ECJ has answered this question in the affirmative in

[55] ECJ 25 July 2018 (Case C-528/16) Confédération paysanne and Others v Premier ministre and Ministre de l'agriculture, de l'agroalimentaire et de la forêt (2018) ECR C-583.

[56] To a considerable extent, the remarks in Sect. 4 draw on preliminary works; these include in particular the presentation: 'Neue Molekularbiologische Techniken zwischen Innovation und Vorsorge' (New genomic techniques between innovation and precaution) and the subsequent discussion at the Federal Ministry of Agriculture and Food (2019) Ministry of Agriculture's Forum NMT on 19 July 2019 in Berlin as well as the contribution Appel (2020), § 51 esp. Recital 3c, 4a, 8a et seq., 18b and 25b et seq.

[57] For more on that, see Appel (2020), § 51 Recital 8a et seq., 18b, and 25b et seq.

principle, thus subjecting the application areas of such new techniques to the regulatory and approval regime of genetic engineering law,[58] meaning that the relevant approval procedures are to be conducted and all preconditions for approval must be met in each case. This imposes considerable restrictive consequences on science and the economy. They have led to increasingly louder calls for a differentiation of the corresponding approval law with respect to individual risk and harm potentials as well as for a reform of the underlying European genetic engineering law, in particular with regard to new genomic techniques.[59]

The question of the outcome of such a reform is a highly consequential one. More recent techniques make it possible to modify the genetic material in the smallest of steps without requiring extensive crossbreeding experiments, as in traditional breeding, or the introduction of foreign genes.[60] Therefore, some see an opportunity in these new techniques to counteract the monopolization in plant breeding. After all, most of these comparatively minor procedures are simple and inexpensive enough to potentially allow not only seed corporations but also small cooperatives to develop new plants—for instance, species more resistant to heat, cold, drought, or humidity—in a short amount of time and without having to transfer foreign genes. To some extent, these new technologies therefore hold the promise of protecting entire harvests from insects, fungal diseases, and other hazards. The utilisation of modified plants is expected to reduce the use of fertilizers, pesticides, and herbicides on a large scale, possibly leading to a better productivity on poor soil and a higher biodiversity. On the other hand, the new genomic techniques are associated with risks that cannot readily be considered unproblematic—at least not without a preventive review of the associated risk and impact potentials. When put into perspective like this, the issue of the classification of the new genomic techniques notably highlights the ever-precarious relationship between the opportunities and risks of innovative techniques, exacerbated further by the fact that the allocation of particular areas to a regulated risk technology sometimes depends on prior knowledge and assumptions that cannot be easily justified in a rational and comprehensible manner. In the medical field, for example, genetically engineered drugs are now as common as they are indispensable. Compared to the area of green genetic engineering, risk assessments in this field lead to decidedly more positive results. This comparison alone suggests that instead of regulating the new genomic techniques as a whole, it would be prudent to proceed

---

[58] ECJ 25 July 2018 (Case C-528/16) Confédération paysanne and Others v Premier ministre and Ministre de l'agriculture, de l'agroalimentaire et de la forêt (2018) ECR C-583; for more on this ruling, see Seitz (2018), p. 757 et seq.; Dederer (2019), p. 236 et seq.; Beck (2019), p. 246 et seq.

[59] Cf. German National Academy of Sciences Leopoldina (2019); Appel (2020), § 51 Recital 3a, 18b; Andersen and Schreiber (2020), p. 168 et seq.; for more on the European Commission's roadmap and the initiative 'legislation for plants engineered using certain new genomic techniques', see https://ec.europa.eu/info/law/better-regulation/have-your-say/initiatives/13119-Legislation-for-plants-produced-by-certain-new-genomic-techniques_en. Accessed 22 Sep 2025; this initiative aims to provide a high level of protection for the human, animal, and environmental health and to safeguard new genomic techniques' contributions to the goals of the European Green Deal and the 'Farm-to-Fork'-strategy precisely through innovations.

[60] For more on that and the following, see Appel (2020), § 51 Recital 8b.

in a more differentiated manner, with graded standards and the exemption of certain areas from regulation, if necessary.

However, this path has not yet been pursued by European and German genetic engineering law.[61] According to the basic premise of genetic engineering law, the actual and, compared to other regulatory matters, unique risk of genetic engineering lies in the genetic modification itself. The assumed difference of genetic modifications alone compared to traditional methods of organism modification leads to the normative conclusion of a general basic risk of genetic engineering, based exclusively on the manufacturing process, requiring a minimum of legal supervision and restriction, and justifying the extensive regulatory framework for genetic engineering in the first place.[62] This particular normative assumption[63] is based on general considerations of precaution and underlies the regulatory regime as a whole, regardless of the specific potential for harm posed by an individual genetically modified organism (GMO).

The issue associated with the general assumption of a basic risk for genetical engineering becomes particularly pressing with the inclusion of new forms of genome editing and genome-editing-based plant breeding because the assumption of a general basic risk for genetic engineering still underlying the European and German genetic engineering law has become disputable as a result of the further development of new genomic techniques. The ECJ has defined the scope of application of European genetic engineering law broadly and has also subjected new forms of genome editing and genome-editing-based plant breeding to the corresponding regulation under European genetic engineering law[64] precisely because the European legislator has not issued more differentiated regulations to take account of the continuous development of genetic engineering and the latest genomic techniques. However, such a classification of the latest genomic techniques under genetic engineering law

---

[61] For more on the amendment efforts on European level, see https://ec.europa.eu/info/law/better-regulation/have-your-say/initiatives/13119-Legislation-for-plants-produced-by-certain-new-genomic-techniques_en. Accessed 22 Sep 2025.

[62] For fundamental and conceptual aspects of 'basic risk', see the first Commentary of 1993 on the German Genetic Engineering Act GenTG Wahl (1993) GenTG, Vorb. Recital 17 et seq.; on the (unspoken) statutory premise of a basic risk, see also Appel (1996), p. 229 et seq.; as well as Sparwasser et al (2003) § 6 Recital 362; The assumption of a basic risk is taken up by the BVerfG 24 Nov 2010 (1 BvF 2/05) BVerfGE 128, 1–90 which allows the legislature to assume a 'basic risk' for genetic engineering as a whole, citing its broad leeway for assessment and evaluation. For more on the reception of the basic risk of genetic engineering in case law, see also VG Hannover 1 Oct 2008 (11 A 4732/07) Beseitigung der Aussaat gentechnisch veränderten Saatguts (2008) NuR 31:67–73, p. 72, each with reference to Mecklenburg (2006), p. 232; as well as BVerwG 29 Feb 2012 (7 C 8/11) Freisetzung gentechnisch veränderter Organismen (2012) BeckRS 50,031, para. 25.

[63] The assumption of such a basic risk should lie within the scope of the legislator's prerogative of assessment and should not presuppose any scientific-empirical evidence of actual risk potentials of the genetically modified organisms and their progeny; c.f. BVerfG 24 Nov 2010 (1 BvF 2/05) Zur Vereinbarkeit von Vorschriften des Gentechnikgesetzes mit dem Grundgesetz BVerfGE 128, 1–90; for more details on the constitutional assessment of the basic risk, see Recital 48.

[64] ECJ 25 July 2018 (Case C-528/16) Confédération paysanne and Others v Premier ministre and Ministre de l'agriculture, de l'agroalimentaire et de la forêt (2018) ECR C-583.

would have required a more detailed examination of the nature of the specific risk—comparable to the risk of genetic engineering via gene transfer—inherent in the latest genomic techniques that could justify the broader assumption of such a basic risk. Both the experience now accumulated in the field of genetic engineering, as well as the bridging of the gap between new genomic techniques and the field of traditional breeding raise considerable doubts as to whether the general assumption of a basic risk can continue to be maintained without introducing significant incongruities. It would either require a more differentiated approach to determine whether and to what extent new genomic techniques actually pose specific risks which, even in comparison to traditional breeding methods not covered under genetic engineering law, justify the assumption of a general basic risk. Alternatively, other forms of 'traditional' breeding would have to be examined more closely in terms of associated risks, and the question would have to be raised as to whether they are also subject to a corresponding basic risk. Since every form of breeding, including conventional breeding, involves genetic modification, it would have to be (more) comprehensively substantiated and justified whether and to what extent the comparatively faster, more targeted, and more precise newer methods pose a more specific risk and are to be subject to the more comprehensive regime of genetic engineering law, while the significantly more undifferentiated and in terms of associated risks and impact far less predictable methods of traditional plant breeding are not. Assuming a basic risk for the new genomic techniques without a more detailed and differentiated examination, thus subjecting them to genetic engineering law, while exempting other forms of breeding from such a basic risk without a more detailed and differentiated examination and thus not subjecting them to a more specific risk regulation, does not appear to be coherent in itself and reinforces the postulate for a more differentiated regulation by the European legislator.[65]

The ECJ's reasoning[66] is problematic in that it derives its conclusion that organisms produced by new genomic techniques are genetically modified organisms (GMOs) as defined in the EU's Deliberate Release Directive partially from statements made for GMOs, and thus already presupposing the presence of GMOs. Such statements, however, cannot provide evidence as to whether or not organisms produced by newer techniques are GMOs as defined under European genetic engineering law. Incidentally, the ECJ's conclusions are based on the statement that organisms produced by using newer techniques could be subject to risks comparable to those associated with transgenic organisms. However, it is not specified in detail that the new genomic techniques are just as risky, but it is assumed based on unspecified information available to the court. Thus, the ECJ's default assumption that all new genomic techniques and the organisms they produce pose a basic risk is not supported by any further studies and/or sources on the effects and risks of these new techniques and the organisms they produce.

[65] See Appel (2020) § 51 Recital 8a et seq., 18b, and 25b et seq.

[66] ECJ 25 July 2018 (Case C-528/16) Confédération paysanne and Others v Premier ministre and Ministre de l'agriculture, de l'agroalimentaire et de la forêt (2018) ECR C-583.

This partially devalues the precautionary principle referenced by the ECJ at key points in its line of reasoning. For in order to be applied with constitutional certainty, the precautionary principle always presupposes that the presumed cause for precaution and the underlying potential for concern are identified as clearly as possible and are supported by arguments. With this in mind, there would be reason, and arguments could certainly be made for classifying, for example, potential risks of certain unnatural procedures as problematic from a precautionary perspective, as long as sufficient experience data on their effects on the organism is lacking. The ECJ, however, does not undertake this justification effort, which would require a (more) differentiated examination of new genomic techniques, thus accepting a rather less compelling recourse to the, for genetic engineering law highly important, precautionary principle with regard to new genomic techniques. Tellingly, at the end of its deliberations, the ECJ concludes flatly that an interpretation 'which excludes organisms obtained by means of techniques/methods of mutagenesis from the scope of that directive, without any distinctions, would compromise the objective of protection pursued by the directive and would fail to respect the precautionary principle which it seeks to implement'.[67] With the same conviction, one could counter this with the following: An interpretation which subjects organisms obtained by means of techniques/methods of mutagenesis to the scope of the Deliberate Release Directive, without having analysed and justified the risk potential of the new techniques in a differentiated manner, contradicts the objective of protection and precaution pursued by this directive, the constitutional requirements (also) for precautionary interventions, as well as the principle of proportionality, which also applies to European genetic engineering law. After all, it is essential that new genomic techniques and their associated risks not be examined 'without distinction', but rather in a well-differentiated manner. This makes it all the more evident that the underlying questions regarding the scope of the European genetic engineering law have not been conclusively and satisfyingly clarified by the ECJ's comparatively broad ruling, but instead require a supplementary ruling by a European legislator regulating in a (more) differentiated manner.

However, these considerations do not invalidate neither the precautionary principle nor the associated precautionary dogma, which are coherent in themselves and can, in principle, be implemented in a legally secure way under the rule of law. They show, however, the sophisticated nature of the precautionary principle and how its implementation under the rule of law depends on a differentiated justification of potentials for concern as a cause for precautionary measures, on a continuous adaptation to constantly changing framework conditions, on the ever-developing knowledge as well as changing expertise, and, not least, on subsequent improvements of regulations in one direction or the other. The general assumption of a basic risk at least does not suffice (anymore) when a field of technology is continuously developing and differentiating itself further over the span of decades without the relevant legal

---

67 ECJ 25 July 2018 (Case C-528/16) Confédération paysanne and Others v Premier ministre and Ministre de l'agriculture, de l'agroalimentaire et de la forêt (2018) ECR C-583.

regulation keeping pace with the development and taking into account the degree of differentiation achieved in the meantime.

6 Conclusions for the Relationship Between Precaution and Innovation

If the precautionary principle is implemented in a way that causes for concern are sufficiently identified and justified in a differentiated manner, and those areas are exempted from precaution that do not (or no longer) entail any identifiable risks or any risks that are assessed as unacceptable, the precautionary principle does not require any supplementation by an innovation principle of any kind. Indeed, it is correct that restrictions on freedoms may be justified by recourse to precaution and thereby development opportunities and innovations may be curtailed as a matter of law.[68] The underlying problem, however, arises from the fact that precautionary measures such as hazard prevention restrict freedoms, while unlike freedoms not possessing any immanent limits since they are associated with situations of uncertainty that are difficult to delimit and cannot be (fully) assessed. The idea of restricting this principal openness of precaution by introducing a countervailing innovation principle, however, already fails in its approach because even an innovation or freedom principle cannot provide a solution for the underlying issue, which goes beyond the mode of constitutional freedoms and the state's prerequisites for justifying any encroachment on these freedoms.

In substance, there is no way around identifying and assessing causes for concern as extensively as possible with procedural standards and a recourse to external expertise in order to subsequently take proportionate precautionary measures corresponding to the cause for concern, whereby the legislator must be granted a limited leeway for assessment, evaluation, or judgment in case of persisting uncertainty and/or ambiguous external expertise. The example of the approach to new genomic techniques demonstrates that the prerequisites of the precautionary principle are possibly not adequately taken into account if, for example, a general basic risk for a technique that has long since been further differentiated is assumed and/or if a leeway for assessment is adopted prematurely and sweepingly. In contrast, it is the legislator's responsibility to continuously, gradually, and promptly adapt the precaution-based law to the current level of knowledge, and if necessary, to further regulate or deregulate it accordingly. However, if it is not possible to eliminate persisting uncertainties, precaution is the appropriate legal instrument: Precautionary measures can be justified to the extent that causes for precaution can be plausibly substantiated, even if they are associated with freedom restrictions.

This makes it obvious that there is no irreconcilable contradiction between precaution and the development of innovative technologies. For reasons of protection and precaution, the approval of innovative technologies and products may be subjected

[68] For more on that and the following, see Appel (2022) § 123 Recital 9, 51.

to a more or less sophisticated preventive procedure, which is not up for disposal even if it were to take longer. This remains true even in times of accelerated technological progress, even if that progress seems necessary in order to meet the global challenges ahead.[69] It is precisely the balance expressed therein that characterises a constitutional state oriented towards progress and precaution.

References

Andersen E, Schreiber K (2020) Neue Regeln für Gentechnik in Europa? NuR 42:168–178
Appel I (1996) Stufen der Risikoabwehr. Zur Neuorientierung der umweltrechtlichen Sicherheitsdogmatik im Gentechnikrecht. Natur und Recht (NuR) 5:227–235
Appel I (2004) Methodik des Umgangs mit Ungewissheit. In: Schmidt-Aßmann, Hoffmann-Riem (eds) Methoden der Verwaltungsrechtswissenschaft, 1st edn. Nomos, Baden-Baden, pp 327–358
Appel I (2005) Staatliche Zukunfts- und Entwicklungsvorsorge, Mohr Siebeck.
Appel I (2006) Konkretisierung rechtlicher Anforderungen durch technische Regeln: Immissionsschutzrecht, Gewässerschutz, Bodenschutz, Umwelt- und Technikrecht. UTR 86:67–105
Appel I (2008) Standardisierung durch Informationsaustausch. Zur Konkretisierung der "Besten Verfügbaren Technik" (BVT) nach dem Konzept der IVU-Richtlinie. In: Möllers T (ed) Standardisierung durch Markt und Recht 18:91–114
Appel I (2009) Aufgaben und Verfahren der Innovationsfolgenabschätzung. In: Eifert M, Hoffmann-Riem W (eds) Innovationsverantwortung. Duncker & Humblot, Berlin, pp 147–182
Appel I (2011) Risiken des Risikorechts. In: Appel I, Hermes G, Schönberger C (eds) Öffentliches Recht im offenen Staat. Festschrift für Rainer Wahl zum 70. Geburtstag. Duncker & Humblot, Berlin, pp. 463–488
Appel I (2016) Bedeutung außerrechtlicher Wissensbestände für das Management von Unsicherheit und Nichtwissen. In: Hill H, Schliesky U (eds) Management von Unsicherheit und Nichtwissen. Nomos, Baden-Baden, pp 113–146
Appel I (2018) Europäisches und nationales Umweltverfassungsrecht. In Koch H-J, Hofmann E and Reese M (eds), Handbuch des Umweltrechts, 5th edn. C.H.Beck, Munich
Appel I (2020) Gentechnikrecht. In: Ehlers D, Fehling M, Pünder H (eds) Besonderes Verwaltungsrecht, 4th edn, vol 2. C.F. Müller, Heidelberg, pp 824–913
Appel I (2022) Reformperspektiven im Zulassungsrecht. In: Kahl W, Ludwigs M (eds) Handbuch des Verwaltungsrechts, vol IV. C.F.Müller, Heidelberg, pp 1197–1239
Appel I, Mielke S (2014) Strategien der Risikoregulierung. Nomos, Baden-Baden
Bechmann G, Jörissen J (1992) Technikfolgenabschätzung und Umweltverträglichkeitsprüfung. KritV 75(2):140–171
Beck F (2019) All about that risk? A (re-) assessment of the CJEU's reasoning in the "genome editing" case. EurUP 17(2):246–255
Böhret C (1989) Neuartige Folgen – eine "andere" Verwaltung. VerwArch 80:13–23
Böhret C (1991) Nachweltschutz: sechs Reden über politische Verantwortung. Lang, Frankfurt a.M. Bern New York Paris
Calliess C (2001) Rechtsstaat und Umweltstaat. Mohr Siebeck, Tübingen
Calliess C (2009) Das Innovationspotential des Vorsorgeprinzips unter besonderer Berücksichtigung des integrierten Umweltschutzes. In: Eifert M, Hoffmann-Riem W (eds) Innovationsverantwortung. Duncker & Humblot, Berlin, pp 119–145
Calliess C (2021) The innovation principle—a new European legal principle? ZEuS 1:125–144
Dederer H-G (2019) Genomeditierung ist Gentechnik. Eine kritische Analyse des EuGH-Urteils Confédération paysanne u.a. EurUP 17(2):236–245

[69] Federal Ethics Committee on Non-Human Biotechnology (ECNH) (2019), p. 3.

Depenheuer O (2011) Solidarität und Freiheit. In: Isensee J, Kirchhof P (eds) Handbuch des Staatsrechts, 3rd edn, vol IX. C.F. Müller, Heidelberg, pp 665–698
Di Fabio U (1994) Risikoentscheidungen im Rechtsstaat. Mohr Siebeck, Tübingen
Di Fabio U (1996) Risikosteuerung durch Öffentliches Recht. In: Hoffmann-Riem W, Schmidt-Aßmann E (eds) Öffentliches Recht und Privatrecht als wechselseitige Auffangordnungen. Nomos, Baden-Baden pp 143–166
Eifert M, Hoffmann-Riem W (eds) (2002) Innovation und rechtliche Regulierung. Nomos, Baden-Baden
Eifert M, Hoffmann-Riem W (eds) (2009a) Innovationsverantwortung. Nomos, Baden-Baden
Eifert M, Hoffmann-Riem W (eds) (2009b) Innovationsfördernde Regulierung. Nomos, Baden-Baden
Fehling M (2004) Kosten-Nutzen-Analysen als Maßstab für Verwaltungsentscheidungen. VerwArch 95:443–461
Franzius C (2001) Technikermöglichungsrecht. Wechselbeziehungen zwischen Technik und Recht am Beispiel der Kommunikationstechnik. VERW 34(4):487–507
Garnett K, van Calster G, Reins L (2018) Towards an innovation principle: an industry trump or shortening the odds on environmental protection? Law Innov Technol 10:1–14. https://doi.org/10.1080/17579961.2018.1455023
Gröpl C (2002) Ökonomisierung von Verwaltung und Verwaltungsrecht. VerwArch 93:459–484
Hausschildt J (1998) Facetten des Innovationsbegriffs. In: Hoffmann-Riem, Schneider JP, Rechtswissenschaftliche Innovationsforschung. Nomos, Baden-Baden, pp 29–39
Hoffmann-Riem W (2006) Innovationsoffenheit und Innovationsverantwortung Durch Recht. Aör 131(2):255–277
Hoffmann-Riem W (2016) Innovation und Recht – Recht und Innovation. Mohr Siebeck, Tübingen
Hoffmann-Riem W, Schmidt-Aßmann E (eds) (1994), Innovation und Flexibilität des Verwaltungsrechts. Nomos, Baden-Baden
Hoffmann-Riem W, Schneider JP (eds) (1998) Rechtswissenschaftliche Innovationsforschung. Nomos, Baden-Baden
Huber P-M, Voßkuhle A (eds) (2024), Grundgesetz GG, 11th edn. Beck München.
Jäckel L (2010) Gefahrenabwehrrecht und Risikodogmatik, Mohr Siebeck, Tübingen
Karthaus A (2001) Risikomanagement durch ordnungsrechtliche Steuerung. Nomos, Baden-Baden
Kloepfer M (2000a) Recht als Technikkontrolle und Technikermöglichung. In: Brandner T, Meßerschmidt K (eds) Umweltschutz und Recht. Duncker & Hublot, Berlin, pp 109–124
Kloepfer M (ed) (2000b) Technikentwicklung und Technikrechtsentwicklung. Duncker & Humbolt, Berlin
Ladeur K-H (1993) Risiko und Recht. Von der Rezeption der Erfahrung zum Prozeß der Modellierung. In: Bechmann (ed) Risiko und Gesellschaft, 1st edn. Westdeutscher Verlag, Opladen, pp 209–236
Lübbe-Wolff G (1997) Präventiver Umweltschutz – Auftrag und Grenzen des Vorsorgeprinzips im deutschen und im europäischen Recht. In: Bizer J, Koch H-J (eds), Sicherheit, Vielfalt, Solidarität. Ein neues Paradigma des Verfassungsrechts? Nomos, Baden-Baden
Mecklenburg W (2006) Zur Störfallbewältigung im Gentechnikrecht – Aussaat von mit gentechnisch veränderten Organismen verunreinigtem Saatgut. NuR 28:229–233
Meßerschmidt K (2011) Europäisches Umweltrecht. C.H.Beck, München
Pelkmans J, Renda (2014) European Commission: how can EU legislation enable and/or disable innovation. https://ec.europa.eu/futurium/en/system/files/ged/39-how_can_eu_legislation_enable_and-or_disable_innovation.pdf. Accessed 28 Sept 2025
Petersen F (1993) Schutz und Vorsorge. Duncker & Humblot, Berlin
Pitschas R (2000) Technikentwicklung und -implementierung als rechtliches Steuerungsproblem: Von der administrativen Risikopotentialanalyse zur Innovationsfunktion des Technikrechts. In: Kloepfer (ed) Technikentwicklung und Technikrechtsentwicklung. Duncker & Humblot, Berlin, pp 73–102

Renda A, Simonelli F (2017) European Commission: Study supporting the interim evaluation of the innovation principle. Final Report. https://www.ceps.eu/ceps-publications/study-supporting-the-interim-evaluation-of-the-innovation-principle/. Accessed 28 Sept 2025
Renda A, Simonelli F (2019) European Commission: Study supporting the interim evaluation of the innovation principle. Final Report. https://op.europa.eu/en/web/eu-law-and-publications/publication-detail/-/publication/e361ec68-09b4-11ea-8c1f-01aa75ed71a1. Accessed 28 Sept 2025
Roßnagel A (2007) Innovation als Gegenstand der Rechtswissenschaft. In: Hof H, Wengenroth U (eds) Innovationsforschung. Ansätze, Methoden, Grenzen und Perspektiven. Hamburg, pp 9–22
Rothstein H et al (2006) The risks of risk-based regulation. Environ Int 32(8):1056–1065
Salomo S (2011) Innovationsmanagement, 5th edn. Vahlen, München
Scherzberg A (2001) Wissen, Nichtwissen und Ungewissheit im Recht. In: Engel C, Halfmann J, Schulte M (eds) Wissen – Nichtwissen – Unsicheres Wissen. Nomos, Baden-Baden pp 113–144
Scherzberg A (2010) Risikoabschätzung unter Ungewissheit. Preliminary risk assessment im Kontext der Nanotechnologie. ZUR 6:303–311
Scherzberg A, Lepsius O (2004) Risikosteuerung durch Verwaltungsrecht: Ermöglichung oder Begrenzung von Innovationen? In: Die Staatsrechtslehre und die Veränderung ihres Gegenstandes. Gewährleistung von Freiheit und Sicherheit im Lichte unterschiedlicher Staats- und Verfassungsverständnisse. Risikosteuerung durch Verwaltungsrecht. Transparente Verwaltung – Konturen eines Informationsverwaltungsrechts. 63rd VVDStRL, Hamburg, October 2003. Lecture Notes. De Gruyter, Berlin Boston, pp 214–343.
Schmitt C (1928) Verfassungslehre, 11th edn. Duncker & Humblot, Berlin
Schneider J-P (2001) Zur Ökonomisierung von Verwaltungsrecht und Verwaltungsrechtswissenschaft. VERW 34:317–326
Seitz C (2018) Modifiziert oder nicht? Regulatorische Rechtsfragen zur Genoptimierung durch neue biotechnologische Verfahren. EUZW 29:757–764
Sparwasser R, Engel R, Voßkuhle A (2003) Umweltrecht: Grundzüge des öffentlichen Umweltschutzrechts. C.F. Müller, Heidelberg
Spiecker I called Döhmann (2025) Staatliche Entscheidungen unter Unsicherheit. Mohr Siebeck, Tübingen
Steinberg R (1998) Der ökologische Verfassungsstaat. Suhrkamp, Berlin
Sunstein C (2005) Laws of fear: beyond the precautionary principle. Cambridge University Press, Cambridge
von Westphalen R, Neubert S (1988) Zur Rolle von Recht und Rechtswissenschaft im Technikfolgenabschätzungs- und -bewertungsprozess. In: von Westphalen (ed) Technikfolgenabschätzung als politische Aufgabe. Oldenbourg, München, pp 257–286
Wahl R (1991) Risikobewertung der Exekutive und richterliche Kontrolldichte: Auswirkungen auf das Verwaltungs- und das gerichtliche Verfahren NVwZ 1991:409–418
Wahl R (1993) GenTG Kommentar. In: Landmann/Rohmer (eds) Umweltrecht II, Beck München 1993 ff.
Wahl R, Appel I (1995) Prävention und Vorsorge. In: Wahl R (ed) Prävention und Vorsorge. Von der Staatsaufgabe zur verwaltungsrechtlichen Ausgestaltung. Economica, Bonn, pp 1–216
Wahl R, Melchinger H (2004) Das Gentechnikrecht nach der Novellierung. JZ 49(20):973–982
Wolff F, Gsell M (2018) Ökonomisierung der Umwelt und ihres Schutzes: Unterschiedliche Praktiken, ihre theoretische Bewertung und empirische Wirkungen. German Environment Agency. https://www.umweltbundesamt.de/sites/default/files/medien/1410/publikationen/2018-09-12_texte_71-2018_umweltpolitik-19-jhd.pdf. Accessed 28 Sept 2025

Cases

BVerfG 17 Apr 1991 (1 BvR 419/81, 1 bvR 213/83) Gerichtliche Prüfungskontrolle (1991) BVerfGE 84, 34–58

BVerfG 24 Nov 2010 (1 BvF 2/05) Zur Vereinbarkeit von Vorschriften des Gentechnikgesetzes mit dem Grundgesetz (2010) BVerfGE 128, 1–90
BVerfG 23 Oct 2018 (1 BvR 2523/13, 595/14) Rotmilan (2018) BVerfGE 149, 407–421
BVerfG 24 Mar 2021 (1 BvR 2656/18) Klimabeschluss (2021) BverfGE 157, 30–177
BVerwG 29 Feb 2012 (7 C 8/11) Freisetzung gentechnisch veränderter Organismen (2012) BeckRS 50031
ECJ 5 May 1998 (Case C-180/96) United Kingdom of Great Britian and Northern Ireland v Commission of the European Communities (1198) ECR I-2265
ECJ 5 May 1998 (Case C-157/96) The Queen v Ministry of Agriculture, Fisheries and Food and Commissioners of Customs & Excise, ex parte National Farmers' Union and Others (1998) ECR I-2211
ECJ 4 July 2000 (Case C-352/98) Laboratoires pharmaceutiques Bergaderm and Goupil v Commission (2000) ECR I-5291
ECJ 11 Sept 2002 (Case T-13/99) Pfizer Animal Health v Council (2002) ECR II-3305
ECJ 11 Sept 2002 (Case T-70/99) Alpharma v Council (2002) ECR II-3495
ECJ 25 July 2018 (Case C-528/16) Confédération paysanne and Others v Premier ministre and Ministre de l'agriculture, de l'agroalimentaire et de la forêt (2018) ECR C-583
VG Hannover 1 Oct 2008 (11 A 4732/07) Beseitigung der Aussaat gentechnisch veränderten Saatguts (2008) NuR 31:67–73

EU documents

European Commission (2016a) Commission Staff Working Document. Better regulations for innovation-driven investment at EU level. https://doi.org/10.2777/987880. Accessed 22 Sep 2025
European Commission (2016b) European Political Strategy Centre. Towards an innovation principle endorsed by better regulation. Issue 14. https://doi.org/10.2872/626511. Accessed 22 Sep 2025.
European Commission (2017a) Commission Staff Working Document. Better regulation guidelines. In: Commission Staff Working Document 350. https://ec.europa.eu/info/sites/default/files/better-regulation-guidelines.pdf. Accessed 22 Sep 2025
European Commission (2017b) Better regulation toolbox, document complementing the better regulation guidelines. In: Comission Staff Working Document 350. https://ec.europa.eu/info/sites/default/files/better-regulation-toolbox_2.pdf. Accessed 22 Sep 2025
European Commission, REFIT—making EU law simpler, more efficient and future-proof. https://commission.europa.eu/law/law-making-process/evaluating-and-improving-existing-laws/refit-making-eu-law-simpler-more-efficient-and-future-proof_en. Accessed 22 Sep 2025

Other documents

Federal Ethics Committee on Non-Human Biotechnology (ECNH) (2019) Does the precautionary principle need to be supplemented? Ethical considerations on the 'innovation principle'. https://www.ekah.admin.ch/inhalte/ekah-dateien/dokumentation/publikationen/EKAH_Innovationsbericht_EN_V.pdf. Accessed 22 Sep 2025
European Risk Forum ERF (2015) The ERF study. European risk forum monograph. Fostering innovation. Better management of risk. https://www.eriforum.eu/uploads/2/5/7/1/25710097/monograph_innovation_principle.pdf. Accessed 22 Sep 2025

German National Academy of Sciences Leopoldina (2019) Towards a scientifically justified, differentiated regulation of genome edited plants in the EU. https://www.leopoldina.org/uploads/tx_leopublication/2019_Stellungnahme_Genomeditierte_Pflanzen_web_02.pdf. Accessed 22 Sep 2025

BusinessEurope/ERF/ERT (2015) Impact of EU regulation on innovation. https://www.businesseurope.eu/sites/buseur/files/media/reports_and_studies/2016-12-02_impact_of_eu_regulation_on_innovation_-_repository_of_industry_cases.pdf. Accessed 22 Sep 2025

Legal Drivers for Sustainable Innovations

Michael von Landenberg-Roberg

Abstract A sustainable transition to ecological sustainability and greenhouse gas neutrality will not be possible without technological and social innovations. Promoting innovation is therefore a central task of environmental law as transformative law. This article illustrates how climate protection law fulfills this role by developing regulatory structures that promote innovation, as well as the challenges that can be expected.

1 Promoting Sustainable Innovation Through Legal Regulation

The relationship between environmental law and innovation is ambivalent. Environmental regulation can either hinder or promote innovation. How it affects innovation activities in the economy and society depends primarily on the actual regulatory design. This was recognized and addressed by legal scholars and innovation researchers early on in the development of modern environmental law.[1] The question of how environmental regulation can best be designed to promote innovation has therefore been an issue in environmental law and economics scholarship for more than 40 years.[2]

The debate on innovation-promoting regulation was initially based largely on a perspective that saw innovation primarily as a necessary means to increase economic

[1] As representative examples, reference is made here only to the standard-setting article by Stewart (1981) and furthermore to Bruce La Pierre (1976/1977); Magat (1979) and Ashford et al. (1985); from a more economic perspective see only the influential debate between Porter and van der Linde (1995) and Palmer et al. (1995).

[2] As a result, the literature is almost impossible to survey in its entirety. For a systematic review of the more recent literature see Westergaard Clausen et al. (2023) and Borsatto and Bazani (2021). For comparable early discussions in technology law see Appel, in this volume, see subsection 1.2.1.

M. von Landenberg-Roberg (✉)
Privatdozent at Faculty of Law, Humboldt–Universität zu Berlin, Berlin, Germany
e-mail: michael.roberg@hu-berlin.de

M. Reese et al. (eds.), *Environmental Law in Transformation*,
https://doi.org/10.1007/978-3-032-31567-0_5

productivity and growth. Environmental regulation should, as far as possible, be designed in such a way that it does not stifle the economically essential process of innovation. From the outset, however, there was also a second strand of the debate that explicitly linked the issue of promoting innovation with the goal of improving environmental protection. The idea was that environmental regulation should lead to precisely those technological and social innovations that would make it possible to achieve a higher level of environmental protection in the future. These lines of thought, which focus equally on the *promotion of* and *normative orientation for* innovation through legal regulation, could be taken up seamlessly in the debate on the promotion of sustainability.[3] In this context, the realisation that not only incremental but also disruptive and transformative innovations are crucial to overcome the many unsustainable development patterns in today's economy and society has led to increased interdisciplinary research on the promotion of innovation and the legal instruments to facilitate it.[4] In Germany, efforts to develop "Law & Innovation Research" as an interdisciplinary field of legal scholarship reached its first peak in the late 1990s and 2000s through the initiation of Wolfgang Hoffmann-Riem at the Centre for Research in Law and Innovation at the University of Hamburg.[5] However, the issue of promoting innovation through regulation has not lost its significance since then. On the contrary. In view of the challenges posed by the irreversibility of biodiversity loss and climate change, it is more urgent than ever. With regard to climate change, this is also due to the specific temporal dimension of climate protection as a task of sustainability transformation[6]: If average global warming is to be limited to "well below 2 °C above pre-industrial levels" in accordance with the temperature target of the Paris Agreement on Climate Change,[7] a comprehensive transformation of the entire human way of life and economy towards greenhouse gas neutrality is imperative by the middle of this century.[8] Given this short timeframe, the transformation to greenhouse gas neutrality would not be possible in time without major technological and social innovations, even if current political ambitions were much higher. The Paris Agreement therefore clearly states: "Accelerating, encouraging and enabling innovation is critical for an effective, long-term global response to

[3] Cf. for instance Ashford and Hall (2011); Leach et al. (2012); Eifert (2016, pp. 371–387); recently on the importance for legally induced public welfare orientation of innovations in the sustainability context Markus (2023, pp. 183 f).

[4] See only the contributions in Weber and Hemmelskamp (2005), Lehmann-Waffenschmidt (2007), Hemmelskamp et al. (2007), Jänicke and Lindeman (2010, pp. 127–141); as well as the more recent contributions in Boons and McMeekin (2019).

[5] See the contributions in Schulte (1997), Hoffmann-Riem and Schneider (1998), Eifert and Hoffmann-Riem (2002), Eifert and Hoffmann-Riem (2009a), Eifert and Hoffmann-Riem (2009b). Consolidating the findings Hoffmann-Riem (2017), §§ 16, 25–27. See also Appel, in this volume, see subsection 1.2.3.

[6] On the temporal dimension of the problem Eifert et von Landenberg-Roberg (2023, p. 10).

[7] Art. 2 I (a) Paris Agreement; for a substantiv analysis see Thorgeirsson (2017, p. 127), Bodansky (2016, pp. 288–319).

[8] Cf. IPCC, sixth Assessment Report, Climate Change 2022: Mitigation of Climate Change, Summary for Policymakers, C.1-C.3.

climate change and the promoting economic growth and sustainable development".[9] In its Communication "The European Green Deal", the European Commission also underlines the particular importance of fostering innovation to achieve sustainability and climate neutrality.[10]

Accordingly, the promotion and dissemination of innovation is one of the principle tasks of climate change law.[11]Against this background, climate change law is a particularly good reference area of law to illustrate how legal regulation can direct and promote sustainable innovation and what challenges regulators may face in this regard. This paper therefore develops the topic of legal drivers for sustainable innovation in four steps: First, based on the findings of interdisciplinary innovation research, the fundamental challenges for the promotion of innovation through legal regulation are identified. Since the notion of the "surprisingly new" is a central component of the concept of innovation,[12] it is not surprising that dealing with knowledge deficits on several levels is a central challenge[13] (2).

Based on this, the second step will be to show how climate protection law as a reference area responds to these challenges by providing normative target orientation for the innovation process and implementing corresponding incentive structures. To this end, the central function of target programming trough climate change laws at the policy planning level is first elaborated, followed by an examination of selected innovation-promoting regulatory strategies at the policy implementation level. The analysis reveals that climate change law makes exemplary use of the entire range of innovation-promoting regulatory tools: from classical "command and control"-regulation and the use of competition and innovative network structures to financial incentive mechanisms and subsidies (3).

In a third step, it is explained how climate protection law, in reaction to recognised deficits in regulatory knowledge, is designed as "adaptive law" or "law capable of learning".[14] The performance of climate protection law is permanently assessed trough procedures of self-monitoring and evaluation, also with regard to its innovation-promoting performance. In this way, innovation-enhancing regulation is applied recursively to create increasingly better innovation-enhancing legal incentive structures over time (4). Since innovations do not necessarily lead to a complete and timely phase-out of greenhouse gas-emitting technologies and behavioral patterns

[9] Art. 10 para. 5 sentence 1 Paris Agreement.

[10] European Commission, The European Green Deal, COM/2019/640 final, p. 4, 22.

[11] Cf. van Fleet (2008, pp. 1–16), Franzius (2015 pp. 180 f.), von Landenberg-Roberg (2022, pp. 281 f.), Ginzky and Ruppel (2022, p. 450).

[12] Cf. Schulz-Schaeffer (2020, p. 26).

[13] Cf. Eifert (2016, p. 375 f.), Rodi (2009, pp. 154 f).

[14] For the "basic philosophy" of "regular review, continuous learning and constant improvement" in Climate Change Law, cf. the German Climate Protection Plan 2050, BT-Drucks. 18/10370, pp. 2, 5, 13, 55. More generally on the need for a "law capable of learning" in administrative law as a consequence of the knowledge of knowledge deficits see Franzius (2022), § 4 para. 90–94, Appel (2004, p. 329); for the European level see Eifert (2008, p. 159).

from social practice, climate protection law, as a transformational law, pays particular attention to the necessary processes of exnovation.[15] Therefore, at the end of the article, the intersection between innovation-promoting and exnovation-forcing regulation in the process of sustainable transformation will be outlined in brief (5).

2 Innovations as the Object of Legal Incentive Regulation

Regulation that promotes innovation presupposes an understanding of the underlying structure of the innovation processes. The concept of innovation itself is as multifaceted as it is complex.[16] Just as there is no uniform innovation research or even interdisciplinary innovation theory, there is also no standardised concept of innovation. How one defines the concept of innovation depends as always on the function intended by it and in particular on the disciplinary perspective. The innovation concepts of technical, economic or social science innovation research are therefore neither inter- nor intradisciplinary necessarily identical.[17] And yet they have common elements that can be drawn upon from a regulatory perspective: Innovations are characterised by a *novelty* that is perceived as *significant* by a social practice to solve a specific problem. It is therefore integrated into this social practice and spreads therein.[18]

2.1 Innovation as a Complex Social Process

With regard to sustainability-relevant innovations, three aspects of the concept are of central importance: First, from a transformation-oriented regulatory perspective, the concept of innovation encompasses not only technological or product innovations, but also social innovations.[19] These include, for example, new forms of processes, organisation or cooperation, as well as new business models and patterns of behaviour. Second, not everything that is new, not every invention, is always an innovation. The novelty must also be judged as something significantly new, as something new

---

[15] On the concept of "exnovation" in sustainability studies, which focuses on the preconditions for the termination of non-sustainable practices, technologies, infrastructures, etc., see only Heyen et al. (2017, pp. 326–331), David (2017, pp. 138–146), Rosenbloom and Rinscheid (2020). On the task of transformative environmental law to focus not only on the promotion of innovation logics, but also on the "exnovation of non-sustainable economic practices", recently also Ginzky and Ruppel (2022, p. 450).

[16] See on the different dimensions of the concept of innovation Hauschildt (1998, pp. 29 f).

[17] Cf. Edwards-Schachter (2018), Linton (2009), Rammert (2020).

[18] See also with slight variations Hauschildt (1998, p. 29 f.), Hoffmann-Riem (2006, p. 255).

[19] On the importance of social innovations for more sustainable development already World Commission on Environment and Development, Our Common Future, 1987, para. 27 ff.; von Hauff and Jörg (2010, pp. 192 f.); On the history of the term Howald and Schwarz (2020, p. 247).

with social relevance, and therefore able to achieve social acceptance and diffusion.[20] This points to the third aspect: innovations are not events but processes.[21] For analytical purposes, these innovation processes can be divided into different phases, following Schumpeter's theory of innovation.[22] The following distinctions are commonly made: The phase of invention, in which the new (e.g. a scientific discovery or a technological invention) is created; the phase of implementation or innovation in the narrower sense, in which the new is prepared for social practice and transferred to it (e.g. through the first market launch of a new product or the first application of a new process); and finally the phase of diffusion, in which the new is established and disseminated within the social practice of at least one social subsystem and is thus recognised as *significantly* new. However, social science research on technology has shown that actual innovation processes do not always follow these phases in a linear fashion, but are characterised by a variety of recursive shifts and discontinuities.[23] For the question of how to approach innovation-promoting regulation, the phase model therefore retains a heuristic value, but the law must take into account a much more complex structure of empirical innovation processes.[24]

2.2 Knowledge Deficits and Subsystem Rationalities as Challenges

The complexity of the innovation process from a social point of view is also illustrated by corresponding theoretical reconstructions from the perspective of the sociology of knowledge: they sensitise us to the very different forms of knowledge that intertwine and influence each other within an innovation process.[25] For a successful innovation process, it is not only the primary invention knowledge that is central to the creation of the innovation. Equally important are emergent forms of knowledge, which are only generated during the innovation process itself, as well as innovation and implementation knowledge, which is crucial for the implementation and widespread recognition of the novelty as an innovation.[26] The innovation process is socially complex because these different forms of knowledge have to interact in an evolutionary innovation process. In a functionally differentiated society, however, they are usually not concentrated but socially distributed among different groups of

[20] For detailed account see Howaldt et al. (2020, p. 103).

[21] On the process character of innovations only Schulz-Schaeffer (2020, pp. 29 f).

[22] Schumpeter (1939). On Schumpeter's theory of innovation Blättel-Mink (2020).

[23] Cf. only Grupp (1997), Kowol and Krohn (2000, p. 135), Grupp et Breitschopf (2006, p. 169).

[24] Likewise, Eifert (2009, p. 18).

[25] Particularly instructive in this regard Boas (2009, pp. 28–30) as well as Braunisch and Knoblauch (2020).

[26] Boas (2009, p. 30).

actors and social subsystems.[27] Moreover, each functional system decides for itself according to which criteria it recognises and accepts novelties as innovative.[28] An innovation in the scientific system does not necessarily have to be recognised as an innovation in the economic system, and vice versa.

2.3 *Setting Normative Targets and Implementing Incentive Structures as Solution*

Regulation enables social innovation processes primarily by ensuring the individual and collective exercise of freedom and by providing the necessary legal infrastructure.[29] However, if legal regulation wants to go beyond this and not only enable innovation processes, but specifically promote them with the goal of fostering sustainability, it is confronted with two central challenges in view of the complexity of the societal "innovation systems"[30] just described:

The first challenge lies in the structural knowledge deficits of government regulators.[31] On the one hand, there is a lack of knowledge about which concrete innovative knowledge is ultimately decisive for the success of an innovation process with regard to the interests of invention, innovation and implementation from the point of view of the actors involved in the societal innovation process. Secondly, there are deficits with regard to the regulatory knowledge itself, i.e. the instruments and policy combinations with which legal regulation can effectively promote and steer innovation processes in the respective societal context.

The second challenge lies in the inherent logic of the social subsystems which legal regulation must take into account. If the law directs the innovation processes in the various social subsystems by means of "command and control" regulation or economic incentives, it must be mindful of the path dependencies that may arise in the individual subsystems as a result. Particularly in the case of technological development paths, this can lead in extreme cases to "lock-in" effects, which prematurely exclude alternatives and perhaps more promising innovation potential.[32]

Innovation-promoting regulation reacts to the described knowledge deficit and the functional inherent logics of the subsystems by not even attempting to interfere with the innovation process itself. Instead, it directs the innovation activity of the functional systems towards politically determined goals by normatively orienting the

---

27 Pyka (2020, pp. 85 f.), Boas (2009, p. 30). More generally on the problem of a lack of regulatory knowledge on the part of the state, see Cancik, in this volume, see sect. 5.

28 Schulz-Schaeffer (2020, pp. 31 f.), Hauschildt (1998, pp. 30 f., 37 f.); with specia regard to to the social subsystem of science Luhmann (1990, pp. 216–224).

29 Eifert (2009, pp. 12 f.) discusses this "basic layer" of innovation-promoting law in detail.

30 See Lundvall (2010), Nelson (1993), Rakas and Hain (2019).

31 Cf. Augsberg (2014, pp. 237 ff.); with specific reference to innovation regulation Boas (2009, pp. 33 f.); Hoffmann-Riem (2017, pp. 191 f).

32 On this problem Foxon (2014, pp. 304–316), Cecere et al. (2014).

innovation space towards goals and targets. This form of normative target programming goes hand in hand with the implementation of a corresponding incentive structures and instruments of context control.[33] The attempt to instrumentalise economic competition as a "discovery process"[34] and innovation mechanism can be observed as a basic feature of most innovation-oriented regulatory approaches.[35]

3 Legal Drivers for Innovation: Examples from Climate Change Law

Climate protection law is particularly suitable as a reference area for innovation-promoting regulation. It provides an example of both: Normative target programming of the societal innovation space (I.) as well as different strategies for promoting innovation at the level of implementing measures of climate policy (II.).

3.1 Setting Legal Targets for Greenhouse Gas Neutrality and Indicating the Pressure to Innovate Through Sector-Specific Transformation Pathways

Target setting framework legislation on climate protection, such as the German Federal Climate Change Act (*Bundes-Klimaschutzgesetz*, KSG), plays a central role also in the promotion of innovation.[36] By aligning national climate policy with the temperature target of the Paris Agreement (Sect. 1 para. 2 KSG) and setting specific national climate targets (Sect. 3 KSG), the legislator has transformed the requirement to achieve climate neutrality by 2045 from a mere imperative of climate policy into a legally binding statutory target. Together with the statutory reduction targets for 2030 and 2040 (Sect. 3 para. 1 KSG) and the annual reduction targets until 2040 in Annexes 2 and 3, this results in a projected transformation path for Germany. This transformation path has the task of structuring the individual climate policy implementation measures in terms of their overall level of reduction and thus indirectly steering the future emissions behavior of the different sectors of society.

However, in its original version, the legal target programming of the Federal Climate Protection Act did not stop at this general level. It also divided the total annual

---

[33] On the innovation-oriented pursuit of public purposes in final-determined innovation spaces as a starting point for innovation-promoting regulation Eifert (2009, p. 15 et seq).

[34] Locus calssicus von Hayek (1969).

[35] Eifert (2009, pp. 15 f.).

[36] On the function and significance of the Federal Climate Protection Act in general only Saurer (2022), § 10; with regard to the consequences for the climate protection laws of the Länder Köck et Kohlrausch (2021, pp. 612 f.) Specifically on the importance of targets see Hilson (2020), Franzius, in this volume, section 3; and Reese, in this volume, section 4.

emissions by 2030 into sectoral budgets.[37] It is precisely this sectoral breaking down of the transformation paths into sector-specific annual emission budgets that sends out two decisive "scarcity signals" to the sectors: One with regard to the remaining emission quantities and one with regard to the remaining emission time. Both scarcity signals are vital for the triggering of innovation processes in the individual sectors. For the emitters in the respective sectors not only know the extent of their current emissions, but they generally also know which reduction or substitution potentials can already be realised technologically or socially. Based on this knowledge, they can then use the annual budgets to calculate not only the transformation time available to the sector, but also the sector-specific innovation pressure. This legally generated innovation pressure results from the interaction of the current emission level, the reduction potentials that can already be realised, and the allocated annual emission budgets. The projection of the future sectoral transformation path, which is carried out with the annual budgets, therefore already sends out innovation incentives, as they also represent the benchmark for the design of the specific emission reduction instruments at policy level.

It was precisely this innovation incentive function of the sector-specific transformation path that prompted the German Federal Constitutional Court in its "Climate Decision"[38] to oblige the legislator to update the sector-specific transformation paths in due time in advance. Because the transformation process is so complex and depends on innovation, a long-term orientation regarding emission budgets for different sectors and industries is crucial. Only such a long-term orientation would allow for anticipation of future impacts, provide a basis for specific expectations and trigger investment and innovation in response to climate change. Therefore, The German Federal Constitutional Court has called for such a long-term orientation as a guideline and incentive for timely planning and innovation.[39] It demanded emission budgets, or at least the criteria for future emissions budgets, to be set by the legislature and continuously developed through 2030. It is clear from these innovation-related passages of the Climate Decision that the dimension of promoting innovation is not purely external to climate change law as transformation law, but is to a certain extent constitutionally inscribed in it.

---

[37] Wickel (2021, p. 335), Frenz (2022, § 4 para. 18–31). In the most recent amendment to the Act, however, the sector targets were downgraded to a sole control parameter for monitoring purposes. This has significantly weakened the governance structure of KSG.

[38] Federal Constitutional Court, Order of the First Senate of 24 March 2021—1 BvR 2656/18. A translation in English is available at http://www.bverfg.de/e/rs20210324_1bvr265618en.html. For an in-depth analysis of the Courts reasoning see Eifert et von Landenberg-Roberg (2023).

[39] Federal Constitutional Court, Order of the First Senate of 24 March 2021—1 BvR 2656/18, para. 252–254. Cf. Markus, in this volume, subsection 4.4.

3.2 Elements of Innovation-Promoting Regulation at the Level of Policy Implementing Climate Law

However, the projected sectoral transformation paths will only achieve their full innovation-promoting stimulating effect if they are translated into concrete emission reduction measures at the implementation level. It is only at the implementation level that the private sector becomes the addressee of emission reduction targets, be it through inclusion in an emissions trading system or, for example, by being addressed with "command and control" regulation.[40] It is only at the implementation level that the sectoral transformation burdens are distributed in a binding manner in the intra-sectoral context.[41] In very simplified terms, for example, a look at the Building Energy Act (Gebäudeenergiegesetz) shows at what point in time which type of building stock has to make which legally binding contribution to reducing emissions. Transformation burdens and pressure to innovate can and will therefore be distributed very differently within the sectors. It is therefore only at the level of policy instruments that innovation-promoting regulatory elements can directly target the relevant innovation areas and specific social innovation systems with the necessary degree of precision.

If climate change law at this level is examined for innovation-promoting regulatory elements, the range is as broad as the range of climate change law instruments themselves. It ranges from command-and-control regulation to the creation of markets and financial support schemes.[42]

3.2.1 Innovation Through Command-and-Control Regulation: Stimulating Innovation in Energy Efficiency Law through Dynamic Standard Setting

From the very beginning, energy efficiency law has been one of the main pillars of climate change law.[43] It is also particularly interesting from the perspective of innovation-promoting regulation because it is at the same time a reference area for target-based dynamic regulation.[44] Due to its objective of using energy as efficiently as possible, which is structured as an optimisation principle, it has an inherent dynamic impulse. In addition, the targets set by climate change law also provide energy efficiency law with an external dynamisation impulse.[45] Energy efficiency

---

40 On the lack of direct obligations of citizens and companies through the KSG Kment (2020, p. 1543), von Weschpfennig (2022, para. 32).

41 Cf. Franzius, in this volume, subsection 2.3.

42 For further instruments of innovation promotion in Climate Law apart from the following see Schneider (2002, p. 264); Franzius (2015), Rodi (2009).

43 Cf. Jordan and Rayner (2010, p. 54), Reimer (2009, p. 147).

44 Insightful on this Britz et al. (2010, pp. 66 f).

45 Britz et al. (2010, pp. 79 f).

law is therefore conceptually oriented towards ambitious energy efficiency targets[46] that are not tied to the limits of what is currently feasible, but also assume the innovative development of additional efficiency potentials in the future.[47] From a regulatory perspective, this makes it necessary to resort to forms of dynamic regulation that aim at a continuous tightening of normative energy efficiency standards which can be used to promote corresponding innovation processes.

However, in-depth studies on the innovation potential of dynamic regulatory technologies have shown that the mere reference to the respective best available techniques ("Stand der Technik") as a minimum efficiency requirement does not necessarily lead to innovation-promoting effects. If, as in the case of the regulation of industrial plants, the regular integration of technology development and plant operation means that there is no sufficient incentive structure to disclose innovations to the regulatory authorities or to other competitors, innovation-promoting effects are unlikely to occur.[48] Whether the promotion of an independent market for energy efficiency services can remedy the resulting knowledge deficit is controversial. On the other hand, dynamic technology standards in product regulation can provide better incentives for innovation if they are combined with consumer-oriented information labelling systems and ensure optimal visibility of the most energy-efficient products ("frontrunners").[49]

Technology forcing through standard-setting can also be seen as a regulatory technique that not only promotes innovation, but actually requires it. In this case, product standards are set for a future date that cannot be met by employing currently existing technology.[50] However, this approach also presupposes a sufficient degree of regulatory knowledge about a realistic innovation potential in order to avoid under- or over-regulation, and it also depends on demanding procedural safeguards in case the expected innovation progress does not materialise.[51]

Empirical evidence of an example of successful innovation promotion through energy standards can be found in an instructive study by *de Fries* and *Verhagen* for the building sector in the Netherlands.[52] The study found that mandatory standards not only increase the amount of innovation carried out in the building industry and improve energy efficiency, but also trigger different types of innovations: While

[46] The European Energy Efficiency Directive (Directive (EU) 2023/1791 of the European Parliament and of the Council of 13 September 2023) in its currently applicable version sets only a EU wide collective energy efficiency target in form of a reduction of energy consumption of at least 11,7% in 2030 compared to the projections of the 2020 EU Reference Scenario (Art. 4 para.1). Each Member State shall set an indicative national energy efficiency contribution based on final energy consumption accordingly (Art. 4 para. 2).

[47] Britz et al. (2010, p. 80).

[48] Cf. Diehl (2014); instructive on the problems of promoting innovation through "best availabe techniques"-standards from an economic perspective Gawel (2009, pp. 200 f).

[49] Diehl (2014, pp. 635, 639 f).

[50] For a discussion of the question why under a regime of direct regulation technology-forcing performance standards have hardly been applied see Nentjes et al. (2007).

[51] On this with an original regulatory proposal Diehl (2014, pp. 520, 591).

[52] de Vries and Verhagen (2016).

innovators in the sector prefer incremental innovations that can be easily integrated into existing building construction, more stringent requirements require systemic innovations, which means changing processes and organisations. The study found that ambitious performance standards can also have an impact on the organisation of an entire sector. They can force integration and the tightening of couplings between firms in order to achieve systemic innovation.[53]

With regard to the general question of the legal stimulation of innovation, it can be learned from energy efficiency law that innovation-promoting regulation is indeed possible by means of direct regulatory standard setting. However, due to the asymmetrical distribution of knowledge between the regulated and the regulator, it is also very conditional in its successful implementation.

3.2.2 Innovation Through Economic Incentives: Emissions Trading Schemes

At first glance, emissions trading appears to be a simpler instrument. Alongside the promotion of energy efficiency and the expansion of renewable energies, emissions trading is the third central pillar of European climate change policy.[54] In Germany, emissions trading has recently been extended by the introduction of an independent "upstream" emissions trading system for the building and transport sectors (Brennstoffemissionshandelsgesetz, BEHG)..[55] For the time being, it will be used alongside the European emissions trading scheme implemented by the Greenhouse Gas Emissions Trading Act (Treibhausgas-Emissionshandelsgesetz, TEHG). In emissions trading systems, the main incentive for innovation is achieved by putting a price on greenhouse gas emissions. In addition to the basic principle of cost minimisation, the setting of a carbon price is expected to create dynamic und continuous incentives for the development and diffusion of low-carbon technologies.[56] Compared to other pricing instruments, such as the CO_2 tax, emissions trading is characterised by a precise control effect on total emissions.[57] Through the conceptually central "cap", total emissions for the covered sectors can be precisely determined and reduced over time in accordance with predefined transformation paths. In addition to the price signal, the transparent predictability of the future emissions structure also promotes innovation. A third innovation factor of emissions trading systems is that the revenues generated by the auctioning of allowances can in turn be used to promote financial innovation. For example, the European emissions trading system has created an "innovation fund", which is fed by auction revenues and

[53] de Vries and Verhagen (2016, p. 67).

[54] Cf. van Asselt (2010), Kreuter-Kirchhof (2019, pp. 398 f).

[55] Cf. Vollmer (2022, § 16 Rn. 46), Ernst (2022, § 1 para. 4 f).

[56] Cf. Fischer (2005), Jaffe et al. (2002, pp. 55 f).

[57] On the relative advantages and disadvantages of emissions trading systems Stavins (2022); Ernst (2022), § 1 para. 24 f.

supports climate-friendly innovations in the energy sector and industry through calls for proposals worth billions of euros.[58]

At second glance, emissions trading is also much more complicated. The price-induced incentive to innovate depends to a large extent on the respective certificate price, and this can only have a steering effect if the overall budget and the certificate allocation process are designed appropriately.[59] The history of the European emissions trading system (EU ETS) to date provides ample evidence of how diverse the challenges are and how laborious the regulatory path of trial and error has been.[60] As far as the promotion of innovation is concerned, the history of the European emission trading scheme shows in particular that the successes in promoting innovation in sectors not covered by emissions trading must be taken into account when setting the cap and taken into account by means of a cap adjustment that is as dynamic as possible. Among other things, it was the inadequately considered success in promoting the expansion of renewable energies that contributed to a structurally oversized budget and thus to the price decline in the early trading periods. With emissions trading, too, everything depends on the specific design, which is highly context-dependent and complex.[61]

The empirical findings on the innovation impact of emissions trading schemes reflect this complexity. While some studies suggest that, at least in the first trading periods, the insufficient price signal and lack of predictability led to only limited innovation effects through European emissions trading,[62] later studies indicate significant increases in innovation. For example, *Calel* und *Dechezleprêtre* found in their 2016 study that despite the still limited price signals, the EU ETS increased low-carbon innovation among regulated firms by up to 10% without crowding out patenting of other technologies.[63] At the same time, the study found evidence that the EU ETS has not influenced patenting beyond the group of regulated companies. Their results imply that the EU ETS accounts for nearly a 1% increase in European low-carbon patenting compared to a counterfactual scenario.[64] Corresponding innovation-promoting effects have also been observed with regard to regional emissions trading systems. In a study on the California Emissions Trading Scheme, a significant increase in the number of environmentally friendly patents registered was also observed for the period 2011–2015.[65]

[58] Cf. Art. 10a para. 8 of EU Directive 2003/87/EC; Skjærseth et Eikeland (2023, pp. 266 f).

[59] Rodi (2009, pp. 163 f).

[60] Cf. Flachsland et al. (2020, pp. 134 f.), Gawel (2016, pp. 351–357).

[61] On the importance of design and context factors see also Rogge et al. (2011, p. 521).

[62] Cf. Rogge et al. (2011, pp. 513–523).

[63] Calel and Dechezleprêtre (2016).

[64] Calel and Dechezleprêtre (2016, p. 173).

[65] da Cruz (2022).

3.2.3 Innovation Through Innovative Network Structures: Regulatory Sandboxes

As a final example, the promotion of innovative network structures through the provision of resources and tailor-made legal frameworks will be discussed. Network structures are considered to have particular potential for innovation processes due to their inherent flexibility, the reduction of uncertainty they bring about and the facilitation of learning.[66] The state can promote them in form through the provision of financial resources and influence their innovation-promoting design through funding guidelines.[67]

In Germany, the "Energy Transition Regulatory Sandboxes" (*Reallabore der Energiewende*)[68] established under the seventh Energy Research Programme are a particularly interesting form of sustainable network promotion. These involve the state funding of collaborative projects in which innovative technologies and integrated energy concepts can be tested under real conditions and in systemic interaction in temporally and spatially limited experimental areas.[69] The aim is to further develop innovative technologies and concepts for the transformation of the energy system close to the market and to test the social consequences of the innovations in reality. To the extent that the regulatory sandboxes create space for participation, they can also contribute to strengthening the social acceptance of the innovations tested there. An example from Germany is the regulatory sandbox "IW3—Integrierte WärmeWende Wilhelmsburg"[70] in Hamburg. This regulatory sandbox aims to show how a reliable and affordable heat supply based on renewable energies can be achieved by efficiently combining heat, electricity and mobility. To this end, a geothermal plant will extract geothermal energy from a depth of around 3500 metres and feed it into a local heating network. During the summer months, the excess heat will be stored in a water-conducting rock near the surface. A cross-system technology platform will then combine heat, power and mobility in the neighbourhood via a virtual power plant for an intelligent, efficient and renewable energy supply.

Regulatory sandboxes can also be developed into testing grounds for innovative regulations by using so-called "experimentation clauses".[71] Experimentation clauses make it possible to temporarily suspend generally applicable regulatory requirements within a limited experimental space. The deliberately created regulatory vacuum can then be used for evidence-based testing and, if necessary, further development of the legal framework in line with requirements. Because of their far-reaching effects,

---

[66] Cf. contributions in Pyka and Scharnhorst (2009), furthermore Tranos (2019).

[67] For a detailed analysis Eifert (2002, pp. 94–97).

[68] See https://www.energieforschung.de/en/home/current-research-topics/living-labs-of-the-energy-transition (last accessed 1.8.2025).

[69] For more details concerning the designing of regulatory sandboxes Federal Ministry for Economic Affairs and Climate Action, Making space for innovation: The handbook for regulatory sandboxes, 2019.

[70] About the project: https://www.iw3-hamburg.de (last accessed 1.8.2025).

[71] On "experimentation clauses" see Bauknecht et al. (2021), Philipsen et al. (2021), Antoni et Schäfer-Stradowsky (2022, § 26 para. 86), Fietze (2022).

however, "experimental clauses" must be provided for by the respective standard-setters themselves.

4 Sustainability Law as "Learning Law": Establishing Self-Referential Evaluation Processes to Improve the Promotion of Innovation

Climate law as a law of sustainability transformation is also paradigmatic with regard to the procedural self-optimisation of innovation-promoting incentive structures. The German Climate Protection Plan 2050 (*Klimaschutzplan 2050*), as Germany's long-term strategy under the Paris Agreement,[72] was already explicitly conceived as a "process" that "takes account of new findings and developments" and follows the "basic philosophy of regular review, continuous learning and constant improvement".[73] With the Federal Climate Change Act, the procedures for climate policy planning, self-monitoring and evaluation have now also been legally anchored and structured at the federal level.[74] The "Climate Protection Program" (*Klimaschutzprogramm*), which must be adopted at the latest after each update of the "Climate Protection Plan", is the central link between the national climate protection targets and the specified sectoral annual emission levels as well as the concrete climate protection measures to be adopted at the implementation level.[75] In addition to the sectoral specification of concrete measures, it also ensures the cross-sectoral coordination of the various reduction instruments and policy measures. In the current Climate Protection Program 2030, measures to promote innovation play a central role alongside direct reduction measures as a "core element" of an "effective and credible climate policy".[76] According to Article 10 (1) of the Climate Protection Act, the status of their implementation is to be evaluated and reported to the German Bundestag every year as part of the preparation of the Climate Protection Report. In this context, it makes sense to evaluate not only the extent to which the climate protection measures envisaged in the plan have been implemented, but also the experience gained with regard to the effectiveness of individual measures to promote innovation. This can then be used as a starting point for a corresponding update or revision of the climate protection program.

---

[72] Cf. Art. 4 para. 19 Paris Agreement.

[73] Klimaschutzplan 2050, BT-Drucks. 18/10370, p. 2.

[74] For more details on the statutory anchoring of climate protection planning, see Guckelberger (2022, § 9 para. 3–7), Saurer (2022, § 10 para. 20–26); on the self-reflexivity brought about by the evaluation obligations, see Franzius (2021, p. 137).

[75] On the legal nature and binding effect of climate protection programmes Schlacke (2020, p. 341). More generellay on planning as a key-element of sustainable development regulation Reese, in this volume, section 3; Durner, in this volume, section 1.

[76] Cf. under Point 3.5.3 of Klimaschutzprogramm 2030, BT-Drucks. 19/13900, p. 116.

With regard to innovation in the energy sector, which is central to successful transformation, this self-reflective evaluation structure, which already exists at national level, is further strengthened at European level. In their "Integrated National Energy and Climate Plans" (INEK plans), which are to be drawn up on the basis of the European Governance Regulation (GovernanceVO)[77] and submitted to the Commission, the member states must, among other things, also explain their objectives, targets and contributions to the "research, innovation and competitiveness" dimension.[78] According to Art. 17 and Art. 25 of the Governance Regulation, progress reports must be submitted every two years on the state of implementation and the progress made. The information generated in this way can be used not only by the Commission in its assessment of progress under Art. 29 of the Governance Regulation, but also provide Member States with an opportunity to critically evaluate and readjust their incentive regulation and support measures for promotion innovation.

5 Sustainable Innovation Through "Exnovation"-Regulation

Inventions of sustainable technologies and social practices are a necessary building block for a successful transformation to a sustainable society. However, they do not always ensure the timely adoption and complete elimination of non-sustainable technologies and behaviours in societal subsystems. Not least, experience in the field of energy system transformation has shown that innovative progress in the field of renewable energies alone does not automatically lead to a corresponding reduction in fossil energy production.[79] A whole range of factors can lead to serious lock-in effects: For example, the sunk costs associated with the current system, the accumulation of experience with carbon technologies und institutions or entrenched interests related to long-standing development trajectories.[80] In social science research on sustainability and transformation, the term "exnovation" therefore draws attention to the processes, actors and structures that are relevant for the targeted elimination or reduction of non-sustainable practices, technologies, infrastructures, and so on.[81]

Climate change law aims at the timely phase-out of greenhouse gas emitting technologies and social practices. On an abstract level, climate protection law as a whole can therefore be understood as a paradigmatic form of exnovation regulation. With its transition from a mere reduction law to a transformation law aiming at complete greenhouse gas neutrality, climate change law is conceptually designed for

[77] Cf. Art. 3 of Regulation (EU) 2018/1999 of the European Parliament and of the Council of 11.12.2018 on the Governance of the Energy Union and Climate Action.

[78] Art. 4 d) of Regulation (EU) 2018/1999.

[79] Cf. David (2018, pp. 520 f).

[80] Rosenbloom and Rinscheid (2020, p. 2).

[81] See Heyen et al. (2017, p. 326); as well as the contributions in Arnold et al. (2015).

the *complete* substitution of greenhouse gas-emitting processes.[82] With its binding targets and the climate protection laws as coordinating framework instruments, climate change law is therefore an illustrative example of regulatory "exnovation governance"[83] par excellence, even if a corresponding instrumental implementation of the transformation path has not yet taken place to a sufficient extent in all sectors. Climate protection law makes use of almost all available regulatory techniques to force substitution processes in the individual sectors: These range from the setting of regulatory standards (e.g. in the field of energy efficiency, where the "phase-out" of the classic incandescent light bulb is one of the prime examples of a politically intended process of ex-novation[84]) to the adaptation of subsidy law to economic incentive regulation through price instruments such as emissions trading. In climate protection law, innovation-promoting and ex-novation-promoting regulation are often only two sides of the same coin, two perspective-dependent facets of the same instrument.

While at the abstract instrumental level only limited insights can be expected from the social science perspective on ex-novation that go beyond the interdisciplinary body of knowledge already integrated into the administrative law perspective on regulation,[85] the situation is different at the concrete instrumental level and for specific problem areas in the individual sectors. Here, the concept of ex-novation and related social science structural analyses, if sufficiently detailed, can sensitise regulators to the subject-specific path dependencies and actor structures that need to be taken into account in regulatory ex-novation strategies.[86] From an ex-novation perspective, the time dimension and socio-economic compensation instruments come into view as central variables of regulatory design with which existing resistance can be overcome and the necessary public acceptance can be generated. The discussion on the appropriate design of the phase-out of coal-fired power generation and the solution found there by way of the so-called "coal compromise" (which includes: gradual reduction phases with recourse to the tendering model, determination of the complete phase-out by 2038 at the latest, provision of compensatory financial support to strengthen the infrastructure in the former coal regions) exemplifies how informative structural analyses from the perspective of sustainability science can be for the regulatory design of concrete processes of ex-novation.[87]

---

[82] For further details on this development of climate change law von Landenberg-Roberg (2022).

[83] See David (2014), Heyen et al. (2017, p. 326).

[84] Cf. Stegmaier et al. (2014, pp. 116–119).

[85] See on the governance approach in administrativ law only Voßkuhle (2022), § 1 para. 19 f., 53 f.

[86] On different types of path dependencies Clausen and Fichter (2016, pp. 8–31).

[87] See Heyen (2016) with further references. On the legal challenges of the coal phase-out Franzius (2018).

6 Conclusion

In conclusion, law can direct innovation towards sustainability goals such as climate neutrality and stimulate innovation through legal incentives. The promotion of innovation is itself normatively inscribed in climate change law. Climate change law thus offers numerous examples of how innovation-promoting regulation can contribute to the transformation towards sustainability. However, it has also become clear that, due to the complex social structure of innovation processes and the resulting knowledge deficits, innovation-promoting regulation is an undertaking that is as fraught with preconditions as it is in need of constant optimisation. Against this background, climate protection law and its innovation-promoting regulatory structures are best conceived as adaptive law or law capable of lerning, and the innovation-promoting approaches are best constantly evaluated and optimised. Innovation-promoting regulation in climate change law must therefore also be applied to the development of the law itself, in order to produce increasingly better innovation-promoting regulatory structures over time. Climate change law as a law of sustainability transformation is thus not only innovation-promoting law, but also innovative law.

References

Antoni J, Schäfer-Stradowsky S (2022) Post-EEG—zukunftsfähiger Rechtsrahmen für erneuerbare Energien. In: Rodi M (ed) Handbuch Klimaschutzrecht. C.H. Beck, München

Appel I (2004) Methodik des Umgangs mit Ungewissheit. In: Schmidt-Aßmann E, Hoffmann-Riem W (eds) Methoden der Verwaltungsrechtswissenschaft. Nomos, Baden-Baden, pp 329–360

Arnold A, David M, Hanke G, Sonnberger M (eds) (2015) Innovation-Exnovation. Über Prozesse des Abschaffens und Erneuerns in der Nachhaltigkeitstransformation. Metropolis-Verlag, Marburg

Ashford N, Hall R (2011) The importance of regulation-induced innovation for sustainable development. Sustainability 3(1):270–292. https://doi.org/10.3390/su3010270

Ashford N, Ayers C, Stone RF (1985) Using regulation to change the market for innovation. Harvard Environmental Law Rev 9:419–466

Augsberg I (2014) Informationsverwaltungsrecht. Mohr Siebeck, Tübingen

Bauknecht D, Heyen D, Gailhofer D, Bizer K, Feser D, Führ M, Winkler-Portmann S, Bischoff T, Proeger T (2021) How to design and evaluate a regulatory experiment?, Project Paper, March 2021

Blättel-Mink B (2020) Das Innovationsverständnis von Joseph A. Schumpeter. In: Bättel-Mink B et al (eds) Handbuch Innovationsforschung. Springer, Berlin, pp 63–82

Boas A (2009) Innovationsregulierung als Wissensregulierung. In: Eifert M, Hoffmann-Riem W (eds) Innovationsfördernde Regulierung. Duncker& Humblot, Berlin, pp 23–43

Bodansky D (2016) The Paris climate change agreement: a new Hope? AJIL 110:288–319

Boons F, McMeekin A (eds) (2019) Handbook of sustainable innovation. Edward Elgar Publishing, London

Borsatto J, Bazani C (2021) Green innovation and environmental regulations: a systematic review of international academic works. ESPR 28:63751–63768

Braunisch L, Knoblauch H (2020) Wissenssoziologische Ansätze der Innovationsforschung. In: Bättel-Mink B et al (eds) Handbuch Innovationsforschung. Springer, Berlin, pp 335–346

Britz G, Eifert M, Reimer F (2010) Charakteristika des Energieeffizienzrechts. In: Britz G, Eifert M, Reimer F (eds) Energieeffizienzrecht. Nomos, Baden-Baden, pp 63–107
Bruce La Pierre D (1976/1977) Technology-forcing and federal environmental protection statutes. Lowa Law Rev 62:771–838
Calel R, Dechezleprêtre A (2016) Environmental policy and directed technological change: evidence from the European carbon market. Rev Econ Stat 98:173–191. https://doi.org/10.1162/REST_a_00470
Cecere G et al (2014) Lock-in and path dependence: an evolutionary approach to eco-innovations. J Evol Econ 24:1037–1065
Clausen J, Fichter K (2016, April) Pfadabhängigkeiten und evolutorische ökonomik, inputpapier im rahmen des projekts evolution2Green—transformationspfade zu einer green economy
da Cruz V (2022) Cap-and-innovate: evidence of regulation-induced innovation in California. Economic working paper series, No. 22/377. ETH Zurich, Zurich
David M (2014) Exnovations-Governance im Nachhaltigkeitskontext, Regierungsforschung.de, 18th November 2014
David M (2017) Moving beyond the heuristic of creative destruction: targeting exnovation with policy mixes for energy transition. Energy Res Soc Sci 33:138–146
David M (2018) Exnovation as a necessary factor in successful energy transitions. In: Davidson D, Gross M (eds) The Oxford handbook of energy and society. OUP, Oxford, pp 519–537. https://doi.org/10.1093/oxfordhb/9780190633851.013.31
de Vries H, Verhagen W (2016) Impact of changes in regulatory performance standards on innovation. Technovation 48(49):58–86
Diehl A (2014) Innovationsfördernde dynamische Regulierung. Nomos, Baden-Baden
Edwards-Schachter M (2018) The nature and variety of innovation. Int J Innov Stud 2(2):65–79
Eifert M (2002) Innovation in und durch Netzwerkorganisation. In: Eifert M, Hoffmann-Riem W (eds) Innovation und rechtliche Regulierung. Nomos, Baden-Baden, pp 88–133
Eifert M (2008) Europäischer Verwaltungsverbund als Lernverbund. In: Spiecker genannt Döhmann I, Collin P (eds) Generierung und Transfer staatlichen Wissens im System des Verwaltungsrechts. Mohr Siebeck, Tübingen
Eifert M (2009) Innovationsfördernde Regulierung. In: Eifert M, Hoffmann-Riem W (eds) Innovationsfördernde Regulierung. Duncker & Humblot, Berlin, pp 11–18
Eifert M (2016) Nachhaltigkeit durch Innovation und Wissensgenerierung. In: Kahl W (ed) Nachhaltigkeit durch Innovation und Verfahren. Mohr Siebeck, Tübingen, pp 371–387
Eifert M, Hoffmann-Riem W (eds) (2002) Innovation und rechtliche Regulierung. Nomos, Baden-Baden
Eifert M, Hoffmann-Riem W (eds) (2009a) Innovationsfördernde Regulierung. Duncker & Humblot, Berlin
Eifert M, Hoffmann-Riem W (eds) (2009b) Innovationsverantwortung. Duncker & Humblot, Berlin
Eifert M, von Landenberg-Roberg M (2023) Climate change challenges constitutional law. In: Bäumler J et al (eds) EYIEL 2022, pp 3–33
Ernst C (2022) Kommentierzug zu § 1 BEHG. In: Fellenberg F, Guckelberger A (eds) Klimaschutzrecht. C.H.Beck, München
Fietze D (2022) Experimentierklauseln für die Energiewende. Nomos, Baden-Baden
Fischer C (2005) Technical innovation and design choices for emissions trading and other climate policies. In: Hansjürgens B (ed) Emissions trading for climate policy—US and European perspectives. CUP, Cambridge, pp 37–52. https://doi.org/10.1017/CBO9780511493485.004
Flachsland C et al (2020) How to avoid history repeating itself: the case for an EU emission trading system (EU ETS) price floor revisited. Clim Pol 20(1):133–143. https://doi.org/10.1080/14693062.2019.1682494
Foxon T (2014) Technological Lock-in and the Role of Innovation. In: Handbook of Sustainable Development. Edward Elgar, Cheltenham, pp. 304–316
Franzius C (2015) Regulierung und Innovation im Mehrebenensystem. Die Verwaltung 48(2):175–201

Franzius C (2018) Rechtsprobleme des Kohleausstiegs. NVwZ 37(21):1585–1591
Franzius C (2021) Ziele des Klimaschutzrechts. ZUR 32(3):131–140
Franzius C (2022) § 4 Modalitäten und Wirkungsfaktoren der Steuerung durch Recht. In: Voßkuhle A et al. (eds.) Grundlagen des Verwaltungsrechts, 3rd edn. C.H.Beck, München
Frenz W (ed) (2022) Klimaschutzrecht, 2nd edn. Erich Schmidt Verlag, Berlin
Gawel E (2009) Technologieförderung durch "Stand der Technik". In: Eifert M, Hoffmann-Riem W (eds) Innovationsfördernde Regulierung. Duncker & Humblot, Berlin, pp 197–220
Gawel E (2016) Der EU-Emissionshandel vor der vierten Handelsperiode. EnWZ 5(8):351–357
Ginzky H, Ruppel O (2022) Experimentierfreude, Innovation und Nachsteuerung durch "transformatives" Recht? ZUR 33(9):449–450
Grupp H (1997) Measuring and explaining technical change. Springer, Berlin
Grupp H, Breitschopf B (2006) Innovationskultur in Deutschland. In: Weingart N, Taubert N (eds) Das Wissensministerium. Velbrück Wissenschaft, pp 169–197
Guckelberger A (2022) Kommentierung zu § 9 KSG. In: Fellenberg F, Guckelberger A (eds) Klimaschutzrecht. C.H.Beck, München
Hauschildt J (1998) Facetten des Innovationsbegriffs. In: Hoffmann-Riemn W, Schneider JP (eds) Rechtswissenschaftliche Innovationsforschung. Nomos, Baden-Baden, pp 29–39
Hemmelskamp J et al (2007) Innovation-oriented Envionmental regulation. Theoretical approaches and empirical analysis. Springer, Berlin
Heyen D et al (2017) Out of the comfort zone! Governing the Exnovation of unsustainable technologies and practices. Gaia 26(4):326–331
Heyen DA (2016) Exnovation: herausforderungen und politische gestaltungsansätze, für den ausstieg aus nicht-nachhaltigen strukturen, öko-Institut working paper 3/2016
Hilson C (2020) Hitting the target? Analysing the use of targets in climate law. J Environ Law 32:195–220
Hoffmann-Riem W (2006) Innovationsoffenheit und Innovationsverantwortung durch Recht: Aufgaben rechtswissenschaftlicher Innovationsforschung. Archiv des öffentlichen Rechts 131(2):255–277
Hoffmann-Riem W (2017) Innovation und Recht–Recht und Innovation. Mohr Siebeck, Tübingen
Hoffmann-Riem W, Schneider J-P (eds) (1998) Rechtswissenschaftliche Innovationsforschung: Grundlagen, Forschungsansätze. Gegenstandsbereiche, Nomos, Baden-Baden
Howald J, Schwarz M (2020) Soziale Innovationen. In: Blättel-Mink B et al (eds) Handbuch Innovationsforschung. Springer, Berlin, pp 247–262
Howaldt J et al (2020) Diffusion von Innovation. In: Bättel-Mink B et al (eds) Handbuch Innovationsforschung. Springer, Berlin, pp 103–119
Jaffe A et al (2002) Environmental policy and technological change. Environ Resour Econ 22:41–70
Jänicke M, Lindeman S (2010) Governing environmental innovations. Environ Polit 19(1):127–141
Jordan A, Rayner T (2010) The evolution of climate policy in the European Union. In: Jorden A et al (eds) Climate change policy in the European Union. CUP, Cambridge, pp 52–80
Kment M (2020) Klimaschutzziele und Jahresemissionsmengen. NVwZ 39(21):1537–1544
Köck W, Kohlrausch L (2021) Klimaschutzgesetzgebung im Bundesstaat–Zur Zukunft der Landesklimaschutzgesetze. ZUR 32(11):610–617
Kowol U, Krohn W (2000) Innovation und Vernetzung: Die Konzeption der Innovationsnetzwerke. In: Weyer J (ed) Soziale Netzwerke, 2000. De Gruyter, Oldenburg, pp 135–160
Kreuter-Kirchhof C (2019) Emissionshandel und Erneuerbare Energien Richtlinie. ZUR 30(7–8):396–404
Leach M et al (2012) Transforming innovation for sustainability. Ecol Soc 17(2):11
Lehmann-Waffenschmidt M (ed) (2007) Innovations towards sustainability. Springer, Berlin
Linton J (2009) De-babelizing the language of innovation. Technovation 29(11):729–737
Luhmann N (1990) Die Wissenschaft der Gesellschaft. Frankfurt a.M, Suhrkamp
Lundvall B-A (ed) (2010) National Systems of innovation: toward a theory of innovation and interactive learning. Anthem Press, London
Magat W (1979) The effects of environmental regulation on innovation. Law Contemp Probl 43:4–25

Markus T (2023) Gemeinwohlorientierte Innovation als Rechtsprinzip? In: Köck W et al (eds) Zukunftsfähiges Umweltrecht I. Nomos, pp 181–184. https://doi.org/10.5771/9783748941521-181

Nelson R (ed) (1993) National Innovation Systems. OUP, Oxford

Nentjes A et al (2007) Technology-forcing through environmental regulation. Eur J Polit Econ 23(4):903–916

Palmer K, Oates WE, Portney PR (1995) Tightening environmental standards: the benefit-cost or the no-cost paradigm? J Econ Perspect 9(4):119–132

Philipsen S et al (2021) Legal enclaves as a test environment for innovative products. Regul & GovAnce 15(4):1128–1143

Porter M, van der Linde C (1995) Toward a new conception of the environment-competitiveness relationship. J Econ Perspect 9(4):97–118

Pyka A (2020) Evolutorische Innovationsökonomik. In: Bättel-Mink B et al (eds) Handbuch Innovationsforschung. Springer, Berlin, pp 83–101

Pyka A, Scharnhorst A (eds) (2009) Innovation networks: new approaches in modelling and analyzing. Springer, Berlin

Rakas M, Hain D (2019) The state of innovation system research: what happens beneath the surface? Res Policy 48:103787

Rammert W (2020) Entwicklungslinien der Technik- und Innovationsforschung. In: Blättel-Mink B et al (eds) Handbuch Innovationsforschung. Springer, Berlin, pp 43–60

Reimer F (2009) Ansätze zur Erhöhung der Energieeffizienz im Europarecht. In: Schultze-Fielitz H, Müller T (eds) Europäisches Klimaschutzrecht. Nomos, Baden-Baden, pp 147–184

Rodi M (2009) Innovationsförderung durch ökonomische Instrumente der Umweltpolitik. In: Eifert M, Hoffmann-Riem W (eds) Innovationsfördernde Regulierung. Ducker & Humblot, Berlin

Rogge K et al (2011) The innovation impact of the EU emission trading system. Ecol Econ 70(3):513–523

Rosenbloom D, Rinscheid A (2020) Deliberate decline: an emerging frontier for the study and practice of decarbonization. WIREs Clim Chang 11(6):e669. https://doi.org/10.1002/wcc.669

Saurer J (2022) Das Bundes-Klimaschutzgesetz. In: Rodi M (ed) Handbuch Klimaschutzrecht. C.H.Beck, München

Schlacke S (2020) Bundesklimaschutzgesetz: Klimaschutzziele und -pläne als Herausforderung des Verwaltungsrechts. EurUP 18(3):338–345

Schneider JP (2002) Klimaschutzorientierte Innovationssteuerung am Beispiel der Kraft-Wärme-Kopplung. In: Eifert M, Hoffmann-Riem W (eds) Innovation und rechtliche Regulierung. Nomos, Baden-Baden, pp 264–289

Schulte M (ed) (1997) Technische Innovation und Recht. CF Müller, Heidelberg

Schulz-Schaeffer I (2020) Innovation im Verhältnis zu Neuheit und Wandel. In: Blättel-Mink B et al (eds) Handbuch Innovationsforschung. Springer, Berlin

Schumpeter J (1939) Business cycles: a theoretical, historical, and statistical analysis of the capitalist process. McGraw-Hill Book, New York

Skjærseth J, Eikeland P (2023) Governing EU low-carbon innovation: from strategic energy technology plan to European green Deal. In: Rayner T et al (eds) Handbook on European Union climate change policy and politics. Edward Elgar Publihing, London, pp 259–273. https://doi.org/10.4337/9781789906981.00031

Stavins R (2022) The relative merits of carbon pricing instruments: taxes versus trading. Rev Environ Econ Policy 16(1):62–82

Stegmaier P et al (2014) The discontinuation of socio-technical systems as a governance problem. In: Borrás S, Edler J (eds) The governance of socio-technical systems. Edgar Elgar Publishing, London, pp 111–131. https://doi.org/10.4337/9781784710194.00015

Stewart R (1981) Regulation, innovation, and administrative law: a conceptual framework. Calif Law Rev 69(5):1259–1377

Thorgeirsson H (2017) Objective (article 2.1). In: Klein D et al (eds) The Paris agreement on climate change. OUP, Oxford

Tranos E (2019) Networks in the innovation process. In: Fischer M, Nijkamp P (eds) Handbook of regional science. Springer, Berlin, pp 853–868
van Asselt H (2010) Emission trading: the enthusiastic adoption of an "alien" instrument? In: Jorden A et al (eds) Climate change policy in the European Union. CUP, Cambridge, pp 125–144
van Fleet D (2008) Legal approaches to promote technological solutions to climate change. Duke Law & Technol Rev 7(1):1–16
Voßkuhle A (2022), § 1 Neue Verwaltungsrechtswissenschaft. In: Voßkuhle A et al. (eds.) Grundlagen des Verwaltungsrechts, 3rd edn. C.H.Beck, München
Vollmer M (2022) BEHG/Nationales Brennstoffemissionshandelssystem. In: Rodi M (ed) Handbuch Klimaschutzrecht. C.H.Beck, München
von Hauff M, Jörg A (2010) Innovationen im Kontext der Nachhaltigkeit. In: Hagemann H, von Hauff J (eds) Nachhaltige Entwicklung: Das neue Paradigma in der Ökonomie. Metropolis-Verlag, Marburg, pp 185–212
von Hayek FA (1969) Der Wettbewerb als Entdeckungsverfahren. In: von Hayek FA (ed) Freiburger Studien. Mohr Siebeck, Tübingen
von Landenberg-Roberg M (2022) Verantwortungsstrukturierung durch Emissionsbudgets. Die Verwaltung 55(2):249–286
von Weschpfennig A (2022) Kommentierung zu § 3 KSG. In: Fellenberg F, Guckelberger A (eds) Klimaschutzrecht. C.H. Beck, München
Weber M, Hemmelskamp J (eds) (2005) Towards environmental innovation systems. Springer, Berlin
Westergaard Clausen L et al (2023) How environmental regulation can drive innovation: lessons learned from a systematic review. Environ Policy GovAnce 33(4):364–373
Wickel M (2021) Das Bundes-Klimaschutzgesetz und seine rechtlichen Auswirkungen. ZUR 32(6):332–339

A New Area of Environmental Planning (Law) for Transformation

Planning Law as an Instrument for Ecological Transformation

Wolfgang Durner

Abstract For a society to achieve ecological transformation necessarily requires some degree of planning and coordination. From an instrumental perspective, therefore, planning is an indispensable element of sustainable development regulation. Over the past two decades, planning law has become an important tool for the European legislator in order to accomplish certain environmental goals. Originally developed as an instrument of international environmental regimes, this approach has shown considerable success under sectoral legislative acts of the EU such as the Water Framework Directive or the Air Quality Directive. As these directives illustrate, legally prescribed environmental planning always involves similar tasks and stages: The planner has to analyse an existing ecological situation, to set realistic goals, to identify ways and opportunities to achieve those goals, to evaluate the effectiveness and feasibility of these measures, to design a legally binding plan of action and eventually to implement the plan. Where implementation fails to show the expected success, the plans must be revised and strengthened and public interest litigation may be encouraged in order to enforce existing plans. Recently, the concept of legally binding action planning has been extended in order to address even more fundamental ecological problems. The German Climate Change Act and the Commission's proposal on a Nature Restoration Law adopt several elements of planning law and seek to influence and to channel environmental policy by means of formal planning. However, planning as a legal instrument has also certain inherent weaknesses: To address environmental problems by providing planning procedures can be a mere formal compromise which postpones substantive decisions. Planning procedures cause considerable bureaucratic costs without guaranteeing a certain outcome. Moreover, in a democracy legal planning cannot circumvent the need to reach political consensus on fundamental ecological policy questions.

W. Durner (✉)
Chair of Public Law, Rheinische Friedrich-Wilhelms-Universität Bonn, Bonn, Germany
e-mail: lehrstuhl.durner@jura.uni-bonn.de

M. Reese et al. (eds.), *Environmental Law in Transformation*,
https://doi.org/10.1007/978-3-032-31567-0_6

1 Planning as a Key-Element of Sustainable Development Regulation

When Joseph interpreted the dream of Pharaoh, he advised him to look for a discerning and wise man in order to take one-fifth of Egypt's harvest during the seven years of abundance. 'The plan seemed good to Pharaoh and to all his officials' and Joseph was put in charge of all Egypt.[1] Even in biblical times, apparently, planning ahead was key in order to cope with ecological crises. A fortiori, societies which seek to achieve even longer-term ecological transformations necessarily need to apply some degree of planning and coordination.[2] In fact, however, almost all countries on earth are facing comprehensive ecological transformations.[3] These require an enormous sequence of adjustments and conversions, such as the construction of new infrastructures, the winding down of old ones or the step by step elimination of sources of pollution. State control is indispensable for the implementation of these processes. To the extent that these transformations can be channelled by law, therefore, planning is an essential tool of sustainable development regulation.[4]

For all these reasons, formalized planning has become a crucial element of EU environmental law.[5] For the past two decades, the European legislator has been increasingly implementing its environmental goals through planning instruments by obliging the member states to draw up so-called action plans. The accumulation of action planning mandates in recent EU law illustrates that this is an overarching form of regulatory engineering. These planning obligations are ultimately intended to accomplish tasks prescribed by European law or to achieve environmental standards, for example in the fight against particulate matter or flood risks. Air quality planning may be the most practically significant use case of the instrument at present.

2 Action Planning in International Environmental Law

Certain origins of this regulation strategy can be found in international law.[6] Principle 2 of the 1972 Stockholm Declaration calls on states to safeguard the natural resources of the earth 'through careful planning or management'.[7] Various international treaties

---

[1] Genesis 41.

[2] Cf. Markus, in this volume, subsection 4.3.3.

[3] See e.g. the various contributions in Reder et al. (2015).

[4] Daniels (2017, p. xxxvii-xxxv), Whitehead (2019).

[5] Durner and Ludwig (2008, pp. 457–462), Gärditz (2009, pp. 40–47), Knappe (2022, pp. 15–67).

[6] On the role of International Law as a Model for the instrument of action planning in European Union Law see Knappe (2022, pp. 42–46).

[7] Declaration of the United Nations Conference on the Human Environment (1972), 11 ILM 416 (1972).

follow this path and commit their contracting parties to develop plans or programmes in order to achieve internationally agreed targets[8]:

The 1997 United Nations Convention on the Law of the Non-Navigational Uses of International Watercourses for instance, the only universally accepted treaty governing freshwater resources, calls for the coordinated management of an international watercourse and defines the concept of management as 'planning the sustainable development of an international watercourse and providing for the implementation of any plans adopted'.[9] This approach is reflected in many regional watercourse conventions. The 1999 Convention on the Protection of the Rhine authorizes the Commission to make proposals for 'programmes of measures', which have to be implemented by the Contracting Parties once they are adopted.[10]

The Parties to the 1992 Convention on Biological Diversity are required 'to develop national strategies, plans or programmes for the conservation and sustainable use of biological diversity' and 'to rehabilitate and restore degraded ecosystems and promote the recovery of threatened species, inter alia, through the development and implementation of plans or other management strategies.'[11]

In the field of climate law, the UN Framework Convention on Climate Change of 1992 obliges its Parties to take precautionary measures to prevent, mitigate or minimize climate change.[12] In order to achieve this goal, they must develop 'policies and measures' which shall comprehensively cover all major sources, sinks and reservoirs of greenhouse gases; these obligations are subject to detailed reporting. Unlike the expired Kyoto Protocol of 1997,[13] the Paris Agreement of 2015 is based on a similar approach. Its article 4 para 2 provides that each Party shall 'prepare, communicate and maintain successive nationally determined contributions that it intends to achieve'.[14] The agreement relies on the national climate plans submitted individually with corresponding national reduction commitments, which are to be reviewed and successively increased in the negotiations with regard to the common global

---

[8] For further examples beyond those mentioned in the subsequent text cf. Sands and Peel (2018, pp. 269, 274, 279, 582, 584, 767).

[9] United Nations Convention on the Law of the Non-Navigational Uses of International Watercourses, 36 ILM 720 (1997), Article 24. Tanzi et al. (2015, p. 120) stress the non-mandatory nature of this instrument.

[10] Convention on the Protection of the Rhine (1999), OJ L 289, 31.10.2013, pp. 31–37, Article 8 para 1 lit. b.

[11] Convention on Biological Diversity (1992), 31 ILM 818 (1992), Article 6 and Article 8 lit. f. According to Sands and Peel (2018, p. 390) 189 parties to the Convention had adopted their national actions plans and bio-diversity strategies by 2017.

[12] Framework Convention on Climate Change, 31 ILM 849 (1992), Article 3 para 3.

[13] Kyoto Protocol to the United Nations Framework Convention on Climate Change, 37 ILM 22 (1998). The Protocol's cornerstone was the establishment of individual quantified emission limitation and reduction commitments for certain developed State Parties. This approach was completely abandoned by the Paris Agreement which is in essence a sort of second Protocol to the Framework Convention. For a comparison of both instruments cf. Fraser (2019).

[14] Paris Agreement, 55 ILM 740 (2016).

target.[15] Both the Climate Change Convention and the Paris Agreement require their signatory states to achieve climate targets through programs which the states have to develop themselves, i.e., ultimately through action plans.

These origins amply illustrate that the instrument is in essence the manifestation of a legislative process aimed at achieving compromises.[16] It is precisely for this reason that this regulatory technique has also become a model for the European Union.[17]

3 Action Planning in EU Environmental Law

Originally developed as an instrument of international environmental regimes, action planning has become a regulatory key strategy of the EU under various sectoral legislative acts. Even older legal acts of the Union, such as the Directive on Environmental Impact Assessment 85/337/EEC, already had the character of a 'planning tool'.[18] However, this approach was greatly intensified after the turn of the century. For two decades now, the European legislator has been increasingly realizing its environmental goals through planning instruments by obliging the member states to draw up so-called action plans.[19] The corresponding obligations to draw up plans are ultimately intended to accomplish tasks prescribed by European law or to achieve environmental standards, for example in the fight against particulate matter or flood risks. Central examples are the program of measures according to the EU Water Framework Directive 2000/60/EC[20] and the Marine Strategy Framework Directive 2008/56/EC,[21] the Air Quality Directive 2008/50/EC,[22] the Environmental Noise Directive 2002/49/EC[23] and the Floods Directive 2007/60/EC.[24]

---

[15] Cf. Sands and Peel (2018, pp. 690–692 and 933). The extent to which substantive legal content is associated with these procedural obligations is subject to controversial legal discussion, cf. Bodansky (2016, pp. 144–150), Lavanya (2016).

[16] This is shown particularly clearly by the example of the climate regime in the contribution of Odell (2021).

[17] Knappe (2022, pp. 50–51).

[18] Craik (2008, p. 5 and 33).

[19] Knappe (2022, pp. 3–7).

[20] Directive 2000/60/EC of the European Parliament and of the Council of 23 October 2000 establishing a framework for Community action in the field of water policy, OJ L 327, p. 1, 22.12.2000.

[21] Directive 2008/56/EC of the European Parliament and of the Council of 17 June 2008 establishing a framework for community action in the field of marine environmental policy (Marine Strategy Framework Directive), OJ L 164, p. 19, 25.6.2008.

[22] Directive 2008/50/EC of the European Parliament and of the Council of 21 May 2008 on ambient air quality and cleaner air for Europe, OJ L 152, p. 1, 11.6.2008.

[23] Directive 2002/49/EC of the European Parliament and of the Council of 25 June 2002 relating to the assessment and management of environmental noise, OJ L 189, p. 12, 18.7.2002.

[24] Directive 2007/60/EC of the European Parliament and of the Council of 23 October 2007 on the assessment and management of flood risks, OJ L 288, p. 27, 6.11.2007.

The original flagship of this model is the European Water Framework Directive 2000/60/EC. It aims to achieve a sustainable quality and quantity-based management of surface waters and groundwater throughout the Union. According to the central target, a 'good water status' must be achieved for all water bodies, which comprises the subcomponents of a good chemical and a good ecological status.[25] The directive leaves the path to this good water status to a certain extent to member state implementation. However, it instrumentally follows the model of action planning and requires that the member states develop both the objectives and the necessary measures in formalized planning procedures in which deficits of the water bodies are systematically identified, objectives are fixed in 'river basin management plans', corresponding solutions are developed in 'programmes of measures' and these plans are then finally implemented.[26] Ultimately, an individual goal must be planned and implemented for each water body.

Another example for this technique is provided by the Directive on Ambient Air Quality 2008/50/EC.[27] This so called 'Air Quality Framework Directive' and some additional daughter directives set limit values and critical levels for key pollutants in the air. Where these objectives are not met, member states must act in order to comply with these standards. 'Air quality plans' have to be developed for zones and agglomerations where concentrations of pollutants in ambient air exceed the relevant air quality targets. Moreover, specific short term 'action plans' must be drawn up indicating the immediate measures to be taken where there is a risk of an exceedance of 'alert thresholds' in order to reduce that risk and to limit its duration.[28]

Dozens of other legislative acts have followed these examples: The European Environmental Noise Directive 2002/49/EC provides for a comprehensive noise mapping and subsequently for drawing up noise action plans 'with a view to preventing and reducing environmental noise where necessary'.[29] The Floods Directive 2007/60/EC requires member states to elaborate 'flood risk maps' and 'flood risk management plans'.[30] Directive 2008/98/EC on Waste contains obligations for the member states to draw up 'waste management plans' and 'waste prevention programmes'.[31] Art. 4 of the Directive (EU) 2019/904 on the Reduction of the Impact of Certain Plastic Products on the Environment supplements these obligations and provides

---

[25] Baranyai (2020, pp. 98–100).

[26] Epiney (2019, pp. 436–466), Langlet and Mahmoudi (2016, pp. 231–232).

[27] Directive 2008/50/EC of the European Parliament and of the Council of 21 May 2008 on ambient air quality and cleaner air for Europe, OJ L 152, p. 1, 11.6.2008.

[28] Cf. Epiney (2019, pp. 482–486), Pedrosa and Vanheusden (2020, pp. 308–310), Langlet and Mahmoudi (2016, pp. 213–215).

[29] See Epiney (2019, pp. 497), Langlet and Mahmoudi (2016, p. 221–222).

[30] Cf. Langlet and Mahmoudi (2016, p. 237).

[31] Directive 2008/98/EC of the European Parliament and of the Council of 19 November 2008 on waste and repealing certain Directives, OJ L 312, p. 3, 22.11.2008, Articles 28 and 29.

that the measures implemented under those plans shall lead 'to a substantial reversal of increasing consumption trends' regarding single-use plastic products.[32]

Whilst these directives show various differences in their structure, terminology and effectiveness, they have striking similarities with respect to the role and the process of planning: The planner always has to analyse an existing ecological situation, to set realistic goals, to identify ways and opportunities to achieve those goals, to evaluate the effectiveness and feasibility of these measures, to design a legally binding plan of action and eventually to implement the plan.[33] Where implementation fails to show the expected success, the plans have to be tightened and public interest litigation may be encouraged in order to enforce existing plans and procedures.

4 Strengths and Problems of Action Planning

The action plan approach combines specific strengths and weaknesses. Its most striking advantage, as stated earlier, is that it simplifies law-making by allowing the legislator to agree on common goals and procedures without deciding on specific measures. It thereby shields state sovereignty and national legal systems from more precise regulatory obligations.[34] Implementing these essentially procedural obligations grants the planning authority maximum flexibility, making it possible to consider local particularities and to make far-reaching policy choices. This allows the member states to integrate the requirements of Union law into their existing national environmental law without fundamental system breaks. State parties and member states have been prepared to accept planning obligations since they leave room for various ways of implementation and prove particularly suitable for dealing with environmental summation effects. Due to its flexibility, action planning has found its way into numerous jurisdictions worldwide.

At the same time, however, action planning has turned out to be a time-consuming process with high bureaucratic costs. The results and the long-term effectiveness of the measures envisaged are often difficult to compare, which hampers supervision of national implementation.

---

[32] Directive (EU) 2019/904 of the European Parliament and of the Council of 5 June 2019 on the reduction of the impact of certain plastic products on the environment, OJ L 155, p. 1, 12.6.2019, Article 4 para 1.

[33] For a more detailed distinction of the various steps in the Environmental Planning Process cf. Daniels (2017, pp. 14–27).

[34] According to Knappe (2022, pp. 51–61), this is only the case at first glance. In his opinion, however, this approach expands the Union's regulatory powers in the long term. For a similar view, cf. Baaner (2011).

5 Legal Classification Issues in Germany

Moreover, at least in Germany, the new concept of action planning has created a bundle of new legal problems and questions, such as the scope and limits of the planning authorities' creative freedom, the delineation of responsibilities between planning and enforcement authorities and, above all, judicial review of the plans: May the planning authority, in order to achieve the specified goals, create obligations for the citizens to an almost unlimited extent like the democratic legislator can?[35] Do statutory-like plan contents have the same effect for the citizens as a substantive law?[36] Must particularly far-reaching planning requirements be established by the legislature itself? What legal protection is available if citizens wish to object to the specifications of the plans or, conversely, consider these specifications to be insufficient in order to achieve the intended ecological goals? Are the courts allowed to review the plans at all? Does this review follow the standards for reviewing legal norms or those for reviewing an executive branch plan?[37]

European Union law has left all these questions to the member states, which must provide answers in the context of their own constitutional systems. At least in Germany, some of these issues remain unresolved to this day, with courts doing their best to sidestep them.

6 Limits of Effectiveness of Action Planning

At the centre of those debates, however, is the limited effectiveness of the instrument. The resilience and feasibility of plans have always been the weak points of any planned state action.[38] The history of mankind is packed with failed plans and failed planned economy states.[39] *Bertold Brecht*, in the lyrics to his 1928 'Threepenny Opera,' even wrote a famous 'Ballad of the inadequacy of human planning' ('*Ballade von der Unzulänglichkeit menschlichen Planens*'):

> 'Aye, make yourself a plan
> They need you at the top!
> Then make yourself a second plan
> Then let the whole thing drop.'[40]

[35] Klement (2024, pp. 216–222).

[36] Durner and Ludwig (2008, pp. 461 and 465).

[37] Knappe (2022, pp. 423–481).

[38] This was one of the central sociological insights of Niklas Luhmann, cf. van Assche and Verschraegen (2008).

[39] This applies to Germany as well, cf. Steiner (2010).

[40] Brecht (1977, p. 64). Brecht himself provided different titles for this song, inter alia ‚Lied von der Unzulänglichkeit menschlichen Strebens.'The most common English translation is „Useless Song".

Some of the weaknesses of any planning also show up with respect to the instrument of action planning. It is always much easier to draw up politically ambitious plans than to implement them. When implementation takes place, however, addressing basic environmental issues with a combination of targets and planning-only procedures often does not provide sufficient guidance to agencies.

Moreover, social resistance usually only arises at this level of implementation. While abstract aim-setting and abstract planning obligations may appear economically and politically neutral, concrete measures fixed in subsequent plans will, at some point, unavoidably burden certain groups of society or sectors of the national economy. Consequently, societies may quite easily agree upon the need to reduce the emissions of greenhouse gases as long as concrete steps are postponed and nobody is burdened by this kind of abstract decision. Nevertheless, an existing consensus on the goals to be achieved doesn't necessarily make it any easier to decide on the measures to be taken. In Germany, in the area of climate protection, this is illustrated by the controversial dispute over heating systems in residential buildings in 2023.[41]

7 Risk of Overstretching the Planning Authorities

To the extent that the choice among these policy options is delegated to a planning authority, its task becomes increasingly political. Frequently, from the perspective of the policy makers, setting targets and providing for subsequent action plans is not just a flexible approach but also an option 'to buy time'. This approach rolls out the crucial decision on the necessary measures to be taken by the administrative planning authorities. More often than not, thus, the use of the action planning instrument indicates unresolved environmental policy decisions. Planning authorities, however, due to their 'inferior role as a part of public administration', are regularly overwhelmed by the task of resolving such fundamental political conflicts.[42] The instrument of action planning thus faces the inherent risk of overburdening the planning authorities.

The proceduralist aim of action planning is to bridge the seemingly insurmountable delta between goals and measures through bureaucratic planning. In some respects, therefore, the use of the instrument of action planning attempts to depoliticize environmental policy issues and to outsource authoritative decision-making to outwardly neutral administrative planning processes. This approach is one of a series of similar policy areas in which Union law has ordered economic transformation processes, especially privatizations of former state industries, to be implemented by independent regulatory agencies.[43] Action planning thus shifts political power

[41] Cf. Best (2023, p. 17).

[42] Kühn (2021, p. 154).

[43] For an analysis of this strategy cf. Rangoni and Thatcher (2023) and Simoncini (2018, pp. 132–176) with the observation at p. 174: '[T]he current regime demonstrates little awareness of the political relevance of the technical tasks exercised by EU agencies'.

from the parliamentary legislature to the planning executive; this raises delicate constitutional questions on the fundamental division of power.[44]

8 The Role of the Judiciary

Administrations are often hardly in a position to make highly political decisions and tend to avoid social conflicts. The first generation of environmental plans, in particular, fell well short of environmental policy expectations in all member states.

The solution of Union law to a considerable degree builds upon the third pillar of the Aarhus Convention.[45] It seeks to make the environmental goals enforceable by private persons and environmental associations, so that the enactment of effective plans can be sought in the courts. Where existing plans are found to be insufficient, this transfers the above-mentioned policy choices from the planning authorities to the courts. In Germany with respect to air pollution by particulate matter and NO_X, this approach led to notable changes in several larger cities as a result of successful spectacular lawsuits filed by the association 'Deutsche Umwelthilfe'.[46]

At least in part, however, certain limits of the courts' enforcement power also became apparent: In one of the most spectacular lawsuits, in 2016, the Bavarian Higher Administrative Court sentenced the State of Bavaria to issue an action plan under the Air Quality Framework Directive that would have closed downtown Munich to older diesel vehicles. The Administrative Court believed that only traffic bans on certain diesel vehicles would enable compliance with the air quality targets set by the EU. According to the Court, the state's planning freedom was therefore limited to taking this particular measure. For several years, the State openly ignored this very unpopular judgement. Eventually, the desperate Bavarian Court asked the Court of Justice of the EU whether it might be possible to place the Bavarian prime minister in preventive detention to enforce the ruling, even without a legal basis to do so; the European Court of Justice eventually ruled in 2019, unsurprisingly, that detention can only be imposed if there is a sufficiently precise legal basis for it in national law.[47] While this preliminary decision was being made, Munich's crucial air quality target was met even without the announced diesel driving ban and has been complied with since then. Overall, this process led to a significant weakening of the judiciary's authority and exemplified the decision-making shifts to the courts that accompany action planning.

---

[44] Cf. Durner and Ludwig (2008, pp. 464–465), Klement (2024, pp. 210–212).

[45] Cf. Jendroska (2005).

[46] Schink and Fellenberg (2018); Pagenkopf (2019).

[47] ECJ, Case C-752/18—Deutsche Umwelthilfe vs. Freistaat Bayern, Judgment of the Court (Grand Chamber) of 19.12.2019, ECLI:EU:C:2019:1114; cf. Misonne (2020).

9 Differing Levels of Success Under Different Action Plan-Directives

Despite the above-mentioned restrictions, in Germany the Air Quality Directive has become a striking example for the idea that courts can enforce binding environmental targets. In fact, at least in Germany, virtually all of the court decisions that called for the inclusion of specific measures into action plans referred to the Air Quality Directive. This directive aims to meet certain air quality limits and thus to achieve a highly specific goal. The potential solutions ultimately remain manageable because they must address a very limited number of emission sources.[48]

The implementation of the EU Water Framework Directive, on the other hand, has been more of a mixed bag.[49] The inclusion of a measure in the action plan presupposes that the planner considers all relevant load paths and adopts a combination of measures that enables an equitable distribution of the burden. As a rule, the existing leeway is so extensive that different lawful solutions are usually conceivable, and a court cannot order a specific plan content. Even at the conceptual level, there are considerable gaps in the understanding of complex causal processes.[50] Consequently, planning duties thus lack the essential quality of typical public law norms: to reduce complexity and to provide clear orientation for state decision-making in overly complex situations.[51] Planning duties rather leave the full complexity to the planning authorities. While the overambitious targets of the Water Framework Directive are still very far from being implemented, the courts have been reluctant to fully enforce the directive. To some extent, this reluctance may be due to the fact that the directive is pretty unrealistic. The ecological objectives in particular, but also some of the 2013 tightened chemical parameters—and thus the achievement of the 'good chemical status'—are objectively not realizable within the deadline of 2027.[52]

Finally, under the Environmental Noise Directive the competent authorities shall draw up action plans for certain polluted areas 'to regulate noise problems and noise

[48] According to Fellenberg (2022, p. 917), in some municipalities the options for action with respect to air pollution by particulate matter and NO_X, had already narrowed to the effect that a route-related traffic ban for diesel vehicles was seen as the only suitable measure for complying with the European limit values. However, even this assessment may provide an oversimplification of the complexity of the causes, cf. de Sadeleer (2020, pp. 394–395).

[49] According to the European Commission's evaluation (Press Release, 12 December 2019) the EU Water Framework Directive proved to be 'fit for purpose'. The assessment of member states' implementation efforts by Maia (2017, p. 3057), on the other hand, concludes that 'although some general improvement occurred along the first cycle of RBMPs, the main objective of the WFD is still quite distant.' For an exemplary view on the rather ambitious implementation in the Netherlands cf. Dieperink et al. (2012).

[50] Maia (2017, p. 3057), points to the fact that 'the relationship between the effect of ecological flow regimes definition on water bodies status is still not clear'.

[51] Cf. Kratochwil (1989, p. 10), observing that the reduction of complexity is an essential function of all legal norms.

[52] Even beyond 2027, Bouleau (2008, p. 235) suggests that the good status 'may include an ecological dream that is difficult to achieve'.

effects.' Ultimately, the directive does not specify a clear objective.[53] This vague material obligation on the one hand, the massive cost of comprehensive noise remediation on the other hand, make the courts rather cautious. Up to now, the Environmental Noise Directive has failed to show any impact in Germany in spite of the fact that noise is a major environmental problem in parts of the country.[54]

10 The German Climate Protection Act

An even more far-reaching and ambitious example of action planning is provided by the German Climate Protection Act which seeks to achieve national climate gas neutrality by 2045 and, following a much-acclaimed ruling of the Federal Constitutional Court of 2021, to reduce emissions by 65 percent of 1990 levels by 2030.[55] The ambitious global target is broken down into individual sectors, including energy, transport and the building sector, which all have to achieve individual targets under individual sectoral timetables. These climate goals are reviewed through continuous monitoring. Where the budgets are not met, the Federal Government is required to adjust its sectoral policies immediately and the existing climate protection programmes must be updated to include certain additional measures.[56]

While the Climate Protection Act explicitly excludes rights of action both by private persons as well as by environmental associations, there are strong legal arguments that some rights of legal action are guaranteed under the Aarhus-Convention[57] and the implementing Aarhus-Directive 2003/35/EC.[58,59] Nevertheless, it is hard to imagine that courts might be in a position to force the governments to adopt plans of a certain content in order to achieve the relevant reduction targets in the transport sector, for example. Basically, this would force the courts to take over the task of the democratic decision maker.

---

53 Therefore, Riedel et al (2022, p. 259) call for the establishment of 'binding standards for noise-related environmental quality'.

54 As the latest report of the Commission, COM(2023)139 - Implementation of the Environmental Noise Directive in accordance with Article 11 of Directive 2002/49/EC, suggests, basically this assessment applies to all EU member states.

55 According to Müller-Brandeck-Bocquet (2022, p. 128), this was 'the world's first law to set binding national climate protection targets'.

56 Kment (2020); Schlacke (2022, pp. 908–910).

57 Convention on Access to Information, Public Participation in Decision-making and Access to Justice in Environmental Matters (Aarhus Convention), OJ L 124, p. 1, 17.5.2005.

58 Directive 2003/35/EC of the European Parliament and of the Council of 26 May 2003 providing for public participation in respect of the drawing up of certain plans and programmes relating to the environment, OJ L 156, p. 17, 25.6.2003.

59 Schlacke (2020, p. 361).

11 The EU Nature Restoration Law

In July 2024 the EU adopted Regulation (EU) 2024/1991 on nature restoration (the 'Nature Restoration Law'). Member States are obliged to restore the relevant terrestrial, coastal and freshwater ecosystems throughout their territory and exclusive economic zones to 'good ecological status' and to restore at least 30% of their habitats by 2030, 60% by 2040 and 90% by 2050. In order to achieve this, they are required to develop 'national restoration plans' under which restoration measures are required until 'good condition' is reached. The plans are subject to specific provisions on public participation, monitoring, evaluation, reporting, and enforcement procedures.[60]

In instrumental terms, the Nature Restoration Law was modelled on the Water Framework Directive again. As to the legal form, however, the regulation creates direct obligations, including through the prohibition of deterioration in Art. 4 para. 11 and 12, the practical effects of which are difficult to predict at present.[61] Furthermore, it de facto excludes the member states' parliaments from any decisive influence on this fundamental transformation. Simultaneously, the Commission submitted similar proposals to reduce the use and risk of chemical pesticides by 50% by 2030.[62]

In the run-up to the enactment of the law, the proposals had been met with some degree of scepticism deriving inter alia from the fact that many of the general conditions that hamper these noble targets are governed by EU policies on traffic, agriculture and chemicals. The proposals thus attempt to bridge significant unresolved policy conflicts at the European level by transferring them to national planning authorities and ultimately to the courts. The implications of this transfer are aggravated by the fact that the directive's overambitious implementation schedule will be difficult to realise.

12 Conclusion

The development of the above-mentioned planning instruments shows an obvious tendency to establish a new form of legally guided 'policy planning' and thus to subjugate environmental policy to internationally agreed environmental targets.[63] At the same time, however, such instruments document the current lack of political consensus to agree on more concrete measures at this stage. Planning as a legislative

---

[60] Regulation (EU) 2024/1991 of the European Parliament and of the Council of 24 June 2024 on nature restoration and amending Regulation (EU) 2022/869, OJ L 1991, 29.7.2024, Chap. 3, Articles 14–19.

[61] Cf. Fellenberg (2025, pp. 126–128), Trouwborst (2025, pp. 374–375).

[62] Proposal for a regulation of the European Parliament and of the Council on the sustainable use of plant protection products and amending Regulation (EU) 2021/2115, COM(2022) 305 final.

[63] Cf. Schlacke (2022, p. 909), Franzius (2023); Franzius, in this volume, subsection 2.1; Reese, in this volume, subsection 2.1.

instrument thus postpones substantial decisions as well as their implementation to the future. The opportunity of this instrument lies in a potential gain in rationality, the danger in planning activism.

The yield of the instrument of action planning depends primarily on how small-scale and precise the goals to be achieved are. There is, so to speak, an inverse proportionality of problem complexity and steering power. Planning can be a good instrument, for example, to reduce the total amount of phosphate inputs into groundwater. Although such a mandate may generate high bureaucratic costs, it can ultimately lead to the identification of appropriate solutions and their implementation in the face of local resistance. With an infinitely more complex problem such as the reduction of greenhouse gases, on the other hand, the performance power of administrative planning will tend to be overstretched. To take the comparison to the extreme: An order to a planning authority to issue action plans in order to achieve 'sustainable development' would entail replacing democratic parliamentary legislation by bureaucratic decision-making.[64] The use of the instrument of action planning, therefore, requires in each case to carefully weigh up the effort and the return. Moreover, legal planning in a democracy cannot circumvent the need to reach political consensus on fundamental environmental policy issues.

References

Baaner L (2011) The Programme of measures of the water framework directive-more than just a formal compliance tool. J Eur Environ & Plan Law 8(1):82–100

Baranyai G (2020) European water law and Hydropolitics. An inquiry into the resilience of Transboundary water governance in the European Union, 1st edn. Springer

Best V (2023) Volkes Herrschaft und Fehlerteufels Beitrag. Zum Zusammenhang von Demokratie und Scheitern. INDES-Zeitschrift für Politik und Gesellschaft 11(2):6–19

Bodansky D (2016) The legal character of the Paris agreement. Rev Eur Community & Int Environ Law 25(2):142–150

Bouleau G (2008) The WFD dreams: between ecology and economics. Water Environ J 22(4):235–240

Brecht B, Manheim R, Willett J (1977) The Threepenny opera in a new translation. Vintage Books, New York

Craik N (2008) The international law of environmental impact assessment. Cambridge University Press

Daniels T (2017) Environmental planning handbook, 2nd edn. Routledge

de Sadeleer N (2020) Light-vehicles emissions standards under EU law in the wake of the 'Dieselgate'. In: Peeters M, Eliantonio M (eds) Research handbook on EU environmental law. Edward Elgar Publishing, pp 379–395

Dieperink C et al (2012) Ecological ambitions and complications in the regional implementation of the water framework directive in The Netherlands. Water Policy 14(1):160–173. https://doi.org/10.2166/wp.2011.223

[64] In principle, however, this vision corresponds at least in part to the ideologically questionable bureaucratic ideal type of administration elaborated by Majone (1996).

Durner W, Ludwig R (2008) Paradigmenwechsel in der europäischen Umweltrechtsetzung? Überlegungen zu Bedeutung und Grundstrukturen des Instruments der Maßnahmenplanung im neueren Umweltrecht der Gemeinschaft. Natur Und Recht (NuR) 30(7):457–467
Epiney A (2019) Umweltrecht der Europäischen Union, 4th edn. Nomos, Baden-Baden
Fellenberg F (2022) Rechtsschutz als Instrument des Klimaschutzes—ein Zwischenstand. NVWZ 41(13):913–920
Fellenberg F (2025) Anwendungsfragen rund um die Europäische Wiederherstellungsverordnung. NVWZ 44(3):124–130
Franzius C (2023) Verfassungsfragen der Planung politischer Transformationsentscheidungen am Beispiel der Klimaschutzplanung. ZUR 34(4):199–204
Fraser T (2019) A comparative architectural analysis of the 1997 Kyoto protocol and the 2015 Paris agreement and other ways to counter environmental ‘ratification fatigue’. In: Popowski V (ed). Routledge, The Implementation of the Paris Agreement on Climate Change, pp 42–56
Gärditz KF (2009) Europäisches Planungsrecht. Grundstrukturen eines Referenzgebiets des europäischen Verwaltungsrechts, Mohr-Siebeck, Tübingen
Jendroska J (2005) Aarhus convention and community law: the interplay. J Eur Environ & Plan Law 2(1):12–21
Klement K (2024) Zeithorizonte von Verwaltung. Krisenmanagement, langfristige Planung und Systemkohärenz. Veröffentlichungen der Vereinigung der Deutschen Staatsrechtslehrer 83:193–250
Kment M (2020) Klimaschutzziele und jahresemissionsmengen–kernelemente des neuen bundes-klimaschutzgesetzes. NVWZ 39(21):1537–1543
Knappe L (2022) Die Maßnahmenplanung im europäisierten Verwaltungsrecht. Carl Heymanns Verlag, Hürth
Kratochwil F (1989) Rules, norms, and decisions on the conditions of practical and legal reasoning in international relations and domestic affairs. Cambridge University Press
Kühn M (2021) Agonistic planning theory revisited: the planner’s role in dealing with conflict. Plan Theory 20(2):143–156
Langlet D, Mahmoudi S (2016) EU environmental law and policy. Oxford University Press
Lavanya R (2016) The 2015 Paris agreement: interplay between hard, soft and non-obligations. J Environ Law 28(2):337–358
Maia R (2017) The WFD implementation in the European member states. Water Resour Manag 31(2010):3043–3060
Majone G (1996) Regulating Europe, 1st edn. Routledge
Misonne D (2020) Arm wrestling around air quality and effective judicial protection. Can arrogant resistance to EU law-related orders put you in jail? J Eur Environ & Plan Law 17(4):409–425
Müller-Brandeck-Bocquet G (2022) Germany and the European Union. How chancellor Angela Merkel shaped Europe, 1st edn. Springer Cham, Switzerland
Odell J (2021) Why did they finally reach agreement? In: Jepsen H et al (eds) Negotiating the Paris agreement. The insider stories. Cambridge University Press, pp 284–313
Pagenkopf M (2019) “Demobilisierung der Städte”–Frage der Grenzen für die Rechtsprechung. NVWZ 38(4):185–194
Pedrosa K, Vanheusden B (2020) EU air pollution law: comprehensive but insufficient. In: Peeters M, Eliantonio M (eds) Research handbook on EU environmental law. Edward Elgar Publishing, pp 296–312
Rangoni B, Thatcher M (2023) National de-delegation in multi-level settings: independent regulatory agencies in Europe. Governance 36(1):81–103
Reder M et al (eds) (2015) Global common good. Intercultural perspectives on a just and ecological transformation. Campus Verlag, Frankfurt, New York
Riedel N, Köckler H, Bolte G (2022) Moving noise action planning towards more environmental health equity. Five Propos Cities & Health 6(2):258–266
Sands P, Peel J (2018) Principles of international environmental law, 4th edn. Cambridge University Press

Schink A, Fellenberg F (2018) Dieselfahrverbote zur Einhaltung der Grenzwerte für NO_2? Neue Juristische Wochenschr (NJW) 71(28):2016–2019
Schlacke S (2020) Klimaschutzrecht im Mehrebenensystem. Zeitschrift für das gesamte Recht der Energiewirtschaft (EnWZ) 9(10):355–363
Schlacke S (2022) Klimaschutzrecht im Mehrebenensystem. NVwZ 41(13):905–912
Simoncini M (2018) Administrative regulation beyond the non-delegation doctrine: a study on EU agencies. Hart Publishing, Oxford
Steiner A (2010) The plans that failed: an economic history of East Germany, 1945–1989. Berghahn Books, New York and Oxford
Tanzi A, Kolliopoulos A, Nikiforova N (2015) Normative features of the UNECE water convention. In: Tanzi A et al (eds) The UNECE convention on the protection and use of Transboundary watercourses and International Lakes. Its Contribution to International Water Cooperation, Brill NV, Leiden, pp 116–129
Trouwborst A (2025) Rewilding and the EU nature restoration law: plotting the course of ecosystem restoration in Europe. J Eur Environ & Plan Law 22(3):364–384
van Assche K, Verschraegen G (2008) The limits of planning: Niklas Luhmann's systems theory and the analysis of planning and planning ambitions. Plan Theory 7(3):263–283. https://doi.org/10.1177/1473095208094824
Whitehead M (2019) Anthropocene: the challenge for environmental planning. In: Davoudi S et al (eds) The Routledge companion to environmental planning. Routledge, pp 73–82

Targets and Measures: How to Build Climate Change Law?

Claudio Franzius

Abstract German climate law has a new layer of planning instruments. This layer is located between rather general goals and quite specific measures which need to be implemented to achieve the goals. The targets of the Federal Climate Protection Act serve as a benchmark for the content of the climate protection programmes. Due to this purpose, the Climate Protection Act will therefore be named "benchmark law". This has implications for project approval, but also raises constitutional issues. The de facto obligation of the legislature to fulfil the target provisions of the Climate Protection Act, which is presented as a simple "super law", does not collide with the democratic principle of the German Basic Law. The famous climate decision of the Federal Constitutional Court is taken up, which shows new ways to better deal with climate change. The judicial enforceability of climate protection programs against the back-drop of EU law is affirmed, and an outlook on the new policy planning law, which is conceptually welcomed here, rounds off the article.

1 Introduction

Climate protection law is organised on several levels—international law, European Union law, national law. It works with targets and measures that do not appear to be sufficient to contain the dangerous consequences of climate change. The diagnosis is not just an ambition gap, but above all an implementation gap.[1] The question is whether the long-term goal of climate neutrality is sufficiently underpinned by measures that not only promise to achieve the goal, but also make it likely.

[1] Cf. Perino et al. (2022, p. 213).

My thanks go to Vincent-Carlos Barduhn (KomUR—Competence Network 'Challenges of Environmental Law') for his support.

C. Franzius (✉)
Chair of Public Law, Administrative Law and Environmental Law, University of Bremen, Bremen, Germany
e-mail: franzius@uni-bremen.de

M. Reese et al. (eds.), *Environmental Law in Transformation*,
https://doi.org/10.1007/978-3-032-31567-0_7

Instead of leaving the target level and focussing solely on the measures, it is important to take a closer look at the interlinking of targets and measures. A new type of policy planning law[2] acts as a hinge for the selection and coordination of measures.[3] This can be observed in the European Union, where the European Climate Law sets the targets and the Governance Regulation introduces new planning instruments, but the concrete measures were only launched with the so-called "Fit for 55" package.[4] The situation is similar in Germany, where the Climate Protection Act formulates the national targets and introduces climate planning in order to coordinate the appropriate policy measures to achieve the targets.

It must not be forgotten that policy planning is not entirely new to the German legal system. The birth of modern environmental law in Germany was marked by the Federal Government's Environmental Programme of 1971, which set out the subsequent legislation for the protection of environmental media. After taking a look at the so-called "emergence of iterative planning processes"[5](2), this paper reconstructs the German Climate Protection Act as a "benchmark law" guiding action (3). Afterwards, the paper examines the evaluation of this control, which cannot be done without referring to the imposing climate decision of the Federal Constitutional Court[6] and finally addresses the enforceability of policy planning (4). The article concludes with an outlook (5).

2 Emergence of Iterative Planning Processes

2.1 Targets

It's no secret that targets alone will not achieve anything. If we were to rely solely on compliance with the temperature limit—limiting global warming to 1.5 degrees Celsius internationally—it would not be a convincing strategy, despite all the arguments in favour of leaving the responsible parties enough freedom to adopt reduction measures at their own will.[7] It is sometimes claimed that setting ambitious reduction targets would politically price in the failure to achieve targets on time and that the unlawful situation in the future would be factored in.[8] Without climate targets, however, implemented measures would lack enough ambition and the necessary

---

[2] In German: "Politikplanungsrecht". This means the law, how the legislator guides the political process to fulfill the objectives.

[3] Lammers (2023, p. 65 et seq).

[4] Cf. Schlacke et al. (2022, pp. 1–13).

[5] Saurer (2023, p. 163).

[6] Order of the First Senate of 24 March 2021—1 BvR 2656/18, http://www.bverfg.de/e/rs20210324_1 bvr265618en.html; see Eifert and von Landenberg-Roberg (2023, pp. 3–33).

[7] On the climate targets see Hilson (2020, p. 195).

[8] Cf. Durner (2021, p. 341).

"planning horizon to promote development" that the Federal Constitutional Court has demanded for the goal of climate neutrality.[9]

2.2 *Measures*

The fact that climate policy targets are legally binding does not change the fact that they are imprecise. If we therefore focus more strongly on the measures, it is clear that these must initiate a transformation process of the economy and society into a climate-neutral world.[10] Neither in theory nor in practice does this work with one measure alone, as is often assumed for European emissions trading. In fact, it is not just a matter of introducing a great number of new measures, but also of refocusing the existing legal instruments onto additional climate protection. In other words, it is no longer just about reducing greenhouse gas emissions, but about transformation in order to achieve the reduction targets. The targets serve in this case as a benchmark. They guide the policy for the measures to be taken, facilitate their justification and serve as a tool to analyse existing inadequacies.[11] Without this benchmark, the measures to be taken would remain piecemeal. Environmental law is open to this kind of "goal-orientation". This also applies to the hinge function of planning in order to make the objectives operationalisable for concrete measures, as European action planning shows.[12]

2.3 *Policy Planning*

There is hardly any other area that is better suited to planning than climate protection, which must be understood from a historical point of view and at different levels. In view of the large number of measures to be taken, harmonisation and coordination is required, which is achieved through overarching planning.[13] Climate law, as a law of transformation and allocation of responsibility,[14] is dependent on planning control, which indicates a change in the forms of action.[15] Even in Union law, a remarkable use of planning instruments can be observed, which is explained by the fact that the European Union assumes the fulfilment of the contractual obligations arising from the Paris Agreement on behalf of the Member States and reports a uniform climate

---

[9] Order of the First Senate of 24 March 2021—1 BvR 2656/18—para 251.

[10] See on transformative climate law Franzius et al. (2025, p. 149).

[11] Cf. Franzius (2022, p. 393 et seq).

[12] Overview: W. Durner, Planning law as an instrument for ecological transformation, in this volume.

[13] See also M. Reese, EU policy planning law for the implementation of the Green Deal, in this volume.

[14] Cf. von Landenberg-Roberg (2022, p. 249).

[15] Saurer (2023, pp. 159–178).

contribution to the Climate Secretariat to replace national climate contributions, which can only be assured if the Union is equipped with suitable possibilities to influence Member States. This has been done with the "European Climate Law"[16] and the Governance Regulation.[17]

The Governance Regulation obliges the Member States to submit "integrated nation-al energy and climate plans" (NECPs) in which they specify measures to fulfil the Union's objectives. The Member States must submit biennial progress reports on the implementation of these plans and the degree to which the targets have been achieved. If the Commission concludes in its assessment that the measures taken are inadequate, it can issue recommendations that must be "duly taken into ac-count". The Member States shall then readjust their plans with the aim of complementing the policies and measures. In this way, iterative planning processes—new under EU law and subject to criticism as "soft" governance[18]—are set in motion, in which the Member States' plans are permanently linked with supranational follow-up mechanisms. Although this may not be considered sufficient, there is much to suggest that the climate plans of Union law aimed at mutual learning not only incorporate structural features of the Open Method of Coordination.[19] It also takes up proceduralisation tendencies that distance themselves to a certain extent from substantive-material steering approaches without losing any of their "toughness".[20] This is not so much due to competence limits[21] as to an adoption of the steering logic of the Paris Agreement[22] and can be understood as a new integration model.[23]

Instead of incorporating these plans into national climate protection law and catalyzing a new planning instrument, the federal German legislator has chosen a special path with the "climate protection programmes" under § 9 KSG,[24] which are not required by either international or Union law. There is no need to criticise

[16] Regulation (EU) 2021/1119 of the European Parliament and of the Council of 30 June 2021 establishing the framework for achieving climate neutrality and amending Regulations (EC) No 401/2009 and (EU) 2018/1999 ('European Climate Law'), OJ L 243, p. 1, 9.7.2021; see Franzius (2024b) Art. 1 EU-KG, in: Hofmann/Heß (Eds.), BeckOK Klimarecht, 2024.

[17] Regulation (EU) 2018/1999 of the European Parliament and of the Council of 11 December 2018 on the Governance of the Energy Union and Climate Action, amending Regulations (EC) No 663/2009 and (EC) No 715/2009 of the European Parliament and of the Council, Directives 94/22/EC, 98/70/EC, 2009/31/EC, 2009/73/EC, 2010/31/EU, 2012/27/EU and 2013/30/EU of the European Parliament and of the Council, Council Directives 2009/119/EC and (EU) 2015/652 and repealing Regulation (EU) No 525/2013 of the European Parliament and of the Council, OJ L 328, p. 1, 21.12.2018; see Knodt et al. (2024). For the whole story M. Reese, EU policy planning law for the implementation of the Green Deal, in this volume.

[18] Schlacke and Knodt (2019, p. 408).

[19] Lammers (2023, p. 448).

[20] Oberthür (2019, p. 24 et seq).

[21] Cf. Franzius (2024a, p. 994 et. seq).

[22] Critically Tomuschat (2019, pp. 579-631).

[23] Chiti (2022, pp. 19–48).

[24] Bundes-Klimaschutzgesetz of 12 December 2019 (BGBl. I p. 2513), which was amended by Article 1 of the Act of 15 July 2024 (BGBl 2024 I No. 235).

this.[25] The Union relies on policy planning by Member States[26] and allows them to go their own way, which does not have to be limited to the implementation of Union law requirements, although better coordination with the European planning regime would be desirable.[27] The German legislator also introduces an intermediate level of planning to link the targets with the measures to be taken in order to make the Federal Government's obligation to comply with the targets operationalisable and to have packages of measures coordinated in planning.[28] When speaking of policy planning in this sense, it should not be overlooked that the federal government, as the addressee of this obligation, can at best be obliged to take legislative initiatives, but for constitutional reasons it is up to the legislator to decide on the corresponding measures. It is important to emphasise this because it is likely to be the legislator who has to decide on and take responsibility for target achievement measures in the climate crisis due to the significant encroachment on the fundamental rights of those affected, but also due to the democratic activation of the legal reservation through the "materiality" of transformational measures. Admittedly, the nudge function of such gubernative policy planning should not be minimised, even if the Federal Government has so far only inadequately fulfilled its legal obligation under § 9 KSG. This raises questions regarding the access to the courts (4).

3 Climate Protection Act as a Benchmark Law

In view of the enormous coordination tasks that are triggered by the reduction and transformation path to climate neutrality, the question arises as to whether the planning instruments of the Climate Protection Act are sufficient to close the gap be-tween ambitious goals and measures that fall short of them. Political doubts are not to be mixed up with deficits in the law itself. An understanding of the Climate Protection Act as a benchmark law could help.

3.1 Article 20a of the Basic Law

The fact that the Climate Protection Act has an orientation function for the measures is as accurate as it is meaningless. The situation is different if the reduction targets are ascribed a benchmark function for the planning described above. This was precisely the legislator's intention when § 9 para. 1 sentence 3 KSG stipulates that compliance with the permissible annual emission quantities specified in § 4 KSG 2021 is

---

[25] Cf. Franzius (2023b, p. 103 et seq).

[26] Lammers (2023, p. 423).

[27] Franzius (2019, p. 436 et seq).

[28] On the innovation-forcing function of legally binding transformation pathways and sectoral emission budgets ("scarcity signals"), see von Landenberg-Roberg in this volume, subsection 3.1.

"decisive" ("maßgeblich") for the measures to be adopted in the climate protection programme.[29] From here, it is not far to the adjective relevant ("maßstäblich"). In this regard, is the Federal Climate Protection Act not merely a framework law, but a benchmark law ("Maßstäbegesetz")?

A benchmark law is a law that provides a benchmark for subsequent legislation. This can be laid down in constitutional law, which raises concerns about the legislator's obligation, as it loses its room for manoeuvre in this respect. However, it can also be understood from an alternative point of view that it is the legislator himself who is bound by the standards. However, this is not a legal obligation, but at best a de facto obligation that exists as long as the law is not called into question politically. And it should therefore be noted that the de facto binding of the legislature to the target provisions of the Climate Protection Act, which is presented as a simple "super law", does not collide with the democratic principle of the German Basic Law.[30]

The concept of a benchmark law is controversial. Introduced by the Federal Constitutional Court for the fiscal equalisation of the federal states[31], binding the legislator deciding on specific allocations to a pre-emptive benchmark law has been criticised. Even at that time, the constitutional viability of the statement that the financial constitution does not contain any directly enforceable standards, but rather obliges the legislature to concretise and supplement the tax distribution and equalisation system, which is only defined in vague legal terms under constitutional law, with standards that are binding on the legislature itself. According to the court, the benchmarks act is designed for long-term validity, which is intended to restore the law to its traditional constitutional function.[32] Although the hoped-for effects did not materialise, the benchmarks act also found advocates in environmental law.[33] Article 20a of the Basic Law obliges the legislator to enact a law on benchmarks that is designed for long-term validity but can be updated in the light of new findings. The precautionary principle should initially be used to formulate environmental goals, which should afterwards be specified by the legislator for the individual protected goods by means of concrete environmental quality and environmental action goals. This argument was taken up by the German Advisory Council on the Environment, which is in favour of such legislative benchmarks.[34] The benchmarks act defines the objectives and requirements to which ecologically sustainable legislation must be orientated.[35]

---

[29] Today, the total annual emission quantities pursuant to § 4 KSG 2024 are decisive. On the amendment of the Climate Protection Act Stäsche (2024, pp. 299-335). Rightly against the unconstitutionality of the reform Faßbender (2024, p. 579 et seq).

[30] Cf. Franzius (2023a, p. 60 et seq).

[31] Order of the Second Senate of 11. November 1999–2 BvF 2/98—BVerfGE 101, 158 (214 et seq).

[32] To the benchmark law von Schweinitz (2003, pp. 95–114).

[33] Cf. Calliess (2001, p. 242).

[34] German Advisory Council of Environment (2019, p. 13).

[35] Calliess (2024, p. 65).

3.2 *Self-Commitment of the Legislator*

Labelling the Climate Protection Act as a benchmark law must not obscure the differences to the constitutional figure of the benchmark law. It is not the constitution that requires such a law. By setting quantified targets, the legislator restricts the freedom of designing other laws. This does not mean that the legislator is bound by constitutional law regarding the adoption of a benchmark law at all. The legislator is not prevented from amending or repealing the Climate Protection Act, provided that the requirements of EU and constitutional law are complied with. It would be a mistake to assume that the Federal Constitutional Court derives an obligation for the legislator to pass climate protection legislation from Article 20a of the Basic Law in its climate decision.[36] On the contrary: The First Senate relies on the Climate Protection Act as a simple law to open up to the global temperature limit and to derive constitutional obligations from Article 20a of the Basic Law. Because the Climate Protection Act could also be laid out differently, the primacy of politics is preserved.

From this point of view, Article 20a of the Basic Law does not impose in any way an obligation on the legislator to create a benchmark law. Rather, Article 20a of the Basic Law is to be understood as a standardised definition of state objectives ("normgeprägte Staatszielbestimmung"). Accordingly, it is the legislator who formulates the standards with the Climate Protection Act and as long as the law exists, it is binding for all parties. There is no normative hierarchical priority over other laws, although it cannot be overlooked that the subsequent legislator of measures is de facto bound by the staggering of objectives, planning processes and measures to be taken. It would be a mistake to assume that the Federal Constitutional Court derives an obligation for the legislator to pass climate protection legislation from Article 20a of the Basic Law. On the contrary: The First Senate relies on the Climate Protection Act as a simple law to open up to the global temperature limit and to derive constitutional obligations from Article 20a of the Basic Law. Because it could also be different, the primacy of politics is preserved. Therefore, the Federal Constitutional Court cannot be accused of overreaching. All that the climate resolution requires is that the legislator must be consistent in its approach. If the legislator commits itself to the goals of the Paris Agreement and sets its own goals, then it must show ways in which these can be achieved.

Even with the discovered "intertemporal dimension of civil liberties", the Federal Constitutional Court did not set the standards, but rather orientated itself on the standards that the legislator set in the Climate Protection Act. This includes the orientation towards the Paris Agreement made clear in § 1 sentence 3 KSG, which is read into Article 20a of the Basic Law in order to not only act as a justification standard for the violations of fundamental rights complained of, but to justify the shift from the duties to protect to the rights to prevent interference.[37] The extent to which the court is orientated towards legislative decisions is also shown by the argumentation with the budget approach, which is neither prescribed by international

[36] Order of the First Senate of 24 March 2021—1 BvR 2656/18–paras 1–270.

[37] Cf. Minnerop (2022, p. 135), Winter (2022, p. 209), critically Kahl (2023), § 19 para 48 et seq.

nor EU law, but is taken up by the legislator in the Climate Protection Act.[38] Summing up, any form of over-constitutionalisation is out of the question.

3.3 Corrections and Their Limits

If the Climate Protection Act is a basic and benchmark law for the measures to be taken, the question arises as to what to make of it. This cannot be analysed in detail here. It is, however, reasonable to see the targets laid down as the substantive benchmark for policy planning. The targets in the form of reduction targets and emissions budgets are translated into political action and measures via the federal government's climate protection programmes, which, with the long-term goal of climate neutrality in 2045, cover a time horizon that extends beyond the legislative period and the term of office of the federal government.[39]

According to the above, however, the legislator is relatively free to decide how to organise this process in detail. The Federal Constitutional Court does indicate that the legislator is not completely free to decide how it controls this process in terms of planning law, even if the policy planning law in question here is not directly required by constitutional law.[40] But the widespread longing in Germany for constitutional guidelines must be resisted. This has consequences: Because national policy planning is an "invention" that is guided by Union law, but is essentially a matter for the national legislator, there are few constitutional limits to its politically motivated modification. Thus, the abandonment of the authoritative nature of sectoral annual emission quantities, non-compliance with which necessitated subsequent control through immediate planning programmes, may weaken the impact of the regulations on climate policy, but is not objectionable under constitutional law and must not obscure the fact that the amendment of the Climate Protection Act strengthens their prospective orientation.[41]

[38] See Buser (2021, p. 1409).

[39] The translation of high-level climate targets into specific spatial and land-use requirements is a key driver of implementation. This process, and the resulting competition for land between energy, biodiversity, and agricultural targets, is examined in detail in Schlacke and Gurreck, in this volume, subsections 3.1-3.4.

[40] Different Lammers (2023, p. 147 et seq).

[41] Critically Wiedmann (2024, p. 876), different Flachsland et al. (2024).

4 Enforceability of Policy Planning

4.1 Requirements

The question remains as to whether the government can be forced to undertake policy planning in court. Climate protection programmes are expressly mentioned in Annex 5 of the german EIA Act[42] under No. 2.13 in the list of plans and programmes subject to SEA. For this reason, the climate protection programmes pursuant to § 9 KSG are among the objects subject to environmental legal remedies pursuant to § 1 para. 1 sentence 1 no. 4 UmwRG[43] and can be challenged in court by environmental associations. Since the unlawful omission of a decision can also be challenged, the failure to update the climate protection programme is also considered actionable. According to the High Administrative Court Berlin-Brandenburg, this also applies to the immediate action programmes under § 8 KSG 2021, which the legislator has not explicitly declared to be subject to SEA.[44] Article 9 para. 3 of the Aarhus Convention and Article 47 CFR require an interpretation of national procedural law in conformity with Union law.[45] If necessary, the provision of national law that contradicts Union law must remain unapplied.

4.2 Jurisdiction

The rule of law binds state authority to law and order, including the federal government which, however, appears to accept failures to fulfil its objectives. This constitutional obligation also includes applying—and not merely taking into account—the case law of the ECJ. According to its more recent case law,[46] the fact that political planning is not subject to SEA should not be a reason to rule out its enforceability by environmental organisations. This is because compliance with all provisions of European environmental law is subject to judicial review. There must be a legal remedy against all actions that may have violated Union environmental law. Because policy planning serves to ensure compliance with the Union's objectives, the delaying of an emergency programme in the transport sector must also be open to legal challenge.[47]

[42] Environmental Impact Assessment Act in the version published on 18 March 2021 (BGBl. I p. 540), last amended by Article 13 of the Act of 8 May 2024 (BGBl. 2024 I No. 151).

[43] Umwelt-Rechtsbehelfsgesetz in the version published on 23 August 2017 (BGBl. I p. 3290), which was last amended by Article 14b of the Act of 22 December 2023 (BGBl. 2023 I No. 405).

[44] Judgment of 30.11.2023, 11 A 27/22, Neue Zeitschrift für Verwaltungsrecht 2024, pp. 598–603.

[45] Cf. Lange (2022, p. 264).

[46] ECJ, judgment of 8.11.2022, Case C-873/19, ECLI:EU:C:2022:857 Vehicle type approval; Federal Administrative Court, judgment of 26.1.2023, 10 CN 1/23 Inntal-Süd, BVerwGE 177, 350.

[47] Lammers (2023, p. 594 et seq).

4.3 Role of the Courts

In contrast, it is often said that the courts are not allowed to take on climate lawsuits without violating the separation of powers. This proposal is inaccurate. If the judiciary is called upon to initiate policy, but not to replace it, an abuse of the third power can hardly be convincingly demonstrated.[48] As long as legal arguments are presented and the court is used as a forum by utilising, but also recognising, its inherent legal nature, there is little to be said against the judiciary dealing with climate complaints within the framework of the possibilities offered by current procedural law. On the contrary, courts provide important impetus for adapting the law to the challenges of climate change.[49]

5 Outlook

In the end, the question remains as to how to deal with this policy planning. Will it put climate protection law on the right track? Despite all the uncertainties as to how it can be legally possible to initiate and frame the climate policy transformation process in such a way that the goals are actually achieved, climate law, with its instruments of policy planning, has a mechanism that, at least in theory, appears suitable for guiding the necessary transformation of the legal system. It is therefore now up to practitioners to undertake policy planning for measures that do not lack the potential to achieve their objectives from the outset. This path takes time, but is laid down in the applicable law and must be pursued with the participation of all state powers. In view of the plethora of legal requirements for shaping climate policy, it would be wrong to simply ignore the courts here. This cannot and must not lead to the misinterpretation of saving the world through the courts, but it will not stop the courts from dealing with climate lawsuits[50] and should not be used against politics, which remains primarily responsible for containing the dangerous consequences of climate change. Policy planning law provides a mechanism for linking law and politics that allows us to avoid burying our heads in the sand. This is the place where the mix of instruments for achieving the targets is decided from the point of view of distributive justice, and it remains a matter for policy-makers to take the appropriate measures to keep the global temperature below the limit.

[48] Eckes (2021).

[49] Cf. Franzius (2022), p. 383 (426). On the role of the courts in climate protection law, see Britz (2025, pp. 115–140).

[50] Cf. Preston (2021, p. 1, 227), Groß (2024).

References

Britz G (2025) Die Rolle von Gerichten im Klimaschutzrecht. Die Verwalt, Beih 13:115–140

Buser A (2021) Of carbon budgets, factual uncertainties, and intergenerational equity—the German constitutional Court's climate decision. Ger Law J 22(8):1409–1422

Calliess C (2001) Rechtsstaat und Umweltstaat. Mohr Siebeck, Tübingen

Calliess C (2024) Abstand halten revisited: Planetare Grenzen, Art. 20a GG und Biodiversitätsschutz. ZUR 35(2):65–66

Chiti E (2022) Managing the ecological transition of the EU: the European green Deal as a regulatory process. Common Mark Law Rev 59(1):19–48

Durner W (2021) Leistungskraft und Regelungstechniken des internationalen Klimaschutzrechts. Zeitschrift für Europäisches Umwelt- und Planungsrecht (EurUP) 19(4):330–341

Eckes C (2021) Separation of powers in climate cases: comparing cases in Germany and the Netherlands. VerfBlog, 10.5.2021, https://verfassungsblog.de/separation-of-powers-in-climate-cases. Accessed 22 Sep 2025

Eifert M, von Landenberg-Roberg M (2023) Climate change challenges constitutional law: contextualizing the German federal constitutional courts climate jurisprudence within climate constitutionalism. Eur Yearb Int Econ Law 2022 13:3–33. https://doi.org/10.1007/8165_2022_100

Faßbender K (2024) Potentiale und Grenzen des Bundes-Klimaschutzgesetzes. ZUR 35(11):579–589

Flachsland C, Edenhofer J, Zwar C (2024) Eine vertane Chance, aber keine Katastrophe: die Novelle des Bundes-Klimaschutzgesetzes. VerfBlog, 6.5.2024. https://verfassungsblog.de/novelle-bundesklimaschutzgesetz. Accessed 22 Sep 2025

Franzius C (2019) Auf dem Weg zum Klimaschutzgesetz. Zeitschrift für das gesamte Recht der Energiewirtschaft (EnWZ) 8(12):435–442

Franzius C (2022) Prävention durch Verwaltungsrecht: Klimaschutz. Veröffentlichungen der Vereinigung der Deutschen Staatsrechtslehrer (VVDStRL) 81:383–436

Franzius C (2023a) Politikplanung im Klimaschutzrecht. In: Brüning et al. (eds), Verwaltungsrecht: Gestaltung–Steuerung–Kontrolle. Festschrift für Ulrich Ramsauer. C.H. Beck, pp 51–64.

Franzius C (2023b) Rechtliche Möglichkeiten einzelner Staaten zum unilateralen Schutz globaler Umweltgüter. In: Markus T, Reese M, Köck W (eds) Zukunftsfähiges Umweltrecht III. Nomos, pp 89–116

Franzius C (2024a) Governance-Strukturen des EU Green Deal. Deutsches Verwaltungsblatt (DVBl) 16:993–997

Franzius C (2024b) Art. 1 EU-KG. In: Hofmann E, Heß F (eds), BeckOK Klimarecht, 1 edn. C.H. Beck

Franzius C et al (2025) Transformatives Klimarecht: Raum, Zeit. Gesellschaft EurUP 23(2):149–157

German Advisory Council of Environment (2019) Democratic government within environmental limits—on the legitimation of environmental policy, Summary. https://t1p.de/y2qh3. Accessed 22 Sep 2025

Groß T (2024) Why courts will not stop global warming, but climate litigation is still useful. VerfBlog, 12.3.2024. https://verfassungsblog.de/why-courts-will-not-stop-global-warming-but-climate-litigation-is-still-useful. Accessed 22 Sep 2025

Hilson C (2020) Hitting the target? Analysing the use of targets in climate law. Journal of Environmental Law 32(2):195–220

Kahl W (2023) Natürliche Lebensgrundlagen und Ressourcenverbrauch. In: Kischel U, Kube H (eds), Handbuch des Staatsrechts, Volume 1. C.F. Müller, § 19.

Knodt M et al (eds) (2024) Governance der Europäischen Energieunion. Springer

Lammers S (2023) Die europäische Governance-Verordnung und das EU-Klimagesetz, 1st edn. Nomos, Baden-Baden

Lange F (2022) Verbandsklagerecht und das Bundes-Klimaschutzgesetz. Archiv des öffentlichen Rechts 147(2):264–296

Minnerop P (2022) The 'advance interference-like effect' of climate targets: fundamental rights, intergenerational equity and the German Federal Constitutional Court. J Environ Law 34(1):135–162
Oberthür S (2019) Hard or soft governance? The EU's climate and energy policy framework for 2030. Polit GovAnce 7(1):17–27
Perino G et al (2022) Closing the implementation gap: obstacles in reaching net-zero pledges in the EU and Germany. Polit GovAnce 10(3):213–225
Preston BJ (2021) The influence of the Paris agreement on climate litigation: legal obligations and norms. J Environ Law 33(1):1–32
Saurer J (2023) Wandel der Handlungsformen im Umweltrecht der EU. Die Verwaltung 56(2):159–178
Schlacke S, Knodt M (2019) Das Governance-System für die Europäische Energieunion und für den Klimaschutz. ZUR 30(7/8):404–412
Schlacke S, Wentzien H, Thierjung EM, Köster M (2022) Implementing the EU climate law via the 'fit for 55' package. Oxf Open Energy 1:1–13. https://doi.org/10.1093/ooenergy/oiab002
Stäsche U (2024) Abschaffung der Sektorziele und des sektorspezifischen Nachsteuerungsmechanismus durch die KSG-Novelle 2024: Risiken für die Erreichung der nationalen Klimaschutzziele? Zeitschrift für Umweltpolitik & Umweltrecht 2:299–335
Tomuschat C (2019) Enforcement of international law: from the Authority of Hard law to the impact of flexible methods. ZaöRV 79:579–631
von Landenberg-Roberg M (2022) Verantwortungsstrukturierung durch Emissionsbudgets. Die Verwaltung 55(2):249–286
von Schweinitz S (2003) Das Maßstäbegesetz. BWV, Berliner Wiss.-Verl., Berlin
Wiedmann JL (2024) Klimaschutz ohne Sektorziele. Das Zweite Gesetz zur Änderung des Bundes-Klimaschutzgesetzes. NVwZ 43(12):876–881
Winter G (2022) The intergenerational effect of fundamental freedom rights: a contribution of the German Federal Constitutional Court to climate protection. J Environ Law 34(2022):209–221

EU Policy Planning Law for the Implementation of the Green Deal

Moritz Reese

Abstract With the so-called Governance Regulation of 2018 and the Climate Law of 2021, the EU has created a comprehensive target and planning system for the climate policy of the Member States in order to put the Union on the path to climate neutrality and keep it there. The contribution provides an overview of this new type of "policy planning law" and discusses key implementation issues using Germany as an example. It is submitted that policy planning law is a necessary institutional prerequisite for the transformation of the EU and its member states to climate neutrality and that it can only fulfill its necessary contributions to the transformation if it is effectively extended by the member states to the subnational levels. Further, it is considered whether functional policy planning law is also required by fundamental rights as an indispensable means of governance to protect life, health, and freedom.

1 Introduction—Policy Planning Law as an Instrument of European Sustainability Policy

With the "European Green Deal" of 2019, the EU Commission gave the Union a comprehensive agenda for the transformation towards ecological sustainability and, in particular, climate neutrality by 2050. As a result, a wide range of fundamental changes to environmental, climate and energy law have been adopted, which now need to be implemented at national level.[1] However, the political tailwind that made the Green Deal possible at the time has now subsided and turned noticeably. The question of how the sustainability goals of the Green Deal can be safeguarded and policy kept on track is therefore particularly topical.

To this end, the Union has increasingly—and particularly in the context of the Green Deal—begun to set out its sustainability targets in law and to oblige the

[1] For an overview, see Jendrośka and Reese (2023), pp. 7–9.

M. Reese (✉)
Department of Environmental and Planning Law, Helmholtz Centre for Environmental Research-UFZ, Leipzig, Germany
e-mail: moritz.reese@ufz.de

M. Reese et al. (eds.), *Environmental Law in Transformation*,
https://doi.org/10.1007/978-3-032-31567-0_8

Member States to use binding action plans to demonstrate how they will implement the targets or contribute to them. The most prominent example of such "policy planning law" is the governance system for implementing the climate neutrality target, which the EU introduced with the Governance Regulation (GR)[2] of 2018 and further developed with the EU Climate Law (CL).[3]

Using the example of climate governance, the article examines the approach of binding political decisions to objectives and plans from a conceptual perspective and with a view to its steering functions, elements and effectiveness. Following an overview of the governance system and its key functional elements (2.), the special characteristics and control purposes of regulated policy planning are highlighted (3.), before going on to address selected implementation issues, namely the inclusion of all relevant levels (4.) and the limits of planning control, including justiciability (5.). The article concludes with an outlook on the future role of policy planning law beyond the area of climate policy (6.).

2 Overview of the EU Governance System for Climate and Energy Policy

The EU's climate policy is essentially based on two overarching management approaches, the European Emissions Trading System (ETS) and the governance system, alongside a variety of sectoral instruments.[4] In the area of application of emissions trading, the Union pursues a market-based approach that leaves the member states little room for national regulation. This is because the selection and allocation of GHG reduction measures are to be controlled by certificate trading in a market-based and cost-efficient manner, and not by direct regulation.[5] The reduction in total emissions is determined by the quantity of certificates issued (cap). European emissions trading initially covers the CO_2-intensive industrial plants listed in Annex I to the Emissions Trading Directive and intra-European air traffic. Maritime transport has also been gradually included in emissions trading since 2024. The additional

---

[2] Regulation (EU) 2018/1999 of the European Parliament and of the Council of 11 December 2018 on the Governance of the Energy Union and Climate Action, amending Regulations (EC) No 663/2009 and (EC) No 715/2009 of the European Parliament and of the Council, Directives 94/22/EC, 98/70/EC, 2009/31/EC, 2009/73/EC, 2010/31/EU, 2012/27/EU and 2013/30/EU of the European Parliament and of the Council, Council Directives 2009/119/EC and (EU) 2015/652 and repealing Regulation (EU) No 525/2013 of the European Parliament and of the Council (Text with EEA relevance.), OJ L 328, 21.12.2018, p.1.

[3] Regulation (EU) 2021/1119 of the European Parliament and of the Council of 30 June 2021 establishing the framework for achieving climate neutrality and amending Regulations (EC) No 401/2009 and (EU) 2018/1999 ('European Climate Law'), OJ L 243, 9.7.2021, p. 1.

[4] Focusing more on the regulatory areas than on the management approaches, Kreuter-Kirchhof (2025), speaks of a "three-pillar strategy" and sees land use and forestry as a third pillar of the climate strategy.

[5] In place of many: Gawel (2016), who discusses the economic logic, but also the performance limits and impact gaps of this instrument.

ETS II, which was adopted in 2023, will also gradually introduce an upstream emissions trading system for fuels used in the transport and building sectors.[6] From 2027, emissions trading will therefore also be a central instrument for implementing the EU climate targets in these areas and must be coordinated with the governance system in this respect.[7]

The purpose of the governance system is to steer and coordinate the climate and energy policy of the Union and the Member States in its multiple sectors, components and levels in such a way that the Union as a whole becomes climate-neutral by 2050 at the latest. This is to be achieved through binding GHG reduction and action targets and through a system of action planning, monitoring, reporting and updating obligations that ensure that the targets are pursued seriously and implemented as far as possible. The GR introduced such a policy planning system at Member State level and for the management of national climate and energy policies, although initially only for the period up to 2030. The EU Climate Law has extended the governance system to the period up to 2050; in addition, the Union itself has committed to the goal of climate neutrality by 2050 and a 55% net reduction by 2030. Besides, it has instructed the Commission to regularly review progress in order to propose additional Union measures if necessary (see in particular Art. 4 CL). The CL has thus introduced a supplementary governance component for the EU level, which provides for regular pathway monitoring, but not medium-term policy planning in the way that the Member States are required to do by the GR. While the policy planning law of the GR serves primarily to align national policy with the Union's objectives, a key purpose of Union governance under the CL is to review the effectiveness of this autonomy-friendly governance in order to take corrective action under Union law if necessary.

The following analysis focuses on the governance of national climate and energy policy by the GR and the targets addressed to the Member States. The question is how this approach of linking political and administrative decision-making to binding targets is conceptually designed, which essential functional elements belong to it, which purposes it serves and which legal classification and implementation issues it raises. The links to the overarching Union objectives from the CL—which are quite complex and problematic—can be largely ignored. In the following, the most important targets for national climate and energy policy are first outlined in an overview, before going on to discuss the planning and control regime that is intended to ensure the implementation of the targets.

2.1 *Targets and Target-Setting Obligations*

The governance system of the GR refers to targets and target-setting obligations that are not regulated in the regulation itself, but by specific legal acts, in particular for

[6] Kreuter-Kichhof (2025), p. 72 et seq.

[7] Kreuter-Kichhof (2025), p. 77.

reducing GHG emissions, increasing net removals of GHGs by sinks, expanding renewable energies and increasing energy efficiency:

- **To reduce net GHG emissions**, the CL first defines the Union target of climate neutrality by 2050 and also sets the interim target of a 55% reduction in emissions by 2030 (compared to 1990). The Commission has also proposed a 90% reduction as an interim target for 2040 in accordance with Art. 4 (3) CL. For the above-mentioned sectors not covered by ETS-I, the EU Effort Sharing Regulation[8] (ESR) most recently set the Member States country-specific reduction targets for the period 2005–2030 in 2023, which range between 10% (Bulgaria) and 50% (including Germany). The ESR also defines a reduction path with annual emission quantities that are allocated to the member states as emission allowances and can be traded between the states to a limited extent. To a limited extent, the member states are also permitted to transfer emission allowances between the annual slices (so-called "banking" and "borrowing"). Furthermore, Member States are permitted to offset net removals of greenhouse gases in the land use sector against their emission budgets for the periods 2021–2025 and 2026–2030 within the maximum quantities specified in Annex III to the ESR.
- **Targets for net removals** of GHGs from the atmosphere are set out in Regulation (EU) 2018/841 "on the inclusion of greenhouse gas emissions and removals from land use, land-use change and forestry in the 2030 climate and energy policy framework", which was amended by Regulation (EU) 2023/839, in particular with regard to the targets. Following these amendments, the EU target is now that the GHG emissions from land use accounted for in the period 2021–2025 are offset by at least an equivalent amount of accounted removals; the land use sector must therefore achieve climate neutrality in this period in order to subsequently achieve net removals. The EU 2030 target for this is a net removal of 310 million t. CO_2equivalent. Annex IIa to the LULUCF Regulation also specifies the net removals to be achieved by the Member States. The target for Germany, for example, is 3751 kt CO_2equivalent by 2030. The regulation also sets out in detail which measures (afforestation, grassland, etc.) can contribute to net removals and how the removals are to be calculated and monitored. Finally, to a certain extent, it gives the Member States the option of transferring reductions in excess of the national target to other Member States or acquiring reductions from other Member States in order to fill gaps in target achievement. To a certain extent, individual member states are also permitted to use surplus allowances from the ETS-I to fill reduction shortfalls.
- The Renewable Energy Directive (RED) sets a **target for the expansion of renewable energies** for the Union as a whole, which was most recently raised to a share

[8] Regulation (EU) 2018/842 setting binding annual national targets for the reduction of greenhouse gas emissions for the period 2021 to 2030, amended by Regulation (EU) 2023/857 of the European Parliament and of the Council of 19 April 2023 amending Regulation (EU) 2018/842 on binding annual greenhouse gas emission reductions by Member States from 2021 to 2030 contributing to climate action to meet commitments under the Paris Agreement, and Regulation (EU) 2018/1999 (Text with EEA relevance), OJ L 111, 26.4.2023, p. 1.

of at least 42.5% of gross final energy consumption by Amending Directive (EU) 2023/2413 (RED III). The RED does not set any national targets. However, the Member States are obliged by the RED to set national targets or contributions to the aforementioned 2030 target (Art. 4 a No. 2 RED). Art. 5 GR provides criteria for this and obliges the Member States to "jointly ensure that their combined contributions add up to the Union target by 2030". In addition, each Member State must determine an "indicative trajectory" for its contribution, for which the GR standardizes certain minimum thresholds (for 2025 and 2027). The national contributions and trajectories must be submitted with the National Energy and Climate Plans (NECP) to be drawn up in accordance with the RED. The RED also sets out the Community legal framework for the national promotion of renewable energies and regulates how the shares of renewables are to be determined and monitored.

- **To increase energy efficiency**, the Energy Efficiency Directive (EU) 2023/955 (EED), as amended in July 2023, sets a Union target of reducing overall energy consumption by 11.7% compared to the EU reference scenario so that final energy consumption in 2030 does not exceed 763 Mt of oil equivalent (toe) (Art. 4 EED). In addition, the "indicative target" stipulates that primary energy consumption should not exceed a total of 992.5 Mtoe. According to Art. 4 (2), the Member States must define an "indicative national energy efficiency contribution" in their NECP, taking into account the criteria specified in Art. 4(3) EED and using the calculation formula specified in Annex I, in order to contribute to achieving the Union target. In addition, they are obliged to achieve annual energy savings rates of at least 1.49% overall and 1.9% in the public sector in the period 2024–2030 and to carry out energy efficiency renovations on at least 3% of public buildings each year. As a basis for this, the EED comprehensively regulates how energy consumption is to be measured locally and calculated and reported nationally.

The national targets set in accordance with the above-mentioned requirements may no longer be lowered by the Member States in the planning and implementation period up to 2050, but may only be maintained or increased (Art. 14(3) GR). In addition to the aforementioned targets and target-setting obligations, all of the above-mentioned legal acts also regulate specific framework conditions and requirements for promoting the respective sectoral targets. At the same time, however, they leave wide scope for action for national and local implementation, which must be filled in by the Member States in such a way that the binding targets are achieved. The purpose of the planning and monitoring system of the GR and in particular the NECP is to ensure this.

2.2 *The Planning System—The National Energy and Climate Plans (NECP)*

The NECPs and the procedure regulated in the GR for their preparation, review and updating form the core of the governance system with which the Union aims to bring and keep its Member States on track. In conjunction with the above-mentioned sectoral legislation, the GR obliges the Member States to define their national targets in the NECPs and to set out the measures they intend to take to achieve these targets. The plans were to be drawn up for the first time in 2019 for the period 2020–2030 and are to be updated for the following decades.

In order to ensure that the Member States define sufficient target contributions in accordance with the above-mentioned requirements and also effective implementation measures, the GR sets out requirements for the content and analytical basis of the plans and also establishes extensive procedural rules for coordination, participation and reporting. In particular, it determines how the plans and their implementation are to be reviewed by the EU Commission.

With regard to the content of the NECP, it should first be emphasized that the plans are to be divided into an analysis and a measures section and that the GR in Art. 8 and Annex I sets out more precise requirements for the analysis of both the initial situation in the relevant fields of climate and energy policy and the expected effects of the planned policies and measures. Pursuant to Art. 8 (3) GR, the Member States are also obliged to publish comprehensive information on the assumptions and methods for the underlying projections so that these can be understood and verified. The required content of the plans explicitly also includes, in addition to targets and measures pursuant to Art. 7 GR, "a general overview of the investments required to achieve the objectives, targets and contributions set out in the national plan and a general assessment of the sources of these investments".

With regard to the plan preparation procedure, it is initially stipulated for the draft phase that the Member States must involve the public at an early stage (Art. 10 GR) and that they must coordinate with other Member States on a cross-border basis in accordance with Art. 12 GR. The completed drafts must be examined by the Commission in accordance with Art. 9 GR to determine whether the objectives and contributions meet the requirements of the GR and the above-mentioned sectoral regulations, whether the measures and policies defined are likely to achieve the objectives and whether the plans meet the formal requirements of the GR.[9] If the Commission comes to the conclusion that this is not the case, it issues country-specific recommendations to increase the level of ambition of the targets and/or measures. The Member State must take "due account" of the recommendations in the final NECP in accordance with Art. 9 Para. 3 and must justify why it is not taking up a recommendation. The final NECPs are reviewed again by the Commission in a final audit in accordance with Art. 13 GR to determine whether the objectives and contributions are sufficient to implement the Union objectives. If the final review

---

[9] Although the formal review is not explicitly provided for in Art. 9, the correct view is that it must be read into the subjects of the draft review from Art. 13, see Lammers (2023), p. 99.

shows that there is still a gap in ambition, the Commission proposes measures at Union level in accordance with Art. 31 (3) GR to close the gap in this way. In the final instance, therefore, the mandate to determine policies and measures shall be (partly) withdrawn from member states and seized by the Union.

To monitor the implementation of targets, the GR provides for a complex system of progress reporting, which cannot be fully described here. This system also serves to fulfill the monitoring and reporting obligations under the Paris Agreement and in relation to the nationally determined contributions (NDCs) pledged within the Paris framework. The main elements of reporting include.

- the greenhouse gas inventories and inventory reports, which must be prepared annually by the Member States in accordance with Art. 26 GR and submitted by 15 March each year and which must indicate both the total emissions and the emissions of the sectors attributable to the sectors subject to the ESR. Technical requirements and procedures for this are regulated in separate legal acts and guidelines.[10]
- the biennial integrated reports on GHG policies and measures and projections on how GHG emissions and removals by sinks are expected to develop, taking into account the measures, in accordance with Art. 18 GR,
- the integrated national progress reports on the implementation of the NECP, in which progress in all dimensions and fields and on all objectives of the NECP is to be reported every two years in accordance with Art. 17 GR.

On the basis of these reports, regular progress assessments are carried out by the Commission in accordance with Art. 29 GR, namely annually in accordance with Art. 29 (5) with regard to the objectives and commitments mentioned therein, as well as every two years in accordance with Art. 29 (1)-(4) GR and on the basis of the biennial progress reports in accordance with Art. 18 GR. If the Commission determines that a Member State has made insufficient progress, it issues recommendations to this state in accordance with Art. 30 (1) GR and the more detailed provisions of Art. 32 GR in order to ensure that the targets are achieved. The recommendations must be published in accordance with Art. 34 GR. The Member State concerned is obliged to "take due account of the recommendation in a spirit of solidarity between the Member States and between the Union and the Member States". It must explain how it does this in its next progress report. If it does not take up a recommendation, it must justify this. A further progress review by the Commission is taking place every five years since September 2023 in accordance with Art. 7 of the EU Act.

Finally, the planning procedure includes the regular updating of the NECP, which, according to Art. 14, is initially to take place after five years and then every ten years, whereby the Member States are given the opportunity to refrain from updating, stating the reasons.[11] The update is to be carried out in accordance with the same substantive and procedural requirements as the initial preparation of the NECP.

[10] Lammers (2023), p. 109.

[11] It is rightly criticized that this option is not compatible with the fact that an update of the first plan generation after the target increases in the Fit-for-55 package is essential, see Lammers (2023),

2.3 The Long-Term Strategy

In addition to the NECP, the member states had to draw up a long-term strategy for their climate and energy policy with a perspective of at least 30 years for the first time by January 2020 in accordance with Art. 15 GR. The strategies should show prospects and reduction paths in the relevant sectors towards climate neutrality by 2050 at the latest. They are to be updated every five years and a new strategy is to be drawn up every ten years with a correspondingly extended 30-year perspective. According to Art. 15 (2) GR, the Commission also had to draw up a long-term strategy for the Union as a whole by April 2019 in order to provide long-term guidance for both EU policy and national policy planning. The NECPs are to be coordinated with the long-term strategies at both levels. In accordance with Article 15(9) of the GR, the Commission shall examine "whether the long-term national strategies are suitable for the joint achievement of the objectives and targets of the Energy Union referred to in Article 1 and shall provide information on any remaining collective gap." A recommendation mechanism along the lines of Art. 34 GR is not provided for in relation to the long-term strategies. In the long-term perspective, the GR is content to make ambition gaps transparent.

3 The EU Governance System as "Policy Planning Law"—Concept, Functions, Significance

The obligations and procedures regulated in the GR serve to commit national climate and energy policy to the long-term Union objectives without taking away its scope for decision-making on ways and means. This steering approach of legally regulated state-led policy planning, which is increasingly being discussed as "policy planning law",[12] has conceptual precursors in EU law,[13] e.g. in the EC Water Framework Directive (WFD) and Directive (EU) 2016/2284 on the reduction of national emissions of certain atmospheric pollutants, but finds a temporary climax of a special kind in the GR. National governments and legislation are obliged to engage in highly complex, cross-sectoral planning that is much more extensive than the above-mentioned directives and affects a wide range of design issues, particularly in terms of energy, transport, agricultural, industrial and structural policy. The governance system for climate

p. 121; however, it should therefore also be impossible for the Member States to give viable reasons that justify a waiver of the update.

[12] Faßbender (2024), Franzius (2022, 2023); Kloepfer and Wiedmann (2022), p. 319, Guckelberger (2022), Köck and Kohlrausch (2021), Schlacke (2021a), section 16 para. 13, 33; Reese (2020), Lammers (2023) has presented a profound and in many respects ground-breaking monographic analysis of the structures, functions and dogmatic classification of the governance system as policy planning law in his dissertation.

[13] A more detailed account of the development of the target orientation and planning approach is provided by Wolfgang Durner in this volume, see Sect. 3.

and energy policy extends even further into the areas of legislation and fiscal policy than the WFD, for example, and thus into in the area of tension between law and politics and at the limits of law and planning as a means of state control.

The policy planning approach is now also being used prominently in biodiversity protection through the new EU regulation on nature restoration.[14] Here, too, medium and long-term transformation targets are set as binding law and the Member States are obliged to undertake iterative, adaptive implementation and restoration planning. Although this planning is likely to include a higher proportion of administrative measures than the NECP, it will also be dependent on contributions from legislation and political choices of ways and means.

The fact that policy planning has been given such a central role despite all the prevalent skepticism about planning,[15] and above all through the legalization of objectives and planning procedures, gives reason for a special legal interest in the more recent forms of policy planning law. The interest here is firstly in understanding the phenomenon, particularly with regard to the reasons that motivate the advance of the policy planning approach, and then the questions that arise regarding the classification under constitutional and administrative law,[16] regarding the effective design and enforcement as well as the limits of this approach. A look at its functions will show that policy planning law should primarily be understood as a response to the special and new challenges of the sustainability transformation that climate change and the biodiversity crisis demand of us, and which—according to a core thesis put forward here—cannot be achieved without long-term orientation and planning of the responsible policy fields.

The EU's policy planning law is aimed at transforming the Union towards climate neutrality and thus at a far-reaching restructuring of the energy, production, transportation and land use systems. This transformation is a multi-generational task of enormous scope that can only be accomplished in the long term and requires that clear common goals are pursued, that the diverse contributions between states, regions and sectors are adequately distributed and coordinated, and that compliance with the target path is continuously monitored and, if necessary, course corrections are made. The transformation to climate neutrality is therefore a planning task per se. It cannot be accomplished without a planning and steering sovereign and without functioning planning institutions to allocate and coordinate responsibilities. It is not to be expected that the transformation can succeed without joint, reliable planning and that countries and people will reach their goal merely through the invisible hand

[14] See Fellenberg (2025), p. 128, Qasem and Rehder (2025), pp. 12–13, Köck (2025), Reese (2024a, b).

[15] Dermine (2024) speaks of "a retour en grace of planning as a public policy approach".

[16] On the classification of climate protection programs in the forms of action, see Schlacke (2020), pp. 339–344 ("Verwaltungsrechtliche Planung"), Schlacke (2021b), section 20 para. 42; Franzius (2023), p. 201 ("neuartige mehrebenenorientierte planerische Handlungsform"). Also Köck (2022), section 36 para. 107 et seq., Lammers (2023), p. 49 et seq., von Weschpfennig (2023), section 156 para. 34, Wickel (2021), p. 333.

of the market, as it were, not even within the framework of comprehensive emissions trading.[17] This is because the transformation to climate neutrality requires to a large extent a restructuring of infrastructure and land use structures which, as public goods, are not generated by the market but must be planned, implemented and financed by public authorities. However, supplementary measures, in particular regulatory control, can also be useful and necessary in the area of emissions trading in order to drive forward the decarbonization of the markets. For this reason, even in combination with the ETS a system of transformative policy planning remains at least useful, if not indispensable, with regard to the following core functions:

- **Long-term orientation**: The policy planning system of the GR and the CL serves to align the policies of both the Member States and the Union with the long-term transformation goals. Objectives and planning obligations are necessary elements of long-term orientation. Without the objectives, there would be no direction, and without planning, policy could not be aligned with the objectives.[18] Legalization makes both binding and ensures that the Member States carry out the required policy planning and seriously pursue the specified objectives. The long-term binding nature of the target and procedural provisions of Union law on climate and energy policy is not in itself a special feature compared to other Union law that applies for an indefinite period, as it were. Rather, the special feature lies in the target orientation and planning framework of the Member States' climate and energy policies.
- **Agreement on targets and burden sharing:** At the target level, an essential function of the policy planning system is to reach a binding agreement within the Union and between the Member States on the targets of European climate policy and also on the distribution of burdens and contributions between the Member States. A binding target and burden-sharing agreement is a fundamental prerequisite for the mutual willingness of all states to make their own contributions in reliance on the contributions of other countries. The binding targets—and also the provisions for their enforcement—lead the Union out of the "prisoner's dilemma", as it were, which inhibits the protection of common goods if the Community members cannot rely on the cooperation of the other members.[19]
- **Reflective, adaptive orientation**: The policy planning system of the GR and the CL is conceptually geared towards the fact that the diverse factors, actors and developments in climate policy cannot be precisely controlled and are subject to unforeseeable influences and that policy must therefore be shaped in an iterative process of ongoing path control and readjustment.[20] The new policy planning law is therefore primarily to be understood as a procedural framework that is intended to ensure an ongoing target-oriented review and further development of the policy program.

---

[17] See also Franzius in his contribution to this volume, subsection 2.3.

[18] See also the contribution of Franzius in this volume, subsection 2.3.

[19] Fundamental Hardin (1968).

[20] For more details, see Lammers (2023), p. 449 et seq., Franzius (2022), p. 2 et seq.

- **Subsidiarity:** The policy planning system is an expression and means of autonomy-friendly and federal state control, because it is aimed at leaving the decision on means and ways of achieving the common objectives to the national and sub-national levels as far as possible.[21] In this way, the governance approach promotes democratic decision-making in the countries, regions and municipalities in their areas of responsibility and in accordance with their respective preferences, as is essentially required by the principle of subsidiarity.[22] With EU emissions trading, on the other hand, the Union prescribes the choice of instrument centrally, in the form of an instrument that largely excludes decentralized control in the areas concerned because it relies on market-based initiation and distribution of GHG avoidance. Emissions trading grants its muchvaunted flexibility to market participants, but not to states, governments and parliaments, which could alternatively use regulatory or promotional means and allocate the reduction burdens according to aspects other than cost efficiency alone.
- **Coordination**: A core function of the policy planning law of the GR and the CL is rightly seen as institutionally strengthening the necessary coordination of energy and climate policy across the dimensions and sectors, between the Union and the Member States and also within the Member States.[23] Coordination between the Union and the Member States is an essential part of the planning, review and revision procedures regulated by the GR. With the formalized and legally binding plans, coordination is significantly strengthened compared to the soft approaches of the "open method" and the European Semester.[24] The bindingly required plans and the status analyses, projections and reports prescribed for this purpose are an indispensable basis for coordination. However, the coordination basis for the national NECPs should also include parallel medium-term planning at EU level, which the EU law does not regulate in a binding manner.
- **Transparency**: The policy planning law of the GR also ensures that transparency is created with regard to the facts (the sources and trends of emissions and sinks) as well as reduction targets and measures and the status of implementation and the impact of the measures. The related investigation, planning and reporting obligations inform the political players themselves, the Commission in its supervisory function and, above all, the public and enable them to actively follow the policy planning, identify ambition and implementation deficits and, if necessary, demand remedial action. Transparency and publicity are also used specifically within the framework of the GR in order to motivate affected member states in the sense of "name-and-shame" and through "peer pressure" to eliminate ambition and implementation deficits.[25]

[21] Cf. 12, 27th recital to the GR.

[22] This "federal" function of the planning approach is also emphazised by Wolfgang Durner in this volume, section 4. On the fundamentals see Reese (2014), p. 200 et seq.

[23] Franzius in this volume, subsection 2.3; Franzius (2022), p. 3, Lammers (2023), p. 423 et seq.

[24] Lammers (2023), p. 446 et seq.

[25] For more on this, see Lammers (2023), p. 574 et seq.

- **Political relief:** Policy planning law and the target commitments it contains also have the unspoken function of relieving the political burden on national elected representatives. In particular, they are relieved of the political responsibility for the necessary impositions on the domestic electorate because they can invoke the obligation under EU law to comply with the defined targets and the NEC plans based on them.
- **Planning basis for the economy**: In the private sector, too, the transformation requires long-term planning perspectives and transition periods that enable a sustainable switch to climate-neutral alternatives. The creation of a comparatively reliable planning basis for markets and investors is also an important function of policy planning law.[26]

In view of the elementary functions that policy planning law has for climate protection in the interplay of states, levels and sectors, it must also be asked whether a policy planning is not also to be appraised as an indispensable institutional foundations of human rights protection, as recently called for by the ECtHR in particular in the case of the Swiss climate seniors.[27] For Germany, the case law of the Federal Constitutional Court and its much-noticed decision of 24th March 2021 are particularly relevant in this regard. In the underlying case, the applicants had claimed that the German Climate Protection Act did not provide for sufficient targets and measures to adequately protect their fundamental rights to life, health and freedom. In its decision, the court did not focus on the protection of life, health or private life, but on the long-term safeguarding of freedom protected by fundamental rights. It saw an unconstitutional interference with the fundamental right to general freedom of action—as stipulated in Article 2(1) of the German Constitution—in the fact that the reduction path set out in the national climate protection law would shift the GHG reduction burden excessively to the future (after 2030) and thus disproportionately restrict the future exercise of freedom. For the "intertemporal" protection of fundamental freedoms, a fair, proportionate distribution of the GHG reduction burdens is required in view of the opportunities for freedom that depend on it. The national targets and reduction pathways must meet this requirement. According to the Federal Constitutional Court it is also necessary "to formulate transparent measures for the further shaping of greenhouse gas reduction at an early stage, which provide orientation for the necessary development and implementation processes and ensure a sufficient degree of development pressure and planning security."[28] Based on the above, it is doubtful that this requirement can be met solely through appropriate medium and long-term targets, but without regulated policy planning, status assessment and coordination. In my opinion, there is much to be said for recognizing a minimum level of regulated policy planning as a *conditio sine qua non* for the constitutionally required protection of the future exercise of freedom and also for the protection of life, health

[26] Cf. in particular the 12th and 34th recitals to the GR.

[27] ECtHR Klimaseniorinnen Schweiz and others v Switzerland App No 53600/20 (2024).

[28] BVerfG, Judgement of 24.3.2021 - 1 BvR 2656/18, 4th guiding principle.

and/or the right to private and family life under Art. 8 ECHR, to which the ECtHR refers in its above-mentioned decision.

The special conceptual feature of policy planning law—as described above—is that it obliges the states addressed to plan measures in a targeted manner in order to program policy-making decisions, especially legislation, over longer periods of time. The approach relies on states developing effective and coherent programs of measures for all responsible sectors and decision-making levels and on the executive and legislative bodies concerned adhering to this planning, even in the long term and across legislative periods and changing majorities. Under the pressure of transformation requirements, such a commitment to planning means that policy planning law is entering areas that were traditionally reserved for the political sphere of democratic decision-making and which are thus not institutionally prepared for "planning law" control. In the field of tension between politics and law, this approach therefore raises a whole series of questions of classification, design and implementation, which can only be touched on in excerpts below, namely with regard to the domestic design and extension to the sub-national levels (4) as well as the means and limits of enforcement, including the role of the judiciary (5).

4 The Domestic Organization and Inclusion of Subnational Levels of Action—The Example of Germany

The policy planning law of the GR is generally directed at the Member States. It is therefore the responsibility of the Member States to determine the national targets, to draw up and submit the NECP, and to monitor and report on the progress of implementation. It is also the task of the Member States—and first and foremost of national legislation—to define national responsibilities in such a way that the target-setting, investigation and planning tasks can be carried out effectively.

The transformation goals of climate and energy policy affect the areas of responsibility of almost all branches and, in particular, all levels of administration and legislation. Not only in federal Germany, but in almost all countries of the Union, important competences for the implementation of climate targets lie in the hands of the sub-national levels, where they are also—more or less immovably—anchored in the constitutions of the federal systems.[29] A planning system that is intended to effectively call up and coordinate the necessary contributions from all levels must therefore also extend to the subnational levels. It is therefore the responsibility of the Member States and their national legislation to expand the governance system nationally and, in particular, to extend it to their implementation levels in order to demand the target contributions and implementation plans required from them. The more federally structured the states are, the more difficult it is to integrate the federal units and sub-levels. This is illustrated below using Germany as an example.

---

[29] Schlacke (2022), p. 910 et seq., Köck and Kohlrausch (2021), Reese (2023).

The vertical distribution of competences in German climate policy is primarily shaped by the general—constitutional—structures of the German federal system. The German federal system is an example of so-called "executive" federalism, in which legislation is the predominant domain of the federal level while the regional states (Länder) are mainly responsible for the implementation of the (federal) laws and for regional infrastructure development, spatial planning and structural fiscal policy. Municipalities even have a constitutional right to regulate their local affairs autonomously according to Article 28(2) GG, and this includes local spatial planning, infrastructure development and various public services.

Despite the far-reaching legislative powers of the federal level, the federal states and municipalities therefore bear a great deal of responsibility for the transformation to climate neutrality, particularly in the fiscal and planning areas of infrastructure, spatial and urban development, public services, public investment and structural policy.[30] Municipalities in particular also have a wide range of opportunities within the scope of their self-government to develop municipal settlement structures, infrastructures and facilities towards climate neutrality. Without a corresponding transformation policy on the part of the federal states and municipalities, the transition to climate neutrality cannot succeed.

Policy planning law can therefore only conceptually fulfill its steering claim if the jointly responsible regional authorities are also obliged, within the scope of their competences, to determine coherent target contributions and draw up programmes of measures. Because this is a necessary condition for the effective implementation of the target and planning obligations under EU law, the creation of a national substructure must also be considered part of the obligation to implement EU law. It cannot be sufficient to leave the implementation of Union law to the regional states and municipalities without a federal legal framework, because the central coordination function of policy planning law cannot be fulfilled by a variety of unconnected decentralized approaches. The policy planning approach of EU law thus inherently presupposes a centrally regulated planning system that spans the entire multi-level system.

However, such a complementary system to EU policy planning law is largely lacking in Germany.[31] As in many EU member states,[32] a national climate protection law (Klimaschutzgesetz—KSG) has been enacted in Germany that sets GHG reduction targets for the entire country and obliges the federal government to draw up a national action plan—as is explained in more detail by *Claudio Franzius* in this volume.[33] However, the KSG is aimed exclusively at the federal level and federal policy and does not set out any target contributions or planning obligations for the

[30] Cf. BVerfG, Judgement of 18.1.2022 - 1 BvR 1565/21 et al., para. 16; Faßbender (2024), p. 587 et seq., Köck and Kohlrausch (2021), Wickel (2021), p. 337, Reese (2023), p. 40 et seq.

[31] See also Franzius (2023), p. 200.

[32] See Evans et al. (2023), Mackaill-Hill and Mascolo (2022).

[33] Bundes-Klimaschutzgesetz (2019) Federal Climate Action Act of 12 December 2019 (Federal Law Gazette I, p. 2513), as last amended by Article 1 of the Act of 15 July 2024 (Federal Law Gazette I No. 235). For an English translation see: https://www.gesetze-im-internet.de/englisch_ksg/

federal states and municipalities. It thus remains up to them to decide whether, how and when they contribute to the implementation of the climate targets.

It is very noteworthy in this context that Germany has not introduced a planning obligation for the federal states and municipalities to reduce GHG emissions, but it has done so for the area of climate adaptation. The Climate Adaptation Act of December 2023[34] obliges the federal states to draw up climate risk analyses and adaptation strategies, and stipulates that adaptation concepts must be developed at local level and coordinated with supra-local planning. The German Climate Adaptation Act thus creates a policy planning law that extends down to the municipal level, although this is neither required by EU law in the area of adaptation, nor does it appear necessary from the point of view of subsidiarity, because both the task of adaptation and the consequences of non-adaptation are predominantly local in nature. Meanwhile, there is no such national planning system for the area of climate protection, although this is a global protected good and the need for coordination is by far greater than for climate adaptation.

In view of the elementary functions of regulated policy planning for the transformation to climate neutrality and thus also for the protection of human and fundamental rights (4. above), the question arises as to whether there is even a constitutional need to include the subnational levels in the national policy planning system over and above the requirements of EU law. In 2022, the German Constitutional Court had to rule on a constitutional complaint aimed at the enactment of climate laws and programs of measures by the federal states.[35] It was argued by the applicants that climate laws and climate protection programs were also indispensable at state level in order to guarantee the intertemporal protection of freedom that the German Constitutional Court had demanded with regard to the national climate law. The constitutional complaints were therefore not directed against the federal government and the lack of a multi-level policy planning law along the lines of the Climate Adaptation Act, but directly against the federal states. In line with the constitutional court procedure, the arguments were based exclusively on constitutional law and did not refer to the concept and implementation constraints of the European policy planning law of the GR.

The German Constitutional Court did not even accept this constitutional complaint for decision with a brief explanation. The court did not address the functional logic of policy planning law but, after a brief reference to the climate resolution, asserted that "in the federal state (…) different regulations for the coordination of constitutionally required climate protection measures are conceivable."[36] The court further held that this "does not have to be done by means of burden-sharing between the regional states, but could also be done, for example, by means of a sector-related regulation that does not contain quotas for the regional states." However, the following paragraph then

[34] Bundes-Klimaanpassungsgesetz (2023) Federal Climate Adaptation Act of 20 December 2023 (Federal Law Gazette I, p. 393). For an English translation see: https://www.bmuv.de/fileadmin/Daten_BMU/Download_PDF/Gesetze/kang_en_bf.pdf

[35] Cf. BVerfG, Judgement of 18.1.2022 - 1 BvR 1565/21 and others.

[36] BVerfG, Judgement of 18.1.2022 - 1 BvR 1565/21 and others, para. 16.

states that it may be necessary "at least for practical reasons, to coordinate further federal and state measures to achieve climate protection targets more closely *under federal law* than has been the case to date."[37]

The decision therefore provides an indication that the responsibility for guaranteeing the elementary coordination functions, even across the federal levels, is primarily to be placed with the federal government. There are good reasons to conclude that there is indeed a need for coordination under federal law, at least due to the target and planning obligations under EU law, and that this includes in particular obliging the federal states and municipalities to make concrete reduction contributions and adaptive policy planning within the scope of their responsibilities. Incidentally, this should apply regardless of the extent to which targets and contributions are related to sectors. In my opinion, it stands to reason that the domestic extension of policy planning law to the federal states and municipalities should also be seen as a necessary condition for effective intertemporal protection of freedom (with the steering approach as a whole). A new constitutional complaint should use this argument to criticize the inactivity of the federal government, not that of the federal states.[38] Consideration could also be given to asserting the necessity of a complete policy planning law that includes all levels of state action as a minimum condition for the protection of human rights within the meaning of the above-mentioned ECtHR case law.

5 Binding Limits and Enforcement of Policy Planning Law

Questions of commitment and enforcement arise in three respects, namely with regard to the planning obligations and procedures, compliance with the objectives and the implementation of the plans. With regard to the obligations of the GR and the CL to prepare and update the NECP, including the requirements for procedures, content, reviews and reports, no special features apply compared to other EU law, because no political leeway is opened up or affected in this respect. The regular instruments of enforcement and, in particular, infringement proceedings therefore apply here without further ado.

The situation is different when it comes to implementing the targets, as this largely requires political decisions on ways and means, which should be reserved for national policy under the planning approach. In order to identify gaps in ambition and implementation and to initiate necessary improvements, the governance system provides for the investigation, reporting, evaluation and review mechanisms described above

[37] BVerfG, Judgement of 18.1.2022 - 1 BvR 1565/21 and others, para. 17.

[38] Lammers (2023), p. 46 and fn. 51 on the federal government's responsibility for federal burden-sharing.

and relies primarily on transparency, on a "permanent dialog"[39] with the Commission and on its recommendations, which are "non-binding" as a form of action by the Union in accordance with Article 288 (5) TFEU.

With regard to the restrained precautions for the "enforcement" of the implementation of targets and plans, *Simon Lammers* has classified the targets and the NECP as a type of "soft law" under European law, which is primarily aimed at influencing the Member States without being directly legally binding, whereby the regulated dialog with the Commission achieves a relevant hardening compared to the general method of open coordination.[40] In fact, the approach suggests recourse to categories of international law and to similarly constructed "compliance" mechanisms of multilateral environmental agreements.[41]

The soft character of the governance system has sometimes been criticized as a weakness of its design.[42] In view of the soft character and the low binding force of the Commission's recommendations, *Schlacke and Knodt* have suggested creating effective sanctions for non-compliance with the targets by linking them to structural fund support.[43] They also submit that the linking of the European Semester with the European Structural and Investment Funds could serve as a model for this.

A further hardening of the targets and NECP by linking them to the structural funds still seems very worthy of consideration. However, it should also be borne in mind that the required target implementation requires a variety of legal measures and the necessary majorities at various levels, which cannot be decreed.[44] Democratic policy planning law must therefore rely on a predominantly procedural, reflective and influencing control[45]; the soft character is inherent to the instrument. If it turns out that the autonomy-preserving policy planning approach does not work because the objectives and plans cannot be implemented through national policy, measures at EU level should be considered as an alternative, with which the Member States are deprived of their policy planning mandate, as it were. As already mentioned, this exit option is also clearly laid out in the governance system.[46]

In view of the soft approach of the GR to ambition and implementation gaps, the question also arises as to the extent to which the targets, planning obligations and plans are justiciable. In any case, a justiciable breach of EU law is likely to exist if a Member State violates the directly binding provisions of the GR and, for example, fails to submit the required planning or plan revision, fails to provide the prescribed planning basis and plan content or fails to comply with the prescribed procedure for public participation and coordination as well as the dialog with the Commission.

---

[39] Thus the 54th recital to the GDPR.

[40] Lammers (2023), p. 446 et seq.

[41] In Lammers (2023), in particular on p. 656 et seq.; fundamental on compliance systems e.g. Zaelke et al. (2005), p. 29 et seq., Brown Weiss and Jacobson (1998).

[42] See Schlacke/Knodt (2019), p. 410; Lorenzen (2022), p. 163 et seq.

[43] Schlacke and Knodt (2019), p. 410.

[44] See also Wolfgang Durner in this volumes, section 7.

[45] In detail Lammers (2023), p. 447 et seq.

[46] Art. 31 (3), 32 (2) and (6) as well as Art. 6 (4) CL; see also recital 51 to the GR.

Such violations of directly binding Union law can—as already mentioned—be reprimanded by the Commission in infringement proceedings before the CJEU. Recognized environmental associations must also have recourse to the competent national courts.[47]

However, there are doubts about the justiciability of ambition and implementation gaps. On the one hand, it can be argued that the GR only claims a soft, influencing effect in this respect for the good reasons mentioned above, and that this must rule out judicial enforcement. However, as a directly binding procedural rule, the GR stipulates that the Commission's recommendations for closing ambition or implementation gaps must be "duly taken into account" and that deviations must be justified.[48] Whether viable reasons are given for deviating from the recommendations should, in principle, be open to careful judicial review and this includes, whether the Member State has made it plausible that it will return to its target path by means other than those recommended.[49] If, on the other hand, no plausible alternatives are presented and the failure to meet the targets is obviously accepted, this should also be open to legal challenge in infringement proceedings before the CJEU and by NGO suits before the competent national courts.

Admittedly, the courts can only determine that there is a lack of ambition or implementation, but cannot determine how it should be closed. Nevertheless, the judicial determination and a possible penalty payment could increase political pressure and at the same time strengthen the above-mentioned political relief function of policy planning law. However, care must also be taken to ensure that the targets and the reality of implementation remain realistically close to each other, on both sides and—if necessary—by adjusting the targets. It is another consequence of having legally binding targets that these regulated targets must remain realistic and achievable. *Ultra posse nemo obligatur*! Otherwise, it is foreseeable that the objectives and policy planning law as a whole will lose the will to comply.[50] Such a loss of authority, which could have repercussions for the whole of EU law, would be fatal and would not only thwart the transformation goals of policy planning law.

---

[47] See Schlacke and Knodt (2019), p. 410. With regard to the Climate Protection Act in particular, also Franzius (2023), p. 203, with further references to the discussion.

[48] This is also emphasized in the 54th recital to the CFR.

[49] Reese (2020), p. 642.

[50] This is currently happening with the objectives of the Water Framework Directive! See Reese (2021a), (b).

6 Conclusion and Outlook: Policy Planning Law as a Necessary But not Sufficient Condition for the Transformation to Climate Neutrality—also Alongside Expanded Emissions Trading

With the GR and the CL, the Union commits its Member States to climate and energy policy targets and to reflective and transparent planning to implement these targets. The hopes of European climate policy now rest on this policy planning law approach—alongside emissions trading. However, the EU's experience with similar approaches to national planning control is not very encouraging. For example, even 20 years after the adoption of the Water Framework Directive and 10 years after the expiry of the regular implementation period, the water status targets of the Water Framework Directive have still not been achieved in large parts of Germany's water bodies.[51] Compared to the goals of climate neutrality and the energy transition, the goals of the WFD seem like child's play.

Experience with the WFD shows "on a small scale" what applies all the more to the major transformation towards climate neutrality: that the famous limits of plannability must not be ignored; and it must not be expected that the diversity of responsible, often parliamentary decision-makers in the many different areas of action can be guided precisely to the goal by planning obligations alone. For this reason, policy planning law must focus its claim to binding force primarily on the process and the adequacy conditions of complex, long-term and reflexive planning, and otherwise remain quite cautious.[52] It should be clear that regulated policy planning is not a sufficient, but nevertheless a necessary prerequisite for sustainability transformation. Without common, bindingly recognized goals and without planning, the transformation of energy, production, transport, land use and settlement systems cannot succeed a priori. With this in mind, the GR and the CL should be recognized and further developed, and at the same time, direct control measures should also be expanded at EU level, above all emissions trading.[53]

ETS II is now in the introductory phase and covers large parts of the sectors that were previously "only" subject to the governance system and sectoral regulation. There is therefore no doubt that governance must be adapted with a view to ETS II, and the governance requirements and contributions of the systems must be readjusted and redefined.[54] In future, the ETS may take on the role of a "lead instrument" for European climate policy, also in the transport and buildings sectors.[55] However, it should be noted that emissions trading alone cannot bring about the transformation to climate neutrality.[56] Particularly in the areas of infrastructure, services of general

[51] Reese (2021a). On the reasons for missing the target, see Reese (2021b).

[52] Franzius (2022), p. 5.

[53] See Reese (2020), p. 642.

[54] Kreuter-Kirchhof (2025), p. 77 et seq.

[55] Ibid.

[56] Appropriate in the sense of Franzius (2022), p. 5, referring to Gawel (2016), p. 352 et seq.

interest and urban and spatial development, the market instrument cannot have a sufficient effect on its own. Planning, regulatory, promotional and fiscal measures will continue to be crucial—and thus also policy planning law.

References

Brown Weiss E, Jacobson H (1998) Engaging countries: strengthening compliance with international environmental accords. MIT Press, Cambridge

Dermine P (2024) The planning method: An inquiry into the constitutional ramifications of a new EU governance technique. Common Mark Law Rev 61(4):959–992. https://doi.org/10.54648/cola2024065

Evans N, Kocher D, Kögel N, Duwe M (2023) The landscape of national climate laws in Europe: a status update. In: Ecologic institute. Berlin, pp 1–14. https://www.ecologic.eu/19399. Accessed 14 Aug 2025

Faßbender K (2024) Potentiale und Grenzen des Bundes-Klimaschutzgesetzes. ZUR 579–589

Fellenberg F (2025) Anwendungsfragen rund um die europäische Wiederherstellungsverordnung. NVwZ 2025:124–130

Franzius, 2022Franzius C (2022) Der „Green Deal" in der Mehrebenenordnung. KlimaR 2–5

Franzius C (2023) Verfassungsfragen der Planung politischer Transformationsentscheidungen am Beispiel der Klimaschutzplanung. ZUR 199–205

Gawel E (2016) Der Emissionshandel vor der vierten Handelsperiode. EnWZ 351–357

Guckelberger A (2022) Klimaschutzinstrumente aus KSG, TEHG und BEHG. NuR 44:221–230

Hardin G (1968) The tragedy of the commons. Science 162(3859):1243–1248. https://doi.org/10.1126/science.162.3859.1243

Jendrośka J, Reese M (2023) Environmental law in transformation - Key developments under the European Green Deal. In: Abrahams D, Gillett, T (eds) Environment & climate change law 2023: Practical cross-border insights into environment and climate change law, international comparative legal guides, 20th edn., pp 7–15. https://t1p.de/ucpg5. Accessed 14 Aug 2025

Kloepfer and Wiedmann, 2022Kloepfer M, Wiedmann J (2022) Die Architektur des deutschen Klimaschutzrechts. EurUP 20(3):304–320

Köck W, Kohlrausch L (2021) Klimaschutzgesetzgebung im Bundesstaat – Zur Zukunft der Landesklimaschutzgesetze, ZUR 610–617

Köck (2022) Plans und andere Formen des prospektiven Verwaltungshandelns. In: Voßkuhle A et al (eds) Grundlagen des Verwaltungsrechts, Band II, 3rd edn. C.H.Beck, München, pp 718–856

Köck W (2025) Deutschland braucht ein Durchführungsgesetz zur EU-Verordnung über die Wiederherstellung der Natur. ZUR 1–2

Kreuter-Kirchhof, 2025Kreuter-Kirchhof Ch (2025) Der neue europäische Emissionshandel II. ZUR 72–78

Lammers S (2023) Die europäische Governance-Verordnung und das EU-Klimagesetz – Politikplanung und Koordinierung als Aufgabe des Rechts, 1st edn. Nomos, Baden-Baden

Lorenzen J (2022) Das EU-Klimagesetz im Lichte von Demokratie- und Effektivitätsprinzip. EurUP 20(2):156–165

Mackaill-Hill H, Mascolo F (2022) Climate Laws in Europe. Essential for achieving climate neutrality. CAN Europe. https://www.germanwatch.org/en/85311. Accessed 14 Aug 2025

Qasem F, Rehder J (2025) Naturwiederherstellung am Beispiel von Moorflächen. ZUR 3–14

Reese M (2014) Zu Deutung und Dogmatik des europäischen Subsidiaritätsprinzips. In: Ewer W et al (eds) Methodik - Ordnung - Umwelt: Festschrift für Hans-Joachim Koch aus Anlass seines siebzigsten Geburtstags, Schriften zum Öffentlichen Recht, Band, vol 1279. Duncker & Humblot, Berlin, pp 181–210

Reese M (2020) Das EU-Klimagesetz – Nachhaltigkeit durch Umweltpolitikplanungsrecht? ZUR 641–643
Reese M (2021a) Offenbarungseid zur Wasserrahmenrichtlinie. ZUR 321–323
Reese (2021b) Transformation to healthy water Ecology - Institutional requirements, deficits and options in European and german perspective. Sustainability 13(6):3368. https://doi.org/10.3390/su13063368
Reese M (2023) Transformation to climate neutrality from a federal perspective – Distribution of powers and regional responsibilities under European law and in the German federal system. Rev d'Etudis Auton i Fed 37:31–60. https://doi.org/10.57645/20.8080.01.2
Reese M (2024a) Das neue Renaturierungsgesetz der EU – Nun zur Umsetzung! ZUR 449–451
Reese M (2024b) The EU's new nature restoration law – now for implementation! JEEPL 21(3–4):361–364. https://doi.org/10.1163/18760104-21030010
Schlacke S, Knodt M (2019) Das Governance-System für die Europäische Energieunion und für den Klimaschutz, ZUR 404–412
Schlacke S (2020) Bundes-Klimaschutzgesetz: Klimaschutzziele und -pläne als Herausforderung des Verwaltungsrechts. EurUP 18(3):338–345
Schlacke S (2021a) Umweltrecht, 8th edn. Nomos, Baden-Baden
Schlacke S (2021b) Planende Verwaltung. In: Kahl W, Ludwigs M (eds) Handbuch des Verwaltungsrechts, Bd. I, C.H.Beck, München, pp 831–876
Schlacke, 2022Schlacke S (2022) Klimaschutzrecht im Mehrebenensystem. NVwZ 905–912
von Weschpfennig A (2023) Plan und Planung. In: Kahl W, Ludwigs M (eds) Handbuch des Verwaltungsrechts, Bd. I, C.H.Beck, München, pp 1349–1392
Wickel M (2021) Das Bundes-Klimaschutzgesetz und seine rechtlichen Auswirkungen. ZUR 332–339
Zaelke D, Stilwell M, Young O (2005) Compliance, Rule of Law and Good Governance. In: Zaelke D, Kaniaru D, Kruzikova E (eds) Making Law Work: Environmental compliance and sustainable development. Cameron, pp 29–52

Cases

BVerfG, Judgement of 24.3.2021 - 1 BvR 2656/18, ECLI:DE:BVerfG:2021:rs20210324.1bvr265618
BVerfG, Judgement of 18.1.2022 - 1 BvR 1565/21 and others
ECtHR Klimaseniorinnen Schweiz and others v Switzerland App No 53600/20

Legal Sources

Bundes-Klimaschutzgesetz (2019) Federal Climate Action Act of 12 December 2019 (Federal Law Gazette I, p. 2513), as last amended by Article 1 of the Act of 15 July 2024 (Federal Law Gazette I No. 235)
Bundes-Klimaanpassungsgesetz (2023) Federal Climate Adaptation Act of 20 December 2023 (Federal Law Gazette I, p. 393)

Multifunctional Land Use as a Key Concept in Planning Law

Sabine Schlacke and Matti Gurreck

Abstract The increasing competition for land—driven partly by legal targets and incentives—intensifies land-use conflicts. This article explores how multifunctional land use, defined as the simultaneous realisation of multiple uses on the same area, can address these pressures. Analysing EU and German law, it finds that while multifunctionality is partly reflected in legislation (for example in the EU's Renewable Energy Directive), it lacks legal clarity and binding effect. To unlock its full potential, multifunctionality should be anchored as a guiding principle in Germany's planning law. The German legislator took a first step towards more efficient and sustainable land use planning by adopting the new section 7(1) sentence 2 of the German Regional Planning Act, which transposes Article 15b(3) RED III into German law and serves as a new guiding principle of multifunctional use.

1 Introduction

The pressure to utilise land as a resource is already high at present. According to the latest scientific findings, it will continue to increase in the future—partly due to legal incentives and requirements (e.g. area-related targets or permission-related prioritisation as part of the energy transition). This development promotes conflicts of use and is explored in section B. Against this background, it is crucial to engage with the idea of multifunctional use of land. This contribution examines the legally embedded objectives and demands of land use (section C) before exploring the concept of multifunctional land use, taking into account the recommendations of the German Advisory Council on Global Change (WBGU) and current European Union

S. Schlacke (✉)
Chair of Public Law, in Particular Administrative and Environmental Law, University of Greifswald, Greifswald, Germany
e-mail: sabine.schlacke@uni-greifswald.de

M. Gurreck
Law School, Faculty of Social Sciences and Business Studies, University of Eastern Finland, Joensuu, Kuopio, Finland
e-mail: matti.gurreck@uef.fi

M. Reese et al. (eds.), *Environmental Law in Transformation*,
https://doi.org/10.1007/978-3-032-31567-0_9

legislation (section D). It further analyses the extent to which multifunctionality is reflected in the current legal framework in Germany, highlighting the pivotal role of planning law. Finally, section E synthesises the findings, drawing key conclusions on the legal implications of multifunctional land use.

2 Starting Point: Increasing Pressure on Land as a Resource

Like soil, land is a finite resource that must be used sensibly in order to preserve the basis of human life. Its allocation and utilization are subject to diverse planning and usage demands, reflecting its critical role in various sectors.

Globally, the total land area encompasses around 13 billion hectares (ha), of which about one-third (4.8 billion ha) is used for agriculture. The agricultural land is further divided into cropland, which accounts for 1.6 billion ha, and permanent meadows and pastures, covering 3.2 billion ha.[1] Urban areas, including human settlement, as well as industry and infrastructure such as transportation networks, occupy around 1% of the world's land surface. The remaining land comprises forests, wetlands, and other natural landscapes.[2] In the European Union (EU), these numbers are similar, with agriculture (39%)—including arable lands, pastures as well as mosaic farmlands—and forests (40%) covering most of the EU's total land area.[3]

Overall, competition for land is likely to increase, the two most significant drivers being the energy sector and the food sector.[4] In the case of Germany, a study commissioned by the Federal Ministry of Agriculture estimates that the competition for land could result in a reduction of more than 300,000 ha of agricultural land by 2030, as new land utilisation often affects areas previously used for agriculture. While the speed of land take for settlement and transport has decreased significantly over the past decade, a sharp increase is expected by 2030. Against this backdrop, the study recommends that land use demands be weighed against each other more carefully in the future and that synergies and multiple uses of land be realised as far as possible.[5] To do so without slowing down the pace of the energy transition and the transformation towards more sustainable and climate-friendly land use is a major challenge for policymakers and for the instrument of spatial planning which coordinates the various land use interests, balances conflicts at the planning levels and regulates land uses and functions.[6]

[1] UN FAO (2023).

[2] WBGU (2024a, b).

[3] European Environment Agency (2024, 2025).

[4] King et al. (2023).

[5] Osterburg et al. (2023).

[6] See section 1(1) of Germany's Regional Planning Act (Raumordnungsrecht, ROG).

3 Legally Embedded Land Use Objectives and Demands

Competition for land is fuelled in particular by legal objectives. In this context, the focus of this contribution is on four current legal developments: area-based targets (I.), prioritising (II.) and privileging (III.) certain projects, in addition to other objectives (IV.), some of which have existed for some time. All four are relevant factors for the increase in land use competition.

3.1 *Area-Based Targets*

Lately, EU law as well as the German federal law have set targets in relation to the utilisation of land by formulating and prescribing new land requirements that can lead to land competition and scarcity. The temperature goals set in the Paris Agreement demand significant and sustained efforts from the international community in terms of climate mitigation and energy policy. At the EU level, these efforts have been formalized through instruments such as the EU Climate Law[7] and the Fit for 55 packages,[8] which aim to achieve climate neutrality by 2050 and a 55% reduction in greenhouse gas emissions by 2030. Central to meeting these ambitious objectives are the contribution of the Land Use, Land Use-Change and Forestry (LULUCF) sector and the rapid and substantial expansion of renewable energy capacities.

3.1.1 LULUCF

From a climate mitigation perspective, land as a resource is primarily addressed through LULUCF activities. Land has a significant role in climate mitigation, as the Intergovernmental Panel on Climate Change's (IPCC) 2019 special report on climate change and land pointed out: It is both a source and a sink of CO_2, accounting for roughly 23% of total net anthropogenic emissions of greenhouse gases (GHGs).[9] It is mainly regulated through the LULUCF Regulation[10] at the EU level and in German climate law through the Federal Climate Action Act (Bundes-Klimaschutzgesetz,

---

[7] Regulation (EU) 2021/1119 of the European Parliament and of the Council of 30 June 2021 establishing the framework for achieving climate neutrality and amending Regulations (EC) No 401/2009 and (EU) 2018/1999 ('European Climate Law'), OJ L 243, 9.7.2021.

[8] On the Fit for 55 package see Schlacke et al. (2022).

[9] Arneth et al. (2019), p. 82. Note that this refers to the Agriculture, Forestry, and Other Land Use (AFOLU) sector, not the LULUCF sector. Both terms describe overlapping but distinct aspects of land-based greenhouse gas (GHG) emissions and removals.

[10] Regulation (EU) 2018/841 of the European Parliament and of the Council of 30 May 2018 on the inclusion of greenhouse gas emissions and removals from land use, land use change and forestry in the 2030 climate and energy framework and amending Regulation (EU) No. 525/2013 and Decision No. 529/2013/EU, OJ L 156, 19.6.2018.

KSG).[11] The aim of both legal acts is to remove more GHG emissions from the atmosphere through sinks such as soils, forests and bodies of water than are emitted by them as GHG sources. To this end, the LULUCF Regulation contains an obligation for the Member States in Article 4(3) to reach the GHG reduction targets set out in Annex IIa. The Regulation represents a significant advancement in accounting for human-induced emissions and removals from the land sector which were for a long time outside the scope of climate mitigation law.[12] The German legislator has included a definition of the LULUCF sector (section 2 No. 8 KSG) and an independent, quantified CO_2 reduction target in section 3a KSG.

The prerequisite for (re)establishing the sink function of land is that land is utilised, converted or protected accordingly. At the same time, corresponding measures should be coherent with other policy objectives, in particular the protection of biodiversity and food security. As not all anthropogenic GHG emissions can be reduced to zero, the LULUCF sector is of central importance for achieving the goal of net GHG neutrality by 2045 (Germany, see section 3(2) sentence 1 KSG) and 2050 (EU, see Article 1(2) of the EU Climate Law) respectively. It is therefore a key sector and possibly poses the greatest challenge for achieving the European and German climate targets.

3.1.2 Renewable Energy

The legal frameworks to increase the deployment of renewable energy also have a distinct spatial dimension. The latest Emissions Gap Report by the United Nations Environment Programme underscores that global climate protection efforts remain insufficient to achieve the objectives of the Paris Agreement, even if current commitments are fully implemented.[13] Decarbonizing the energy system stands as a cornerstone of climate mitigation and the first global stocktake has emphasized the need to triple renewable energy capacity by 2030—a critical goal for UNFCCC parties.[14] Yet, progress toward achieving this goal remains severely lacking, with only solar photovoltaics showing potential to meet the required scale of expansion.[15]

Beyond the technical and financial challenges of this transition, a pressing yet often overlooked issue is the growing competition for land. Renewable energy infrastructure—including solar and wind farms, energy storage facilities, and grid networks—requires substantial space, competing directly with other essential land uses such as transport, housing, biodiversity conservation, and agriculture. In this context, land

---

[11] Bundes-Klimaschutzgesetz (KSG) of 12 December 2019 (BGBl. 2019 I p. 2513) as last amended by Article 1 of the law of 15 July 2024 (BGBl. 2024 I Nr. 235). English translation available at https://www.gesetze-im-internet.de/englisch_ksg/. On the KSG see Franzius, in this volume, subsection 2.3, Sects. 3, and Sect. 4.1.

[12] Savaresi et al. (2020).

[13] United Nations Environment Programme (2024).

[14] UNFCCC (2024), Outcome of the first global stocktake, FCCC/PA/CMA/2023/16/Add.1, Decision 1/CMA.5, para. 28, lit. a.

[15] International Renewable Energy Agency (2024).

has become the "currency of the energy transition,"[16] in which its allocation and management determine the success or failure of decarbonization efforts.

Renewable Energy Directive III

The recently amended Renewable Energy Directive of the EU,[17] called RED III because it is the third major amendment,[18] introduces spatial planning obligations and significantly changes the provisions on permitting.[19] Articles 15b, 15c, and 16a of the RED III represent the foundation of the EU's updated strategy for accelerating renewable energy deployment. Member States are tasked with identifying so-called Renewable Acceleration Areas (RAAs) where simplified permitting procedures will apply. This process involves two main steps: mapping the areas necessary to achieve renewable energy targets (Article 15b RED III) and formally designating RAAs based on certain criteria (Article 15c RED III).

As part of the mapping process, Member States need to identify the domestic potential and the available areas necessary for the installation of renewable energy plants and their related infrastructure. This does not require measures in the form of a legally binding act since it only constitutes the initial selection of areas potentially available for renewables deployment.[20] The German government has commissioned a study titled "Analyse der Flächenverfügbarkeit für Windenergie an Land post-2030" (Analysis of land availability for onshore wind energy post-2030), to fulfil the mapping obligation of Article 15b(1) RED III.[21]

Following the mapping of necessary areas, Member States have to designate RAAs,[22] which Article 2(2) No. 9a RED III defines as "a specific location or area, whether on land, sea or inland waters, which a Member State designated as particularly suitable for the installation of renewable energy plants". Article 15c RED III contains the criteria to be applied in the designation process which aim at upholding standards of environmental protection, in particular: certain environmentally sensitive areas like Natura 2000 sites are excluded as possible RAAs; the plans designating the RAAs have to be accompanied by a so-called "mitigation rulebook",[23]

---

[16] German Federal Agency for Nature Conservation (BfN) (2021).

[17] Directive (EU) 2018/2001 of the European Parliament and of the Council of 11 December 2018 on the promotion of the use of energy from renewable sources, OJ L 328, p. 82, 21.12.2018.

[18] Directive (EU) 2023/2413 of the European Parliament and of the Council of 18 October 2023 amending Directive (EU) 2018/2001, Regulation (EU) 2018/1999 and Directive 98/70/EC as regards the promotion of energy from renewable sources, and repealing Council Directive (EU) 2015/652, OJ L, 2023/2413, 31.10.2023.

[19] On the role of planning law in the ecological transformation in the EU, see Durner, in this volume, section 3.

[20] Römling (2024), p. 238.

[21] Proposal for the transposition of the RED III into German law, Deutscher Bundestag, Drucksache (BT-Drs.) 20/12785, p. 31.

[22] Article 15c(1), point (a)(ii) RED III.

[23] Terminology used by the European Commission, SWD(2024) 333 final, p. 8.

meaning appropriate rules to prevent or, where prevention is not feasible, significantly reduce the adverse environmental impacts of renewables projects have to be established[24]; the plans have to undergo a strategic environmental assessment under the Strategic Environmental Assessment Directive (SEA Directive)[25] and an appropriate assessment according to Article 6(3) of the Habitats Directive,[26] if they are likely to have a significant impact on Natura 2000 sites.[27] In addition, Member States need to ensure public participation in the designation process.[28] As a result, renewable energy projects inside RAAs do not have to comply with certain environmental regulations.[29]

Germany: Acceleration of Renewables Deployment Through the Wind Energy Area Requirement Act

Even before the transposition deadlines of the RED III provisions mentioned above have expired,[30] Germany had already adopted a similar approach to accelerate the roll-out of renewable energy: The Wind Energy Area Requirement Act (Windenergieflächenbedarfsgesetz, WindBG) sets individual area targets for the German federal states, which requires the designation of a certain percentage of the land surface area as wind energy areas at the planning level.[31] According to the explanatory memorandum to the WindBG, this will lead to a doubling of the area currently designated for wind energy.[32] The federal states can fulfil their area designation obligations by including them in their state-wide or regional spatial development plans or by means of regional or municipal area designations that are bindingly determined by law or spatial planning objectives vis-à-vis the spatial planning authorities or municipalities.[33] At the permitting stage, renewable energy projects within wind energy

---

[24] Article 15c(1), point (b) RED III.

[25] Directive 2001/42/EC of the European Parliament and of the Council of 27 June 2001 on the assessment of the effects of certain plans and programs on the environment, OJ L 197, p. 30, 21.07.2001.

[26] Article 12(1) Council Directive 92/43/EEC of 21 May 1992 on the conservation of natural habitats and of wild fauna and flora, OJ L 206, p. 7, 22.07.1992, in short: Habitats Directive.

[27] Article 15c(2) RED III.

[28] As detailed in Article 6 of the SEA Directive (2001/42/EC), see Article 15d RED III. For a critical reflection on public participation see Cancik, in this volume, section 3.

[29] Article 16a RED III.

[30] The mapping of necessary areas has to be completed by 21 May 2025; for the designation of RAAs the date is 21 February 2026.

[31] Section 3(1) in conjunction with Annex 1 WindBG (Law of 20 July 2022 (BGBl. I S. BGBl 2022 I, p. 1353), as last amended by Article 12 of the Law of 8.5.2024, (BGBl. 2024 I Nr. 151). Analyses of the WindBG are provided by Kment (2022), p. 1154, Schmidt-Eichstaedt (2023), p. 10, Groneberg (2023).

[32] See the legislative materials: BT-Drs. 20/2355, p. 1. For the status of implementation see Schlacke et al. (2025), p. 441.

[33] Section 3(2) sentence 1 No. 1 WindBG and section 3(2) sentence 1 No. 2 WindBG.

areas benefit from provisions such as section 6 WindBG, according to which neither an environmental impact assessment nor a species protection assessment must be carried out at project level if a strategic environmental assessment has been carried out at planning level.[34]

3.2 Prioritisations

Besides the direct obligations to designate areas, legal requirements in the form of prioritisations for renewable energy projects have an impact on land use. Prioritisation means assigning a predominant or even overriding public interest to specific concerns or projects and/or qualifying them as serving public safety. Such interests and projects are thus given a higher weight compared to other concerns within the framework of weighing and balancing decisions by public authorities and courts.

Within the RED III this is reflected in Article 16f, which requires Member States to ensure that, in the permit-granting procedure, the planning, construction and operation of renewable energy plants as well as the grid and storage infrastructure "are presumed as being in the overriding public interest and serving public health and safety when balancing legal interests in individual cases for the purposes of" certain environmental law provisions.[35] Article 3 of the Emergency Regulation contains a similar provision.[36] Such provisions are also included in several German laws to favour projects needed for the energy transformation, most notably section 2 sentence 2 of the German Renewable Energy Act (Erneuerbare-Energien-Gesetz, EEG). According to section 2 sentence 2 EEG, renewable energies will be prioritised in the weighing and balancing of interests until electricity generation in Germany is almost GHG neutral.

Although this balancing priority can be refuted in individual cases, it imposes a high burden of substantiation and justification on the competent authority. As a result, renewable energy plants and related infrastructure are more likely to prevail within the scope of the authorities' discretionary powers.

---

[34] See Schlacke and Thierjung (2023), p. 637 et seq., Rieger (2023), p. 1043.

[35] Decisions according to Article 6(4) and Article 16(1), point (c) of the Habitats Directive, Article 4(7) of the Water Framework Directive (Directive 2000/60/EC) and Article 9(1), point (a), of the Birds Directive (Directive 2009/147/EC).

[36] Council Regulation (EU) 2022/2577 of 22 December 2022 laying down a framework to accelerate the deployment of renewable energy, OJ L 335, p. 36, 29.12.2022.

3.3 Privileges

In addition to prioritisation, the German legislator is increasingly expanding the catalogue of privileged projects under section 35(1) of the Building Code (Baugesetzbuch, BauGB) in favour of renewable energy projects. Section 35 regulates which projects are permissible outside of build-up areas. Those projects listed as privileged in section 35(1) are much easier to realize than non-privileged ones because a permit can be obtained provided that the project does not conflict with public interests and adequate site development is ensured. In recent years, the legislator has added wind energy (No. 5), biomass (No. 6), solar energy on rooftops and external wall surfaces, along motorways and railways (No. 8) and solar installations and businesses in connection with an agricultural, forestry or gardening business (No. 9) to the list of privileged projects in section 35(1). This effectively facilitates the realisation of renewable energy projects because permits according to the Building Code can be obtained provided the renewables projects in question do not conflict with public interests and adequate development is ensured.

3.4 Other Objectives Affecting Land Use

Like climate mitigation and renewable energy infrastructure, biodiversity conservation also requires areas on which conservation measures can be implemented. The Kunming-Montreal Global Biodiversity Framework adopted in December 2022 under the Convention on Biological Diversity (CBD), includes 3 area-based targets. Inter alia, the CBD members aim to ensure that by 2030 at least 30% of areas of degraded terrestrial, inland water, and marine and coastal ecosystems are under effective restoration" (target 2) and that "by 2030 at least 30% of terrestrial and inland water areas, and of marine and coastal areas […] are effectively conserved and managed through ecologically representative, well-connected and equitably governed systems of protected areas […]" (target 3).[37] This commitment is closely linked to target 15.5 of the UN Sustainable Development Goals (SDGs), which calls for immediate and significant action to reduce the degradation of natural habitats and halt biodiversity loss.

The overarching climate and biodiversity goals will also increase land-use competition. This is because the previous clearing of forest areas, destruction of wetlands, drainage of peatlands or the conversion of pasture into arable land have not only led to considerable biodiversity losses, but also to GHG emissions. Almost a quarter of global greenhouse gas emissions are attributable to agriculture, forestry and other anthropogenic land uses.[38] In order to counteract this trend and compensate for GHG emissions, more land needs to be utilised to create near-natural habitats and

[37] Kunming-Montreal Global Biodiversity Framework. CBD/COP/DEC/15/4, in: https://www.cbd.int/doc/decisions/cop-15/cop-15-dec-04-en.pdf. Accessed 22 Sept 2025.

[38] Arneth et al. (2019), p. 82.

carbon sinks in the interests of climate protection, climate adaptation and biodiversity conservation. This will be accompanied by quantitative and qualitative changes in land use in the direction of increased afforestation, restoration of wetlands and rewetting of peatlands as well as conversion of arable land into pastureland, which—in Germany—will probably primarily affect areas previously used for agriculture.[39]

The EU Nature Restoration Law[40] points in a similar direction, albeit not as ambitious as the international, non-binding new Global Biodiversity Framework. Its Article 1(2) stipulates that Member States shall put in place restoration plans as well as effective and area-based restoration measures with the aim to jointly cover, as a Union target, at least 20% of land areas and at least 20% of sea areas by 2030, and all ecosystems in need of restoration by 2050.[41]

Agriculture is both a significant driver of biodiversity loss and climate change and one of the sectors most vulnerable to the adverse impacts of these planetary crises. The growing competition for land could raise concerns about food security, particularly when agricultural land is diverted for non-agricultural purposes. However, food security is not currently at risk in Germany or the EU. Globally, the issue of food security is less about insufficient agricultural production or the availability of land and more about the equitable distribution of resources.[42] Agricultural land has substantial potential to contribute more effectively to food security, as a considerable portion is currently allocated to non-food purposes, such as the production of bioenergy and animal feed.[43] These uses are relatively inefficient in terms of producing energy[44] and food[45] respectively, highlighting the need for more sustainable and effective land use practices.

In summary, the diverse legal objectives, prioritisations, privileges and other objectives will intensify land-use pressure and exacerbate competition among the various uses of land. As outlined above, a monofunctional land use in favour of renewable energy generation is (legally) encouraged without any balancing of other interests.

---

[39] Osterburg et al (2023), p. 38 et seq.

[40] Regulation (EU) 2024/1991 of the European Parliament and of the Council of 24 June 2024 on nature restoration and amending Regulation (EU) 2022/869, OJ L, 2024/1991, 29.7.2024.

[41] The planning component is an example of so-called policy planning law, see Reese, in this volume, section 3.

[42] Pörtner et al. (2022).

[43] Globally, the majority of agricultural land is used for livestock rearing, Ritchie and Roser (2019).

[44] European Academies Science Advisory Council (2019), p. 8.

[45] See the comparison of the land use footprints of animal products and crops by Ritchie and Roser (2019).

4 Multifunctional Land Use as an Element to Mitigate Competition for Land

Addressing these competing demands for land requires robust spatial planning that integrates multifunctional land use. Innovative solutions, such as combining renewable energy projects with biodiversity conservation or agricultural production can reduce land use conflicts. In this way, the energy transition must be seen not only as a technical or economic challenge but also as a spatial one, where strategic land management plays a decisive role in its success.

4.1 The Concept of Multifunctionality

The terms "multifunctionality" or "multifunctional land use" are not explicitly defined in legal documents, including the EU's Renewable Energy Directive, which speaks of "multiple uses" of areas. Elements mentioned in scholarship include the strategic integration of multiple land use functions within the same spatial area such as nature conservation, economic activities, and social services.[46] An explicit and comprehensive engagement with the concept of multifunctionality was undertaken by the German Advisory Council on Global Change (WBGU) in its 2020 flagship report "Rethinking Land in the Anthropocene: from Separation to Integration". It refers to multifunctional land use as the simultaneous realisation of two or more different uses on the same area. It does not mean a use that fulfils several functions at the same time.[47] The WBGU recommends a fundamental global change in the use of land as a resource to mitigate climate change, avert the dramatic loss of biodiversity, and to make the global food system more sustainable. It proposes a multifunctional and multiple use of land, rather than a monofunctional one, to take sufficient account of the threefold global challenge, the so-called 'trilemma' of climate change, biodiversity decline and food security. It elaborates on the diverse synergies that go hand in hand with multifunctional land use.

In line with the Kunming-Montreal Global Biodiversity Framework and in order to implement the area-based targets set out therein, the WBGU proposes in a recently published policy paper an orientation towards the guiding concept of a 'multifunctional mosaic for land'.[48] The basic idea behind this guiding concept is that conservation and use should be combined and designed across the entire area in such a way that significant additional benefits for nature and people are achieved.[49] In practical terms, this can mean combining intensive and small-scale land use (e.g. industry and agriculture) with biodiversity-friendly and sustainable utilisation.

---

[46] See for example Mander et al. (2007).

[47] WBGU (2020), Rethinking Land in the Anthropocene: from Separation to Integration. Flagship Report, 2020.

[48] WBGU (2024a), Biodiversity: Act Now for Nature and Humanity, Policy Paper 13, April 2024.

[49] See also Pörtner et al. (2023).

4.2 *Potential and Examples of Multifunctionality in the Context of Energy Policy*

This, according to the WBGU, should lead to "multiple-benefit strategies" for land use.[50] The potential of combined land uses is great, in particular for combinations with energy production, as illustrated by a recent study: In the case of Germany, 97–98% of the land surface area needed for wind turbines could at the same time be used for other purposes.[51] Examples of multiple land uses in the field of agriculture include agroforestry, in which trees and shrubs are added to an agricultural area to diversify production. Aquaponics combines the cultivation of vegetable plants with fish farming and biochar can be used to store CO_2 in agricultural waste in the long term or be utilised as a source of energy. In what follows, two applications of multifunctional uses are highlighted—combining photovoltaics with the rewetting of peatlands and wind power plants.

4.2.1 Peatland Photovoltaics

To illustrate the potential and the challenges of multifunctionality, combining the rewetting of peatlands with ground-mounted photovoltaics (PV) on the same site, so-called peatland PV, serves as an example. It can be distinguished from agri PV, where the open-space PV plants are installed above or alongside agricultural crops,[52] and paludi PV, where the agricultural use occurs on rewetted peatland.[53] The rewetting of peatlands can make a significant contribution to climate protection as they cover only about 3% of the earth's surface yet hold nearly 30% of the soil carbon.[54] This requires water levels to be raised and kept close to the surface.[55] Besides the climate mitigation function, peatlands provide other essential ecosystem services like preventing floods or soil erosion as well as storing and filtrating water.[56]

The scale of the potential is significant: In Germany alone, 1.45 million ha of drained peatlands used for agriculture must be rewetted by 2050 at the latest to meet the international climate targets established by the Paris Agreement and the European Green Deal. To support the energy transition while protecting these critical

---

[50] WBGU (2020), p. 3.

[51] Bampinioti et al. (2023).

[52] Also called 'agrivoltaics'. This also has significant potential in terms of renewables capacity: Deploying Agri-PV systems on just 1% of the EU's utilized agricultural land could enable the installation of 1 TW of photovoltaic capacity, see A. Chatzipanagi et al. (2023). On the implementation in German law see Baars (2024), p. 39.

[53] Seidel et al. (2024), p. 2.

[54] IUCN, About Peatlands, https://www.iucn-uk-peatlandprogramme.org/about-peatlands. Accessed 22 Sept 2025.

[55] Greifswald Moor Centrum (2022).

[56] Harenda et al. (2017).

ecosystems, it is essential to prioritize the use of sealed and low-environmental-value areas for PV deployment—such as rooftops and parking lots. Environmentally valuable areas should be exempt from peatland PV projects.[57] To ensure realising the potential of PV in combination with other land uses, a multi-faceted and simultaneous approach is required.[58]

From a legal perspective, research by Seidel et al. suggests privileging peatland PV within the German Building Code (BauGB) and recognizing peatland PV deployment as serving an overriding public interest as measures that could contribute to overcoming legal hurdles hindering the rapid deployment of peatland PV. This approach should also include the designation of specific areas for peatland PV projects, akin to the area designation requirements already in place for wind energy described above.[59]

4.2.2 Combining Wind and PV Plants

Deploying wind energy and PV on the same site is another example of multifunctionality. In Germany, the designation of areas for wind energy has recently been pushed forward.[60] This development also bears potential for the multiple use of land: For example, areas that have been designated wind energy areas are often suitable to be combined with open-space PV plants. Depending on the local topographical conditions (for example the intensity and duration of solar radiation where PV systems are concerned or the right wind conditions in case of wind energy), this can significantly increase the energy yield of the area. The example illustrates the synergy effects resulting from the multiple use of land in favour of wind and open-space PV which range from the joint use of technical infrastructure (joint connection to a transformer station or feed-in cable, joint use of access roads and storage areas) to overcoming the volatility characteristic of renewable energy generation, e.g. wind still periods and periods with limited or no solar radiation.[61] Furthermore, using an area where renewable energy plants are already deployed can increase the acceptance among the local population for new plants because it limits additional land use.[62] Also, in an area already shaped by wind power plants, adding solar PV panels usually does not have as great an impact on the landscape as building a free-standing solar park on otherwise undeveloped land. Regarding potential conflicts with species conservation law, solar PV modules can deter wind turbine-sensitive species from the areas beneath wind turbines, which can enhance wind energy production. This could reduce the need for

---

[57] Greifswald Moor Centrum (2022).

[58] Fraunhofer-Institut für Solare Energiesysteme ISE (2025).

[59] See recommendations by Seidel et al. (2024), p. 26 et seq.

[60] See above Sect. 3.1.2.2.

[61] See the statement of the Academy for Territorial Development in the Leibniz Association (ARL) (2022), p. 15.

[62] Schlacke and Plate (2024), p. 328.

temporary shutdowns that would otherwise be required during specific agricultural activities to safeguard birds.[63]

4.3 Legal Framework for Multifunctionality

The described need for multifunctionality is reflected only to some degree in legislation.

4.3.1 EU Law

Within EU law, the RED III and the Nature Restoration Law are particularly noteworthy for their references to multiple uses.

Multiple Uses in the RED III

As part of the mapping of necessary areas,[64] Article 15b(3) RED III requires Member States to "favour multiple uses of the areas" to be mapped. Also, renewable energy projects need to be compatible with pre-existing uses of the areas concerned. Article 15b(3) RED III is a step in the right direction. However, its effectiveness in reducing land-use conflicts depends largely on the Member States' implementation. The provision merely calls for Member States to "favour" multiple uses without defining the term or specifying concrete measures, aside from ensuring compatibility with pre-existing land uses.[65] This wording makes enforcement by the European Commission unlikely, as "favouring" constitutes an obligation of effort rather than result, which will probably be fulfilled easily unless a Member State completely disregards the option of multiple uses.[66] Hence, the responsibility lies with Member States to develop detailed rules on multiple uses, though the European Commission has announced issuing a guidance document to assist in this process.[67]

---

63 Baars (2024), p. 44.

64 See Sect. 3.1.2.1.

65 Similarly, recital 27 of the RED III merely encourages Member States to "explore, enable, and favour multiple uses" and to facilitate land-use changes where activities can coexist.

66 Gurreck (2025), p. 104, 105.

67 SWD(2024) 333 final, p. 4.

Nature Restoration Law

The EU's 2024 Nature Restoration Law (NRL) aims to restore degraded ecosystems by setting binding restoration targets.[68] Among other things, Member States are required to adopt restoration plans (Articles 14–19 NRL).[69] The NRL explicitly recognises the need to create the kinds of multi-benefit strategies proposed by the WBGU. When drafting the restoration plans, synergies with climate change mitigation, climate change adaptation, land degradation neutrality and disaster prevention and according prioritisations of the restoration measures have to be identified. In doing so, Member States need to take the renewable energy targets of the RED into account,[70] in particular the "potential for renewable energy projects to contribute towards fulfilling nature restoration objectives".[71] When areas designated as RAAs are concerned, the NRL states that the Member States must ensure the functioning of the RAAs, "including the permit-granting procedures applicable in those areas [...], remains unchanged."[72] As described above, combining the rewetting of peatlands with PV can create the kinds of synergies envisioned by the NRL.[73] Promoting peatland PV is thus also a way of implementing the NRL.

4.3.2 National Law

At the level of national law, multifunctional land use will be particularly relevant in the transposition of the RED III. Furthermore, urban planning law in Germany already contains elements of multifunctional use.

Transposition of the RED III by the Member States

The RED III's ambitious deadline required Member States to transpose most of the provisions, including Article 15b(3), into national law by 21 May 2025.[74] The German Government intended to include this provision on multiple uses in its Building Code (BauGB) and in the German Regional Planning Act (Raumordnungsgesetz, ROG): A draft section 1c(5) No. 2 foresaw that the responsible planning authorities need to take multifunctional uses of land into account as one among other

68 See Articles 1 and 4 of the Regulation (EU) 2024/1991.

69 This planning approach is modelled on the EU Water Framework Directive, see Durner, in this volume, section 11.

70 Article 14(9) point (c) of the NRL.

71 Recital 67 of the NRL.

72 Recital 68 of the NRL.

73 Seidel et al. (2024), p. 22.

74 Article 5(1) of Directive (EU) 2023/2413.

concerns in their decision-making processes.[75] This was supposed to establish multifunctional use of land as a guiding principle of land use planning, also outside the context of renewable energy deployment. With a similarly worded provision, a draft section 7(1) sentence 2 of the ROG would have allowed competent planning authorities to explicitly designate multifunctional land uses in regional plans.[76] Moreover, a new section 249b(6) of the BauGB was supposed to promote multifunctional land use and the bundling of areas for wind and solar energy by stipulating that priority is to be given to the use of wind energy if solar energy areas overlap with wind energy areas. In practice, this would have been implemented via a declaration of commitment as a prerequisite for the authorisation of a solar energy project, with which the dismantling of the project is ensured, insofar as this is necessary for the construction, modification or operation of a wind turbine.[77] However, due to the collapse of the coalition government in 2024, the described draft section 249b(6) BauGB and section 1c(5) No. 2 BauGB were dropped.

Nevertheless, the German legislator adopted the amendments of the German ROG in July 2025: The explicit mention of multifunctional land uses as possible designations in regional plans is now included in section 7(1) sentence 2 ROG, which reads: "It may be stipulated that certain areas within the planning zone [...] are allocated for multiple compatible uses and functions (multifunctional use); [...]".[78] While the parliament's leading committee on the amendment considers this a mere clarification of the existing rules,[79] it's significance should not be underestimated. Even though area designations for multifunctional uses were already possible before the amendment, in practice, uptake by the competent planning authorities was low and designations for monofunctional uses common. With the new section 7(1) sentence 2 ROG, the legislator has effectively established a new guiding principle of multifunctional use, sending important signals to planning authorities and project developers.[80] Therefore, the transposition of Article 15b(3) RED III can be considered a success and a step towards more efficient and sustainable land use.

---

[75] See the draft „Referentenentwurf des Bundesministeriums für Wohnen, Stadtentwicklung und Bauwesen Entwurf eines Gesetzes zur Stärkung der integrierten Stadtentwicklung" of 3.9.2024.

[76] See the draft "Referentenentwurf des Bundesministeriums für Wirtschaft und Klimaschutz, des Bundes-ministeriums für Wohnen, Stadtentwicklung und Bauwesen und des Bundesministeriums für Umwelt, Naturschutz, nukleare Sicherheit und Verbraucherschutz—Entwurf eines Gesetzes zur Umsetzung der Richtlinie (EU) 2023/2413 in den Bereichen Windenergie an Land und Solarenergie sowie für Energiespeicheranlagen am selben Standort", 19.07.2024, p. 25.

[77] Proposal for the transposition of the RED III into German law, Bundestag Drucksache 20/12785, 09.09.2024, p. 17.

[78] Own translation of the original German: „Es kann festgelegt werden, dass bestimmte Flächen des Planungsraums [...] für mehrere miteinander vereinbare Nutzungen und Funktionen vorgesehen werden (Mehrfachnutzung); [...]", Bundesrat Drucksache 329/25 (Beschluss), 11.07.2025, p. 16.

[79] Bundestag Drucksache 21/797, p. 56.

[80] On the role of guiding principles in the ecological transformation, see Markus, in this volume, Sect. 4.3.

Urban Planning Law in Germany

Besides the energy sector, multifunctionality is a useful concept in urban planning where it has been discussed and partially implemented for some time now. In cities, competition for space is also increasing with housing, commercial use, climate adaptation, recreation, culture and transport being the most important functions of a city that need to be accommodated on a limited surface area.[81] Among the initiatives addressing this challenge is the New Leipzig Charter—a strategic policy framework adopted by the ministers for urban development from 27 EU countries to promote sustainable, resilient, and inclusive urban development across Europe—which includes the concept of "a city of short distances". What that means is a move away from the practice in urban planning to favour monofunctional uses where the main uses (work, housing, recreational areas, traffic, etc.) were kept apart from one another.[82]

Examples of multifunctional uses in urban areas include green urban spaces which can also serve as retention areas, helping to manage excess rainwater.[83] Additionally, they can support decentralised rainwater management through measures such as infiltration troughs or trenches and serve as recreational areas.[84] In practice, playgrounds or parking spaces could become temporary retention areas in times of extreme rainfall.[85] The challenge of coping with extreme weather events including heavy precipitation will intesify in the future as a result of climate change.[86] Conventional sewage systems and other infrastructure in most cities are not yet adapted to this challenge.[87] Multifunctional retention areas can therefore be part of an adaptation strategy. Their explicit mention was foreseen in a draft law to amend the German Building Code, where a new section 9(1) No. 14c BauGB was supposed to allow for the designation of multifunctional retention rooftops by the competent municipalities in the planning process.[88] This law could not be passed before the 2025 snap election and has so far not been adopted by the new legislator.

Prior to that, the German parliament introduced a new category of "urban areas" into the Federal Building Utilisation Ordinance (Baunutzungsverordnung, BauNVO) in 2017. This law defines land use categories, establishing which types of buildings and activities are permitted within designated zones (e.g., residential, commercial, etc.). It serves as a legal framework that enables municipalities to structure urban development, ensuring a functional and harmonious allocation of land uses while maintaining spatial coherence. With the introduction of the category of "urban areas",

---

81 Comprehensively: WBGU (2016).

82 The New Leipzig Charter. https://t1p.de/0jtek. Accessed 22 Sept 2025.

83 Benden et al. (2017).

84 Sachverständigenrat für Umweltfragen (2018), p. 27.

85 Siekmann et al. (2012), p. 620.

86 Dodman et al. (2022), p. 909.

87 Siekmann et al. (2012), p. 611; WBGU (2024b), p. 70.

88 See the draft „Referentenentwurf des Bundesministeriums für Wohnen, Stadtentwicklung und Bauwesen Entwurf eines Gesetzes zur Stärkung der integrierten Stadtentwicklung", 03.09.2024.

the legislator intended to give the competent authorities the necessary tools to implement the Leipzig Charter, including the concept of "a city of short distances".[89] In urban areas, various uses (housing, commercial, social, cultural) can be combined provided they do not interfere with residential living, see section 6a(1) sentence 1 BauNVO. It can thus be seen as a manifestation of the concept of multifunctional use.[90]

5 Conclusions

Space is a scarce resource, the competition for which is likely to increase in the future. Among the various pressures on land are legally embedded land-use objectives and demands, in particular in the area or energy law. These take the form of, inter alia, area-based targets, prioritising and privileging certain projects. Area-based targets are now included in the RED III and the German WindBG, both of which seek to accelerate the deployment of renewable energy through area designations at the planning level.

Multifunctional land-use, defined as the simultaneous realisation of multiple uses on the same area, offers a transformative approach to addressing this challenge. It can mitigate land use conflicts and create "multiple-benefit strategies" for land use, for example in the case of peatland PV which combines the rewetting of peatlands with open-space photovoltaics (PV) on the same site. Combining wind and PV plants is another example of a more efficient use of space.

The great potential of multifunctional land-use is still insufficiently reflected in the legislation at the EU level and in Germany. While the RED III contains in its Article 15b(3) a requirement to "favour multiple uses of the areas", it lacks further details including a definition of multiple uses, thus leaving significant discretion to the Member States. The latter should therefore specify this provision in their national laws. The EU Nature Restauration Law also recognises the need for multifunctional uses, as does draft legislation in Germany. However, to maximise the benefits provided by multifunctional land use concepts, the legal framework in Germany should be amended to include multifunctional land use as a guiding principle in its planning law, specifically the Regional Planning Act (Raumordnungsgesetz, ROG).[91] While the current legal framework already allows for multifunctional uses, explicitly introducing such a new guiding principle has the potential to actually change the planning practice.

---

[89] Bundestag Drucksache 18/11439, 08.03.2017, p. 18.

[90] Lorenzen (2024), p. 335, 339.

[91] See the proposals by Schlacke and Plate (2024), p. 329 et seq.

References

Academy for Territorial Development in the Leibniz Association (ARL) (2022) Regionalplanung für einen raumverträglichen Ausbau von Freiflächen-Photovoltaik-Anlagen. https://www.arl-net.de/de/shop/freiflachen-photovoltaikanlagen.html. Accessed 22 Sept 2025

Arneth A, Denton F, Agus F et al (2019) Framing and Context. In: Shukla PR et al (eds) Climate change and land: an IPCC special report on climate change, desertification, land degradation, sustainable land management, food security, and greenhouse gas fluxes in terrestrial ecosystems. https://doi.org/10.1017/9781009157988.003

Baars A (2024) Steuerung multifunktionaler Flächen im Außenbereich. In: Schlacke S (ed), Multifunktionale Flächennutzung. Lexxion, pp 38–47

Bampinioti S, Christakou N, Paulitz B et al (2023) Land: a crucial resource for the energy transition. https://www.mckinsey.com/industries/electric-power-and-natural-gas/our-insights/land-a-crucial-resource-for-the-energy-transition. Accessed 22 Sept 2025

Benden J, Broesi R, Illgen M et al (2017) Multifunktionale Retentionsflächen. Teil 1: Wissenschaftliche Grundlagen, MURIEL Publikation. https://opac.dbu.de/ab/DBU-Abschlussbericht-AZ-32223_01.pdf. Accessed 22 Sept 2025

Chatzipanagi A, Taylor N, Jaeger-Waldau A (2023) Overview of the potential and challenges for agri-photovoltaics in the European Union. https://doi.org/10.2760/208702. Accessed 22 Sept 2025

Deutscher Bundestag (2024) Drucksache 20/12785. https://dserver.bundestag.de/btd/20/127/2012785.pdf. Accessed 22 Sept 2025

Dodman D, Hayward M, Pelling V et al (2022) Cities, settlements and key infrastructure. In: Pörtner H-O, Roberts DC, Tignor M et al (eds) Climate change 2022: impacts, adaptation and vulnerability. Cambridge University Press, Cambridge, UK and New York, NY, USA, pp 907–1040. https://doi.org/10.1017/9781009325844.008

European Academies Science Advisory Council (2019) Forest bioenergy, carbon capture and storage, and carbon dioxide removal: an update. https://easac.eu/publications/details/forest-bioenergy-carbon-capture-and-storage-and-carbon-dioxide-removal-an-update. Accessed 22 Sept 2025

European Environment Agency (2024) Forests and forestry, 4.12.2024. https://www.eea.europa.eu/en/topics/in-depth/forests-and-forestry?activeAccordion=4268d9b2-6e3b-409b-8b2a-b624c120090d. Accessed 22 Sept 2025

European Environment Agency (2025) Agriculture and food systems, 6.3.2025. https://www.eea.europa.eu/en/topics/in-depth/agriculture-and-food?activeTab=fa515f0c-9ab0-493c-b4cd-58a32dfaae0a. Accessed 22 Sept 2025

Fraunhofer-Institut für Solare Energiesysteme ISE (2025) Recent facts about photovoltaics in Germany. https://www.ise.fraunhofer.de/en/publications/studies/recent-facts-about-pv-in-germany.html. Accessed 22 Sept 2025

German Federal Agency for Nature Conservation (BfN) (2021) „Mehr Flächen für Windenergie" — natur- und landschaftsverträglich verteilt. https://t1p.de/tycwl. Accessed 22 Sept 2025

Greifswald Moor Centrum (2022) Informationspapier des Greifswald Moor Centrum zu Photovoltaik-Anlagen auf Moorböden. https://www.greifswaldmoor.de/files/dokumente/Infopapiere_Briefings/Positionspapier_PV-auf-Moor_fin.pdf. Accessed 22 Sept 2025

Groneberg S (2023) Die Windenergie-an-Land-Strategie: Überblick und erste Bewertung. Energiekriese-Aktuell 2(11):010136

Gurreck M (2025) The EU's renewable energy directive – planning and permitting under the RED III. Stud Prawa Publicznego 1(49):85–108. https://doi.org/10.14746/spp.2025.1.49.5

Harenda K, Lamentowicz M, Samson M, Chojnicki B (2017) The role of peatlands and their carbon storage function in the context of climate change. In: Zielinski T, Sagan I, Surosz W (eds) Interdisciplinary approaches for sustainable development goals, 1 edn. Springer, Cham, pp 169–187

International Renewable Energy Agency (2024) Delivering on the UAE consensus: tracking progress toward tripling renewable energy capacity and doubling energy efficiency by 2030. https://www.ourenergypolicy.org/resources/delivering-on-the-uae-consensus/. Accessed 22 Sept 2025

King R, Benton TG, Froggatt A et al. (2023) The emerging global crisis of land use: How rising competition for land threatens international and environmental stability, and how the risks can be mitigated. Royal Institute of International Affairs. https://doi.org/10.55317/9781784135430. Accessed 22 Sept 2025

Kment M (2022) Eine neue Ära beim Ausbau von Windenergieanlagen. NVwZ 41(16):1153–1159

Lorenzen J (2024) Steuerung multifunktionaler Flächen im urbanen Raum. ZUR 35(6):333–340

Mander Ü, Helming K, Wiggering H (2007) Multifunctional land use: meeting future demands for landscape goods and services. In: Mander Ü, Wiggering H, Helming K (eds) Multifunctional land use, 1st edn. Springer, pp 1–13

Osterburg B, Ackermann A, Böhm J et al (2023) Flächennutzung und Flächennutzungsansprüche in Deutschland, Thünen Working Paper 224. https://literatur.thuenen.de/digbib_extern/dn067046.pdf. Accessed 22 Sept 2025

Pörtner H-O, Scholes RJ, Arneth A et al (2023) Overcoming the coupled climate and biodiversity crises and their societal impacts. Science 380(6642). https://doi.org/10.1126/science.abl4881

Pörtner LM., Lambrecht N, Springmann M et al (2022) We need a food system transformation – in the face of the Ukraine war, now more than ever. https://zenodo.org/records/6461468

Rieger W (2023) § 6 WindBG – die nächste Runde im Konflikt zwischen dem Ausbau der Windenergie und dem Artenschutz. NVwZ 42(14):1042–1046

Ritchie H, Roser M (2019) Our world in data: land use, published September 2019 and last revised in May 2024. https://ourworldindata.org/land-use. Accessed 22 Sept 2025

Römling D (2024) Die Novelle der Erneuerbare-Energien-Richtlinie (EU) 2018/2001 (RED III). Zeitschrift für Europäisches Umwelt- und Planungsrecht 22(3):237–246

Savaresi A, Perugini L, Chiriacò M (2020) Making sense of the LULUCF Regulation: Much ado about nothing? Review of European, Comparative & International Environmental Law 29(2):212–220. https://doi.org/10.1111/reel.12332

Sachverständigenrat für Umweltfragen (2018) Wohnungsneubau langfristig denken – Für mehr Umweltschutz und Lebensqualität in den Städten. https://www.umweltrat.de/SharedDocs/Downloads/DE/04_Stellungnahmen/2016_2020/2018_11_Stellungnahme_Wohnungsneubau.htm. Accessed 22 Sept 2025

Schlacke S, Wentzien H, Thierjung E-M et al (2022) Implementing the EU Climate Law via the 'Fit for 55' package. Oxford Open Energy. https://doi.org/10.1093/ooenergy/oiab002

Schlacke S, Plate C (2024) Multifunktionale Flächennutzung: Potentiale und Grenzen des Raumordnungsrechts. ZUR 35(6):323–332

Schlacke S, Plate C, Thierjung E (2025) Beschleunigung des WEA-Ausbaus: Befund, Umsetzung, role model - eine Zwischenbilanz. NVwZ 44(7):441–446

Schlacke S, Thierjung E (2023) Im Dschungel der Beschleunigungsgesetzgebung zum Ausbau von erneuerbaren Energien: EU-Notfall-VO, section 6 WindBG und RED III und IV. DVBL 11:635–643

Schmidt-Eichstaedt G (2023) Die Festlegung von Windenergieflächen – Terminkalender und Pflichtenheft. Zeitschrift für deutsches und internationales Bau- und Vergaberecht 46(1):10–17

Seidel M, Wichmann S, Pump C, Beckmann V (2024) Combining photovoltaics with the rewetting of Peatlands - A SWOT analysis of an innovative land use for the case of North-East Germany. Land 13:1548. https://doi.org/10.3390/land13101548

Siekmann M, Vomberg N, Mirgartz M et al (2012) Multifunctional land use in urban spaces to adapt urban infrastructure. In: Leal F (ed) Climate change and sustainable use of water resources, 1 edn. Springer, pp 611–625

SWD (2024) 333 final, commission staff working document guidance on designating renewables acceleration areas accompanying the document Commission Recommendation on speeding up permit-granting procedures for renewable energy and related infrastructure projects. https://t1p.de/l87v0. Accessed 22 Sept 2025

United Nations Environment Programme (2024) Emissions gap report 2024: no more hot air ... please! With a massive gap between rhetoric and reality, countries draft new climate commitments. Nairobi. https://doi.org/10.59117/20.500. 11822/46404. Accessed 22 Sept 2025

UN FAO (2023) Land statistics and indicators 2000–2021. Global, regional and country trends, FAOSTAT Analytical Brief 71. https://openknowledge.fao.org/items/ddc2584a-9d58-4cde-a9a2-789a0bb93835. Accessed 22 Sept 2025

WBGU (2016) Humanity on the move: unlocking the transformative power of cities, 2016, available at https://www.wbgu.de/en/publications/publication/der-umzug-der-menschheit-die-transformative-kraft-der-staedte

WBGU (2020) Rethinking land in the Anthropocene: from separation to integration. Flagship report. https://www.wbgu.de/en/publications/publication/landwende. Accessed 22 Sept 2025

WBGU (2024a) Biodiversity: act now for nature and humanity, policy paper 13. https://www.wbgu.de/en/publications/publication/pp13. Accessed 22 Sept 2025

WBGU (2024b) Water in a heated world. Flagship report 2024, available at: https://www.wbgu.de/en/publications/publication/wasser. Accessed 22 Sept 2025

Thou Shalt not Ignore: Knowledge-Obligations as a Fragile Implementation Incentive in the Law of Environmental Quality Management*

Pascale Cancik

Were you naïve?—Of course! I thought knowledge would lead to action. (Mojib Latif)

Abstract Planning and planning law have long traditions. Practical experience has led to sceptical assessments, though. Without planning, however, the necessary environmentally oriented "transformation" will not take place. A key element of planning as conceived in EU law is public participation in the generation of information and knowledge. The described functions of generating "public" or "participatory" knowledge, as I call it, are manifold. They include the creation of solutions, but also the creation of acceptance for solutions. In order for these functions to be fulfilled in reality, possible weaknesses of the concept of "public knowledge" must be discussed. Given the dearth of research in this field, only preliminary questions will be addressed here. In particular, it is EU environmental quality management law in which the production of "public information and knowledge" about the environmental problem at hand plays an important role. Specific "knowledge-generation-obligations" of the respective administration are supposed to guarantee this specific form of knowledge. Of course, information and knowledge have always been a key element for governing, and the corresponding rules and literature are hard to keep track of. Yet, in our context, the EU seems to follow a rather elaborate concept of what I call participatory or public knowledge used as a form of "nudge" to mobilise administrations to implement the law. This type of public-including-knowledge shall apparently serve as an incentive, as a mobilising factor that generates pressure effects on administrations. Comparing

* I owe Jan Markgraf thanks for his support. I would also like to thank all members of the Competence Network Environmental Law, especially Till Markus, for their helpful comments.

Mojib Latif, early climate researcher, DIE ZEIT No. 19, 2 May 2024.

P. Cancik (✉)
Faculty of Law, University of Osnabrück, Osnabrück, Germany
e-mail: lscancik@uni-osnabrueck.de

M. Reese et al. (eds.), *Environmental Law in Transformation*,
https://doi.org/10.1007/978-3-032-31567-0_10

the relative success of air quality planning with the rather disappointing results of ambient noise planning will raise the question, however, whether public participation and the production of public/participatory knowledge possibly may be overrated as long as they are not integrated into a regulatory framework with limit values and legal protection. In view of overburdened administrations and diffuse assignments of responsibility, more or less deliberate "ignorance", i.e. ignoring knowledge that is actually accessible, can be an almost unavoidable element in administrative decision-making. It is highly probable that statutory duties of knowledge alone are not sufficient to combat this phenomenon of more or less conscious disregard of knowledge. Even if the law adds the public and its presumed mobilising pressure as a motivating factor, i.e. as a "nudge" for the administrations, this is not a sufficient solution.

1 A Noise Walk and a Question: Crowd-Knowledge-Production?

On a sunny late afternoon around 2012, some citizens and two employees of the municipal administration of a medium-sized city in Germany met for a so-called noise walk. Equipped with a kind of old-fashioned noise measuring device, they went to various places that were considered noisy in order to record the noise situation and discuss related problems. Why did they do this?

The noise walk was a creative attempt by the administration to implement the new regulation on environmental noise action planning. In further public events, draft noise action plans were presented, measures discussed with the public, and the plan finally adopted by the responsible authorities. The procedure resembles a sort of crowd-funding related to local people's knowledge about local noise problems and possible countermeasures: crowd-knowledge-producing.

The obvious reason for these and similar actions all over Germany were the novel provisions of the EU Environmental Noise Directive to involve the public in the "management" of environmental noise.[1] They were implemented in Germany in the *Bundes-Immissionsschutzgesetz* (Federal Immission Control Act) which provided for a quite elaborate concept of public participation in "noise management"-planning.[2] Historians looking at the ups and downs of participatory approaches since the 1960s might perhaps later discover a trace of the *zeitgeist* in that type of regulation framed by the rhetoric of knowledge management. Meanwhile, one can ask whether the concept

---

[1] Directive 2002/49/EC of the European Parliament and of the Council of 25 June 2002 relating to the assessment and management of environmental noise - Declaration by the Commission in the Conciliation Committee on the Directive relating to the assessment and management of environmental noise, OJ L 189, 18.7.2002, pp. 12–25.

[2] § 47d sec. 3 BImSchG (roughly translated): The public is consulted on proposals for noise action plans. The public is given timely and effective opportunities to participate in the development and review of noise action plans. The results of the participation shall be taken into account. The public shall be informed of the decisions taken. Appropriate deadlines shall be provided with sufficient time for each stage of participation.

and the (presumed) motivation behind it can convince. The EU-Commission puts it recently as follows: "The Environmental Noise Directive aims to protect human health by requiring Member States to assess noise pollution so that authorities and citizens can choose the best solutions as part of binding action plans."[3]

2 The Concept of Environmental Quality Management Laws

Since the 1970s, the perceived crisis of command-and-control regulation led to reflections on other ways of managing behaviour for the benefit of the environment. Law enforcement deficits were to be countered through more intelligent "governance" mechanisms, sometimes labelled as "smart" or "better regulation", and that meant: through a different legal design. European environmental law at the forefront has taken this up. A type of regulation has emerged that can be called "environmental quality management law". The approach is characterised by comprehensive planning procedures, with action plans or programmes at their core, which are designed to define and achieve quality objectives for specific areas.[4]

Since the 1990s, a number of directives pursued this specific regulatory approach with the objective of improving the quality of the air, water, noise situation and so on.[5] All these directives have been adapted in the meantime. Still the basic approach has not been changed.[6] It will be illustrated here by using four examples.[7]

[3] European Commission (2024), March infringements package: key decisions. Press Release, 13.3.2024. https://t1p.de/crd9x. Accessed 22 Sep 2025. Press release on an additional letter of formal notice to **Germany** (INFR(2016)2116) within the infringement procedure for failing to establish noise action plans for all major roads under the END-Directive.

[4] On the "programmatic approach" see Braaksma (2023); Durner, in this volume, section 3.

[5] For comprehensive analysis see Knappe (2022). For precursors in international law see Durner, in this volume, section 2.

[6] Environmental Impact Assessment (EIA) will not be considered here in detail. It is, of course, of great importance for the production of information on environmental issues. However, the EIA-Directive is not primarily focused on area/ quality management, but on the planning and approval of concrete projects. Thus, the generation of knowledge is embedded in a different procedural and functional context. The central question of my contribution about the mobilisation effect of shared knowledge does not arise in the same way. But of course, we can see effects of public access to the information generated by EIA, as the participation of environmental NGOs and respective court trials show. For the SEA-Directive see below (fn. 22). Also omitted is the Waste Framework Directive, Directive 2008/98/EC of the EP and of the Council of 19.11.2008 on waste and repealing certain Directives, OJ L 312, p. 3, 22.11.2008. It regulates the recording of waste-related information for the respective area. Optionally, "the use of awareness-raising campaigns and the provision of information to the general public or a specific group of consumers" (Art. 28 para. 4 c) WFD) can also be included. Public participation and information must be ensured, e.g. through publication on a "publicly accessible website" (Art. 33, 31 WFD).

[7] This approach can be also found in the Marine Strategy Framework Directive, Directive 2008/56/EC of the European Parliament and of the Council of 17 June 2008 establishing a framework for community action in the field of marine environmental policy, OJ L 164, p. 19, 25.06.2008.

(1) The Air Quality Directive 1996 (AQD) with the subsequent daughter directives marked the beginning.[8] According to this directive, all member states had to define "zones" and "agglomerations" and prepare a "preliminary assessment" of air quality for them. Where such data were not available, they had to be determined by "measurement, investigation or assessment campaigns", as stated in Art. 5 of the AQD 1996. In a second step—after limit values and alert thresholds had been set by the (then) EC—the air quality had to be assessed again with regard to these values. This step, at the latest, turns the information into knowledge that can trigger measures if limit values are exceeded in a relevant way. This was the case with certain fine dusts at the beginning of 2005 when the respective limit value came into force. By this time at the latest, action plans had to be drawn up to counter exceedances and the risk of exceedances.[9] The 2008 AQD continued this approach.[10]

The regulatory structure established since then is as follows: definition of the area—recording of the area with a view to certain knowledge (quality assessment)—preparation of an "action plan" with the necessary measures.[11] Similar to the emerging territorial states of the early modern period, it seems, a space is recorded and made controllable through territorial definitions, mapping, data collection—in our context to improve environmental situations.

(2) The second example of this approach is the Water Framework Directive of 2000.[12] Information has to be gathered on existing water body conditions and on "good" conditions to be achieved. Article 5 stipulates that the "river basin districts"—i.e. the territorial units relevant for water protection purposes—must also be recorded for information purposes. To get there, these territorial units must first be defined, then their characteristics described; the effects of human activities on the water status in this area must be examined, and finally the use of water there must be analysed in

[8] Council Directive 96/62/EC of 27 September 1996 on ambient air quality assessment and management, OJ L 296, p. 55, 21.11.1996. Pedrosa and Vanheusden (2020). The terminology Framework and Daughter Directive is not European, cf. Jarass (2003), p. 259. Particularly well-known became the so-called Fine Particulate Matter Directive, Directive 1999/30/EC for sulphur dioxide, for nitrogen dioxide and for nitrogen oxides, for particulate matter and for lead, OJ L 163, p. 41, 29.6.1999.

[9] Art. 11 of the AQD 1996 sets out accompanying information and reporting obligations.

[10] Directive 2008/50/EC of the European Parliament and of the Council of 21 May 2008 on ambient air quality and cleaner air for Europe, OJ L 152, p. 1, 11.06.2008.

[11] Or in the terminology of other directives, e.g. the EU Water Framework Directive: "programme of measures".

[12] Directive 2000/60/EC of the European Parliament and of the Council of 23 October 2000 establishing a framework for community action in the field of water policy, OJ L 327, p. 1, 22.12.2000. Transposed in Germany with the seventh WHG amendment in 2002. Similar: Marine Strategy Framework Directive (Directive 2008/56/EC of the European Parliament and of the Council of 17 June 2008 establishing a framework for community action in the field of marine environmental policy, OJ L 164, 25.06.2008, pp. 19–40) and the Flood Directive (Directive 2007/60/EC of the European Parliament and of the Council of 23 October 2007 on the assessment and management of flood risks, OJ L 288, p. 27, 6.11.2007).

economic terms.[13] Detailed requirements for the collection, evaluation and contextualisation of the information are set out in Annexes II and III to the Directive. In addition to environmental data in the narrower sense, economic information is also requested, which is intended to serve, among other things, the appropriate enforcement of the polluter pays principle via the requirement of cost recovery for water services (taking water uses into account).[14] The "management plans" and "programmes of measures" to be drawn up on the basis of the new knowledge are to be submitted to the EU. In addition, further reporting obligations are foreseen (Art. 15). Information to the public is also specifically regulated (Art. 14). A consultation procedure is only provided for with regard to the management plans. However, in connection with EIA law, various forms of participation in the preparation of programmes of measures are also standardised in Land law.[15]

To sum up: In water law, too, the step-by-step process of area-related knowledge gathering—management planning—concretisation in a programme of measures—implementation of the measures—is established. As mentioned, this regulatory pattern is found in many directives now.

(3) A third example is the Environmental Noise Directive of 2002 (END) which we started with that provides for a similar approach.[16] For certain defined areas, comprehensive information on the state of the area was to be collected in a first round, within the framework of a "noise mapping".[17] This was followed by the obligation to draw up so-called action plans, which define targets to be achieved in the future and are to contain short- and long-term measures to achieve the targets. The (public) collection of information on specific noise situations forms the starting point for such action planning.

(4) Our last example is the draft Soil Protection Framework Directive 2006 which never entered into force. It provided for the identification of so-called "risk areas" that are endangered by erosion, compaction, salinisation and the like. To counteract the risks, "programmes of measures" with target definitions and individual concrete

---

[13] Cf. Art. 5 seq. Directive 2000/60/EC.

[14] Cf. the 38th recital as well as Art. 9 (Costs for water services) and Annex III (Scope of information for economic analysis).

[15] Cf. e.g. § 86 NWG (Northrhine-Westfalian Water Act). Public participation may be required via the SEA regulations in the UVPG, cf. Annex 5 to the UVPG No.1.4 - Programmes of measures under § 82 of the WHG are subject to mandatory SEA.

[16] Directive 2002/49/EC of the European Parliament and of the Council of 25 June 2002 relating to the assessment and management of environmental noise, OJ L 189, p. 12, 18.07.2002.

[17] The obligation to map noise follows from Art. 7 of the END, which contains requirements for structuring the information; assessment methods for noise measurements are provided for in Art. 6 in conjunction with Annex II.

measures were to be drawn up.[18] In the recitals of the draft, the problem of knowledge was explicitly mentioned.[19]

Public participation and "raising awareness" played an important role: "Member States shall take appropriate measures to raise awareness of the important role of soil [...] and promote the *transfer of knowledge and experience* in the field of sustainable soil use."[20] The rhetoric of knowledge management already seemed to be couched in legal language here. We will return to soil protection later. With regard to public participation, the proposal refers to Art. 2 of the Strategic Environmental Assessment Directive (SEA-Directive).[21] This norm defines in general the valid standards of participation of the public and the "public concerned", not least with regard to turning the public into an informed one. It can be seen as a kind of fundamental norm, expressing the idea of shared or public knowledge as governance factor relevant in EU environmental law today.

3 (Participatory) Knowledge as Incentive to Act: First Thesis

As we have seen, the complex planning structures contain sophisticated rules for the production of information and knowledge.[22] But is this not a trivial point? Of course, administrations always have (had) a need for gathering information, and the generation of knowledge has always been a "classic" part of planning law and its implementation. And yet, it makes sense to take a second look, a look at what I want to call: Member state administrations' knowledge obligations.

---

[18] Art. 6 et seq. COM(/2006)232 final—COD 2006/0086, Proposal for a Directive of the EP and of the Council establishing a framework for the protection of soil and amending Directive 2004/35/EC, 22.09.2006. Criteria for site identification are given in Annex I. Secondly but not relevant here, a list of "contaminated sites" was to be drawn up. Art. 10 et seq. of the Proposal. In German soil protection and contaminated site law, registers of contaminated sites, old deposits and suspected contaminated sites had already been in place for some time (BBodSchG 1998 in conjunction with Land law).

[19] Recital 14 Proposal of a Soil Protection Directive, (fn. 19), with a poorly phrased German version. Cf. also recitals 15; and 22 (on site recording); 30 f. on the public.

[20] Art. 15 No. 1 Proposal of a Soil Protection Directive (fn. 19) (emphasis mine).

[21] Directive 2003/35/EC of the European Parliament and of the Council of 26 May 2003 providing for public participation in respect of the drawing up of certain plans and programmes relating to the environment and amending with regard to public participation and access to justice Council Directives 85/337/EEC and 96/61/EC, OJ L 156, p. 17, 25.06.2003.

[22] Regularly a difference is made between data, information and knowledge. For the purposes here, it is sufficient to understand knowledge as a third step, as it were, characterised by its pragmatic reference, see Lenk and Wengelowski (2004), p. 150 et seq.; (Lenk and Wengelowski (2004), p. 147: Administration as dealing with information). On the distinction between data - information - knowledge, which in turn can be understood in different ways, Trute (2010) with many references. Vesting (2022), who with others calls for the precise separation of these categorical terms.

The legal acts provide for the creation and dissemination of new and regularly updated information between the authorities and for the publication of knowledge. Increasingly, the public is also involved in the production of environmental knowledge, what I have called shared or participatory or—somewhat vaguely—public knowledge.[23]

I would like to argue that the commitment to the production of specific knowledge together with the intense involvement of the public in the generation of shared knowledge makes a difference not only in procedural terms.[24] It also has specific functions,[25] one of which should be emphasised here: Knowledge should serve as an incentive, as a mobilising factor that potentially generates pressure effects on administrations. Above all, "ordinary" people, civil society, those affected, should be mobilised and—again through their pressure—persuade the administrations of the member states to implement the laws, to translate the legal texts into practice, into "reality". In my opinion, this is a central motivation for the European legal design: If the public knows that the administration knows the problem, it is assumed that the administration will act to solve it.

"Knowledge obligations", thus, imply action, as the European 'legislator' apparently expects. This seems to be based on social science in that knowledge is also defined as the ability to act.[26] However, the question arises as to whether the expectation raised by this knowledge-as-incentive-design will be fulfilled. Overall, it is plausible that the intense generation of information is of central importance for successful environmental policy. But is it as plausible that the production of public, of shared knowledge works as an instrument to support law implementation?

The implicit assumptions behind this idea are hardly made explicit. However, it is plausible that they roughly follow the line outlined here: In a (very simplified) rational perspective, we assume that administrations and political bodies, just like "normal" people, are always trying to improve their information and thus their knowledge. We assume, that we try to learn in order to identify and solve problems and to improve our

---

[23] On participatory administration cf. Grohs (2021), who describes more recent developments of participation as "co-production". Our topic could be linked to the subcategories of "co-design" and "co-evaluation". On a "collaborative approach" as part of "better regulation" at least in the view of the EU-Commission shortly: Braaksma and Tolsma (2020), p. 320. The case of Citizens Science also belongs to the participatory age, but lies a bit differently: The citizens involved do not support or exert pressure on legally bound administrations which were obliged to act anyway, but support a scientific project by collecting information.

[24] The involvement in administrative knowledge through active information-duties of the administrations under EU-Law are part of that knowledge-as-incentive-design, but cannot be detailed here.

[25] Not to be further elaborated here is the obvious function of obtaining "Europe-wide" information and knowledge at EU level to enable the EU institutions to act through (then more detailed) EU law. In a second step, the aim is to gain further knowledge to monitor and evaluate the implementation and impact of the new EU rules in the member states. With regard to the 'epistemic power' of different EU actors to define which knowledge is relevant and which scientific and methodological standards will be employed in the process of generating information see Markus (2013), pp. 145–165.

[26] Stehr (2004), p. 20; Lenk and Wengelowski (2004), p. 151.

lives.[27] In this perspective, more knowledge is linked to better problem solving, i.e. better management, or in public-managerial language: better governance. In short, we follow a common-sense concept of "knowledge leads to (improved) action".[28] This concept is connectable to an old basic idea of the Enlightenment, but also to rational choice theory and a kind of everyday theory in our so-called "knowledge society".

The underlying assumptions and theories have been contested in many ways, of course.[29] Nevertheless, there is a 'reasonable reason' for this expectation of (better) knowledge leading to action. Thus, it also seems conceptually coherent that EU knowledge obligations force administrations to acquire knowledge and that also means: not to ignore the accumulated knowledge. Using behavioral science terms, one could state, that this shared public knowledge about environmental problems shall act as a kind of administrative "nudging" to motivate administrations to solve the identified environmental problem—together with the "public concerned", if you will.[30] Environmental law scholars welcomed this new management approach as innovative with arguments that are, of course, still worth considering today: In Germany, too much emphasis was placed on conflict resolution or problem solving by the courts anyway.[31] The scholars emphasised the enforcement deficits of the 'old' approach as well as the necessary density of regulation ('flood of norms') if one follows the limit value and legal protection path: The EU concept, however, relied on the participatory political process [...] leading to an improvement in the noise situation. "It is about activating the expertise (also of laypeople) outside the professional administration in favour of the administration's decision-making process".[32]

---

[27] This "desire for knowledge" as a supposedly common motivation is itself controversial. Cf. Mair, Kelly and High (2012), p. 1.

[28] Short overview of the history of the learning state: Stolleis (2009/2011).

[29] Cf. only the short overview on related questions and the state of research on this, in: Bundeszentrale für politische Bildung (2013). Short overview on the relevance of non-knowledge: Wehling (2013); Gill (2004).

[30] For this term as a legal term cf. Art. 3 of the SEA-Directive mentioned above (Directive 2003/35/EC of the European Parliament and of the Council of 26 May 2003 providing for public participation in respect of the drawing up of certain plans and programmes relating to the environment and amending with regard to public participation and access to justice Council Directives 85/337/EEC and 96/61/EC, OJL 156, p. 17, 25.6.2003): "'the public concerned' means: the public affected or likely to be affected by, or having an interest in, the environmental decision-making procedures referred to in Article 2(2); for the purposes of this definition, non-governmental organisations promoting environmental protection and meeting any requirements under national law shall be deemed to have an interest". The concept of nudging, which aims to control the behaviour of citizens, was developed by Thaler and Sunstein (2008).

[31] For instance: Schulze-Fielitz (2008), esp. p. 36 et seq., who outlines and welcomes the replacement of subjective legal protection as an enforcement concept by extended participation.

[32] Schulze-Fielitz (2008), p. 43 (my translation); also p. 53: "[…] endeavour to activate the citizens through public participation within the noise abatement planning process."

4 Ignoring as "Administrative Resource" and Exit Option: Second Thesis

However, the further developments in Germany have shown that not only have successes in air quality been achieved primarily with the help of the courts, but that successes in reducing environmental noise are also rather rare (cf. below 5).[33] So, if environmental quality management via shared knowledge is not as successful as intended and necessary,[34] could this also be due to the governance concept itself?

In other words: What prevents knowledge from leading to action? What are the conditions that enable the desired mobilisation of this shared knowledge? Under what conditions does knowledge actually lead to action, in our case: Noise abatement or other improvements in environmental quality?

These are far too big questions, of course. My second thesis, which is to be put up for discussion here, only addresses part of them: It is that the 'rational assumption' outlined above is both, right and wrong. Non-knowledge, ignoring is not seldom a central resource for the 'survival' of administrations (and other organisations)—as is knowledge and non-ignoring.

Knowledge production is not only timely, costly and exhausting, and therefore suffering from all the deficits of authorities not adequately equipped for their tasks, as is well known from public administration research. But even more: The concept of the pushing effect of knowledge itself implies a normative surplus, an expectation regarding the motivation to act, which might be debatable.

Although there is, of course, research on the problem of knowledge or communication deficits in administrations, and the problem of so to speak organised ignoring of administrative failures has also been addressed recently,[35] research on ignoring as—to a certain extent—an administrative "necessity" is still rare.[36] Therefore, only initial questions can be posed for discussion. Many of the raised questions fall in the domain of psychology,[37] of social and political science. Also, a comparative discussion on the situation in other EU-member states could be productive, since the EU regulatory approach might have been influenced from the legal and administrative culture of other member states, especially the Netherlands.[38] The considerations

---

[33] Riedel et al. (2022), p. 258 et seq.

[34] With regard to noise: Cf. EEA (2020); EEA (2014). EU Commission, Environmental Implementation Review 2022—Country Report—GERMANY, SWD/2022/265 final, p. 22. https://t1p.de/hirmu; in German: https://t1p.de/qa492, p. 27. A similar legal design, delegating the setting of targets to Member State administrations and subsequent inadequate further implementation, is reported for the Marine Strategy Framework Directive. Weiß (2017); Markus, Schlacke and Maier (2011).

[35] Seibel (1996); with regard to concrete "administrative desasters" Seibel, Klamann and Treis (2017).

[36] I would like to thank Wolfgang Seibel for affirmation of this information on the state of research in administrative science.

[37] For example: Mandl and Gerstenmaier (2000).

[38] For a comparing view with regard to water cf. Baaner (2011), with regard to air quality (and legal protection) Backes (2012).

made here would therefore require contributions from other disciplines, which are beyond my expertise. But we can at least shed light on the questions and encourage further research.

5 A Brief Look Back at Knowledge and Jurisprudence

In the 1990s at the latest, the knowledge perspective became a leading scientific perspective also in law. It follows the perception and description of our present as being characterised in a special way by knowledge, culminating in the term "knowledge society". Since then, the phenomenon of "non-knowledge" and its sub-cases (uncertain knowledge, conscious non-knowledge, unconscious non-knowledge) has been discussed.[39] The fact that the state, that administrations have to make decisions despite or "under" not-knowing[40] and that we know about it publicly marks a fundamental problem of the "knowledge society".

In addition to not being able to know (and still having to decide), the overload of knowledge and information ("informational overkill") was considered a main problem of administration in a knowledge society.[41] The "reduction of complexity",[42] "stop rules" for the search for knowledge[43] and the outsourcing of knowledge acquisition tasks to the private sector[44] are discussed as reactions to this phenomenon. We spoke of the "knowledge of the state",[45] of the state or legal "knowledge order"

---

[39] In recent times Courts have addressed the question, how administrations have to handle scientific uncertainty; see Köck and Markus (2023), with regard to habitat and species conservation law. Here, as well, concrete standards are lacking, thus administrations are forced to develop their own approach, that is: methods for specifiying vague standards and evaluating the needs for protection.

[40] Cf. some of the sociology of knowledge-contributions in: Böschen et al. (2004).

[41] This is embedded in a long tradition of theoretical approaches and descriptions to grasp the 'real reality' of administration (organisation), of planning with its information processing and its conflicts of interest; and these theories often lead to, ultimately, theories of *non-rational* decision-making (Bogumil and Jann). Some keywords are: bounded rationality (Herbert A. Simon 1945); muddling through (Lindblom 1959) or—more elegantly—incremental politics; organisation of hypocrisy (Brunsson 1989); street level bureaucracy (Lipsky 2010); negotiating or co-operative state; to name just a few. Jann and Bogumil speak of "implementation ignorance of the legislator", who does not take into account the realities of implementation and refer to Frido Wagener, who has stated very critically that administrations pursue "pragmatic reduction of regulations in implementation", especially in the case of overload (Wagener 1979), an ultimately unconstitutional behaviour. For an overview and references see Bogumil and Jann (2020), esp. pp. 211–236.

[42] A term coined by Luhmann, but used here in a more concrete sense of selecting information and sorting out others.

[43] Ladeur (1995), p. 24 et seq., pp. 87, 89 et seq. Preclusion regulations as "information stop regulations" in Durner (2008), p. 219 et seq., pp. 234, 238: these limit the obligations to investigate by limiting the balancing requirement, which would otherwise lead to information overload.

[44] Cf. only Spieker (2008).

[45] Cf. Collin and Horstmann (2004). The contributions in Röhl (2010).

or at least "information order", and we developed "public information management law".[46] The handling of information/knowledge was discussed from different perspectives.[47] In the administrative sciences, the focus was on the organisation of information procurement, dissemination and storage in organisations, on 'knowledge management' and 'organisational learning'. But what applies when 'the state' does not want to know about certain—perceptible—developments that one could know about—what I have called 'ignorance'—this aspect was, as far as I can see, not the focus of the knowledge discourse, although it 'flashed up' again and again in individual places, so to speak.[48]

The importance of forgetting, of not knowing, of repression for individuals but also for institutions has been emphasised time and again in recent years.[49] Not least the pandemic, but even more so the climate crisis, has shown, how difficult it is to literally bring knowledge to the institutions and those actors respectively, which are responsible and able to decide on the necessary measures and apply them.[50] We should not ignore the well-known fact that organisations and their representatives may behave irrational.

So, if the concept of 'knowledge is welcome and leads to action' is to some extent naive and in danger of failing, what does this mean for the EU regulatory concept of participatory knowledge as an impetus, a "nudge"?

6 Public Knowledge as Mobilising Tool in Air Quality and Environmental Noise: With or Without Legal Protection

Notwithstanding the similar structure, the mentioned and other directives of that type show many differences, of course, not least with regard to the participatory elements, especially to *which* "public" is participating. With regard to water, it is

[46] Cf. Trute (2010), p. 21 et seq.; on the concept of information management law only Vesting (fn.22), esp. marginal Nos. 1 et seq. and 47 et seq.

[47] Excellent in its multidisciplinary consideration recently Reich (2024).

[48] Short hints on non-knowledge as (also strategically usable) resource at: Böschen et al. (2004), pp. 8, 10. Dealing with non-knowledge: Hoffman-Riem (2010). But ignorance implies forms of knowledge refusal. The perspective of a duty related to knowledge that affects the state is used in the construction of "observation duties" of the legislature, developed by the German Constitutional Court.

[49] On ignorance in the sense of ignoring as a given, often necessary human characteristic: Salecl (2020). On the rationality of ignorance: Wehling (2013), pp. 41–47; Wehling (2006); Michael Stolleis, (2009/2022), p. 1043 et seq. Refers to the *"Eigenlogik"* of the institution (inherent logic of the organization) as one factor for "dumb", knowledge-resisting administrations.

[50] Another example of "conscious ignorance" is the lack of information about water use in the Länder, as made known by journalists: cf. https://correctiv.org/aktuelles/kampf-um-wasser/2022/10/25/klimawandel-grundwasser-in-deutschland-sinkt/. 19.06.2024.

mainly the specific public to be included. The relevant questions were so particular that only specialised interest groups, like water associations, agricultural associations, environmental associations stepped in.[51] They are the drivers of a huge, ongoing learning process. However, the general public (citizens, ...) tended not to participate in the foreseen procedures. General public pressure as an incentive to act could consequently hardly arise in this way.[52]

We will therefore focus on two directives that are easier to compare due to their characteristics and with regard to how exactly mobilisation through shared knowledge is supported: The Ambient Air Quality Directive (AQD) and the aforementioned Environmental Noise Directive (END). They are similar in key aspects (general aim: health protection; participation of a general public, that is "ordinary" citizens; action plans as tool for long-term and short-term measures; local administrations as competent authorities for planning) but differ in one essential aspect. While binding limit values came into force in the area of air quality, expressly characterized by EU law as protective of health,[53] this is not the case with environmental noise. In the German legal system, this meant—after lengthy legal disputes—[54] that citizens can, under certain conditions, demand the adoption of air quality programs (action plans) and the enforcement of measures provided for in an action plan.[55]

Yet, in the area of environmental noise, all attempts to obtain similar legal protection have so far failed. The German courts have denied standing for such claims: the necessary individual right, the possible violation of which the plaintiff would have to assert, is not provided for, the Federal Administrative Court recently argued.[56] Even if one considers a different decision to be possible, the statement made by the court is dogmatically sound and comprehensible within the concept of the END and the German implementation.

---

[51] The practice of the Water Framework Directive shows that participation in Germany is in fact only carried out by certain interested "publics", but not by a general public, as the topic is hardly accessible to them. Schneider (2014), pp. 250, 261.

[52] For implementation problems following primary knowledge generation and the perception as work in progress (learning system) see Köck and Henn (2020).

[53] Art. 1 No. 1, Art. 13, 15, 16 of Directive 2008/50/EC of the European Parliament and of the Council of 21 May 2008 on ambient air quality and cleaner air for Europe, OJ L 152, p. 1, 11.06.2008.

[54] The German Federal Administrative Court did at first not follow this idea of standing / judicial protection but had to be convinced by the ECJ C-237/07 (Janecek). On the long (non)implementation history cf. Cancik (2011).

[55] Notwithstanding that the current forms of legal protection in Germany (and some other states) can still be criticised as not effective enough, cf. Backes (2012), pp. 472–476; Pedrosa and Vanheusden (2020), p. 312.

[56] Bundesverwaltungsgericht (Federal Administrative Court), BVerwG, Urteil vom 28.11.2019—BVerwG 7 C 2.18., margin No. 10 seq.; for a critical comment cf. Altehenger (2022). So far, there have only been a few attempts to sue for missing or insufficient noise action plans in court and to induce the administrations to take more efficient measures through court rulings. This was because the strongly prevailing opinion was and is based on the assumption that there is no legal standing of individual citizens to sue for the preparation of a noise action plan or for the inclusion of certain measures. Critical: Cancik (2007), p. 171 et seq.; Cancik (2014), margin No. 34; Knappe (2022), p. 458 et seq.

Of course, one could ask whether this German implementation of the END in the *BImSchG*, which has not set any clear limit values, really fulfills the requirements of the directive. However, this has hardly been discussed so far. In any case, there is much to suggest that the lack of success in Germany—with the delayed, at this point more or less existant, but not very effective action plans—is also due to the lack of enforceability (legal protection/right of appeal) and thus ultimately little progress has been made in the area of environmental noise reduction.[57] The fact that this also applies to other EU countries is of little consolation in view of the health relevance of noise pollution,[58] which has come to the fore ever more in recent years.

7 Lessons (to be) Learned for Transformation by Environmental Quality Management Law

Is this criticism to be understood as a plea for less participation or knowledge? Nothing could be further from the truth. It is a plea for a better and maybe also more honest design.[59] "Offers" of participation or pure information gathering within vague regulatory frames are in danger of being misused in the political game of shifting responsibilities; in danger of remaining purely symbolic, which can lead to frustration among those supposedly involved; or in danger of making legal instruments too weak.[60]

In brief, the considerations presented here confirm three proposals that are, of course, also discussed elsewhere:

1. If participation shall work as empowerment, "citizens have to witness meaningful involvement."[61]
2. For (participatory) knowledge to drive action, binding standards,[62] when to act, are necessary, be it on EU-Level or mandated for development by the Member States. These standards (limit or at least orientation values) must be objects of

---

[57] Not to mention that even the formal implementation is not completed yet: Germany has still not drawn up noise action plans for all major roads. As of March 2024, the EU-Commission decided to send a supplementary letter of formal notice to Germany within the infringement proceedings. INFR(2016)2116 under Art. 258 TFEU, https://t1p.de/crd9x. Accessed 22 Sep 2025.

[58] Cf. Report of the Commission, COM(2023)139—Implementation of the Environmental Noise Directive in accordance with Article 11 of Directive 2002/49/EC; therefore, Riedel, Köckler and Bolte (2022) call for the establishment of "binding standards for noise-related environmental quality" (see Durner, section 10, in this volume).

[59] See von Landenberg-Roberg in this volume, section 4 (on climate protection law as "adaptive law" or "law capable of learning," establishing self-referential evaluation processes to enhance innovation promotion).

[60] On problems of newer forms of participation see Grohs (2021), p. 312 et seq. and p. 323 et seq.; Squintani and Perlaviciute (2020).

[61] Riedel et al. (2022), p. 263.

[62] With regard to noise also: Riedel et al. (2022), p. 259 et seq.

evaluation or legal protection with regard to health protection.[63] Finally, simply drawing up a plan as such is not a sufficient "action" in that sense.

3. We need legal protection options that can be activated by citizens to support overburdened or disinterested administrations.[64]

Judicial legal protection helps to uncover enforcement deficits of the administrations. The high relevance of legal protection for the implementation of EU-air quality law in Germany, seems to prove that mobilisation via individual rights and judicial decisions works better than the rather romantic idea that shared knowledge alone serves as a relevant motor for administrations, especially in not uncommon overload situations. The intrinsically appealing idea of forcing solutions through local planning and political pressure from local communities is likely to fail due to a lack of resources on all sides, including those of interested citizens. Insofar, the constructed opposition of "governance perspective" versus "legal protection perspective", or the reduced relevance of legal protection within German governance theories respectively since the 1990s, may have been too sharp.[65]

Ignoring something can be both: an expression of power and a reaction to information overload or - as far as resources are concerned—to a lack of real capacity to act.[66] Ignoring knowledge can then prove to be a relatively easy or even necessary way out. Understanding these restrictions on the mobilising effects of (shared) knowledge is part of the administrative and legislative literacy we need for the transformation.[67] The problem of ambient noise may not seem very relevant in this respect. But there are also corresponding, possibly inadequate, regulatory concepts in other areas. The most recent example is the attempt to introduce a new soil protection regime as part of the Green Deal,[68] which is closely linked to the biodiversity and the climate adaptation strategy. After the old Soil Protection Directive was blocked in 2007 by some member states,[69] and withdrawn by the Commission as part of the bureaucracy reduction campaigns in 2014,[70] a new draft was issued in 2023.[71] Compared to the

---

[63] And when it comes to problems other than noise, possibly also climate damage minimisation.

[64] Shifting the burden of conflict solving to the local level underestimates the possible interest conflicts and the lack of possibilities to solve them on that level.

[65] I owe this consideration to Claudio Franzius. On the relevance of legal protection as instrument of governance, see Buchheim and Möllers (2022), p. 1747 et seq.

[66] "Impossible to realize" is the dry judgement on the IPPC-Directive, Braaksma and Tolsma (2020), p. 316.

[67] On administrative literacy cf. Seckelmann (2022), margin No. 57; M. Döring (2021), p. 1155 et seq.; Cancik (2025), p. 684 et seq.

[68] COM(2021) 699 final, European Commission, Communication from the Commission to the European Parliament, the Council, the European Economic and Social Committee and the Committee of the Regions, EU Soil Strategy for 2030 Reaping the benefits of healthy soils for people, food, nature and climate, 17.11.2021, https://t1p.de/l2moj. Accessed 22 Sep 2025.

[69] Wurster and Olbert (2010), p. 564.

[70] On the history of de-bureaucratisation-claims and their backgrounds see Cancik (2020).

[71] COM/2023/416 final, European Commission, Proposal for a Directive of the European Parliament and of the Council on Soil Monitoring and Resilience (Soil Monitoring Law), 5.7.2023, https://t1p.de/2olqf. Accessed 22 Sep 2025. The compromise reached between the European Parliament and the

first approach and to the Health Soil Strategy of 2021,[72] the proposal is unambitious. It does not even contain an obligation to draw up action plans with any measures, but is centered mainly around administrative knowledge obligations. According to the Commission, landowners and authorities could find and take appropriate measures to improve soil condition based on the soil assessments. In the words of the Commission, to quote just one example: "Farmers will be provided with data and knowledge on the state of their soil, so that they can take informed action to improve the health of their soil."[73] Here again, the concept of knowledge supposedly leading to action is expressed.[74] The possible development of limit or target values is left entirely to the responsibility of the Member States within a very vague frame. One can guess the shifts just from the names: The originally intended "Soil Health Law" has become a "Soil Monitoring Law".

Despite all the doubts one may have about the effectiveness of a concept focused on legal protection, it seems to me, based on current experience, that a combination of (shared) knowledge production, predetermined limit values and judicial prosecution is necessary if the goal of mobilisation of the administration not least through EU citizens is really to be achieved. Knowledge alone will too often not lead to action. And we should not claim that we could not have known.

Acknowledgment I owe Jan Markgraf thanks for his support. I would also like to thank all members of the Competence Network Environmental Law, especially Till Markus, for their helpful comments.

Council in May 2025 further weakened this proposal: Member States are no longer required to define binding sustainable soil management practices. Instead, Member States shall merely "encourage, facilitate and support landowners and land managers to improve soil health and soil resilience" (Art. 10 para. 1 of the Proposal for a Directive of the European Parliament and of the Council on Soil Monitoring and Resilience, 9266/25 of 23.05.2025).

[72] See fn. 68.

[73] Questions and Answers on a Directive on Soil Monitoring and Resilience, 05.07.2023 (https://t1p.de/0secn. Accessed 22 Sep 2025). The de-bureaucratization-approach remains quite explicit: "The administrative burden of the proposal will be limited because Member States are not required to prepare soil plans or programmes, but to use the assessment on soil health to inform the development of plans and programmes under existing policies […]."

[74] Cf. recital 37 of the compromise between the European Parliament and the Council (fn. 72), "[t]he results of the soil health assessment performed under the Directive will inform the process of identifying the specific practices needed to manage soil sustainably and thus the support that Member States should provide to increase soil health and soil resilience. Without prejudice to obligations stemming from other Union and national law, the provisions of this Directive on support to soil health and soil resilience do not impose additional obligations on land owners and managers".

References

Altehenger R (2022) Klagemöglichkeiten im Zusammenhang mit der Lärmaktionsplanung? Zugleich Urteilsanmerkung zum BVerwG, Urteil vom 29.11.2019—7 C 2.18. Natur und Recht (NuR) 44:466–468. https://doi.org/10.1007/s10357-022-4027-3

Baaner L (2011) The Programme of Measures of the Water Framework Directive - More than Just a Formal Compliance Tool. Journal for European Environmental & Planning Law 8(1):82–100

Backes C (2012) Hauptsache wir haben einen guten Plan!—Effektiver Rechtsschutz zur Einhaltung von Immissionsgrenzwerten? In: Ruffert M (ed), Dynamik und Nachhaltigkeit des Öffentlichen Rechts, Duncker & Humblot (ed), pp 459–476

Böschen S, Schneider M, Lerf A (eds) (2024) Handeln trotz Nichtwissen. Vom Umgang mit Chaos und Risiko in Politik, Industrie und Wissenschaft, Campus Verlag

Bogumil J, Jann W (2020) Verwaltung und Verwaltungswissenschaft in Deutschland. Eine Einführung, 3rd edn. Springer VS, Wiesbaden

Braaksma LS (2023) The programmatic approach in environmental law. Towards a legal design in the European Union and the Netherlands that pursues sustainability. University of Groningen Press

Braaksma LS, Tolsma HD (2020) Integrated Pollution Prevention and Control: A Critical Legal Perspective on All-inclusive Integration. In: Peeters M, Eliantonio M (eds) Research Handbook on EU Environmental Law. Edward Elgar Publishing, pp 313–327

Buchheim J, Möllers C (2022) Gerichtliche Verwaltungskontrolle als Steuerungsinstrument. In: Voßkuhle A, Eifert M, Möllers C (eds), Grundlagen des Verwaltungsrechts, Vol. II, 3rd. edn. C.H.Beck, pp 1715–1893

Bundeszentrale für politische Bildung (ed) (2013) Wissen. Aus Politik und Zeitgeschichte (APuZ):18–20

Cancik P (2025) Administration and Self-Government. In: Herdegen M, Masing J, Poscher R, Gärditz KF (eds.), Constitutional Law in Germany, § 14. C.H.Beck, pp 689–736

Cancik P (2020) „Bürokratie“ als negative Markierung: Zur Semantik von Staats- und EU-Kritik. Leviathan 48(4):612–636

Cancik P (2014) § 47d Bundesimissionsschutzgesetz. In: v. Landmann R, Rohmer G (eds), Umweltrecht. Commentary, Vol. III. C.H.Beck, 102. Suppl. Delivery 2023; status: 71. Suppl. Delivery

Cancik P (2011) Europäische Luftreinhalteplanung—zur zweiten Phase der Implementation. ZUR 22(6):283–296

Cancik P (2007) Aktionspläne zur Lärmminderung—effektives Instrument oder “Aktionismus“? ZUR 18(4):169–176

Collin P, Horstmann T (eds) (2004) Das Wissen des Staates. Geschichte, Theorie und Praxis, 1 edn. Nomos

Döring M (2021) How-to Bureaucracy: A Concept of Citizens’ Administrative Literacy. Administration & Society 53(8):1155–1177. https://doi.org/10.1177/0095399721995460

Durner W (2008) Materieller Konflikt, Informationsgewinnung und informationelle Kooperation in der Raumplanung. In: Spiecker I gen. Döhmann, Collin P (eds.), Generierung und Transfer staatlichen Wissens im System des Verwaltungsrechts. Mohr Siebeck, pp. 219–238

European Environment Agency (EEA) (2020) Environment noise in Europe—2020, EEA Report 22/2019. https://www.eea.europa.eu/en/analysis/publications/environmental-noise-in-europe. Accessed 22 Sep 2025

EEA (2014) Noise in Europe 2014, EEA Report 10/2014. https://www.eea.europa.eu/en/analysis/publications/noise-in-europe-2014. Accessed 22 Sep 2025

Gill B (2004) Nichtwissen in der postsäkularen Wissensgesellschaft—der Zuwachs an selbst- und fremddefinierten Nichtwissen. In: Böschen S, Schneider M, Lerf A (eds) Handeln trotz Nichtwissen. Vom Umgang mit Chaos und Risiko in Politik, Industrie und Wissenschaft, Campus Verlag, pp 19–36

Grohs S (2021) Participatory Administration and Co-production. In: Proeller I, Schimanke D, Ziekow J (eds) Kuhlmann S. Public Administration in Germany, Palgrave Macmillan, pp 311–327

Hoffman-Riem W (2010) Wissen, Recht und Innovation. In: Röhl HC (ed), Wissen—Zur kognitiven Dimension des Rechts. Die Verwaltung, Beiheft 9:159–212

Jarass HD (2003) Luftqualitätsrichtlinien der EU und die Novellierung des Immissionsschutzrechts. NVwZ 22(3):257–266

Knappe L (2022) Die Maßnahmenplanung im europäisierten Verwaltungsrecht, 1st edn. Carl Heymanns Verlag

Köck W, Henn E-V (2020) Die Rechte der Wasserversorger bei der Grundwasserressourcenbewirtschaftung. Dargestellt am Beispiel der PFC-Grundwasserbelastungen in Mittelbaden, NVwZ 39(8):504–511

Köck W, Markus T (2023) Legal Approaches to Scientific Uncertainty in Germany—The Case of EU Nature Conservation Law. In: Eliantonio M, Lees E, Paloniitty T (eds) EU Environmental Principles and Scientific Uncertainty before National Courts. The Case of the Habitats Directive, 1st edn. Bloomsbury Publishing, pp 163–189

Ladeur KH (1995) Das Umweltrecht der Wissensgesellschaft. Von der Gefahrenabwehr zum Risikomanagement. Duncker & Humblot, Berlin

Lenk K, Wengelowski P (2004) Wissensmanagement für das Verwaltungshandeln. In: Jann W, Wagner D (eds) Edeling T. Wissensmanagement in Politik und Verwaltung, VS Verlag für Sozialwissenschaften, pp 147–165

Mandl H, Gerstenmaier J (eds) (2000) Die Kluft zwischen Wissen und Handeln. Empirische und theoretische Lösungsansätze, Hogrefe, Bern

Markus T (2013) Changing the Base: Legal Implications of Scientific Criteria and Methodological Standards on what Constitutes Good Marine Environmental Status. Transnational Environmental Law 2(1):145–165

Markus T, Schlacke S, Maier N (2011) Legal Implementation of Integrated Ocean Policies: The EU's Marine Strategy Framework Directive. Int J Marine Coastal L 26(1):59–90

Pedrosa K, Vanheusden B (2020) EU Air Pollution Law: Comprehensive but Insufficient. In: Eliantonio M (ed) Peeters M. Research Handbook on EU Environmental Law, Edward Elgar Publishing, pp 296–312

Reich J (2024) Information als Voraussetzung des Verwaltungshandelns, in: VDStRL (ed), Bestimmungsfaktoren „guter Verwaltung". Veröffentlichungen der Vereinigung der Deutschen Staatsrechtslehrer (VVDStRL), Vol. 83, De Gruyter, pp 317–366

Riedel N, Köckler H, Bolte G (2022) Moving noise action planning towards more environmental health equity. Five propositions. Cities & Health 6(2):258–266. https://doi.org/10.1080/23748834.2021.1876391

Röhl HC (ed) (2010) (2010) Wissen—Zur kognitiven Dimension des Rechts, Die Verwaltung, Beiheft 9. Duncker & Humblot

Salecl R (2020) Passion for Ignorance: What We Choose Not to Know and Why. Princeton University Press

Schneider C (2014) Verwaltungskoordinierung im Rahmen der Flussgebietsbewirtschaftung. Verlag Dr. Kovač, Hamburg

Schulze-Fielitz H (2008) Umgebungslärm als neuartige rechtliche Herausforderung. In: Hendler R et al. (eds), Jahrbuch des Umwelt- und Technikrechts, E. Schmidt-Verlag, pp 7–53

Seckelmann M (2022) Partizipation und Akzeptanz bei der Zulassung von Großvorhaben. In: Kahl W, Ludwigs M (eds), Handbuch des Verwaltungsrechts, Vol. IV, § 112. C.F. Müller

Seibel W (1996) Successful Failure. An Alternative View on Organizational Coping. American Behavioral Scientist 39(8):1011–1024

Seibel W, Klamann K, Treis H (2017) Verwaltungsdesaster. Campus Verlag, Frankfurt, New York, Von der Loveparade bis zu den NSU-Ermittlungen

Spiecker I gen. Döhmann (2008) Die informationelle Inanspruchnahme des Bürgers im Verwaltungsverfahren: Der Amtsermittlungsgrundsatz nach § 24 VwVfG. In: Spiecker I gen. Döhmann,

Collin P (eds), Generierung und Transfer staatlichen Wissens im System des Verwaltungsrechts, Mohr Siebeck, pp 196–216
Squintani L, Perlaviciute G (2020) Access to Public Participation: Unveiling the Mismatch between what Law Prescribes and what the Public Wants. In: Eliantonio M (ed) Peeters M. Research Handbook on EU Environmental Law, Edward Elgar Publishing pp, pp 133–147
Stehr N (2002) Soziologie. In: Engel C, Halfmann J, Schulte M (eds), Wissen—Nichtwissen—Unsicheres Wissen. Nomos, pp 17–34
Stolleis M (2009) Der lernfähige und lernende Staat. In: Fried J, Stolleis M, Wissenskulturen: über die Erzeugung und Weitergabe von Wissen. Campus Verlag, pp 58–78
Thaler RH, Sunstein CR (2008) Nudge: Improving Decisions About Health, Wealth, and Happiness. Yale University Press, New Haven
Trute H (2010) Wissen - Einleitende Bemerkungen, in: H.C. Röhl (Ed.). Wissen - Zur kognitiven Dimension des Rechts, Die Verwaltung, Beiheft 9:11–38
Vesting T (2022) Die Bedeutung von Information und Kommunikation für die verwaltungsrechtliche Systembildung. In: Hoffmann-Riem W, Schmidt-Aßmann E, Voßkuhle A (eds) Grundlagen des Verwaltungsrechts, vol 1 § 20, 3rd edn. C.H. Beck, München
Wehling P (2013) Soziale Praktiken des Nichtwissens. APuZ 18–20:41–47
Wehling P (2006) Im Schatten des Wissens?: Perspektiven der Soziologie des Nichtwissens. UVK Verlagsgesellschaft, Konstanz
Weiß A (2017) Meeresstrategie-Rahmenrichtlinie: Auf dem Weg zu einem guten Umweltzustand der Meeresgewässer in Europa? ZUR 28(6):331–338
Wurster B, Olbert T (2010) Der europäische Bodenschutz wird diskutiert—und nichts passiert. EuZW 21(15):564

FSC
www.fsc.org
MIX
Papier | Fördert gute Waldnutzung
FSC® C083411

Kolibri 360 GmbH
Ferdinand-Jühlke-Straße 7
99095 Erfurt, Deutschland
produktsicherheit@kolibri360.de